PRACTICUM AND INTERNSHIP

PRACTICUM AND INTERNSHIP

Textbook for Counseling and Psychotherapy
Second Edition

John C. Boylan, Ph.D.

Professor
Graduate Counseling and Psychology Department
Marywood College
Scranton, Pennsylvania

Patrick B. Malley, Ph.D.

Associate Professor
Department of Psychology in Education
University of Pittsburgh
Pittsburgh, Pennsylvania

Judith Scott, Ph.D.

Associate Professor
Department of Psychology in Education
University of Pittsburgh
Pittsburgh, Pennsylvania

ACCELERATED DEVELOPMENT
A member of the Taylor & Francis Group

USA	Publishing Office:	ACCELERATED DEVELOPMENT
		A member of the Taylor & Francis Group
		1101 Vermont Ave., N.W., Suite 200
		Washington, DC 20005
		Tel: (202) 289-2174
		Fax: (202) 289-3665
	Distribution Center:	ACCELERATED DEVELOPMENT
		A member of the Taylor & Francis Group
		1900 Frost Road, Suite 101
		Bristol, PA 19007-1598
		Tel: (215) 785-5800
		Fax: (215) 785-5515
UK		Taylor & Francis, Ltd.
		4 John Street
		London WCIN 2ET
		Tel: 071 405 2237
		Fax: 071 831 2035

PRACTICUM AND INTERNSHIP: Textbook for Counseling and Psychotherapy, Second Edition

1 2 3 4 5 6 7 8 9 0 BRBR 0 9 8 7 6 5

⊗ The paper in this publication meets the requirements of the ANSI Standard Z39.48-1984 (Permanence of Paper)

This book was set in Times Roman by Princeton Editorial Associates. Technical development by Cynthia Long. Prepress Supervisor was Miriam Gonzalez. Cover design by Michelle Fleitz. Printing and binding by Braun-Brumfield, Inc.

A CIP catalog record for this book is available from the British Library.

Library of Congress Cataloging-in-Publication Data
Boylan, John Charles.
    Practicum and internship : textbook for counseling and psychotherapy / John C. Boylan, Patrick B. Malley, Judith Scott.—2nd ed.
        p.   cm.
    Includes bibliographical references and index.

    1. Psychotherapy—Study and teaching (Internship)—Outlines, syllabi, etc.   2. Psychotherapy—Study and teaching—Supervision—Outlines, syllabi, etc.   3. Psychotherapy—Study and teaching (Internship)—Forms.   4. Psychotherapy—Study and teaching—Forms.   I. Malley, Patrick B.   II. Scott, Judith, date.   III. Title.
RC459.B68   1995
616.89′ 14′0711—dc20   95–12439

                                                                                                                          CIP

ISBN 1-56032-392-2

TABLE OF CONTENTS

92823

CHAPTER 3
INTERNSHIP EXPERIENCE
John C. Boylan, Ph.D.

CHAPTER 6
ETHICAL AND LEGAL GUIDELINES
Patrick B. Malley, Ph.D.

CHAPTER 7
CONSULTATION IN SCHOOLS AND MENTAL HEALTH AGENCIES: MODELS AND METHODS   253
John C. Boylan, Ph.D.

LIST OF FIGURES

LIST OF SAMPLES

LIST OF TABLES

CONTRIBUTORS

Roxanne J. Bogo received her master's degree in student personnel services at the University of Pittsburgh. She is presently a residence director at the University of Pittsburgh, Pittsburgh, PA.

David E. Botwin, Ph.D., is an associate professor in the Department of Psychology and Education, University of Pittsburgh, Pittsburgh, PA.

Collie W. Conoley is an associate professor of education psychology and the director of the Counseling Psychology Training Program at University of Nebraska, Lincoln, NE.

Patsy A. Donn, Ed.D., is Director of Counseling and Psychological Services Center and Professor of Psychological Counseling, Ball State University, Muncie, IN.

A. Michael Dougherty is professor and head, Department of Human Services, Western Carolina University, Cuyllowhee, NC.

Leslie P. Dougherty is a teacher at Waynesville Junior High, Waynesville, NC.

William P. Erchul is an associate professor of psychology and the director of the School Psychology Program at North Carolina State University, Raleigh, NC.

Jeffrey B. Hersh is Assistant Director, Mental Health Service, University of Massachusetts, Amherst, MA.

Joseph W. Hollis, Ed.D., is Professor and Chairperson Emeritus, Department of Counseling Psychology and Guidance Services, Ball State University, Muncie, IN.

Francis R. Kush is a licensed psychologist on the clinical staff in the Adult Mood Disorder/Dual Diagnosis Module at Western Psychiatric Institute and Clinic, University of Pittsburgh. In addition, Dr. Kush is the Clinical Director for The University of Pittsburgh School of Education.

Nancy T. Malley is a licensed psychologist and professor in the social sciences, Robert Morris College, Pittsburgh, PA.

Dale Malecki, M.A., is Elementary School Counselor at Abington Heights School District, Clarks Summit, PA.

Nancy Murdock is assistant professor in the Division of Counseling Psychology and Counselor Education, University of Missouri—Kansas City, MO.

Diana Purcell is head counselor at Georgia Highlands Treatment Services Center, Dalton, GA.

Karen S. Pfost received her Ph.D. in counseling psychology at the University of Missouri—Columbia. She is a staff psychologist at the Student Counseling Center and Assistant Professor of Psychology at Illinois State University. She is in private practice in Bloomington, IL. Her current professional and research interests include group therapy, women's issues, and eating disorders.

Kent Poey is Coordinator of Psychology Internship Training, Mental Health Service, University of Massachusetts, Amherst, MA.

Nan R. Presser received her Ph.D. in psychology from the University of Texas at Austin. She is on the faculty of the Department of Psychology at Illinois State University and is a staff psychologist at the Student Counseling Center. She is also active as a psychologist in private practice. Her current professional interests focus on clinical training, supervision, and individual and group psychotherapy.

Lou Ann Schrock-Brutz is a master's degree student in the Counseling Program, Psychology in Education, University of Pittsburgh.

Cal D. Stoltenberg is a professor and chair of the Department of Educational Psychology at the University of Oklahoma, Norman, OK.

PREFACE

The purpose of this text is to assist supervisors, and practicum students and interns in their practicum/internship training. *Practicum and Internship Textbook for Counseling and Psychotherapy, second edition,* contains theoretical components that are valuable and essential to the training of student counselors and psychotherapists. In addition to the theoretical aspects presented, training activities germane and necessary to the development of applied counseling skills are explicated.

In the last several years, a great many changes have occurred in professional organizations, the ethical codes, and the legal system as related to the practice of counseling. These changes are having an impact on the training of counselors and psychotherapists. This text contains the necessary information and activities to aid supervisors and students in responding to these changes. It also includes theory and guidelines to innovative instructional approaches that are basic to the education of professional counselors and psychotherapists.

Specifically, this text responds to major changes that have taken place in the professional, legal, and ethical aspects of training. In the professional area, we have referred to two accreditation organizations throughout the text. One accreditation organization is the Council for Accreditation of Counseling and Related Educational Programs (CACREP), which is an independent council created by the American Counseling Association (ACA) and now is recognized by many colleges and universities as the organization that implements the standards of the counseling profession in preparatory programs. Through their efforts, the number of credits and consequently the length of time in training has been increased significantly. Counseling students who, immediately after being graduated, wish to sit for certification by the National Board for Certified Counselors (NBCC) must be graduates of counseling programs approved by CACREP. Many changes regarding practicum and internship experiences for counselors also have taken place in response to the CACREP standards. These differences are reflected in the increased number of hours required in the practicum/internship experience, in the expectations and differentiation of functions between practicum and internship experiences, and in the extent and identification of supervisory services. Another accreditation organization is the American Psychological Association, which continues to define and influence the standards set for practicum and intern experiences for psychologist preparation programs. In response to these standards, internship sites can apply directly to the certifying board to become APA approved internship sites. The standards for each certifying agency are updated continually. This text has been written to respond to current professional standards.

The legal and ethical context in which the practicum student or intern now functions also has changed quite drastically. Today, experienced supervisors and students often are faced with perplexing situations where nuance flourishes relative to their responsibility to themselves, their clients, the legal system, and the professional ethical standards. In this text, we have included the latest data and theory regarding the legal and ethical responsibilities of supervisors, practicum students, interns, and the training institution.

In conclusion, we believe that this text will provide an opportunity to orient practicum/intern supervisors, practicum/intern students, and training institutions to their ethical/legal responsibilities. In addition, the text includes instructional guidelines, details, and mechanics for initiating and maintaining a practicum or internship, student counselor/client monitoring techniques, guidelines for supervision, evaluation techniques, and ethical/legal issues related to selected problem areas in the practice of counseling and psychology.

Chapter 1

DEFINITIONS, PHASES, AND STANDARDS

Judith Scott, Ph.D.

This text provides an overview of the elements and procedures related to practicum and internship experiences, which are an integral part of professional preparation programs in the helping professions. It is written for practicum students and interns, for practicum and intern professors, and for field site supervisors to structure and guide the applied component of professional training programs. Practicum and internship experiences are required in a broad variety of counselor preparation programs in the helping professions. Counseling and psychology training programs and the national associations and accrediting bodies related to these specializations continue to clarify the definitions of practicum and internship within their field experience requirements. They also specify activities and experiences that are appropriate to each component. The trend has been toward an increase in the number of hours required in practicum and internship experience at the master's and doctoral levels, as reported by Hollis and Wantz (1994) based on their 25-year longitudinal study. Also, the standards of supervision have become more stringent.

All involved in the applied training components in counseling and psychology need to examine carefully the expectations they bring to practicum and internship. The practicum and intern professor, the practicum student and/or intern, the site supervisor, and professional accrediting agencies all have expectations that may vary. We have developed a list of questions that are examples of those that could be directed to each source. Students can add to or modify these as they apply to students' specific situations.

Practicum and Internship Professor

- How do these persons define the knowledge, skills, and activities appropriate to practicum and internship?

- What are the concepts that provide a foundation for the practicum and internship experiences?

- What is the relationship between the professor and the field site? Does the professor provide an active liaison function between the practicum and internship course activities and the field site? How does the professor provide site-based or campus-based supervision and training activities?

- How is the student expected to demonstrate the identified competencies and how are they evaluated? Will the student be retained in practicum until minimal competencies are demonstrated?

- How does the professor view the responsibility for site placement? Is the student's responsibility clearly stated?

- How does the professor view his/her role in the field experience, i.e., instructional leader, evaluator, manager, role model, resource person?

Practicum Student and Intern

- What kinds of experiences are expected and needed by the student or intern?

- What approaches are used in supervision?

- Will practicum and internship experiences lead to the appropriate certification and licensing from the state and/or national certification and licensing boards?

- How do the experiences afforded in practicum and internship reflect the breadth and depth of professional counseling and psychology? Will both individual and group counseling or therapy be part of the experience?

- With what range of clients can the student expect to work? Are these clients representative of the client population with whom the student expects to work when employed?

- Who are the other practicum students and interns? What kinds of experiences and points of view might they add to group supervision sessions?

- How will the student be evaluated and what kinds of records of counseling or therapy practice (written or taped) will be expected?

- What are the procedures for placement in practicum and internship? What field placement sites are recommended and available?

- Are practicum students and interns expected to have their own insurance?

Practicum and Internship Site Supervisors

- What are the credentials and experiences of the site supervisors? What are their views on professionalism? Are they active or inactive in professional organizations?

- How does the site supervisor define the role of practicum student or intern? How much time is expected for record keeping, report writing, and case conferences? How much time each week will the supervisor devote to supervision and/or interaction with the practicum student or intern?

- How does the site supervisor interact and communicate with the university training program?

- Has the site had previous experience with practicum students and interns?

Standards Set by Professional Organizations, Certifying Boards, Accrediting Agencies, and University Units

- How many hours of practicum or internship are required in the program, and what number of these hours is spent in direct service? What is the ratio of direct service to supervision?

- What kinds of supervisory support are required? Are both individual and group supervision recommended? How many hours of supervision are needed?

- What kinds of procedures apply for the protection of clients? How are the clients informed about practicum students and interns?

- What are the prerequisites to an internship? How is it placed in the program?

- What number of credit hours are devoted to practicum and internship?

DEFINITIONS

A few terms must be defined to promote a clear understanding of the meanings intended in this text.

Counselor: a graduate student in either counselor or psychologist preparation programs that require field based training experiences as part of the curriculum.

Practicum Student: a student in training who is enrolled in a specific practicum course.

Intern: a student in training who has completed the academic and experiential prerequisites for an internship in a counseling or psychology specialization and is enrolled in the internship component of the program.

Student: a term used in certain places in this manual to refer to the person enrolled in either practicum or internship.

Practicum Site Supervisor: the person at the field site who shares or has primary responsibility for supervision of the practicum student at the site.

Practicum/Internship Professor: the agent of the university (generally a university faculty member) who is directly responsible for the university course in practicum or internship to which the student is assigned.

Practicum Site: the place where the practicum experiences occur. The site may be within the university, i.e., counseling practicum clinic or counseling center. The site may be within a school or community agency, i.e., correctional clinic, diagnostic center, mental health center, employment agency, hospital, pastoral counseling agency, or rehabilitation agency.

Internship Site: the place where the internship experiences occur. The site meets the university training program's standards for internship experiences and provides the intern with the opportunity to perform all the activities that a regularly employed staff member who occupies the professional role to which the intern is aspiring would be expected to perform. It may be within a school, university, or community agency.

Internship Site Supervisor: a clearly designated professional staff member at the internship site who is directly responsible for providing systematic, intensive on-site supervision of the intern's professional training activities and performance. The internship supervisor has professional credentials appropriate to the role to which the intern aspires.

PHASES OF PRACTICUM AND INTERNSHIP

Phases of practicum and internship can be described from a number of perspectives. For example, one might describe the practicum and internship from the categories of level of skill, such as beginner level, intermediate level, and advanced level. Another way of categorizing phases might be according to functions, such as stating goals, acquiring knowledge, and refining skills and techniques. The author prefers to describe the phases in practicum and internship from a developmental perspective.

Several principles regarding development can be identified within practicum and internship:

1. Movement is directional and hierarchical. Early learning establishes a foundation for later development.

2. Differentiation occurs with new learning. Learning proceeds from the more simplistic and straightforward toward the more complex and subtle.

3. Separation/individuation can be observed. The learning process leads to progressively more independent and separate functioning on the part of the counselor/therapist.

These developmental principles can be identified within the program structure, the learning process, and the supervisory interactions encountered by the trainee.

Development Reflected in Program Structure

Students generally can expect to proceed through the experiential component of their training programs in an orderly and sequentially planned progression. A typical sequence would be as follows:

Pre-practicum

Practicum

Internship

Full Professional Status

Some variation exists in counseling and psychology training programs regarding the number of hours required in each component. Also some variation exists in training programs regarding the range of expected skills and competencies that are necessary before the student can move on to the next component in the field experience.

At the pre-practicum end of the continuum, the student could appropriately expect more instructional and active participation with the professor. Basic skill development, role-playing, peer interaction, and observation activities in a counseling lab setting may be emphasized. In the practicum component, the student is likely to be functioning in a field site with supervision and supportive instructional functions being provided by both university faculty and field site supervisor(s). Observation of functioning professionals at the field site, coleading counseling activities, and initial contact with a limited range of clients are likely activities in the initial stages of practicum. These activities gradually are expanded to include counseling/therapy with a broader range of clients and increased opportunities to expand and develop the full range of professional behaviors. At the internship end of the continuum, the student is expected to be able to participate in the full range of professional activities within the field site under supervision directed primarily by approved field site personnel.

Development Reflected in Learning Processes

A sequence in the learning process engaged in by the counselor or therapist in training has been described by Hogan (1964). The trainee is characterized as progressing across four levels of development in his/her learning to function in a clinical setting. At Level 1, the trainee is influenced heavily by method or technique and most likely will function out of an imitative or recipe oriented approach to counseling or therapy. At Level 2, the trainee is less method-bound and is concerned primarily with investing and using his/her own personality in the counseling or therapy work. Developing insight and differentiating personal reactions from client realities are recurring struggles in the learning process. At Level 3, the trainee is more able to assume a peer relationship with other professionals and has greater and more stable insight into professional and personal concerns. At Level 4, the trainee approaches the master level and functions independently and/or with consultation to use his/her capacity to bring full range of personal insight and creativity to the counseling or therapy work.

As the trainee progresses across the four levels, the role of counselor or therapist becomes more internalized and integrated. At the initial levels, counseling role and professional behaviors are viewed as being taken in and learned from the outside. At the higher levels of learning, the trainee integrates the role of counselor or therapist into his/her personal identity and becomes the one who knows. New methods and techniques are reflected upon, considered, and tried rather than merely read about and applied.

In Figure 1.1. are outlined four levels of learning as the trainee progresses.

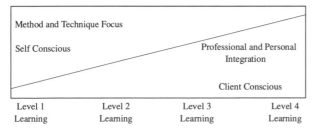

Figure 1.1. Schematic outline of trainee across four levels of learning.

Development Reflected in Supervisor Interaction

Supervisory interaction between supervisor and trainee begins with the trainee's high level of dependence upon the supervisor for instruction, feedback, and support. This interaction is modified as skill, personal awareness, and confidence increase for the trainee. The trainee becomes more likely to explore new modes of practice that reflect his/her unique personality and style. The interaction continues to move gradually toward higher levels of independent judgment by the trainee and a more collegial and consultative stance on the part of the supervisor.

In Figure 1.2. is charted the changing balance of trainee and supervisor interaction.

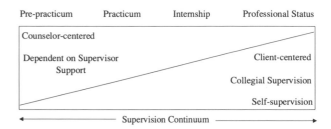

Figure 1.2. Schematic representation of trainee-supervisor interaction over time within practicum and internship.

STANDARDS FOR PRACTICUM AND INTERNSHIP

Accreditation of counselor preparation programs has become increasingly important in the last several years, and this has brought about changes in counselor preparation programs. The two most influential factors causing these changes have been identified as national accreditation and state certification and licensing (Hollis & Wantz, 1993, 1994). Practicum and internship have become a significant part of counselor and psychotherapist preparation and are affected similarly by accreditation and licensing requirements. Graduation from an accredited program can influence obtaining a job and state certification and/or licensure, and achieving professional acceptance. Five accreditation bodies—APA, CACREP, COAMFTE, CORE, and AAPC—have published standards that influence state certification and licensing of psychologists and counselors. These standards also influence academic units to develop preparation programs which meet national standards. More and more hiring officials are recognizing what accreditation may mean in terms of a program for a graduate. This trend has caused students to seek admission to accredited programs, thus giving accreditation significantly more meaning in the last few years. The acceptance of national standards is not universal; however, standards are accepted widely and are influencing what is offered in counselor preparation programs (Hollis & Wantz, 1994).

The major experiential components in counselor preparation—practicum and internship—have had three major changes in recent years: (1) the amount of time spent in practicum and/or internship; (2) the setting where the experience occurs; and (3) the specifications for qualifications of the supervisor doing the clinical supervision of the practicum and/or internship person. These three aspects—clock hours spent, setting, and supervisor qualifications—could make major differences in job opportunities, kind of practice, clientele, philosophical orientation, and techniques emphasized throughout the student's professional life. For these reasons as well as others (i.e., personalities involved, practicum and internship sites available) each student needs to give considerable attention to *where* he/she does practicum and internship, under *whose* clinical supervision, and for *what* period of time.

Each of five accreditation bodies (national organizations) has established separate and somewhat different standards—each to meet preparation needs for counselors within particular areas (Hollis & Wantz, 1994, pp. 27–35). Even though only one of these five probably will be applicable to you, an understanding of all five will assist you in better understanding qualifications of others within the mental health profession with whom you may be co-worker, team member, consult, or referrer of clients.

Professional Counselors

The Council for Accreditation of Counseling and Related Educational Programs (CACREP) met for the first time in September, 1981. This independent Council was created by what is now called the American Counseling Association and its divisions in order to implement standards of the counseling profession in preparation programs. The Council agreed to honor all previous accreditation decisions rendered by the Association for Counselor Education and Supervision (ACES) and those previously made by the California Association of Counselor Education and Supervision (CACES).

CACREP accredits entry level programs at the master's degree level in five areas: community counseling, marriage and family therapy/counseling, mental health counseling, school counseling, and student affairs practice (counseling) in higher education. Within the community counseling area, further specializations in gerontological counseling and career counseling are denoted. At the entry level, those statements related to practicum and internship are as follows:

> The program must provide curricular experience and demonstrated knowledge and skills in different specialization areas so that the student may gain experience in the professional setting where the student intends to practice. The direct service hours required for practice should include work with the population with whom the student intends to work.
>
> Practica will extend over a minimum of one academic term and should provide for the development of individual and group work skills. Individual and group supervision by approved faculty and field site supervisors should be provided on a weekly basis and include ongoing evaluation as well as a formal evaluation at the end of practicum.
>
> A supervised internship that provides opportunities for students to engage in both individual and group work is recommended. The internship provides an opportunity for the student to perform, under supervision, a variety of activities that a regularly employed staff member in the setting would be expected to perform. A regularly employed staff member is defined as a person occupying the professional role to which the student is aspiring.
>
> Ordinarily, internships will be full-time of a work week extended over a minimum of one academic term or half-time of a work week extended over two academic terms. Individual and group supervision by approved faculty and field site supervisors should be provided on a weekly basis. Formal evaluation of the student's performance during the internship by faculty and site supervisors is required.

In summary form related to the three aspects identified as being of primary interest (setting, clock hours, and supervisor), the following would be applicable:

Community Counseling

Setting: occurs in a community setting

Clock Hours:

Practicum: 100 hours with 40 hours of direct client contact

Internship: 600 hours internship with 240 hours of direct service to clients including but not limited to using preventive, developmental, and remedial interventions with appropriate clientele and community interventions consistent with the program.

Supervisor: NCC certification or a degree in a counseling related field. A minimum of two years of pertinent professional experience.

Gerontological Specialization in Community Counseling

Setting: Community agency serving older persons (50 years of age or older).

Clock Hours:

Practicum: 100 hours with 40 hours of direct contact working with older persons.

Internship: 600 hours with 240 hours of direct contact with clients (which is defined as older persons, their families and caregivers).

Supervisor: NCC certification or a degree in a counseling related field. Minimum of two years of pertinent professional experience.

Career Counseling Specialization in Community Counseling

Setting: A setting where career counseling regularly occurs.

Clock Hours:

Practicum: 100 hours with 40 hours of direct client contact including work with clients seeking career counseling.

Internship: 600 hours with 240 hours of direct client contact.

Supervisor: NCC certification or degree in counseling related field. Minimum of two years of pertinent professional experience.

Mental Health Counseling

Setting: A setting where the applicant is provided opportunities to develop skills relevant to the practice of clinical mental health counseling.

Clock Hours:

Practicum: 100 hours with 40 hours of direct client contact including individual counseling and group work.

Internship: 900 hours, with a minimum of 240 hours of direct client contact.

Supervisor: 300 clock hours of supervised experience must be under the direct supervision of a qualified mental health professional (CCMHC, licensed psychologist with clinical credentials, or licensed clinical social worker).

Marriage and Family Counseling/Therapy

Setting: A setting that regularly offers counseling services to couples and families.

Clock Hours:

Practicum: 100 hours with 40 hours of direct client contact including work with couples and families.

Internship: 600 hours with 240 hours of direct client contact defined as work demonstrating systemic approaches and completed primarily with couples and families.

Supervisor: NCC certification or counseling related degree. A minimum of two years pertinent clinical experience.

School Counseling

Setting: A school setting

Clock Hours:

Practicum: 100 hours with 40 hours of direct client contact.

Internship: 600 hours with 240 clock hours of direct service including, but not limited to, individual counseling, group work, developmental classroom guidance, and consultation.

Supervisor: NCC certification or counseling related degree. Certified school counselor. A minimum of two years pertinent counseling experience.

Student Affairs Practice in Higher Education, College Counseling Emphasis

Setting: Post-secondary setting.

Clock Hours:

Practicum: 100 hours with 40 hours direct service.

Internship: 600 hours with 240 hours of direct service including, but not limited to, individual counseling, group work, career planning, consultation, student advisement, leadership training, and developmental programming.

Supervisor: NCC certification or counseling related degree. Minimum of two years pertinent counseling experience.

CACREP also accredits counselor education programs at the Ph.D. and Ed.D. levels. The statement applicable to practicum and internship is as follows:

Doctoral students are required to participate in a supervised advanced practicum in counseling. Doctoral students are required to complete at least one doctoral level counseling internship of 600 clock hours. The 600 hours may include supervised experiences in clinical settings, teaching, and supervision and includes most of the activities of a regularly employed professional in the setting.

Counseling Psychologists

The American Psychological Association (APA) has for several years accredited programs for preparation of counseling psychologists at the doctoral level only. Additionally, APA has developed guidelines and requirements for accrediting doctoral level internships. The trend is for employers and state licensing boards to require completion of an APA approved internship or its equivalent. Accreditation criteria for practicum and internship are as follows:

Setting:

Practicum: Setting not specified but implied within a clinical setting.

Internship: An APA approved site or its equivalent.

Clock Hours:

Practicum: 300 hours (Division 17 currently is considering raising this to 600 hours)—150 of these hours in direct service with 75 hours of formally scheduled supervision.

Internship: Full-time for one academic or calendar year or part-time for two years with a minimum of two hours per week for formally scheduled individual supervision.

Supervisor: Psychologists who are licensed or certified in the state in which they work and who have completed an internship in the appropriate specialty. Collaborative work with representatives of other disciplines is desirable.

Marriage and Family Therapists

The American Association for Marriage and Family Therapy (AAMFT) through its Commission on Accreditation for Marriage and Family Therapy Education (COAMFTE) serves as an accreditation body for graduate programs and post degree clinical training programs. The major items pertaining to practicum and internship are as follows:

Clinical training must integrate didactic with clinical material. A practicum is a part-time clinical experience completed concurrently with didactic coursework. A practicum typically results in 5–10 direct client contact hours per week; it also includes such activities as supervision, staff meetings, community relations, and record-keeping.

Students are required to spend a minimum of 500 face-to-face hours with clients. Although students may treat individual clients, at least 50 percent of the 500 direct client hours must be completed with couples or families physically present in the therapy room.

In summary form related to the three aspects identified, the following are applicable:

Setting: Clinical setting implied

Clock Hours:

Supervised Clinical Practice: 500 direct contact hours, 50 percent of which are with couples or families; a minimum of 100 hours of supervision required.

Internship: Required at the doctoral level, 9 to 12 months of no fewer than 30 hours per week, comprising at least 500 client contact hours, and a minimum of 100 hours of supervision.

Supervisor: AAMFT approved supervisor or supervisor in training. Alternate supervisor as approved by AAMFT on a case-by case basis.

Rehabilitation Counselors

The Council on Rehabilitation Education (CORE) is the accrediting body for master's degree programs in rehabilitation counselor education. Those statements applicable to practicum and internship are as follows:

> Practicum must be done under supervision with disabled persons and include case conferences, client staffing, plan development, client evaluation, referral, case recording, and caseload management.

> Internship is a fieldwork experience in an accredited rehabilitation agency or facility, supervised by a certified rehabilitation counselor for a minimum of one hour per week. The intern must be involved in tasks performed by a regularly employed rehabilitation counselor.

In summary, the requirements for the three aspects are as follows:

Setting: An accredited rehabilitation agency or facility. The site must provide services to individuals with disabilities.

Clock Hours:

Practicum: 100 hours of supervised rehabilitation counseling experience.

Internship: 600 hours of supervised rehabilitation counseling experience.

Supervisor: Certified Rehabilitation Counselor or Rehabilitation Counselor Education Faculty member.

Pastoral Counselors

The American Association of Pastoral Counselors (AAPC) accredits training programs and service centers. The training programs are for preparation of pastoral counselors, and the two types of accreditation are "approved" and "have provisional approval."

Those statements applicable to supervised practice are as follows:

> Educational preparation for certified membership should contribute to the pastoral counselor's training and develop

a broad experience-related understanding of people. This should take place in a setting in which both the school and practical situation are in mutual relation.

> 375 hours of pastoral counseling together with 125 hours of supervision of that counseling are required with one third of such supervision to have been with an AAPC approved Center for Training in Pastoral Counseling or from a Diplomate of the Association.

In summary, the following apply:

Setting: Not specified.

Clock Hours: 375 hours of pastoral counseling with 125 hours of supervision.

Supervisor: One third of supervision hours with AAPC approved center or a diplomate of the association.

Counselor Certification

Certifying bodies, in addition to accreditation organizations, are stipulating what is expected within the preparation program and are being more specific about practicum and internship experiences. As a result, counselors-in-preparation need to keep abreast with these requirements and trends so as to obtain those practicum and/or internship experiences that will enable them to be eligible for the certificate(s) they may desire after graduation.

The National Board for Certified Counselors (NBCC) awards the designation of National Certified Counselor (NCC) to those applicants who successfully fulfill certain criteria. Applicants graduating from CACREP accredited programs may sit for the National Counselors Examination immediately upon completion of their master's degree programs. Those who successfully pass the exam are awarded National Certified Counselor status. Effective July 1, 1995, applicants graduating from programs that are not CACREP accredited will need to complete a minimum of 48 semester or 72 quarter hours of graduate study in the practice of counseling or a related field. This includes a master's degree from a regionally accredited counselor preparation program in which coursework in eight identified areas and a minimum of two academic terms of supervised field experiences in a counseling setting have been completed. In addition, a minimum of two years of field experience (3,000 hours) in counseling at the post-master's level under the weekly supervision (100 hours face-to-face supervision) of a National Certified Counselor (NCC) or the equivalent as determined by the Board is required, as well as successful passing of the National Counselors Examination.

NBCC also awards specialty counseling credentials in Career, Gerontological, School, Clinical Mental Health, and Addictions Counseling. The requirements for specialty certifications require coursework and experience as well as the passing of an examination. With any NBCC specialty certification, the requirements for the general practice certification (NCC) are a prerequisite.

The Academy of Clinical Mental Health Counselors provides and implements standards for the independent practice of mental health counseling. Applicants for the Certified Clinical Mental Health Counselor (CCMHC) credential must meet or exceed Academy requirements in each of the following four areas: (1) academic preparation, (2) clinical experience and supervision, (3) examination, and (4) clinical skill. Pre-application requirements include completion of a CACREP accredited 60 semester hour master's degree program (1988 or more recent standards) in mental health counseling or its equivalent and two years of clinical practice after the master's degree. This experience must include 3,000 hours of direct client contact in a supervised clinical setting. Applicants also must document 100 hours of face-to-face supervision by an Academy approved supervisor.

The Commission on Rehabilitation Counselor Certification provides and implements standards for qualifying as a Certified Rehabilitation Counselor (CRC). Applicants who have completed a CORE accredited master's degree program are eligible to take the CRC examination upon graduation. Those who have graduated from a rehabilitation master's degree program that is not fully accredited by CORE must complete a 600-hour internship supervised by a Certified Rehabilitation Counselor and/or additional acceptable employment experience under the supervision of a Certified Rehabilitation Counselor. Those not supervised by a CRC must complete a Provisional Supervision Contract as well as pass the examination.

The American Association for Marriage and Family Therapy provides a professional credential entitled Clinical Member status. The eligibility criteria requires a master's or doctoral degree in marriage and family therapy or an equivalent degree, including a supervised practicum as defined by the AAMFT. In addition, a minimum of two years of post-master's degree experience in clinical work supervised by an AAMFT supervisor or supervisor-in-training is required. This post-master's degree experience includes 1,000 hours of face-to-face marriage and family therapy with individuals, couples, and families and at least 200 hours of supervision completed concurrently.

The American Association of Pastoral Counselors (AAPC) has established certification guidelines delineated by membership status in the organization. Categories of membership are Member, Fellow, and Diplomate. Each category of certified membership requires explicit levels of education and supervised practice, an oral examination, and an endorsement from a recognized religious body.

IMPLICATIONS

Implications for students-in-preparation are becoming very clear. In addition to requirements for practicum and internship as stipulated by the counselor preparation program, each student in light of his/her own projected future will need to give careful consideration to five items: (1) selection of sites where practicum and/or internship is experienced, (2) review of the credentials of the supervisor, (3) availability of the supervisor to devote time to supervision, (4) clients usually served in the setting to assure a wide spectrum of experiences consistent with the students' career directions, and (5) credentialing requirements of organizations with which the student hopes to affiliate.

Certification requirements as they develop often are being established with more requirements than the standards for graduation. Thus, students must look beyond the local college or university requirements and must consider trends in certification by professional organizations and state licensure/certification requirements.

CHAPTER BIBLIOGRAPHY

American Association for Marriage and Family Therapy. (1994, March). *Membership requirements and applications.* Washington, DC: Author.

American Association of Pastoral Counselors. (1993). *General information on individual membership/affiliation.* Fairfax, VA: Author.

American Psychological Association Committee on Accreditation. (1983, revised July, 1993). *American Psychological Association accreditation handbook.* Washington, DC: Author.

Bradley, R. (1989). *Counselor supervision: Principles, process, practice* (2nd ed.). Muncie, IN: Accelerated Development.

Commission on Rehabilitation Counselor Certification. (1993). *CRCC certification guide.* Rolling Meadow, IL: Author.

Council for Accreditation of Counseling and Related Educational Programs. (1994). *CACREP accreditation standards and procedures manual.* Alexandria, VA: Author.

Commission on Accreditation for Marriage and Family Therapy Education. (1991). *Manual on accreditation.* Washington, DC: Author.

Council on Rehabilitation Education, Inc. (1991). *Accreditation manual for rehabilitation counselor education programs.* Rolling Meadows, IL: Author.

Delaney, D. J. (1978). Supervising counselors in preparation. In J. Boyd (Ed.), *Counselor supervision: Approaches, preparation, practices* (pp. 341–374). Muncie, IN: Accelerated Development.

Drapela, V. J., & Drapela, G. B. (1986, November). The role of the counselor in intern supervision. *The School Counselor,* 92–99.

Hogan, R. (1964). Issues and approaches in supervision. *Psychotherapy Theory, Research, and Practice, 1,* 139–141.

Hollis, J.W., & Wantz, R.A. (1993). *Counselor preparation, 1993–1995, volume I: Programs and personnel* (8th edition). Muncie, IN: Accelerated Development.

Hollis, J.W., & Wantz, R.A. (1994). *Counselor preparation, 1993–1995, volume II: Status, trends, and implications* (8th edition). Muncie, IN: Accelerated Development.

Lamb, D. H., Baker, J., Jennings, M., & Yarris, E. (1982, October). Passages of an internship in professional psychology. *Professional Psychology, 13*(5), 661–669.

National Board for Certified Counselors, Inc. (1994). *Specialty certification.* Greensboro, NC: Author.

PRACTICUM EXPERIENCE

Judith Scott, Ph.D.

Students often are required to complete both a practicum and an internship. In Chapter 1 we reviewed the definitions and summarized the professional standards that currently are influencing the applied practice components of programs. Chapter 2 focuses on the practicum site, and Chapter 3 focuses on the internship site. Current CACREP and APA guidelines are utilized as much as possible in the format presented. The practicum student or intern and the professor/supervisor may need to make adaptations in the format presented in order to meet particular needs of their institutions and/or setting.

GUIDELINES FOR CHOOSING A PRACTICUM SITE

The practicum placement is often the first opportunity that the student has to gain experience of working with a client population. Prior counseling experience probably occurred in pre-practicum or practicum lab situations with volunteers or peer counseling interactions. Many counselor preparation programs offer the student an opportunity to have some say in determining the practicum placement. The practicum student may be able to gain experience at more than one practicum site. The university practicum supervisor has the responsibility for deciding where the practicum student might gain the best experiences for professional development given his/her particular needs and professional goals. The practicum site personnel have responsibility to select practicum students who the site's professional staff believe will be able to benefit from the placement and who serve the needs of the client population. The practicum student tentatively can select sites of interest and then, with university supervisor's approval, visit and apply for placement. A list of approved sites can be provided by your program.

Going about the selection and application process can be confusing. A helpful procedure is to have criteria in mind as you are considering a practicum placement. The usual categories that are considered in the selection process are personnel available, professional associations of the site, professional practices of the site, administrative support, and other related information. Within these categories the following questions may be helpful in determining selection of a practicum site.

Professional Staff and Supervisor

- What are the professional credentials of site personnel? What are the educational backgrounds and ranges of experiences of the director and practicum supervisor?

- What values regarding training and supervision are verbalized and demonstrated?

- Will the supervisor be available for individual supervision for a minimum of one hour a week?

- What are the special counseling/therapy interests of the practicum supervisor(s)?

- Do the staff members regularly update their skills and participate in continuing education?

Professional Associations of the Site

- In what association does the site hold membership?

- Does the site hold approval of national certifying agencies?

- What is the reputation of the site among other organizations?

- Does the site have affiliations or working cooperations with other institutions?

Professional Practices of the Site

- Does the site follow the ethical guidelines of the profession (APA, ACA, NASW, AAPC, AAMFT)? Which one(s)?

- What kinds of resources are available to personnel (i.e., library, computer programs, ongoing research, professional consultation)?

- What are the client procedures, treatment modalities, and staffing and outreach practices? How are these consistent with goals of practicum?

- How are client records kept? What are the policies and procedures regarding taping (audio and/or video) and other practicum support activities?

- Will practicum students have opportunity for full participation?

Administration

- What resources, if any, are directed toward staff development?

- How is policy developed and approved (corporate structure, board of directors, contributors)?

- How stable is the site (hard money or soft money support, length of service of director and staff, purposes or mission statements)?

Other Information

- Who is the client population served, i.e., restricted group or open; age range narrow or wide; services remedial, preventive, and/or developmental; socioeconomic level low, middle, and/or high?

- Are adequate facilities available for practicum students?

- Does the site and its professional staff demonstrate high regard for human dignity and support civil rights of clients?

NEGOTIATING THE PRACTICUM PLACEMENT

After the initial stage has been completed for site selection, the next step is to negotiate the practicum placement. This process works best when a written exchange of agreement is made so that all parties involved in the practicum placement understand roles and responsibilities involved. Specific guidelines followed in the practicum can be stated as part of the agreement. Guidelines identified by national certifying agencies often are used or referenced in formalizing the practicum placement.

In APA practicum guidelines, statements concerning the development of the following capacities are included:

- understanding of and commitment to professional and social responsibility as defined by statutes of the ethical code of the profession (see Chapter 6 of this manual);

- the capability to conceptualize human problems;

- awareness of the full range of human variability among the dimensions of ethnicity, sub-culture, affirmative action, race, religion, sexual preference, handicap, sex, and age;

- understanding of one's own personality and biases and of one's impact upon others in professional interaction;

- skills in relevant interpersonal interactions such as systematic observation of behavior, interviewing, psychological testing, psychotherapy, counseling and consultation; and

- ability to contribute to current knowledge and practice.

In CACREP guidelines, the development of individual counseling and group work skills is recommended. Statements related to practicum activities include the following:

- experience in individual and group interactions (At least one fourth of the direct service hours should be in group work.);

- opportunities for students to counsel clients representative of the ethnic, lifestyle, and demographic diversity of their community;

- familiarizing students with a variety of professional activities other than direct service work; and

- use of a variety of professional resources such as measurement instruments, computers, print and non-print media, professional literature, and research.

State Licensing Board and state Departments of Education also may provide guidelines and set standards regarding field experience activities and minimum number of hours required in practicum. In addition, university and program faculty may have their own guidelines. We suggest that the counselor preparation program identify the guidelines that it follows and include the guidelines in the practicum contract.

Many counselor preparation programs exchange a formal agreement with the field site in the placement of practicum students. A Sample Letter (Sample 1) and contract (Form 2.1) are included and can be adapted to the specific needs of your training program. The contract includes a statement concerning guidelines to be followed, conditions agreed upon by the field site, conditions agreed upon by the counselor or psychologist preparation program, and a list of practicum activities.

ROLE AND FUNCTION OF THE PRACTICUM STUDENT

The practicum student, who has been accepted to the field site, will start as a novice in the counseling profession; however, he/she will be a representative of the University and other student counselors or psychologists. The student is working in the setting as a guest of the practicum site. The site personnel have agreed to provide the student with appropriate counseling experiences with the clientele they serve. Although the individual freedom of the student counselor is understood and respected, the overriding concern of the site personnel is to provide role appropriate services to the client population. The role of the practicum student is to obtain practice in counseling or psychotherapy in the manner in which it is provided in the practicum setting. The student counselor is expected to adhere to any dress codes or expected behaviors that are existent at the field site. In some instances the student may disagree with some of the site requirements; however, the role of the student counselor is not to change the system but to develop his/her own abilities in counseling practice. Privileges extended to the student counselor may be revoked by the site staff at their own discretion.

If conflicts arise between the student counselor and the site personnel, this can provide the student with a good opportunity to develop personal insight. The first order of work for the student is to reflect on what about himself/herself makes this situation problematic rather than to focus upon what about the system is flawed. The faculty liaison is always available to assist the student in the process of understanding himself/herself within the system and to facilitate the student's ability to function in the setting. When the student counselor is accepted into practicum, he/she enters into an agreement with the site and the university regarding expected professional behaviors.

A *Student Profile Sheet* (Form 2.2) and a *Student Practicum/Internship Letter* (Form 2.3) have been included. The profile sheet guides the documenting of the student counselor's academic preparation and relevant experience prior to practicum. The agreement form demonstrates a formal agreement being entered into by the student.

CONCEPTS IN PRACTICUM

Concepts about the practicum experience influence the kinds and range of activities, the process of supervisory and consulting interaction, and the nature of the teaching contract between the practicum student and the professor. Such concepts provide the foundation of this beginning experiential component of professional training. Although no one right way exists to develop a conceptual framework for practicum, the practicum professor must be able to articulate the framework and to share this with the student.

The following example represents a possible conceptual framework. It can be used as a reference for the practicum professor who is structuring the practicum with the students. Some concepts may be used as a point of departure for discussion, others may be modified, and others may be challenged.

1. Practicum is a highly individualized learning experience in which the practicum student is met at the level of personal development, knowledge, and skills that he/she brings to the experience.

   In any group of practicum students, one can expect a wide range of talents, unique perspectives regarding human behavior, and varying

(Continued on p. 25)

SAMPLE LETTER

(Use University Stationery)

                                                            Date

Dear Practicum Site Supervisor,

    The enclosed contract is designed to formalize the arrangement between _____ (University Program) and _____ (Practicum Site) for student counselors enrolled in the practicum at _____ (University). The practicum activities have been selected based upon APA and CACREP guidelines, state licensing or certification requirements, and the university and program faculty recommendations.

    If the guidelines, agreements, and practicum activities are followed closely, the student counselor should have the opportunity to demonstrate counseling competencies at an increasing level of complexity in the amount of time contracted. We realize that a practicum site may not be able to provide access for the student to every activity because of the differences that exist in individuals and institutions. The contract for each practicum experience will indicate those activities that can be provided.

    We appreciate and thank you for your interest and cooperation in helping to prepare professional counselors/psychologists.

                                                Sincerely,

                                                _____
                                                (Name of Professor)
                                                Ph. # _____

Sample 1. Letter sent to practicum site supervisor.

PRACTICUM CONTRACT

This agreement is made on _____ by and between_____

(Date)   (Field Site)

and _____ . The agreement will be effective for a period

(University Program)

from _____ to _____ for _____ per week for _____ .

(No. Hours)   (Student Name).

Purpose

The purpose of this agreement is to provide a qualified graduate student with a practicum experience in the field of counseling/psychology.

The University Program agrees

1. to assign a university faculty liaison to facilitate communication between university and site;

2. to provide the site prior to placement of the student the following information

    a. profile of the student named above and

    b. an academic calendar that shall include dates for periods during which student will be excused from field supervision;

3. to notify the student that he/she must adhere to the administrative policies, rules, standards, schedules, and practices of the site;

4. that the faculty liaison shall be available for consultation with both site supervisors and students and shall be immediately contacted should any problem or change in relation to student, site, or university occur; and

5. that the university supervisor is responsible for the assignment of a fieldwork grade.

The Practicum Site agrees

1. to assign a practicum supervisor who has appropriate credentials, time, and interest for training the practicum student;

2. to provide opportunities for the student to engage in a variety of counseling activities under supervision and for evaluating the student's performance (suggested counseling experiences included in the "Practicum Activities" section);

3. to provide the student with adequate work space, telephone, office supplies, and staff to conduct professional activities;

4. to provide supervisory contact that involves some examination of student work using audio/visual tapes, observation, and/or live supervision; and

5. to provide written evaluation of student based on criteria established by the university program.

With the specified time frame, _____ (Site Supervisor) will be the primary practicum site supervisor. The training activities (checked below) will be provided for the student in sufficient amounts to allow an adequate evaluation of the student's level of competence in each activity. _____ (faculty liaison) will be the faculty liaison with whom the student and practicum site supervisor will communicate regarding progress, problems, and performance evaluations.

PRACTICUM ACTIVITIES

1. Individual Counseling/Psychotherapy
   Personal/Social Nature
   Occupational/Educational Nature

2. Group Counseling/Psychotherapy
   Coleading
   Leading

3. Intake Interviewing
   Including taking social history
      information

4. Testing
   Administration
   Analysis
   Interpretation of Results

5. Report Writing
   Record-keeping
   Treatment Plans
   Treatment Summaries

6. Consultation
   Referrals
   Professional Team Collaboration

7. Psychoeducational Activities
   Parent Conferences
   Outreach
   Client Orientation
   Contact with Community Resources
   In-service

8. Career Counseling

9. Individual Supervision

10. Group or Peer Supervision

11. Case Conferences or Staff Meetings

12. Other (Please list) _____
   _____
   _____

Practicum Site Supervisor: _____ Date: _____

Student: _____ Date: _____

Faculty Liaison: _____ Date: _____

Form 2.1, p. 2 of 2, Copy 1

PRACTICUM CONTRACT

This agreement is made on _____ by and between_____
(Date)   (Field Site)
and _____ . The agreement will be effective for a period
(University Program)
from _____to _____ for _____ per week for _____ .
(No. Hours)   (Student Name).

Purpose

The purpose of this agreement is to provide a qualified graduate student with a practicum experience in the field of counseling/psychology.

The University Program agrees

1. to assign a university faculty liaison to facilitate communication between university and site;

2. to provide the site prior to placement of the student the following information

   a. profile of the student named above and

   b. an academic calendar that shall include dates for periods during which student will be excused from field supervision;

3. to notify the student that he/she must adhere to the administrative policies, rules, standards, schedules, and practices of the site;

4. that the faculty liaison shall be available for consultation with both site supervisors and students and shall be immediately contacted should any problem or change in relation to student, site, or university occur; and

5. that the university supervisor is responsible for the assignment of a fieldwork grade.

The Practicum Site agrees

1. to assign a practicum supervisor who has appropriate credentials, time, and interest for training the practicum student;

2. to provide opportunities for the student to engage in a variety of counseling activities under supervision and for evaluating the student's performance (suggested counseling experiences included in the "Practicum Activities" section);

3. to provide the student with adequate work space, telephone, office supplies, and staff to conduct professional activities;

4. to provide supervisory contact that involves some examination of student work using audio/visual-tapes, observation, and/or live supervision; and

5. to provide written evaluation of student based on criteria established by the university program.

Form 2.1, p. 1 of 2, Copy 2

With the specified time frame, _____ (Site Supervisor) will be the primary practicum site supervisor. The training activities (checked below) will be provided for the student in sufficient amounts to allow an adequate evaluation of the student's level of competence in each activity. _____ (faculty liaison) will be the faculty liaison with whom the student and practicum site supervisor will communicate regarding progress, problems, and performance evaluations.

PRACTICUM ACTIVITIES

1. Individual Counseling/Psychotherapy
   Personal/Social Nature
   Occupational/Educational Nature

2. Group Counseling/Psychotherapy
   Coleading
   Leading

3. Intake Interviewing
   Including taking social history
      information

4. Testing
   Administration
   Analysis
   Interpretation of Results

5. Report Writing
   Record-keeping
   Treatment Plans
   Treatment Summaries

6. Consultation
   Referrals
   Professional Team Collaboration

7. Psychoeducational Activities
   Parent Conferences
   Outreach
   Client Orientation
   Contact with Community Resources
   In-service

8. Career Counseling

9. Individual Supervision

10. Group or Peer Supervision

11. Case Conferences or Staff Meetings

12. Other (Please list) _____
   _____
   _____

Practicum Site Supervisor: _____ Date: _____

Student: _____ Date: _____

Faculty Liaison: _____ Date: _____

Form 2.1, p. 2 of 2, Copy 2

PRACTICUM CONTRACT

This agreement is made on _____ by and between_____
                     (Date)   (Field Site)

and _____ . The agreement will be effective for a period
                   (University Program)

from _____to _____ for _____ per week for _____ .
                                   (No. Hours)   (Student Name).

Purpose

The purpose of this agreement is to provide a qualified graduate student with a practicum experience in the field of counseling/psychology.

The University Program agrees

1. to assign a university faculty liaison to facilitate communication between university and site;

2. to provide the site prior to placement of the student the following information

    a. profile of the student named above and

    b. an academic calendar that shall include dates for periods during which student will be excused from field supervision;

3. to notify the student that he/she must adhere to the administrative policies, rules, standards, schedules, and practices of the site;

4. that the faculty liaison shall be available for consultation with both site supervisors and students and shall be immediately contacted should any problem or change in relation to student, site, or university occur; and

5. that the university supervisor is responsible for the assignment of a fieldwork grade.

The Practicum Site agrees

1. to assign a practicum supervisor who has appropriate credentials, time, and interest for training the practicum student;

2. to provide opportunities for the student to engage in a variety of counseling activities under supervision and for evaluating the student's performance (suggested counseling experiences included in the "Practicum Activities" section);

3. to provide the student with adequate work space, telephone, office supplies, and staff to conduct professional activities;

4. to provide supervisory contact that involves some examination of student work using audio/visual tapes, observation, and/or live supervision; and

5. to provide written evaluation of student based on criteria established by the university program.

With the specified time frame, _____ (Site Supervisor) will be the primary practicum site supervisor. The training activities (checked below) will be provided for the student in sufficient amounts to allow an adequate evaluation of the student's level of competence in each activity. _____ (faculty liaison) will be the faculty liaison with whom the student and practicum site supervisor will communicate regarding progress, problems, and performance evaluations.

PRACTICUM ACTIVITIES

1. Individual Counseling/Psychotherapy
    Personal/Social Nature
    Occupational/Educational Nature

2. Group Counseling/Psychotherapy
    Coleading
    Leading

3. Intake Interviewing
    Including taking social history
      information

4. Testing
    Administration
    Analysis
    Interpretation of Results

5. Report Writing
    Record-keeping
    Treatment Plans
    Treatment Summaries

6. Consultation
    Referrals
    Professional Team Collaboration

7. Psychoeducational Activities
    Parent Conferences
    Outreach
    Client Orientation
    Contact with Community Resources
    In-service

8. Career Counseling

9. Individual Supervision

10. Group or Peer Supervision

11. Case Conferences or Staff Meetings

12. Other (Please list) _____
    _____
    _____

Practicum Site Supervisor: _____ Date: _____

Student: _____ Date: _____

Faculty Liaison: _____ Date: _____

Form 2.1, p. 2 of 2, Copy 3

STUDENT PROFILE SHEET

Directions: The student counselor is to submit this information in duplicate to the university practicum liaison who will submit a copy to the field site.

Practicum Student Counselor/Psychologist

Name: _____

Address: _____

Telephone: (Home) _____

                (Office) _____

Date: _____

    I hold the degree of _____
from _____ and have completed the following courses
as part of the _____ (degree) program with a
major in _____ from _____ .

Psychology of Human Development _____   Tests & Measurements _____

Psychology of Learning _____   Personality Development _____

Counseling Skills _____   Career Development_____

Intro to Counseling _____   Legal & Ethical Issues _____

Theories of Counseling_____   Process & Techniques of Group
                                        Counseling _____
        Other (Please list):

        _____   _____
        _____   _____
        _____   _____

Professional and Nonprofessional Work Experience:

STUDENT PRACTICUM/INTERNSHIP AGREEMENT

Directions: Student is to complete this form in duplicate and submit a copy of this agreement to the university practicum supervisor or internship coordinator.

1. I hereby attest that I have read and understood the American Psychological Association and the American Counseling Association ethical standards (Chapter 6 in this manual) and will practice my counseling in accordance with these standards. Any breach of these ethics or any unethical behavior on my part will result in my removal from practicum/internship and a failing grade, and documentation of such behavior will become part of my permanent record.

2. I agree to adhere to the administrative policies, rules, standards, and practices of the practicum/internship site.

3. I understand that my responsibilities include keeping my practicum/internship supervisor(s) informed regarding my practicum/internship experiences.

4. I understand that I will not be issued a passing grade in practicum/internship unless I demonstrate the specified minimal level of counseling skill, knowledge, and competence and complete course requirements as required.

Signature: _____

Date: _____

STUDENT PROFILE SHEET

Directions: The student counselor is to submit this information in duplicate to the university practicum liaison who will submit a copy to the field site.

Practicum Student Counselor/Psychologist

Name: _____

Address: _____

Telephone: (Home) _____

(Office) _____

Date: _____

I hold the degree of _____
from _____ and have completed the following courses
as part of the _____ (degree) program with a
major in _____ from _____ .

Psychology of Human Development _____

Psychology of Learning _____

Counseling Skills _____

Intro to Counseling _____

Theories of Counseling _____

Other (Please list):

_____
_____
_____

Tests & Measurements _____

Personality Development_____

Career Development _____

Legal & Ethical Issues_____

Process & Techniques of Group
Counseling_____

_____
_____
_____

Professional and Nonprofessional Work Experience:

Form 2.2, p. 1 of 1, Copy 2

STUDENT PRACTICUM/INTERNSHIP AGREEMENT

Directions: Student is to complete this form in duplicate and submit a copy of this agreement to the university practicum supervisor or internship coordinator.

1. I hereby attest that I have read and understood the American Psychological Association and the American Counseling Association ethical standards (Chapter 6 in this manual) and will practice my counseling in accordance with these standards. Any breach of these ethics or any unethical behavior on my part will result in my removal from practicum/internship and a failing grade, and documentation of such behavior will become part of my permanent record.

2. I agree to adhere to the administrative policies, rules, standards, and practices of the practicum/internship site.

3. I understand that my responsibilities include keeping my practicum/internship supervisor(s) informed regarding my practicum/internship experiences.

4. I understand that I will not be issued a passing grade in practicum/internship unless I demonstrate the specified minimal level of counseling skill, knowledge, and competence and complete course requirements as required.

Signature: _____

Date: _____

capacities to perceive accurately and engage emotional content. One function of the practicum professor is to role model the optimal facilitative behavior to support the growth and development of students to increase the level of role function. This process parallels the counseling or therapy process. The practicum professor has a unique opportunity to demonstrate respect for the learner as an individual with a unique set of meanings who is capable of accepting responsibility for his/her own learning. The student has the responsibility to bring in material about his/her counseling practice and to share concerns related to practice. The practicum professor and student are partners-in-learning.

2. Practicum facilitates an understanding of one's self, one's biases, and one's impact upon others.

Counseling or therapy is an enterprise that has at its core the assumption that individuals develop by a process of differentiating self from other. It may be viewed as the process of bringing more of one's experiences into the conscious domain. It may be viewed as being able to determine what is my problem and what is your problem. It may be viewed as challenging thinking patterns inappropriately imposed on experience. Whatever the theoretical orientation of the counseling work, the practicum student must examine, on a personal level, those qualities about himself/herself that may enhance or impede this work. The practicum experience provides a setting in which personal qualities related to counseling practice can be examined. Therefore, activities that help clarify the counselor's own feelings, values, background, and perceptions in the context of the counseling work are an appropriate and necessary part of the practicum experience. Focus in practicum is not only directed toward determining the dynamics and personal meanings of the client but also upon examining how the student views others and how his/her behaviors and attitudes affect others.

3. Each member of a practicum group is capable of and responsible for facilitating professional growth and development.

The practicum experience usually involves dyadic, individual, and group activities designed to enhance the quality of counseling practice. Usually peer counseling and peer feedback are selected training activities. Also, usually the group interaction provides a forum in which practicum members can give and receive feedback regarding counseling techniques and concerns. Each member of the practicum participates not only as a student but also as someone who is ale to provide valuable feedback to others regarding the impact particular responses and attitudes may make upon clients. The practicum professor is not the only credible source of feedback regarding student counseling behaviors but rather only one among many whose responses can be examined. The practicum experience, therefore, tends to be more member-centered than leader-centered.

4. Practicum is composed of varied experiences to be determined by the particular needs, abilities, and concerns of the practicum group members and the practicum professor.

Two conditions contribute to the variety and kinds of learning activities that are part of practicum. First, program considerations about how the practicum is placed within the overall curriculum are influential. In some programs, basic skill training is an integral part of practicum. In other programs, skill training activities are included in other courses. Some programs require more hours of field experience, and the practicum is followed by an extensive internship. While in others, the practicum is the only experiential component in the program.

A second condition influencing the kinds and variety of experiences included in practicum is the unique needs that the student brings to the group. These may be personal concerns of the student or concerns related to client needs brought back to the practicum class for discussion. Therefore, practicum, by necessity, must have a flexible and formative approach to planning learning activities.

A range of activities that often are included as part of the practicum could be

structured skill development exercises

unstructured group interaction

role-playing

peer counseling, taping, and critiquing

selected assigned readings regarding special problem areas

keeping personal journals

videotaping and observing counseling sessions

giving and receiving feedback

preparing case presentations for review

interacting with supervisor

5. Supervision and consultation form the central core of practicum.

Intensive supervision and consultation allow the student to move more quickly toward competence and mastery in counseling or therapy. The supervisory interaction can help bring obstacles to the counseling process to awareness so that they can be examined and modified. The supervisory interaction also provides the opportunity for the role modeling process to be strengthened.

The student usually can expect both intensive one-to-one supervision and regular group supervision to be standard parts of the practicum. These not only provide skill development opportunities but also implicitly guide the counselor or therapist toward an openness and appreciation for collegial supervision and self-supervision.

6. Self-assessment by student and practicum professor is essential.

Because of the flexible and formative nature of the practicum, regular reviews need to be made as to how the practicum experiences are meeting the learning needs of the student. Self-assessment allows the student to be consciously aware of and responsible for his/her own development and also provides information for the practicum professor in collaborating about appropriate practicum activities.

The format for this self-assessment can be structured in a variety of ways. One possible approach is to identify current strengths, current weaknesses, and current concerns or confusions. The assessments should be defined as concretely

as possible. Once the assessment of current functioning is described, a contract can be made with the practicum professor and other group members regarding the particular aspects of counseling practice that have been targeted by the student for improvement or development. Ongoing self-assessment is needed to give direction to the practicum.

7. Evaluation is an integral and ongoing part of the practicum.

Evaluation in practicum provides both formative and summative information about how the counseling development goals of the student and practicum professor are being reached. A variety of activities supports this evaluation process. Among these are self-assessment, peer evaluations, regular feedback activities, practicum site supervisor ratings, and audiotape and videotape review. The attitude from which evaluations are offered is characterized by a constructive coaching perspective rather than a critical judgmental perspective.

SUGGESTED COURSE REQUIREMENTS

The practicum has been described as a complexly interwoven set of counseling practices and support activities designed to promote skill development, personal growth, and application of knowledge on the part of the trainee. Activities entered into at the practicum site are directed and monitored by the practicum supervisor based upon site opportunities and student abilities. During the first week of activities, the usual emphasis is on orientation to site policies and practice, observation of professional activities, and review of client records and treatment plans in preparation for counseling practice. As the practicum progresses through the several weeks, activities gradually are expanded to include intake interviewing, testing, new client orientation, coleading, and contacts with referral sources. Individual counseling sessions are increased, group work and outreach are added, and the student participates in in-service and case conferences. In the final weeks of practicum, experiences include individual and group counseling or psychotherapy, and consultation and referrals.

In addition to actual site-based counseling practice, course requirements are designed to support and monitor the evolving skill and personal and knowledge bases of the student.

Class Meetings

Practicum students generally are expected to spend a minimum of two hours per week in a group session with the university supervisor. This time can include didactic and experiential activities and usually includes some form of review of counseling practices. A typical class session would begin by addressing any specific concerns a student has regarding his/her fieldwork. After immediate concerns are addressed, student counselors might engage in the following:

1. role-play situations encountered in fieldwork.

2. listen to and discuss various recorded counseling sessions.

3. review previously taped counseling sessions made by class members.

4. discuss theories and techniques related to common problems and client work of concern to group members, and/or

5. give and receive feedback with peers regarding personal and professional interaction.

Counseling Sessions

In addition to the weekly group meetings, students are required to engage in a specified number of counseling sessions each week. These may be both individual and group sessions. Early in the course, the number of sessions required would be less than at the middle and final phases of the course. A specific minimum number of sessions is required for the course. One-time sessions with clients as well as continuing series of sessions with a client are specified.

Individual Supervision Sessions

The student is expected to spend one or more hours per week throughout the length of the course in individual supervision with site and/or university supervisors. These meetings provide an intensive focus on the student's counseling/therapy work and are often regarded by the student counselor as one of the most valuable practicum components. Typical questions addressed during individual sessions include the following: Is the student counselor providing a facilitative interaction with the client? Is the student counselor accurately perceiving the client? What are the goals of the counseling process? Is the counselor able to facilitate the desired growth or change in the client? What obstacles may be present in the counseling work?

Tape Critiques

If at all possible, the student is expected to tape (audio and/or video) his/her counseling sessions. Of course, permission must be obtained from each client prior to taping the session. The practicum site will have policies and procedures that are to be followed to ensure the informed consent of the client. (See Form 4.2 in Chapter 4 of this manual.) The tapes are to be submitted weekly to the practicum supervisor and/or university supervisor to allow for sharing and evaluation.

Each tape should be reviewed by the student counselor prior to submission and be accompanied by a written or typed critique. The critique should consist of the following information:

1. student counselor's name;

2. client identification, number of the session with client;

3. brief summary of content of the session and intended goals;

4. comment regarding the positive aspects of the counselor's work during the session;

5. comment regarding areas of the counselor's work that need improvement;

6. concerns, if any, regarding client dynamics, and

7. plans for further counseling with the client.

Every effort must be taken to ensure the confidentiality of the counseling session. When the tape has been reviewed and discussed with the student counselor, appropriate notes regarding counseling performance can be made for the student's records. The tape(s) then should be erased.

An example of a completed *Tape Critique Form* is shown in Sample 2 for your review and reference. Several blank *Tape Critique Forms* (Form 2.4) have been included for your use.

DOCUMENTING PRACTICUM ACTIVITIES

Because of national accreditation guidelines and state and university requirements, a necessary procedure is to document both the total number of hours in practicum and the total number of hours spent in particular practicum activities. Two forms are provided for your use. The *Weekly Schedules* (Form 2.5) that are included can be used in two ways. First, the weekly schedule can be used by the practicum student and the practicum supervisor to plan the activities the student will be doing from week to week. Second, the weekly schedule can be used to document the weekly activities the student has completed.

The *Monthly Practicum Log* (Form 2.6) provides a summary of the number of hours of work per month in which the student has engaged within the activity categories established in the practicum contract. A file can be kept for each student for the duration of the practicum.

CHAPTER BIBLIOGRAPHY

American Psychological Association. (1986). *Accreditation handbook*. Washington, DC: Author.

Council for the Accreditation of Counseling and Related Education Programs. (1994). *CACREP Accreditation standards and procedures manual*. Alexandria, VA: Author.

TAPE CRITIQUE FORM

(Sample)

Jane Smith
: Student Counselor's Name

Tom D. Session #3
: Client I.D. & No. of Session

Brief summary of session content:
Tom is citing his reasons for being unhappy in his job situation and reviewing all he has attempted to do to make his boss like and respect his work.

Intended goals:
1. To help Tom explore all of his feelings and experiences related to the job situation.
2. To help Tom be able to assess and value his work from is own frame of reference rather than his boss'.

Comment on positive counseling behaviors:
I was able to accurately identify Tom's feelings and to clarify the connection of feelings to specific content.

Comment on areas of counseling practice needing improvement:
I sometimes became hooked into Tom's thinking about how to please his boss and would work with him about problem-solving in this way.

Concerns or comment regarding client dynamics:

Plans for further counseling with this client:
Continue weekly appointments; move focus back onto the client and try to identify other ways he worries about approval.

Tape submitted to:
Dr. Judith Scott

Date:
1/17/95

Sample 2. An example of a completed Tape Critique Form (Form 2.4).

TAPE CRITIQUE FORM

_____

Student Counselor's Name

_____

Client I.D. & No. of Session

Brief summary of session content:

_____
_____
_____
_____

Intended goals:

_____
_____
_____
_____

Comment on positive counseling behaviors:

_____
_____
_____
_____

Comment on areas of counseling practice needing improvement:

_____
_____
_____
_____

Concerns or comment regarding client dynamics:

_____
_____
_____
_____

Plans for further counseling with this client:

_____
_____
_____
_____

Tape submitted to:

_____

Date:

_____

Form 2.4, p. 1 of 1, Copy 1

TAPE CRITIQUE FORM

Student Counselor's Name

Client I.D. & No. of Session

Brief summary of session content:

Intended goals:

Comment on positive counseling behaviors:

Comment on areas of counseling practice needing improvement:

Concerns or comment regarding client dynamics:

Plans for further counseling with this client:

Tape submitted to:

Date:

TAPE CRITIQUE FORM

Student Counselor's Name

Client I.D. & No. of Session

Brief summary of session content:

Intended goals:

Comment on positive counseling behaviors:

Comment on areas of counseling practice needing improvement:

Concerns or comment regarding client dynamics:

Plans for further counseling with this client:

Tape submitted to:

Date:

Form 2.4, p. 1 of 1, Copy 3

TAPE CRITIQUE FORM

Student Counselor's Name
_____

Client I.D. & No. of Session

Brief summary of session content:
_____
_____
_____
_____

Intended goals:
_____
_____
_____
_____

Comment on positive counseling behaviors:
_____
_____
_____
_____

Comment on areas of counseling practice needing improvement:
_____
_____
_____
_____

Concerns or comment regarding client dynamics:
_____
_____
_____
_____

Plans for further counseling with this client:
_____
_____
_____
_____

Tape submitted to:
_____

Date:
_____

Form 2.4, p. 1 of 1, Copy 4

TAPE CRITIQUE FORM

Student Counselor's Name

Client I.D. & No. of Session

Brief summary of session content:

_____
_____
_____
_____

Intended goals:

_____
_____
_____
_____

Comment on positive counseling behaviors:

_____
_____
_____
_____

Comment on areas of counseling practice needing improvement:

_____
_____
_____
_____

Concerns or comment regarding client dynamics:

_____
_____
_____
_____

Plans for further counseling with this client:

_____
_____
_____
_____

Tape submitted to:

_____

Date:

_____

TAPE CRITIQUE FORM

Student Counselor's Name

Client I.D. & No. of Session

Brief summary of session content:

Intended goals:

Comment on positive counseling behaviors:

Comment on areas of counseling practice needing improvement:

Concerns or comment regarding client dynamics:

Plans for further counseling with this client:

Tape submitted to:

Date:

TAPE CRITIQUE FORM

Student Counselor's Name
_____

Client I.D. & No. of Session
_____

Brief summary of session content:
_____
_____
_____
_____

Intended goals:
_____
_____
_____
_____

Comment on positive counseling behaviors:
_____
_____
_____
_____

Comment on areas of counseling practice needing improvement:
_____
_____
_____
_____

Concerns or comment regarding client dynamics:
_____
_____
_____
_____

Plans for further counseling with this client:
_____
_____
_____
_____

Tape submitted to:
_____

Date:
_____

Form 2.4, p. 1 of 1, Copy 7

TAPE CRITIQUE FORM

Student Counselor's Name

Client I.D. & No. of Session

Brief summary of session content:

Intended goals:

Comment on positive counseling behaviors:

Comment on areas of counseling practice needing improvement:

Concerns or comment regarding client dynamics:

Plans for further counseling with this client:

Tape submitted to:

Date:

TAPE CRITIQUE FORM

_____

Student Counselor's Name

_____

Client I.D. & No. of Session

Brief summary of session content:

_____
_____
_____
_____

Intended goals:

_____
_____
_____
_____

Comment on positive counseling behaviors:

_____
_____
_____
_____

Comment on areas of counseling practice needing improvement:

_____
_____
_____
_____

Concerns or comment regarding client dynamics:

_____
_____
_____
_____

Plans for further counseling with this client:

_____
_____
_____
_____

Tape submitted to:

_____

Date:

_____

TAPE CRITIQUE FORM

Student Counselor's Name

Client I.D. & No. of Session

Brief summary of session content:

_____
_____
_____
_____

Intended goals:

_____
_____
_____
_____

Comment on positive counseling behaviors:

_____
_____
_____
_____

Comment on areas of counseling practice needing improvement:

_____
_____
_____
_____

Concerns or comment regarding client dynamics:

_____
_____
_____
_____

Plans for further counseling with this client:

_____
_____
_____
_____

Tape submitted to:

_____

Date:

_____

Form 2.4, p. 1 of 1, Copy 10

WEEKLY SCHEDULE
(Sample)

Day of Week	Location	Time	Practicum Activity	Comment
Mon	UCC	9-10	Intake Interview John W.	1st session Prob. Exploration
		10-11	Ind. Cnslg. Jane D.	5th session, taped personal/social
		11-12	Ind. Supervision	Reviewed reports Tape Critique
		1-3	Group Cnslg.	Eating Disorder Group
			Co-lead	3rd Session
		3-4	Report Writing	
		4-5	Testing Mary B.	Interpreted Strong/ Campbell
Wed	University	6-8	Group Supervision	Case Presentation Jane D.

Student Counselor Name: _____Jane Smith_____

Week beginning: ___1/17/95_____   Ending: ____1/21/95_____

Sample 3. An example of a completed Weekly Schedule (Form 2.5).

WEEKLY SCHEDULE

Day of Week	Location	Time	Practicum Activity	Comment
___	___	___	___	___
___	___	___	___	___
___	___	___	___	___
___	___	___	___	___
___	___	___	___	___
___	___	___	___	___
___	___	___	___	___
___	___	___	___	___
___	___	___	___	___
___	___	___	___	___
___	___	___	___	___
___	___	___	___	___
___	___	___	___	___
___	___	___	___	___
___	___	___	___	___
___	___	___	___	___
___	___	___	___	___
___	___	___	___	___
___	___	___	___	___
___	___	___	___	___
___	___	___	___	___
___	___	___	___	___

Student Counselor Name: _____

Week beginning: _____   Ending: _____

WEEKLY SCHEDULE

Day of Week	Location	Time	Practicum Activity	Comment
_____	_____	_____	_____	_____
_____	_____	_____	_____	_____
_____	_____	_____	_____	_____
_____	_____	_____	_____	_____
_____	_____	_____	_____	_____
_____	_____	_____	_____	_____
_____	_____	_____	_____	_____
_____	_____	_____	_____	_____
_____	_____	_____	_____	_____
_____	_____	_____	_____	_____
_____	_____	_____	_____	_____
_____	_____	_____	_____	_____
_____	_____	_____	_____	_____
_____	_____	_____	_____	_____
_____	_____	_____	_____	_____
_____	_____	_____	_____	_____
_____	_____	_____	_____	_____
_____	_____	_____	_____	_____
_____	_____	_____	_____	_____
_____	_____	_____	_____	_____
_____	_____	_____	_____	_____
_____	_____	_____	_____	_____
_____	_____	_____	_____	_____
_____	_____	_____	_____	_____
_____	_____	_____	_____	_____

Student Counselor Name: _____

Week beginning: _____   Ending: _____

WEEKLY SCHEDULE

Day of Week	Location	Time	Practicum Activity	Comment
___	___	___	___	___
___	___	___	___	___
___	___	___	___	___
___	___	___	___	___
___	___	___	___	___
___	___	___	___	___
___	___	___	___	___
___	___	___	___	___
___	___	___	___	___
___	___	___	___	___
___	___	___	___	___
___	___	___	___	___
___	___	___	___	___
___	___	___	___	___
___	___	___	___	___
___	___	___	___	___
___	___	___	___	___
___	___	___	___	___
___	___	___	___	___
___	___	___	___	___
___	___	___	___	___
___	___	___	___	___
___	___	___	___	___
___	___	___	___	___

Student Counselor Name: _____

Week beginning: _____   Ending: _____

WEEKLY SCHEDULE

Day of Week	Location	Time	Practicum Activity	Comment
_____	_____	_____	_____	_____
_____	_____	_____	_____	_____
_____	_____	_____	_____	_____
_____	_____	_____	_____	_____
_____	_____	_____	_____	_____
_____	_____	_____	_____	_____
_____	_____	_____	_____	_____
_____	_____	_____	_____	_____
_____	_____	_____	_____	_____
_____	_____	_____	_____	_____
_____	_____	_____	_____	_____
_____	_____	_____	_____	_____
_____	_____	_____	_____	_____
_____	_____	_____	_____	_____
_____	_____	_____	_____	_____
_____	_____	_____	_____	_____
_____	_____	_____	_____	_____
_____	_____	_____	_____	_____
_____	_____	_____	_____	_____
_____	_____	_____	_____	_____
_____	_____	_____	_____	_____
_____	_____	_____	_____	_____
_____	_____	_____	_____	_____
_____	_____	_____	_____	_____

Student Counselor Name: _____

Week beginning: _____   Ending: _____

WEEKLY SCHEDULE

Day of Week	Location	Time	Practicum Activity	Comment
___	___	___	___	___
___	___	___	___	___
___	___	___	___	___
___	___	___	___	___
___	___	___	___	___
___	___	___	___	___
___	___	___	___	___
___	___	___	___	___
___	___	___	___	___
___	___	___	___	___
___	___	___	___	___
___	___	___	___	___
___	___	___	___	___
___	___	___	___	___
___	___	___	___	___
___	___	___	___	___
___	___	___	___	___
___	___	___	___	___
___	___	___	___	___
___	___	___	___	___
___	___	___	___	___
___	___	___	___	___
___	___	___	___	___
___	___	___	___	___
___	___	___	___	___

Student Counselor Name: _____

Week beginning: _____   Ending: _____

WEEKLY SCHEDULE

Day of Week	Location	Time	Practicum Activity	Comment
_____	_____	_____	_____	_____
_____	_____	_____	_____	_____
_____	_____	_____	_____	_____
_____	_____	_____	_____	_____
_____	_____	_____	_____	_____
_____	_____	_____	_____	_____
_____	_____	_____	_____	_____
_____	_____	_____	_____	_____
_____	_____	_____	_____	_____
_____	_____	_____	_____	_____
_____	_____	_____	_____	_____
_____	_____	_____	_____	_____
_____	_____	_____	_____	_____
_____	_____	_____	_____	_____
_____	_____	_____	_____	_____
_____	_____	_____	_____	_____
_____	_____	_____	_____	_____
_____	_____	_____	_____	_____
_____	_____	_____	_____	_____
_____	_____	_____	_____	_____
_____	_____	_____	_____	_____
_____	_____	_____	_____	_____

Student Counselor Name: _____

Week beginning: _____   Ending: _____

WEEKLY SCHEDULE

Day of Week	Location	Time	Practicum Activity	Comment
_____	_____	_____	_____	_____
_____	_____	_____	_____	_____
_____	_____	_____	_____	_____
_____	_____	_____	_____	_____
_____	_____	_____	_____	_____
_____	_____	_____	_____	_____
_____	_____	_____	_____	_____
_____	_____	_____	_____	_____
_____	_____	_____	_____	_____
_____	_____	_____	_____	_____
_____	_____	_____	_____	_____
_____	_____	_____	_____	_____
_____	_____	_____	_____	_____
_____	_____	_____	_____	_____
_____	_____	_____	_____	_____
_____	_____	_____	_____	_____
_____	_____	_____	_____	_____
_____	_____	_____	_____	_____
_____	_____	_____	_____	_____
_____	_____	_____	_____	_____
_____	_____	_____	_____	_____
_____	_____	_____	_____	_____
_____	_____	_____	_____	_____
_____	_____	_____	_____	_____
_____	_____	_____	_____	_____

Student Counselor Name: _____

Week beginning: _____   Ending: _____

WEEKLY SCHEDULE

Day of Week	Location	Time	Practicum Activity	Comment
_____	_____	_____	_____	_____
_____	_____	_____	_____	_____
_____	_____	_____	_____	_____
_____	_____	_____	_____	_____
_____	_____	_____	_____	_____
_____	_____	_____	_____	_____
_____	_____	_____	_____	_____
_____	_____	_____	_____	_____
_____	_____	_____	_____	_____
_____	_____	_____	_____	_____
_____	_____	_____	_____	_____
_____	_____	_____	_____	_____
_____	_____	_____	_____	_____
_____	_____	_____	_____	_____
_____	_____	_____	_____	_____
_____	_____	_____	_____	_____
_____	_____	_____	_____	_____
_____	_____	_____	_____	_____
_____	_____	_____	_____	_____
_____	_____	_____	_____	_____
_____	_____	_____	_____	_____
_____	_____	_____	_____	_____
_____	_____	_____	_____	_____
_____	_____	_____	_____	_____

Student Counselor Name: _____

Week beginning: _____   Ending: _____

Form 2.5, p. 1 of 1, Copy 8

WEEKLY SCHEDULE

Day of Week	Location	Time	Practicum Activity	Comment
_____	_____	_____	_____	_____
_____	_____	_____	_____	_____
_____	_____	_____	_____	_____
_____	_____	_____	_____	_____
_____	_____	_____	_____	_____
_____	_____	_____	_____	_____
_____	_____	_____	_____	_____
_____	_____	_____	_____	_____
_____	_____	_____	_____	_____
_____	_____	_____	_____	_____
_____	_____	_____	_____	_____
_____	_____	_____	_____	_____
_____	_____	_____	_____	_____
_____	_____	_____	_____	_____
_____	_____	_____	_____	_____
_____	_____	_____	_____	_____
_____	_____	_____	_____	_____
_____	_____	_____	_____	_____
_____	_____	_____	_____	_____
_____	_____	_____	_____	_____
_____	_____	_____	_____	_____
_____	_____	_____	_____	_____
_____	_____	_____	_____	_____
_____	_____	_____	_____	_____

Student Counselor Name: _____

Week beginning: _____   Ending: _____

WEEKLY SCHEDULE

Day of Week	Location	Time	Practicum Activity	Comment
———	———————	———	———————————	———————————
———	———————	———	———————————	———————————
———	———————	———	———————————	———————————
———	———————	———	———————————	———————————
———	———————	———	———————————	———————————
———	———————	———	———————————	———————————
———	———————	———	———————————	———————————
———	———————	———	———————————	———————————
———	———————	———	———————————	———————————
———	———————	———	———————————	———————————
———	———————	———	———————————	———————————
———	———————	———	———————————	———————————
———	———————	———	———————————	———————————
———	———————	———	———————————	———————————
———	———————	———	———————————	———————————
———	———————	———	———————————	———————————
———	———————	———	———————————	———————————
———	———————	———	———————————	———————————
———	———————	———	———————————	———————————
———	———————	———	———————————	———————————
———	———————	———	———————————	———————————
———	———————	———	———————————	———————————
———	———————	———	———————————	———————————
———	———————	———	———————————	———————————
———	———————	———	———————————	———————————

Student Counselor Name: _____

Week beginning: _____   Ending: _____

Form 2.5, p. 1 of 1, Copy 10

WEEKLY SCHEDULE

Day of Week	Location	Time	Practicum Activity	Comment
_____	_____	_____	_____	_____
_____	_____	_____	_____	_____
_____	_____	_____	_____	_____
_____	_____	_____	_____	_____
_____	_____	_____	_____	_____
_____	_____	_____	_____	_____
_____	_____	_____	_____	_____
_____	_____	_____	_____	_____
_____	_____	_____	_____	_____
_____	_____	_____	_____	_____
_____	_____	_____	_____	_____
_____	_____	_____	_____	_____
_____	_____	_____	_____	_____
_____	_____	_____	_____	_____
_____	_____	_____	_____	_____
_____	_____	_____	_____	_____
_____	_____	_____	_____	_____
_____	_____	_____	_____	_____
_____	_____	_____	_____	_____
_____	_____	_____	_____	_____
_____	_____	_____	_____	_____
_____	_____	_____	_____	_____
_____	_____	_____	_____	_____
_____	_____	_____	_____	_____

Student Counselor Name: _____

Week beginning: _____   Ending: _____

WEEKLY SCHEDULE

Day of Week	Location	Time	Practicum Activity	Comment
———	———————	———	———————————	———————————
———	———————	———	———————————	———————————
———	———————	———	———————————	———————————
———	———————	———	———————————	———————————
———	———————	———	———————————	———————————
———	———————	———	———————————	———————————
———	———————	———	———————————	———————————
———	———————	———	———————————	———————————
———	———————	———	———————————	———————————
———	———————	———	———————————	———————————
———	———————	———	———————————	———————————
———	———————	———	———————————	———————————
———	———————	———	———————————	———————————
———	———————	———	———————————	———————————
———	———————	———	———————————	———————————
———	———————	———	———————————	———————————
———	———————	———	———————————	———————————
———	———————	———	———————————	———————————
———	———————	———	———————————	———————————
———	———————	———	———————————	———————————
———	———————	———	———————————	———————————
———	———————	———	———————————	———————————
———	———————	———	———————————	———————————
———	———————	———	———————————	———————————

Student Counselor Name: _____

Week beginning: _____   Ending: _____

MONTHLY PRACTICUM LOG

Name: _____

Practicum Site: _____

Practicum Supervisor: _____ (Signature)

Month of	Intake Interview	Ind. Counseling	Group Counseling	Testing	Report Writing	Consultation	Psycho-Educational	Career Counseling	Case Conference	Other (Specify)
Week 1										
Dates:										
Total Hours:										
Week 2										
Dates:										
Total Hours:										
Week 3										
Dates:										
Total Hours:										
Week 4										
Dates:										
Total Hours:										

Form 2.6, p. 1 of 1, copy 1.

MONTHLY PRACTICUM LOG

Name: _____

Practicum Site: _____

Practicum Supervisor: _____
(Signature)

Month of	Intake Interview	Ind. Counseling	Group Counseling	Testing	Report Writing	Consulta-tion	Psycho-Educa-tional	Career Coun-seling	Case Conference	Other (Specify)
Week 1										
Dates:										
Total Hours:										
Week 2										
Dates:										
Total Hours:										
Week 3										
Dates:										
Total Hours:										
Week 4										
Dates:										
Total Hours:										

Form 2.6, p. 1 of 1, copy 2.

MONTHLY PRACTICUM LOG

Name: _____

Practicum Site: _____

Practicum Supervisor: _____

(Signature)

Month of	Intake Interview	Ind. Counseling	Group Counseling	Testing	Report Writing	Consulta-tion	Psycho-Educa-tional	Career Coun-seling	Case Conference	Other (Specify)
Week 1										
Dates:										
Total Hours:										
Week 2										
Dates:										
Total Hours:										
Week 3										
Dates:										
Total Hours:										
Week 4										
Dates:										
Total Hours:										

Form 2.6, p. 1 of 1, copy 3.

MONTHLY PRACTICUM LOG

Name: _____

Practicum Site: _____

Practicum Supervisor: _____
(Signature)

Month of	Intake Interview	Ind. Counseling	Group Counseling	Testing	Report Writing	Consulta-tion	Psycho-Educa-tional	Career Coun-seling	Case Conference	Other (Specify)
Week 1										
Dates:										
Total Hours:										
Week 2										
Dates:										
Total Hours:										
Week 3										
Dates:										
Total Hours:										
Week 4										
Dates:										
Total Hours:										

Form 2.6, p. 1 of 1, copy 4.

56

INTERNSHIP EXPERIENCE

John C. Boylan, Ph.D.

In Chapter 2 is addressed the training and program requirements of practicum activities both on and off campus. Emphasis was placed upon the university training program assuming responsibility for providing coursework and supervision of students. Often the supervision is by university faculty and site supervisor.

In Chapter 3 is addressed the internship component of the students training program. Emphasis is placed upon the procedures for evaluating and obtaining internship placement in an agency or a school.

This section is based upon the assumption that the student has completed all or almost all formal coursework at the training institution and is completing his/her internship experience in an approved internship site. An important concept to note is that the internship experience is typically quite different form previous pre-practicum and practicum experiences. In the internship, the major responsibility for the supervision of the intern is the site supervisor. Thus, the student needs to formalize the relationship with the site supervisor to ensure that the requirements of the internship are consistent with goals of the institution and with the student's personal and professional goals.

This section will provide the student with an overview of what are considered to be the fundamental steps in selecting and evaluating an internship placement.

The transition from practicum to internship can create considerable concern for the student. Selecting an internship site without adequate knowledge of the requirements of both the university training program and the specific internship sites to be considered prevents the student from making an informed decision regarding placement.

Although the selection process may be viewed by some students as an opportunity to explore experiences that are available for training and supervision, often other students feel pressured to make a decision based upon limited information without adequate thought and preparation.

SELECTION AND EVALUATION OF AN INTERNSHIP SITE

A major issue to be addressed by the perspective intern is the appropriateness of the internship experience in relationship to the student's personal and professional goals. A well recognized fact is that the completion of an internship experience that meets the student's career needs and program needs, as well as providing good supervision and training, enhances the student's professional viability.

The initial step in the selection of an internship site requires that the student gather as much information as possible about each potential internship site and personnel.

In preparation, a number of questions need to be addressed:

- Will the internship site provide me with a wide variety of professional activities in keeping with my training and professional goals?

- Does the internship client/patient population represent the type of population with whom I want to work?

- Will I be exposed to all the activities that a regular employed staff member would experience?

- Will I be provided with direct supervision by a trained qualified supervisor?

- Have the internship site personnel had experience in working with interns or is this the first time an intern has been placed there?

- Do/will appropriate liaison activities occur between the university training program and the internship staff?

Answers to these questions enable the student to gain an initial overview of the proposed internship experience at one or more different sites. Consulting with university faculty, the internship coordinator, and other professionals is an invaluable source of internship information. Data about the type of setting, the client population, the types of services, and the staff size aid in the process of determining if the internship site is in keeping with the student's professional needs. The *Intern Site Preselection Data Sheet* (Form 3.1) included in this chapter can be used to gather appropriate information about the internship site. The information needed to complete the form can be obtained by consulting with professionals familiar with the site, by informally visiting the site, or by writing to the site to obtain available descriptive materials and answers to specific questions.

Once the student has selected several possible internship sites, the next step in the process should be to set up a personal interview at each internship site that holds potential. Taking an interview helps the student to gain first hand knowledge about the internship site and provides the opportunity to meet with the staff and other professionals. Hersh and Poey (1984) have developed an interviewing guide to assist the intern in preparing for an on-site interview. Their guide is provided in the next section.

——————————— ★ ★ ★ ———————————

A PROPOSED INTERVIEWING GUIDE FOR INTERN APPLICANTS*
Jeffery B. Hersh and Kent Poey

Many internship centers either require or strongly encouraged an on-site interview. Some may consider a phone interview. Most only will offer an interview to those applicants who have passed through an initial selection process based on completed written application materials. From our observation, the interview is a critical part of selecting intern candidates.

*This article appeared in *Professional Psychology: Research and Practice,* 1984, Vol. 15, p. 305. Reprinted with permission.

Yet many intern applicants appear unprepared to answer rather standard questions. In the interest of clarifying our expectations and hopefully those of other internship centers, we have outlined a series of questions that interns should consider asking intern directors, because such questions typically indicate initiative and interest. There are, however, some questions that are heard in the context of the interview with mixed reactions by intern directors and that may place the intern's evaluation in some negative light. Generally speaking, the best questions are those that reflect motivation to learn and take part in many work activities rather than questions that promote a speculation that the intern may be demanding or complaining.

The listing below is probably more inclusive than encountered in any particular setting. It should be used as a general guide. It is important that the intern applicant prepare himself/herself for the special emphasis of each internship site by anticipating more questions in certain categories than others. For instance, a long discussion of inpatient treatment is unlikely to develop in a training site that primarily provides outpatient services. Our hope is that these lists will be an aid for intern applicants in their preparation for interviews and will be used in conjunction with the published *Survival Guide for Intern Applicants* (Belar & Orgel, 1980). Obviously, preparing for an interview involves more than rehearsing answers to several anticipated questions. We hope the intern candidate will take the opportunity to reflect on his or her learning needs, clinical strengths, and future directions. This contemplative process is invaluable to growth and meaningful challenge in general and will aid the intern candidate in setting his/her priorities for the next year specifically. The intern candidate is advised also to meet with the director of clinical training and other intern applicants for support and feedback.

Common Questions Asked by Internship Directors

1. General:
   What interests you in this internship program?

   Have you worked with client populations similar to those we see here?

   What are some books or articles that you have read recently?

   What are some of your specialized skills?

(Continued on p. 63)

INTERN SITE PRESELECTION DATA SHEET

Name of Agency _____

Address _____

Type of Agency _____ Staff Size _____

Client/patient population _____

Type of Direct Services Rendered

Inpatient therapy	Yes _____	No _____
Outpatient therapy	Yes _____	No _____
After Care	Yes _____	No _____
Addiction therapy	Yes _____	No _____
Individual therapy	Yes _____	No _____
Group therapy	Yes _____	No _____
Marital therapy	Yes _____	No _____
Occupational therapy	Yes _____	No _____
Physical therapy	Yes _____	No _____

Intern Experience Provided (Direct Service)

Inpatient therapy	Yes _____	No _____
Outpatient therapy	Yes _____	No _____
Addiction therapy	Yes _____	No _____
Individual therapy	Yes _____	No _____
Group therapy	Yes _____	No _____
Marital therapy	Yes _____	No _____
Family therapy	Yes _____	No _____

Administrative Experience

Intake Interviewing	Yes _____	No
Testing	Yes _____	No _____
Scoring	Yes _____	No _____
Interpreting	Yes _____	No _____
Report Writing	Yes _____	No _____
Record Keeping	Yes _____	No _____
Treatment Planning	Yes _____	No _____
Consultation	Yes _____	No _____
Referral	Yes _____	No _____
Case Summaries	Yes _____	No _____
Staff Meetings	Yes _____	No _____

Supervision Provided

Direct supervision	Yes _____	No _____
Individual	Yes _____	No _____
Group	Yes _____	No _____

Education Provided

Professional training seminars	Yes _____	No _____
In-service training	Yes _____	No _____
Research	Yes _____	No _____

Form 3.1, p. 1 of 1, Copy 1

INTERN SITE PRESELECTION DATA SHEET

Name of Agency _____

Address _____

Type of Agency _____   Staff Size _____

Client/patient population _____

Type of Direct Services Rendered

Inpatient therapy	Yes _____	No _____
Outpatient therapy	Yes _____	No _____
After Care	Yes _____	No _____
Addiction therapy	Yes _____	No _____
Individual therapy	Yes _____	No _____
Group therapy	Yes _____	No _____
Marital therapy	Yes _____	No _____
Occupational therapy	Yes _____	No _____
Physical therapy	Yes _____	No _____

Intern Experience Provided (Direct Service)

Inpatient therapy	Yes _____	No _____
Outpatient therapy	Yes _____	No _____
Addiction therapy	Yes _____	No _____
Individual therapy	Yes _____	No _____
Group therapy	Yes _____	No _____
Marital therapy	Yes _____	No _____
Family therapy	Yes _____	No _____

Administrative Experience

Intake Interviewing	Yes _____	No _____
Testing	Yes _____	No _____
Scoring	Yes _____	No _____
Interpreting	Yes _____	No _____
Report Writing	Yes _____	No _____
Record Keeping	Yes _____	No _____
Treatment Planning	Yes _____	No _____
Consultation	Yes _____	No _____
Referral	Yes _____	No _____
Case Summaries	Yes _____	No _____
Staff Meetings	Yes _____	No _____

Supervision Provided

Direct supervision	Yes _____	No _____
Individual	Yes _____	No _____
Group	Yes _____	No _____

Education Provided

Professional training seminars	Yes _____	No _____
In-service training	Yes _____	No _____
Research	Yes _____	No _____

Form 3.1, p. 1 of 1, Copy 2

INTERN SITE PRESELECTION DATA SHEET

Name of Agency _____
Address _____
Type of Agency _____ Staff Size _____
Client/patient population _____

Type of Direct Services Rendered

Inpatient therapy	Yes _____	No _____
Outpatient therapy	Yes _____	No _____
After Care	Yes _____	No _____
Addiction therapy	Yes _____	No _____
Individual therapy	Yes _____	No _____
Group therapy	Yes _____	No _____
Marital therapy	Yes _____	No _____
Occupational therapy	Yes _____	No _____
Physical therapy	Yes _____	No _____

Intern Experience Provided (Direct Service)

Inpatient therapy	Yes _____	No _____
Outpatient therapy	Yes _____	No _____
Addiction therapy	Yes _____	No _____
Individual therapy	Yes _____	No _____
Group therapy	Yes _____	No _____
Marital therapy	Yes _____	No _____
Family therapy	Yes _____	No _____

Administrative Experience

Intake Interviewing	Yes _____	No _____
Testing	Yes _____	No _____
Scoring	Yes _____	No _____
Interpreting	Yes _____	No _____
Report Writing	Yes _____	No _____
Record Keeping	Yes _____	No _____
Treatment Planning	Yes _____	No _____
Consultation	Yes _____	No _____
Referral	Yes _____	No _____
Case Summaries	Yes _____	No _____
Staff Meetings	Yes _____	No _____

Supervision Provided

Direct supervision	Yes _____	No _____
Individual	Yes _____	No _____
Group	Yes _____	No _____

Education Provided

Professional training seminars	Yes _____	No _____
In-service training	Yes _____	No _____
Research	Yes _____	No _____

INTERN SITE PRESELECTION DATA SHEET

Name of Agency _____

Address _____

Type of Agency _____ Staff Size _____

Client/patient population _____

Type of Direct Services Rendered

Inpatient therapy	Yes _____	No _____
Outpatient therapy	Yes _____	No _____
After Care	Yes _____	No _____
Addiction therapy	Yes _____	No _____
Individual therapy	Yes _____	No _____
Group therapy	Yes _____	No _____
Marital therapy	Yes _____	No _____
Occupational therapy	Yes _____	No _____
Physical therapy	Yes _____	No _____

Intern Experience Provided (Direct Service)

Inpatient therapy	Yes _____	No _____
Outpatient therapy	Yes _____	No _____
Addiction therapy	Yes _____	No _____
Individual therapy	Yes _____	No _____
Group therapy	Yes _____	No _____
Marital therapy	Yes _____	No _____
Family therapy	Yes _____	No _____

Administrative Experience

Intake Interviewing	Yes _____	No _____
Testing	Yes _____	No _____
Scoring	Yes _____	No _____
Interpreting	Yes _____	No _____
Report Writing	Yes _____	No _____
Record Keeping	Yes _____	No _____
Treatment Planning	Yes _____	No _____
Consultation	Yes _____	No _____
Referral	Yes _____	No _____
Case Summaries	Yes _____	No _____
Staff Meetings	Yes _____	No _____

Supervision Provided

Direct supervision	Yes _____	No _____
Individual	Yes _____	No _____
Group	Yes _____	No _____

Education Provided

Professional training seminars	Yes _____	No _____
In-service training	Yes _____	No _____
Research	Yes _____	No _____

Form 3.1, p. 1 of 1, Copy 4

2. Individual Adult Therapy:
   What kinds of client problems have you worked with and in what modalities?

   What experiences have you had doing emergency work and crisis therapy?

   What kinds of cases do you work well with and what kinds of cases present particular problems?

   What is your therapeutic orientation? How would you describe your therapeutic style?

   Describe your conceptualization and treatment of a recent or current case.

   What are your strengths as a therapist and what areas need improvement?

3. Group Therapy:
   Have you led groups? What kinds—therapeutic, educational?

   Have you had cotherapy experience with groups?

   What in the cotherapy relationship was helpful or difficult?

4. Child/Family/ Couples Therapy:
   What is your experience with child therapy? Family? Couples?

   Describe the kinds of cases you have worked with, including your theoretical orientation.

   What have your cotherapy experiences in family and couples work been like?

5. Inpatient:
   Have you had inpatient experiences? Acute care? Long-term care?

   Milieu therapy?

   What are your strengths in this area and what areas do you need to improve?

6. Psychological Testing:
   What is your background in testing?

   What tests are you familiar with?

   In what specific areas do you want/need further training?

7. Consultation and Education:
   What is your background in consultation and education?

   Have you collaborated with other professional groups including teachers, lawyers, physicians, and nurses?

   Describe your experiences in conducting workshops.

8. Supervision:
   What styles of supervision best facilitate your learning?

   What styles of supervision tend to inhibit your learning?

   What theoretical orientation would you be most comfortable with in supervision?

   Describe a rewarding supervision experience.

9. Work with Special Populations:
   Have you worked with people with physical complaints?

   Have you worked with clients who present handicapped, gay, minority, or cross-culture concerns?

10. Closing:
    What areas of your interest are not addressed by this internship?

    What areas are especially attractive?

    What are your future plans and goals?

Suggested Questions to Ask Internship Directors

1. How are supervisors assigned? What are their theoretical orientations?

2. How much opportunity is there for me to pursue special learning interests?

3. What kind of activities will I be involved in each week?

4. What is the diversity of the client population?

5. What is the relationship between disciplines and working relationships among the staff and interns?

6. Are there any changes in the stipends, vacations, or medical benefits from what is published in the brochure?

7. What office arrangements are provided for an intern, and what clinical support is available?

8. Is it possible to speak with a current intern?

9. Have past interns found jobs available in this area after internship?

10. How many people are you interviewing? For how many positions? What is the process by which the selection decision is made? (If there are nonfunded intern positions, ask how decisions are made between funded and nonfunded slots.)

11. What are the strengths and limits of this program?

Examples of Questions to Avoid Asking Internship Directors

1. How long does an intern work each week?

2. I want to complete by dissertation during my internship year. Could I have time off to do this?

3. Are there any opportunities to earn extra money in private practice during the internship year?

4. Persistent or antagonistic questions and comments showing a lot of interest in a work area that the internship program only minimally provides.

5. Questions and comments indicating a resistance to learning the major theoretical orientation presented by the internship center.

In conclusion, the interview and selection process is highly charged for intern applicants and internship directors. Both want to be evaluated positively. Unfortunately sometimes the pressure is handled by trying to make arrangements contrary to the Association of Psychology Internship Centers guidelines (APIC, 1982). An intern should discuss any procedural or ethical concerns with his/her university director of training. An area that is clearly unethical is encountered when the possibility of "early" acceptance is raised either by the internship applicant or internship director. An example of a potentially problematic area is when an intern is asked to rank the internship among his/her potential choices. We hope this question is asked in a flexible and nondemanding way. Our suggestion is for the intern to respond either by saying that more time is needed to sort out his/her priorities or to answer by placing the internship within a range unless it is definitely and unalterably the first choice. Finally, because our remarks reflect our experiences in one internship site, a survey of internship directors regarding their philosophy of interviewing and the questions asked may add subsequential support to our remarks or significantly extend them in impor-

tant ways. We will conduct such a survey that we hope will benefit both intern applicants and internship settings by clarifying priorities and expectations and by opening the interviewing process to inspection.

References

Association of Psychology Internship Centers. (1982). *Directory of internship programs in professional psychology* (11th ed.). Iowa: Author.

Belar, C., & Orgel, S. (1980). Survival guide for intern applicants. *Professional Psychology, 11,* 672–675.

———————— ■ ■ ■ ————————

A helpful source in obtaining an internship position is *A Guide to Obtaining a Psychology Internship,* second edition, revised and expanded, by Edwin Megargee (1992), published by Accelerated Development, Muncie, IN. This publication provides advice to survive and succeed in obtaining the internship best for the doctoral student. It outlines four steps in preparing a professional resume. Also included are effective interviewing skills for internship position interviewing. Suggestions are provided on what to avoid.

THE INTERNSHIP AGREEMENT

Prior to the start of the internship experience, a formal agreement is made between the student's training program (college or university) and the agency or school in which the internship will take place. In most instances, training programs have internship agreements available that serve as the formal contract between the training programs have internship agreements available that serve as the formal contract between the training program and the agency or school. A sample of an internship (Sample 4) is included. This may be adapted for use by either counseling or psychology interns.

INTERN ROLES AND RESPONSIBILITIES

The beginning intern approaches his/her internship experience with considerable amount of anticipation and anxiety. A contributing factor to the intern's uneasiness can be attributed to lack of familiarity with the role and responsibilities of the organization. Initial confusion and anxiety is lessened when the intern makes an early effort to

(Continued on p. 67)

MEMORANDUM OF AGREEMENT

This agreement is made this _____ day of _____ by and between
_____ (hereinafter referred to as the AGENCY/INSTITUTION/
SCHOOL) and _____ (hereinafter referred to as the UNIVER-
SITY). This agreement will be effective for a period from _____ to _____
for student _____ .

Purpose:

The purpose of this agreement is to provide a qualified graduate student with an internship experience
in the field of counseling/therapy.

The UNIVERSITY shall be responsible for the following:

1. Selecting a student who has successfully completed all the prerequisite courses and the
   practicum experience.

2. Providing the AGENCY/SCHOOL with a course outline for the supervised internship
   counseling that clearly delineates the responsibilities of the UNIVERSITY and the
   AGENCY/INSTITUTION/SCHOOL.

3. Designating a qualified faculty member as the internship supervisor who will work with the
   AGENCY/INSTITUTION/SCHOOL in coordinating the internship experience.

4. Notifying the student that he/she must adhere to the administrative policies, rules, standards,
   schedules, and practices of the AGENCY/INSTITUTION/SCHOOL.

5. Advising the student that he/she should have adequate liability and accident insurance.

The AGENCY/INSTITUTION/SCHOOL shall be responsible for the following:

1. Providing the intern with an overall orientation to the agency's specific services necessary
   for the implementation of the internship experience.

2. Designating a qualified staff member to function as supervising counselor/therapist for the
   intern. The supervising counselor/therapist will be responsible, with the approval of the
   administration of the AGENCY/INSTITUTION/SCHOOL, for providing opportunities for
   the intern to engage in a variety of counseling activities under supervision, and for evaluating
   the intern's performance. (Suggested counseling/therapy experiences are included in the
   course outline.)

Equal Opportunity:

It is mutually agreed that neither party shall discriminate on the basis of race, color, nationality, ethnic
origin, age, sex, or creed.

Sample 4. An example of an internship contract.

Financial Agreements:

Financial stipulations, if any, may vary from one AGENCY/INSTITUTION/SCHOOL to another. If a financial stipulation is to be provided, the agreement is stipulated in a separate agreement and approved by the INTERN, the AGENCY/INSTITUTION/SCHOOL, and the UNIVERSITY.

Termination:

It is understood and agreed by and between the parties hereto that the AGENCY/INSTITUTION/SCHOOL has the right to terminate the internship experience of the student whose health status is detrimental to the services provided the patients or clients of the AGENCY/INSTITUTION/SCHOOL. Further, it has the right to terminate the use of the AGENCY/INSTITUTION/SCHOOL by an intern if, in the opinion of the supervising counselor/therapist, such person's behavior is detrimental to the operation of the AGENCY/INSTITUTION/SCHOOL and/or to patient or client care. Such action will not be taken until the grievance against any intern has been discussed with the intern and with UNIVERSITY officials.

The names of the responsible individuals at the two institutions charged with the implementation of the contract are as follows:

_____   _____
Internship Supervisor at the UNIVERSITY   Agency Supervising Counselor/Therapist at
                                                                                  the AGENCY/INSTITUTION/SCHOOL

In witness whereof, the parties hereto have caused this memorandum of agreement to be signed the day and year first written above.

_____   _____
AGENCY/INSTITUTION/SCHOOL Administrator   Witness

_____   _____
UNIVERSITY Representative   Witness

Sample 4. Continued.

understand the role and responsibilities that he/she is expected to perform in the organization. Similarly, the intern needs to "fit" his/her skills and competencies into the structure of the organization. Prior to the start of the internship experience, the intern needs to address a number of critical issues and questions about his/her role.

1. Do I understand the mission, purpose, and goals of the organization?

2. Do I understand the duties and responsibilities required by my university supervisor and my site supervisor?

3. Do I understand my position in the structure of the organization?

4. Am I capable of articulation what I consider to be my assets, strengths, liabilities?

5. Do I understand the specific objective measures upon which my performance will be evaluated?

6. Do I understand the legal, ethical, and liability issues regarding my work in the organization?

7. Do I have a contract/agreement that delineates my duties and responsibilities? (Sample 4 is included as an example of a typical contract.)

Having reviewed his/her professional role and knowing the specific tasks that are required, the intern needs to formulate a tentative plan for carrying out the internship. Egan (1987) pointed to the need for the student to develop an *Individual Performance Plan* when entering a system. Egan's categories have been adapted here to provide suggestions for the intern.

Establish essential linkage. The intern develops a plan that is linked to the overall mission, strategic plans, and major aims of the organization. The plan is developed in keeping with the university program requirements and the intern's personal training needs.

List all personal performance areas. The intern lists all tasks for which he/she is responsible either alone or with others. Specific behaviors should be identified and planned.

Identify key performance areas. The intern determines what areas in the agency he/she can become a major contributor. Consideration is given to the students perceived strengths and competencies.

Set priorities. The intern develops objectives in each performance area and determines some of the critical accomplishments in that area. Specific objectives that are attainable in a planned time period are specified.

Develop personal performance indicators. The intern lists the formative and summative measures that can be used to indicate personal progress and accomplishments. (pp. 9–170)

With the completion of the individual performance plan, the intern is ready to enter into his/her internship experience armed with information essential to the successful completion of the internship experience.

In summary, the understanding of roles and responsibilities of the intern in the organization enables the intern to avoid any role conflict and prevents other professionals from having different expectations of the intern. A clear understanding of the division of responsibility and a well developed performance plan enable the intern to work collaboratively and cooperatively with other helping professionals in the agency/institution.

BEGINNING COUNSELING SUPERVISION

Counselor supervision is an interactional process between an experienced person (supervisor) who supervises a subordinate (supervisee). Hart (1982) defined supervision as an "ongoing educational process in which one person in the role of supervisor helps another person in the role of supervisee acquire appropriate professional behavior through an examination of the supevisee's professional activities" (p. 12). According to Bradley (1989), counselor supervision has three main purposes:

Facilitation of the counselor's personal and professional development,

promotion of counselor competencies, and

promotion of accountable counseling and guidance services and programs (p. 8).

To meet these ends, the supervisor must be a serious, committed professional who has chosen counseling and supervision as a long-term career goal (Hart, 1982). Similarly, the supervisor needs to assist the new supervisee to "ease" into the process of supervision. The following means of assisting oftentimes are accomplished by the supervisor:

1. communication a caring, empathic, and genuine understanding of the supervisee;

2. providing security to the supervisee as he/she faces training anxieties and vulnerabilities;

3. recognizing typical organizational and role responsibilities required of the supervisee;

4. understanding the supervisee rather than judging the supervisee's behavior in the early stages of supervision;

5. helping the supervisee identify strengths and weaknesses in an attempt to change or modify these behaviors;

6. attending to and accepting supervisee's needs;

7. permitting the supervisee to problem solve, experiment, and make mistakes; and

8. helping foster the development of a professional identity in the supervisee.

Helping the intern "ease" into the process of direct service, while at the same time encouraging the supervisee to test his/her skills and competencies, contributes significantly to development of professional and personal confidence in the supervisee.

STAGES IN THE PROCESS OF SUPERVISION

Friedman and Kaslow (1986) discussed six stages in the early learning and supervisory process. An adaptation of their writing illustrates the six-stage process.

Stage One—Excitement and Anticipatory Anxiety

Stage One begins with the intern's initial acquaintance with the training agency and ends upon contact with either the first patient or patient information. Marked by diffuse anxiety and excitement,

this stage creates uncomfortable feelings because the trainee has no specific task on which to focus and bind the anxiety until he/she is assigned a patient.

Stage Two—Dependency and Identification

Stage Two begins with the assignment of a case and ends with the trainee's realization that he/she has significant impact on a given patient. This stage is marked by the trainee's lack of confidence, skill, and knowledge about what psychotherapeutic work entails and leads to a high degree of dependency on the supervisor as well as to the idealization of the supervisor's skill and understanding.

Stage Three—Activity and Continued Dependency

Stage Three may begin within several months or a year after a trainee has been doing psychotherapy. It is marked by a direction of growth from passivity and dependence to a more active less dependent mode. It is a shift from being done to, to doing. this shift is observed both in the trainee's supervisory relationship and in the trainee's therapeutic work with patients.

Stage Four—Exuberance and Taking Charge

Stage Four begins with the trainee's realization that he/she really is a therapist. It is marked by the trainee's awareness that his/her psychotherapeutic armamentarium is in a large measure responsible for treatment "cures" that he/she effects.

Stage Five—Identity and Independence

Stage Five signals the emergence of the trainee's own capacity to begin to envision survival without the full support of the supervisor. This stage usually lasts several years. Supervisee initiated power struggles of one sort or another are seen. The stage represents a developmental achievement despite the negativistic phenomena with which the supervisee may be confronted. The trainee is aware of areas in which his/her professional strengths either exceed or seem to exceed the supervisor's.

Stage Six—Calm and Collegiality

Stage Six is marked by both the therapist's sense of calm and stability and by his/her feelings of collegiality with peers, senior staff, and supervisors. This stage is marked by risk taking, reexamining and challenging psychotherapy "truths," and increasingly personalizing his/her own styles of treatment.

The following article discusses a model of clinical supervision for the intern and highlights trainee needs and characteristics.

_____ ★ ★ ★ _____

Supervising Consultants in Training: An Application of a Model of Supervision*

Cal D. Stoltenberg

In this article the author delineates a model of supervision for consultation training. The model is based on Stoltenberg and Delworth's (1987) Integrated Developmental Model of supervision of counselors and has been adapted for supervision of consultations trainees. The model describes trainee characteristics and supervision needs across three levels of development, culminating in an integrated (3i) level with developed skills across eight domains of consultation activity. Development is tracked by monitoring changes in three crucial structures: self- and other awareness, motivation, and autonomy. Suggestions for supervision approaches for all three levels are presented, and relevant research is discussed.

Consultation has been developing into an important area of practice for psychologists and counselors for many years. This attention has yielded some important discussions and innovations in the training of consultants, particularly as it affects models of consultation and academic training (Bergan, Kratochwill, & Luiten, 1980; Brown, 1985; Froehle, 1978; Gallessich, 1974, 1985; Kratochwill & Van Someren, 1984; Stum, 1982). Consultation remains an important part of counseling psychology programs with 31% of American Psychological Association (APA) accredited programs requiring a course in consultation and 52% including it as part of direct service in practicum hours (Stoltenberg & Galloway, 1991). In addition, survey data indicate that consultation is included in coursework for about 90% of reporting master's programs in counselor education, and fieldwork in consultation is available in about 82% (Brown, Spano, & Schulte, 1988). The process of supervising consultants in training and attention to their development as consultants has received less attention (Brown, Pryzwansky, & Schulte, 1991) with only a couple of models, Conoley (1981) and Brown (1985), having

* This article appeared in *Journal of Counseling & Development*, 1993, November/December, Vol. 72, pp. 131–138. Reprinted with permission.

focused to any significant extent on the supervision of consultants.

In this article I examine some of the parallels between training consultants and training counselors, particularly focusing on trainee development and supervision environments. The basis for the discussion is the Integrated Developmental Model of clinical supervision proposed by Stoltenberg and Delworth (1987a). The model will be adjusted to fit a framework for training consultants. A working assumption of this article is that there are similar processes in both types of supervision and that trainees will develop in similar ways as they become seasoned professionals.

Training in Consultation

In some ways consultation has suffered from some of the same problems in recent years as has the area of clinical supervision. Considerable work has been done in attempting to define what consultation is (e.g., Gallessich, 1982, 1985) and the different forms it may take. Similar to clinical supervision, professionals who engage in the practice may not have had any (or very little) prior training (Gallessich, 1982; Gallessich, Long, & Jennings, 1986). Thus, "models" of consultation may be subsumed under some generic categories (e.g., mental health, process, behavioral, advocacy) but how consultation is done may be quite idiosyncratic and grow from the experiences of the consultant more than from some basis in theory and empirical literature (Bardon, 1985). This, of course, makes training difficult and suggests that supervisors of consultation trainees may be working from a model that is effective for them, but possibly not a model that will work for the trainee.

In the early stages of the growth of clinical supervision as a scholarly and empirical literature, training and supervision models were focused primarily on applying techniques and processes from the focal model of counseling to the process of supervision. These approaches included psychodynamic (Ekstein & Wallerstein, 1972), client centered (Rogers, 1957; Truax & Carkhuff, 1967), behavioral (Horan, 1972; Krumboltz, 1966), and cognitive orientation, which, according to Leddick and Bernard (1980), spawned the growth of skills training approaches (Hackney & Nye, 1973; Ivey, Normington, Miller, Morrill, & Haase, 1968). Kell and Burrow (1970) proposed a blended model that purportedly incorporated psychodynamic theory with a facilitative (client centered) style while using behavioral terminology. A similar process has occurred in consultation training in reference to behavioral and competency models (e.g., Bergan et al., 1980; Brown, 1985) and consultation models (see Conoley, 1981).

The models of supervision having the greatest impact lately have focused on developmental aspects of the training process. As recently as 1987, Worthington identified 16 models linking counselor development to supervision. Some of these models assume that the theory of supervision should reflect the same crucial constructs as the preferred theory of counseling, suggesting that developmental issues of the trainee in becoming a professional should be congruent with developmental issues encountered by the client (see Goodyear & Bradley, 1983, for a review). Other developmental models are described as being specific to the development of the trainee and address supervision from a unique perspective apart from the counseling process (Loganbill, Hardy, & Delworth, 1982; Stoltenberg, 1981; Stoltenberg & Delworth, 1987a). Loganbill et al. (1982) suggested that supervision is a significantly different process than is counseling and warrants a separate model—one that is able to accommodate various counseling theories and techniques. Crego (1985) has noted that the increase in coursework and training in consultation has not been accompanied by a systematic approach to training or extended across the developmental stages of supervisee competence. He has called for a long-term training model spanning didactic, experiential, and postdoctoral training. Dustin (1985) has called for a stage model of consultation supervision focusing on the development of the supervisee rather than the stages of consultation. The current model is an attempt to address this need.

Developmental models of supervision have stimulated considerable research into the process of supervision. Although some authors have concluded that there is insufficient evidence in support of developmental models of supervision (Borders, 1989; Holloway, 1987), others have determined that there is considerable empirical support and that these models show promise in continuing to guide future research and serve as helpful guides to the process of clinical supervision (McNeill & Stoltenberg, 1992; Russell, Crimmings, & Lent 1984; Stoltenberg & Delworth, 1987a, 1987b; Worthington, 1987). In my opinion, the strength of some of the models rests in their attention to changes that occur in the trainee over time that necessitate changes in the process of supervision to promote professional growth. In basing the models on developmental theory, one is able to understand these changes by examining the varying roles of constructs such as assimilation and accommodation, conflict, and disequilibrium.

Integrated Developmental Model

The Integrated Developmental Model of supervision (IDM) (Stoltenberg & Delworth, 1987a) relies heavily on theories of human development and earlier developmental models of supervision (Hogan, 1964; Loganbill et al., 1982; Stoltenberg, 1981) as well as recent research in clinical supervision. For current purposes, a definition of consultation supervision can be paraphrased from that of clinical supervision (Loganbill et al., 1982); that is, an intensive, interpersonally focused, one-to-one (or, in the case of group supervision, one-to-many) relationship where the supervisor facilitates the development of competence in the trainee. Supervisor responsibilities include evaluation of the trainee while encouraging development and protecting the welfare of the consultee and the client(s).

The model proposes three levels of development culminating in an integrated level called 3i (integrated). Developmental progress is monitored by attending to changes in three crucial structures (self- and other-awareness, motivation, autonomy) across specific domains of competence relevant to consultation. The domains are not considered to be orthogonal or comprehensive in their coverage of consultation activities but are indicative of important aspects of the process of consultation. Indeed, the type of consultation being practiced will have important ramifications for what may constitute specific domains (e.g., mental health consultation will require some different sets of activities than will organizational or process consultation). This, of course, is consistent with differences in activities and skills required for individual versus group versus family counseling. Figure 3.1 is depicting a modification of a figure by Jones (1991) of the relationships between levels, structures, and domains in the ever-popular "cube" configuration.

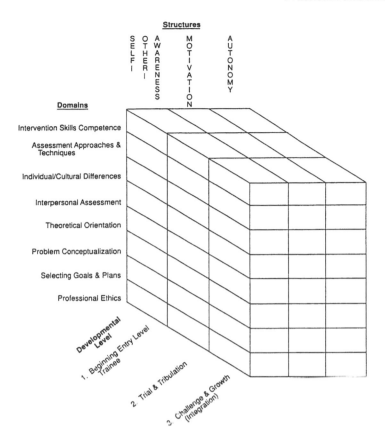

Figure 3.1. Integrated development model of supervision for consultation.

Stage theories of human development rely on sequences of stages that individuals pass through in invariant order. Stages have been described as a heuristic device useful in understanding knowledge development (Vuyk, 1981). The work of a given stage must be complete before the individual can progress to a higher level. In addition, qualitative changes in the trainee's cognitive and affective processes will occur in addition to quantitative changes in skill level. The constant influence of assimilation and accommodation (Piaget, 1970) account for trainee development. Within a given level of development, the trainee will attempt to *assimilate* or integrate new data into existing cognitive structures until those structures are no longer able to account for differential information. This creates disequilibrium or conflict which forces the trainee to loosen existing structures and develop new ones that can *accommodate* the new information and reduce the internal conflict. Without this disequilibrium or conflict, there would be no impetus to reorganize or develop new constructs, and change would be merely horizontal (adding new congruent information, quantitative change) and not vertical (changing structures or schemas and developing to a higher level, qualitative change).

Although debate continues among developmental theorists concerning the necessity of the equilibration construct (Case, 1985; Pascual-Leone & Goodman, 1979), Juckes (1991) has argued that it is essential in avoiding a learning paradox. Loevinger (1977) described this process as an amoeboid movement of development where small areas of insight occur constituting a higher level of development within a lower level. This continues to expand until the individual is largely functioning with higher order structures. Thus, as trainers, we want to elicit in our trainees new and more complex ways of conceptualizing the process of consultation in addition to acquiring an armamentarium of skills and knowledge. As you will see in the next section, the structures identified as important in the IDM are useful in tracking the qualitative changes in trainees that occur as they develop to higher levels of professional competence.

Structures within Levels. As noted earlier, changes in the three structures of self- and other-awareness, motivation, and autonomy mark the growth of trainees through the developmental levels. The following discussion describes trainees at each level in terms of these structures.

Level 1 trainees are those individuals who are new, or relatively new, to the practice of consultation. Depending on the type of academic program they are in (assuming they are initially learning consultation within an academic program), they may have had considerable coursework in psychology, counseling, organizational behavior, and so on, as well as exposure to and practice in other forms of intervention (e.g., individual or group counseling). Prior to receiving supervision in consultation, the trainee should have had some academic preparation introducing him/her to the consultation literature. As suggested by others (Brown et al., 1991; Conoley, 1981; Gallessich, 1974), a laboratory experience in consultation also is preferred as an introduction to consultation process and interventions. Although these laboratory experiences often do not include individual supervision, they approximate the dynamics typically found in group supervision. It should be expected that trainees in laboratory experiences, as well as those entering into an initial practicum in consultation, will be at Level 1.

It is important to be aware of trainees' levels of development in other aspects of training to understand their preparation for consultation training. Often consultation skills are acquired after an individual has attained competency in other areas (Lambert, Yandell, & Sandoval, 1975). Although we would expect all new consultation trainees to be initially at Level 1, they may be at higher levels (2 or 3) regarding certain domains of consultation activity such as interviewing skills. Of course, translation of these skills to the consultation context will be necessary, and one will still expect the structures to largely reflect Level 1 processes.

Regarding the structure of *self-and other-awareness,* the Level 1 trainee will be focusing primarily on himself/herself in both cognitive and affective areas. This *self-focus,* however, is not particularly insightful, but is more a function of being self-conscious and apprehensive about developing a new area of competence and being evaluated by the supervisor and the consultee (or, in the case of laboratory and group supervision experiences, peers). This initial anxiety tends to result in the trainee's focusing on his/her own fears and lack of knowledge and leaves little remaining attention capacity to attend effectively to the consultee. This process is consistent with the notion in developmental theories of available M-power and the action of other silent operators (Pascual-Leone & Goodman, 1979), and the roles of total processing space, operating space, and short-term storage capacity (Case, 1985).

The *motivation* of the Level 1 trainee will be quite high and tends to be a consequence of this heightened anxiety. The trainee is motivated to learn and to become an effective consultant so that the level of anxiety can be reduced and confidence and feelings of self-efficacy can develop. This motivation is not a function of deep self-knowledge and career certainty, but more a function of wanting to become an effective consultant so that this uncomfortable stage can pass. There is typically a strong desire to learn the "correct" model or style of consultation, and there may be some confusion and frustration when different orientations are discussed.

It is probably evident at this point that the Level 1 trainee will exhibit very limited *autonomy* and will be largely *dependent* on the supervisor and others viewed as experts in consultation. This limited knowledge about the practice of consultation, perhaps limited knowledge about oneself, causes the trainee to rely heavily on the supervisor to make important decisions, approve of (or develop) goals and plans, and so on. He/she typically will seek advice on many issues on a regular basis.

Over time, the trainee will become more comfortable with and confident in his/her skills and ability to implement various techniques, and the initial anxiety will diminish. It becomes more clear to the trainee how the techniques and interventions affect the consultee (and the client) and facilitate the process of consultation within a particular domain. This reduces the anxious self-focus and allows the trainee to be less distracted and more able to attend carefully to the needs of the consultee. At this point, the trainee may become quite confident (perhaps overly so), and the stage is set for movement into Level 2.

The *Level 2* trainee is now ready to focus more on the emotional and cognitive experience of the consultee. This *other-awareness* allows the trainee to comprehend more fully the affective reaction of the consultee to the problem at hand and allow for more careful (and accurate) assessment by being able to carefully attend to the consultee's view of the problem and the environment. On the down side, this increased focus on elements outside the trainee (the consultee, client, system) can result in an over-identification with the consultee or the client. This can cause the trainee to experience the same or similar emotions as the other person regarding the problem, which can cloud the trainee's objectivity and ability to function adequately in the consultant role. In addition, considerable confusion can result from attending too closely to the consultee's view of the problem and getting "lost" in irrelevant details or inaccurate perceptions. This level of trainee may become as confused and immobile as is the consultee and thus be unable to work effectively to assist in developing appropriate goals and intervention plans. Over time, the trainees will become more aware of the impact the consultee and the client may have on them, but this information alone is often not sufficient to alter their reactions.

The trainee's *motivation* is likely to *fluctuate* during Level 2, being high when confidence is high and low when confusion or strong negative affect is experienced. A more complex view of the consultation process has developed by now, and uncertainty about how powerful this mode of intervention is may develop, which can have a negative impact on motivation to learn and practice consultation. In addition, under ideal training situations, more complex consultation experiences will be arranged for the trainee, which can challenge his/her level of competence. Also, this more experienced trainee is more likely to be assigned to field experiences with a greater spectrum of needs requiring implementation of diverse models of consultation and competence in a broader range of intervention skills. Thus, a mixture of successes and failures will have an impact on the day-to-day motivation of these trainees.

Similarly, the Level 2 trainee will be striving for more autonomy, desiring to be less dependent on the supervisor and other experts. When success is ex-

perienced, the trainee will want to function more independently and take greater responsibility for the structure of supervision. When frustration and confusion are experienced, the trainee may revert back to a dependent stance with the supervisor and desire specific direction in what to do. Thus, the fluctuating motivation is accompanied by a *dependency-autonomy conflict* in the trainee.

The *Level 3* consultant is able to gauge the emotional impact of the consultee, client, and system on him/her and understand how various techniques and approaches to consultation affect these elements. The trainee exhibits heightened *self- and other-awareness* and remains able to engage in empathic understanding of the impact of the problem on the consultee, client, and the system while now being able to "pull back" into a more objective truly "third person" view of the situation. This allows the consultant to collect adequate (and accurate) information from all necessary sources and use this information in light of previously learned theory and research to make reasoned decisions and recommendations. The dual processes of assimilation and accommodation can now be used to take in and integrate data while adapting to the needs of the situation. This process is consistent with Labouvie-Vief's (1985) description of postformal thought, or mature thinking, which allows one to take his/her own feelings and experiences into account while personalizing the reasoning process.

The *motivation* of this individual is more *constant* with less extreme fluctuation from day to day. The consultant is grounded in a firm understanding of the consultation process and his/her own strengths and weaknesses, which enables the development of a more personalized approach to consultation. Greater *autonomy* consisting of a *conditional dependence* is characteristic of the Level 3 trainee. The trainee is aware of his/her areas of competence and will seek advice when experiencing a situation beyond his/her range of expertise without giving up responsibility for the final decision making. At this point, supervision itself becomes more of a consultation arrangement, with less a need for intensive guidance and advice and more of a collegial sharing of impressions and experiences.

Supervision Environments. The brief discussions of the structures that mark important characteristics of trainees at each level of development are now expanded to examine the supervision process. A basic assumption is that the approach of the supervisor should be varied to provide sufficient structure and guidance to enable learning to occur, yet allow for facilitative levels of conflict (disequilibrium) to be experienced by the trainee to stimulate growth to higher levels.

It is important to remember that trainees are likely to be at different levels for different domains, as opposed to being entirely at Level 1, 2, or 3. In fact, depending on the timing of consultation training in the supervisee's program, we might expect the trainee to be at Level 2 (or even Level 3) in certain aspects of intervention skills competence (e.g., interviewing skills) while clearly at Level 1 in most other domains relevant to consultation. For the purposes of the following discussion, however, rather "pure" examples of trainees at different levels will be used to clarify the process of supervision.

The Level 1 trainee. A considerable amount of supervision conducted in training programs and associated field placements will be with Level 1 trainees who have little or no experience with consultation but may, as noted earlier, have significant experience in other areas of practice. It is important to keep in mind that the trainee will be functioning largely in Level 1 structures with respect to consultation regardless of his/her expertise in other areas. Thus, considerable structure, guidance, and support will be required to assist the trainee in learning necessary skills (Brown, 1985; Conoley, 1981; Meyers, 1984) and to keep the anxiety at manageable levels.

The supervisor typically will be viewed as an expert role model, and regular requests for direction will usually come from the trainee. Confidence will develop in response to greater conceptual clarity of the skills required for consultation and associated models of assessment and intervention when accompanied by positive feedback and shaping by the supervisor. The trainee's professional awareness is low at this point, so easily understandable standards of performance will be the primary form of self-evaluation as opposed to attending to consultee or client progress. As the confidence grows, the supervisor should reduce the amount of structure provided in supervision and encourage more autonomy on the part of the trainee (cf. Meyers, 1984; Dustin, 1985). Some risk taking should be encouraged;

however, it is often more productive to rely more on instruction than on trainee focused problem solving at this stage. Much remains to be learned, and teaching and exemplification are appropriate methods to encourage this learning.

Supervision mechanisms used for this level of trainee will center on providing information, support, role-playing, and modeling to encourage growth (Brown, 1985; Conoley, 1981; Meyers, 1984; Zins, 1989). Direct observation by the trainee of the supervisor, or others, engaging in the practice of consultation can serve a very important role in demystifying the process and providing a template for the trainee to use in his/her own work. Role-playing within individual or group supervision sessions is another important method for demonstrating consultation skills to the trainee (Signell, 1974). Additional readings beyond those required for coursework in consultation can be useful in providing the trainee with more information and perspectives on the process.

If appropriate (e.g., in mental health consultation), assisting the trainee in conceptualizing client problems and dynamics is necessary. Translating skills and perspectives learned from other prior training in related areas (like individual counseling) can be an important function of consultation supervision. One needs to be careful in attending to the trainee's primary focus when dealing with this approach to consultation. There is a tendency for trainees to focus too much on diagnosing the client and designing intervention plans when the focus might more appropriately be on the consultee and his/her interactions with the client. Martin (1983) has argued that the reverse may also be true—that any perceived difficulties may be attributed to the consultee rather than the client because of his/her dominance in the supervisee's perceptual field. Regardless, the trainee will tend to rely on previously acquired skills in this new arena, and the supervisor must assist the trainee with the appropriate translation of these skills to this context. Although some similarities exist (Bardon, 1985), mental health consultation is not mental health counseling.

As with most situations where trainees are learning new skills in a new area, it is important to provide support and frame feedback in a positive manner. For example, trainees are usually more able to accept and integrate criticism or negative feedback if the supervisor first has addressed and reinforced some of the positive things the trainee has demonstrated. Consultee and client progress must be monitored carefully with Level 1 trainees. Preferred modes of supervision will include live observations and videotapes, which allow the supervisor to actually observe the process rather than rely on notoriously unreliable sources of information like trainee verbal and written self-reports. Some field settings, however, will make this difficult or impossible.

The supervisor needs to monitor the anxiety level of the trainee constantly to ensure adequate motivation for growth. As confidence increases, it is usually helpful for the supervisor to introduce increasing degrees of ambiguity into an examination of the consultation process. Focusing on different models of consultation, intervention options, and so on can serve to maintain functional levels of disequilibrium or conflict on the part of the trainee, which stimulates growth. Although we do not want our trainees to experience unreasonable anxiety and uncertainty, facilitative levels of both must be maintained for development to occur. The "too" comfortable trainee is likely to stagnate at a given level, and further growth will be frustrated.

It is important, I believe, to avoid the tendency to take a consultation approach to supervision of consultation, particularly for Level 1 (and Level 2) trainees. Conoley (1981) has delineated carefully some of the differences between consultation and supervision and noted with considerable candor some of the difficulties she encountered when the two processes became blurred. Such an approach becomes more functional for higher level trainees (Level 3), although it is doubtful that much supervision of consultation occurs for individuals at this level because, in part, the amount of training necessary to acquire credentials in clinical practice leaves insufficient time for consultation training (Gallessich, 1985). Nonetheless, the characteristics of the Level 1 trainee and the developmental needs preclude the use of a consultation model and strongly suggest the need for more structure and a didactic approach common to some of the current descriptions of training programs (Brown et al., 1991).

The Level 2 trainee. The structured learning experience provided for the Level 1 trainee should have a positive impact on his/her confidence and self-efficacy regarding aspects of the consultation process. Translating experience and skills from other areas has helped the trainee become more comfortable with dealing with system entry, interviewing and assessment, and selecting interventions and plans to share with the consultee. Prior to this point, for most trainees, experiences will have consisted mostly of laboratory training and some initial consultation experiences. Successes from these early interactions increase the trainee's level of confidence and require less supervisor-imposed structure on the process of supervision.

Supervisors of Level 2 trainees should be able to begin to play less of a teaching role and encourage more autonomy on the part of the trainee. A major function of supervision will be to assist the trainee in clarifying ambivalence regarding becoming a consultant and dealing with some of the limitation imposed by the process. Distinctions between consultation and other activities will continue to be important to address. For example, examining the similarities and differences between how one approaches an organizational consultation (designing, implementing, and evaluating interventions) and how one approaches diagnosis and intervening with counseling systems (like the family) can be useful in helping the trainee conceptualize the process building on existing strengths and adding new ones.

This level of trainee is inclined to experience fluctuations in motivation and confidence. Successes elicit confidence and a desire for more autonomy, whereas frustrating experiences shake this confidence and bring back a desire for more dependence on the supervisor. The trainee has moved beyond an anxious self-focus and is now able to empathize with and strive to understand more fully the experience of the consultee. It is important at this level for the supervisor to encourage this "other" awareness and assist the trainee in assessing the impact he/she is having on the consultee (Conoley, 1981) and, equally important, the impact of the consultee on the trainee. The supervisor should help the trainee sort out affective reactions into those that are a result of empathizing with key individuals in the consultation experience (thus sharing their feelings), those reactions that may be a function of personal issues that resonate with the issues arising in consultation (countertransference, emotional contagion), and others that may be associated with being in the role of an expert and not feeling like one.

Loganbill et al. (1982) identified five general classifications of supervisor interventions that may prove helpful in conceptualizing how one approaches the Level 2 trainee. The first category is *facilitative* interventions that largely consist of mechanisms of support for the trainee. It is advisable for the supervisor to remain supportive in response to all levels of trainees, but the occasional reactance of Level 2 trainees (resisting authority) makes it important not to overlook this type of intervention. *Confrontive* interventions are not usually appropriate for Level 1 trainees (they can't take the increase in anxiety accompanying confrontation of any but the most gentle type), but they are required for Level 2. It is important to challenge trainees during periods of emerging confidence to consider alternative conceptualizations of the consultation problem and expand their competence to include additional forms of interventions and evaluations beyond those with which they feel comfortable. *Conceptual* interventions can assist the trainee in tying together theory with practice by challenging the preferred theory and mode of intervention selected by the trainee and encouraging him/her to become aware of the range of possible consultation interventions (Fuqua & Newman, 1985; Kurpius, 1985). This is particularly important at this stage when the other-awareness can cause confusion and limit the trainee's ability to be objective and rely on theory or the literature in dealing with the problem. Modeling alternative models of intervention can still be very helpful at this stage. When possible, however, the trainee should be given an appropriate degree of autonomy in selecting a given approach with a consultee.

Prescriptive interventions, or telling the trainee what to do, while appropriate for Level 1, are often not appropriate for Level 2 trainees. When the trainee is feeling dependent, prescribing the diagnosis, interventions, and so on will only encourage the dependency and delay growth. When the trainee is feeling confident, prescriptions by the supervisor are likely to be met with resistance (either overt or covert) and can result in passive-aggressive behavior or open rebellion. Offering alternatives is important, but requiring compliance with suggestions should be avoided within the constraints of consultee and client welfare (cf. Robinson & Gross, 1985).

Catalytic interventions, those intended to "stir up" the process, are most appropriate for Level 2.

These interventions include process comments by the supervisor intended to highlight important interpersonal dynamics within the trainee-consultant, trainee-client, and trainee-supervisor relationships. The intent of these interventions is to increase the trainee's awareness of his/her impact on the other party and the other's impact on him/her. Countertransference issues, affective reactions, conceptual confusions, and resistance to feedback are some of the important focuses of catalytic or process interventions. Although these issues may become apparent through discussions with the trainee about current consultation assignments or through written conceptualizations, intervention plans, and so on, the issues are more readily identified in viewing videotapes, conducting live observations, or reviewing audiotapes. Coordination between the on-site and campus supervisors also can highlight these issues. In fact, close coordination between supervisors in different settings, although always important, is crucially so with Level 2 trainees who are more likely than other trainees to gloss over current problems or pit one supervisor against the other.

The Level 2 trainee probably is nearing the end of formal training in consultation if training is occurring within an academic training program. Typically, the trainee will begin demonstrating Level 2 structures for some domains during the latter part of an initial practicum or during a second practicum (if one is available). Other times, the trainee experiencing Level 2 structures will be entering an internship setting where consultation is an important part of the training process. If experiences have been structured during early training and expanded with more complex experiences across a wide variety of consultation environments, the individual can be expected to have firmly established some self-perceived areas of competence combined with some confidence. An increasing awareness of others, a stronger understanding of theory and practice, and a growing awareness of how one's own personal characteristics affect his/her role as a consultant should also be developing.

Unfortunately, for many, this will end formal supervision. They may or may not grow beyond the Level 2 structures for most domains and will either limit their involvement in consultation or retreat to Level 1 structures and remain stagnant in their competence and growth as consultants, or seek out informal supervision in the training or work environment.

Level 3 trainees. As suggested earlier, you are likely to encounter the Level 3 trainee only in internship sites or as staff members in employment settings. Interns who have reached this level of development likely will have had important and well-organized training experiences in their training programs, or will have had "other lives" where consultation served an important role. Supervision of interns, or post-doctoral supervision of psychologists or professional counselors, provides one with the formal structure to continue to engage in supervision where there is a clear definition of role and an evaluative component. If it occurs, supervising individuals in consultation beyond these experiences tends to be more of a clear consultation relationship with less evaluation included, unless there is a formal hierarchical relationship between the supervisor and supervisee (e.g., agency director). Often, it will consist of informal sessions where the "supervisee" seeks advice and perspective from someone who is perceived to be a more senior, experienced, and knowledgeable colleague.

This consultative relationship, while inappropriate for less advanced trainees, is quite appropriate for Level 3. Here the "storms" of Level 2 have subsided, and the individual has developed a more clear picture of approach to consultation incorporating a variety of approaches and techniques (cf. Bardon, 1985; Conoley, 1981). A clear sense of relative strengths and weaknesses will allow this trainee to function in an autonomous manner in some consultation relationships while seeking specific advice and recommendations in others. Facilitative and conceptual supervisory interventions remain important. A supportive relationship with a supervisor or colleague is always important in enabling the individual to consolidate gains and explore areas where further development is desired. Prescriptive interventions are rarely needed, although examining other orientations, theories, or perspectives remains important. Confrontive and catalytic interventions tend to be needed less as the trainee is more open to experience and less in need of a "jolt"; however, some regression still can occur in reaction to strong content emerging in interviews or personal life stressors that are having an impact on one's performance.

At this point in the trainee's development, it is important for a supervisor to assess the particular domains where the trainee is functioning at Level 3 and the domains where less development has occurred. The role of the supervisor here is to encourage growth in domains where Level 3 structures are not yet being utilized by helping the trainee apply higher order understandings from related areas. The supervisor should be attending to bringing the trainee up to Level 3 in all crucial domains relevant to the specific position and move toward integrating across domains. This integration in more of a horizontal change for the trainee and consists of moving comfortably across domains using perspectives and information from all of them to address the process of consultation from a complete and more sophisticated perspective within a personalized approach. This process is consistent with the notion of "chunking" schemas through practice or applying newly created performance rules (Juckes, 1991).

Supervisors at this stage should be alert to certain events or problems that are more likely to be encountered with this level of trainee. The first problem is with trainees who mimic Level 3 structures but are really still struggling with Level 2 issues. In the book on supervision (Stoltenberg & Delworth, 1987a), this type of trainee was referred to as a "pseudo Level 3." Usually because of significant conceptual skills and an understanding of some of the models and jargon of consultation, this individual may be able to "talk" a good game in supervision and present plausible conceptualizations of the process and explain away (again, plausibly) poor outcomes. This individual may have an intellectual grasp of the process, but is not able to adequately empathize with or understand the consultee's world or the organization under study. The result is a sophisticated "cookbook" approach to the problem and the key players, usually resulting in less than satisfactory outcomes if evaluation is conducted adequately (or very positive outcomes with poor quality evaluation). Catalytic and confrontive interventions will be required with this type of trainee to encourage adequate resolution of Level 2 issues and allow for growth to a real Level 3.

Another aspect of supervising Level 3 trainees, and one that is more accessible to discussion than with less developed trainees, is the issue of parallel process. This tends to be more common (or, at least, apparent) in mental health consultation, but also can occur in a different form in other types of consultation. Parallel process has a long history of discussion in the counseling supervision literature (see

McNeill & Worthen, 1989), although little research has been conducted to investigate the process. At this level, parallel process can be addressed with trainees as it may affect the consultee-client relationship and play itself out in the consultant-consultee relationship. Briefly, the consultee may bring emotions, conflicts, and other reaction tapped by his/her work with the client into consultation sessions and "play them out" with the consultant. Depending on the theory one follows, this can either be a conscious (Williams, 1987) or unconscious (Hora, 1957; Searles, 1955) process. Nonetheless, helping the trainee sort out these issues (often involving reactions to perceived authority figures) and their impact on the consultation relationship is an important part of understanding the consultation process and variables that can influence the dynamics of the relationships and implementation of intervention plans.

In most situations, supervising the Level 3 trainee is a rewarding experience allowing for mutual sharing of impressions, experiences, and information. The relationship truly can be collaborative at this point, and the trainee occasionally can provide perspectives useful to the supervisor in his/her own consultative relationships. Personal-professional integration is an important topic for this type of supervision, and one is likely to spend a portion of supervision time dealing with career issues and professional directions. Assisting the trainee in discussing the best fit for him/her in a professional setting, pursuing what types of professional activities, and to what extent consultation will remain a part of this focus is an important process for the trainee and a goal of the supervisor. Answers are not necessary, but a supportive and interested stance on the part of the supervisor showing a real investment in the professional development of the trainee is the crucial, and final, goal of supervision with this level of trainee.

Conclusion

In this article I have argued that a developmental perspective is useful in conceptualizing change over time in the consultation trainee and the supervision process. A three-stage model of trainee development was proposed based on Stoltenberg and Delworth's (1987a) Integrated Developmental Model, which describes in three structures across eight domains of professional activity culminating in an integrated Level 3i. Characteristics of trainees and their supervision needs were described in terms of

self- and other-awareness, motivation, and autonomy. Recommendations for supervisor interventions were tied to these structures and the need to meet trainee needs while encouraging growth. Although the proposed model answers calls in the literature for models of supervision of consultation that address trainee development (Dustin, 1985) and conceptualize the process from entry level to postdoctoral (Crego, 1985), no direct empirical support exists within the consultation literature to support its formulations. Related research relevant to the model as it relates to clinical supervision, however, has been supportive (McNeill & Stoltenberg, 1992; Stoltenberg & Delworth, 1987a; Worthington, 1987). Specific studies examining key constructs of the model for supervision of consultation are needed to examine the unity of a developmental perspective for this discipline. For example, the descriptions of trainees at various levels and their approaches to information processing and problem solving need to be examined using qualitative research designs as well as quantitative cross-sectional and longitudinal approaches. Similarly, the validity of the prescriptions for supervision behavior across trainee levels needs to be investigated. In addition, the framework presented here could benefit from a more detailed focus on each level of trainee within various training contexts across the spectrum of consultative environments. This task, however, is beyond the scope of this article.

Apart from the pros and cons of a developmental approach, the field could benefit from a more systematic focus on training beyond the single course, laboratory, and field experience. To reach one's potential as a consultant will require supervised experience across a number of environments over an extended period of time. Crego's (1985) call for post-doctoral training in consultation is a good start, as are the detailed training programs that address skills training and competency for beginning trainees. A comprehensive formulation of training is necessary, however, for the field to reach its potential as a discipline. In my opinion, attention to developmental changes in trainees as they become skilled consultants is one path to reach this goal.

References

Bardon, J. I. (1985). On the verge of a breakthrough. *The Counseling Psychologist, 13,* 355–362.

Bergan, J.R., Kratochwill, T.R., & Luiten, J. (1980). Competency-based training in behavioral consultation. *Journal of School Psychology, 18,* 91–97.

Borders, L.D. (1989). A pragmatic agenda for developmental supervision research. *Counselor Education and Supervision, 29,* 16–24.

Brown, D. (1985). The preservice training of supervision consultants. *The Counseling Psychologist, 13,* 410–425.

Brown, D., Pryzwansky, W.B., & Schulte, A.C. (1991). *Psychological consultation: Introduction to theory and practice* (2nd ed.). Needham Heights, MA: Allyn & Bacon.

Brown, D., Spano, D.B., & Schulte, A.C. (1988). Consultation training in master's level counselor education programs. *Counselor Education and Supervision, 27,* 323–330.

Case, R., (1985). *Intellectual development: Birth to adulthood.* Orlando, FL: Academic Press.

Conoley, J.C. (1981). Emergent training issues in consultation. In J.C. Conoley (Ed.), *Consultation in schools: Theory research procedures* (pp. 223–263). New York: Academic Press.

Crego, C.A. (1985). Ethics: The need for improved consultation training. *The Counseling Psychologist, 13,* 473–476.

Dustin, D. (1985). On Brown's training and supervision of consultants. *The Counseling Psychologist, 13,* 436–440.

Ekstein, R., & Wallerstein, R. (1972). *The teaching and learning of psychotherapy* (2nd ed.). New York: International University Press.

Froehle, T.C. (1978). Systematic training of consultants through competency. *The Personnel and Guidance Journal, 56,* 436–441.

Fuqua, D.R., & Newman, J.L. (1985). Individual consultation. *The Counseling Psychologist, 13,* 390–395.

Gallessich, J. (1974). Training the school psychologist for consultation. *Journal of School Psychology, 12,* 138–149.

Gallessich, J. (1982). *The profession and practice of consultation.* San Francisco, CA: Jossey-Bass.

Gallessich, J. (1985). Toward a meta-theory of consultation. *The Counseling Psychologist, 13,* 336–354.

Gallessich, J., Long, K.M., & Jennings, S. (1986). In F.V. Mannino, E.J. Trickett, M.F. Shore, M.G. Kidder, & G. Levin (Eds.), *Handbook of mental health consultation* (pp. 279–317). Rockville, MD: National Institute of Mental Health.

Goodyear, R.K., & Bradley, F.O. (1983). Theories of counselor supervision: Points of convergence and divergence. *The Counseling Psychologist, 11,* 59–67.

Hackney, H., & Nye, L.S. (1973). *Counseling strategies and objectives.* Englewood Cliffs, NJ: Prentice-Hall.

Hogan, R.A. (1964). Issues and approaches in supervision. *Psychotherapy: Theory, Research and Practice, 1,* 139–141.

Holloway, E.L. (1987). Developmental models of supervision: Is it development? *Professional Psychology: Research and Practice, 18,* 209–216.

Hora, T. (1957). Contribution to the phenomenology of the supervisory process. *American Journal of Psychotherapy, 11,* 769–773.

Horan, J.J. (1972). Behavioral goals in systematic counselor education. *Counselor Education and Supervision, 11,* 286–291.

Ivey, A.E., Normington, C., Miller, C., Morrill, W., & Haase, R. (1968). Microcounseling and attending behavior: An approach to prepracticum counselor training. *Journal of Counseling Psychology, 15*(Part 2), 1–12.

Jones, L.K. (1991). *Stoltenberg & Delworth's integrated developmental model.* Unpublished handout, North Carolina State University, Raleigh, NC.

Juckes, T.L. (1991). Equilibration and the learning paradox. *Human Development, 34,* 261–272.

Kell, B.L., & Burrow, J.M. (1970). *Developmental counseling and therapy.* Boston, MA: Houghton Mifflin.

Kratochwill, T.R., & Van Someren, K.R. (1984). Training behavioral consultants: Issues and directions. *Behavior Therapist, 7,* 19–22.

Krumboltz, J.D. (1966). Behavioral goals for counseling. *Journal of Counseling Psychology, 13,* 153–159.

Kurpius, D.J. (1985). Consultation interventions: Success, failures and proposals. *The Counseling Psychologist, 13,* 368–389.

Labouvie-Vief, G. (1985). Intelligence and cognition. In J.E. Birren & K.W. Shaire (Eds.), *Handbook of the psychology of aging* (2nd ed.) (pp. 500–530). New York: Van Nostrand Reinhold.

Lambert, N.M., Yandell, W., & Sandoval, J.H. (1975). Preparation of school psychologists for school-based consultation: A training activity and a service to community schools. *Journal of School Psychology, 13,* 68–75.

Leddick, G.R., & Bernard, J.M. (1980). The history of supervision: A critical review. *Counselor Education and Supervision, 19,* 186–196.

Loevinger, J. (1977). Ego maturity and human development. *Pupil Personnel Services Journal, 6,* 19–24.

Loganbill, C., Hardy, E., & Delworth, U. (1982). Supervision: A conceptual model. *The Counseling Psychologist, 10,* 3–42.

Martin, R.P. (1983). Consultant, consultee, and client explanations of each other's behavior in consultation. *School Psychology Review, 12,* 35–41.

McNeill, B.W., & Stoltenberg, C.D. (1992). Agendas for developmental supervision research: A response to Borders. *Counselor Education and Supervision, 31,* 179–183.

McNeill, B.W., & Worthen, V. (1989). The parallel process in psychotherapy supervision. *Professional Psychology: Research and Practice, 20,* 329–333.

Meyers, J. (1984). Training in consultation. *American Journal of Community Psychology, 12,* 233–239.

Pascual-Leone, J., & Goodman, D. (1979). Intelligence and experience: A neo-Piagetian approach. *Instructional Science, 8,* 301–367.

Piaget, J. (1970). *Structuralism.* New York: Basic Books.

Robinson, S.E., & Gross, D.R. (1985). Ethics of consultation: The Canterville ghost. *The Counseling Psychologist, 13,* 444–465.

Rogers, C.R. (1957). The necessary and sufficient conditions of therapeutic personality change. *Journal of Counseling Psychology, 21,* 95–103.

Russell, R.K., Crimmings, A.M., & Lent, R.W. (1984). Counselor training and supervision: Theory and research. In S.D. Brown & R.W. Lent (Eds.), *Handbook of counseling psychology* (pp. 625–681). New York: Wiley.

Searles, H.F. (1955). The informational value of supervisor's emotional experiences. *Psychiatry, 18,* 135–146.

Signell, K.A. (1974). An interaction method of teaching consultation: Role-playing. *Community Mental Health Journal, 10,* 205–215.

Stoltenberg, C.D. (1981). Approaching supervision from a developmental perspective: The counselor complexity model. *Journal of Counseling Psychology, 28,* 59–65.

Stoltenberg, C.D., & Delworth, U. (1987a). *Developmental supervision: A training model for counselors and psychotherapists.* San Francisco, CA: Jossey-Bass.

Stoltenberg, C.D., & Delworth, U. (1987b). Developmental models of supervision: It is development—response to Holloway. *Professional Psychology: Research and Practice, 19,* 134–137.

Stoltenberg, C.D., & Galloway, R.J. (1991, August). *1991 survey of counseling psychology doctoral training programs.* Report presented at the annual meeting of the American Psychological Association, San Francisco, CA.

Stum, D.L. (1982). DIRECT—A consultation skills training model. *The Personnel and Guidance Journal, 60,* 296–301.

Truax, C.B., & Carkhuff, R.R. (1967). *Toward effective counseling and psychotherapy: Training and practice.* Chicago, IL: Aldine.

Vuyk, R. (1981). *Overview and critique of Piaget's genetic epistemology, 1965–1980* (Vols. 1 & 2). London, England: Academic Press.

Williams, A. (1987). Parallel process in a course on counseling supervision. *Counselor Education and Supervision, 27,* 245–254.

Worthington, E.L. (1987). Changes in supervision as counselors and supervisors gain experience: A review. *Professional Psychology: Research and Practice, 19,* 189–208.

Zins, J.E. (1989). Building applied experiences into a consultation training program. *Consultation, 8,* 191–201.

■ ■ ■

CHAPTER BIBLIOGRAPHY

Babad, E. & Solomon, G. (1987). Professional dilemmas of the psychologist in an organizational emergency. *American Psychologist, 33,* 840–846.

Bradley, L. (1989). *Counselor supervision: Principles, process, practice.* Muncie, IN: Accelerated Development.

Egan, G. (1987). *Change agent skills in helping in human services settings.* Monterey, CA: Brooks/Cole.

Friedman, D., & Kaslow, N. (1986). The development of professional identity in psychotherapists: Six stages in the supervision process. In F. Kaslow (Ed.), *Supervision and training: Models, dilemmas, and challenges* (pp. 29–47). New York: The Hayworth Press.

Hart, G. (1982). *The process of clinical supervision.* Baltimore, MD: University Park Press.

Hersh, J., & Poey, K. (1984). A proposed interview guide for intern applicants. *Professional Psychology: Research and Practice, 15,* 305.

Koslow, N.J., & Rice, D.G. (1985). Developmental stressor of psychology internship training: What training staff can do to help. *Professional Psychology: Research and Practice, 16*(2), 253–261.

Solway, K.S. (1985). Transition from graduate school to internship: A potential crisis. *Professional Psychology: Research and Practice, 16*(1), 50–54.

Stoltenberg, C.D. (1993, November/December). Supervising consultants in training: An application model of supervision. *Journal of Counseling & Development, 72,* 131–138.

Chapter 4

MONITORING THE INTERACTIONS WITH THE CLIENT

John C. Boylan, Ph.D.

This chapter is designed to assist the practicum student or intern in assessment and data gathering activities conducted prior to and during counseling/ therapy.

The gathering of client data, a requirement of both practicum and internship experiences, can be a difficult task for the beginning counselor/therapist. The amount of client data required, as well as the manner in which data are to be recorded in the client's files, varies from institution to institution and agency to agency. Generally, however, most settings have developed clear guidelines for the obtaining and recording of client data.

The practicum student or intern must first gain a working knowledge of the procedures that are followed and then must develop his/her own framework and style of gathering data. Thus, care must be taken to ensure that the student can process and report data in a clear and concise manner.

INITIAL CONTACT, ASSESSMENT, AND DATA GATHERING

The initial contact with the client is a crucial point in the process of counseling and therapy. It provides the counselor/therapist with the opportunity to begin structuring the therapeutic relationship.

The process of structuring includes the therapeutic relationship, the rationale, and interventions and treatment goals employed in the helping process. Included in the structure are the setting in which the counseling occurs; issues of confidentiality, expectations, and roles; and goals and purposes of therapy. A valuable time-saver and a method of committing to the structure was suggested by Weinrach (1989). Weinrach advocated basing written guidelines on issues most frequently raised by clients as well as areas where potential conflicts may exist. These guidelines include the following:

- How often can I expect to have an appointment?

- How might I reach you if I feel I have to?

- What happens if I forget an appointment?

- How confidential are therapy sessions?

- What do I do in an emergency?

- When is it time to end treatment?

- What are my financial responsibilities?

- How often do I obtain reimbursement from insurance?

According to Hutchins and Cole (1992), structuring such concerns in writing makes for effective and efficient use of time as well as stimulating open discussion about a variety of concerns before they become problems. Similarly, Hutchins and Cole (1992) suggested that the helper think through the kinds of things that are expected to happen in the helping process. The following list of questions can help serve as a starting point.

Am I personally and professionally qualified to work with this client who has this particular concern or problem in this specific situation?

Do I understand the unique personal, educational, social, and cultural aspects of this client enough to be able to assist in this situation?

Should the client be referred to a helping professional who has more or different specialized training or skills—such as a licensed psychologist? Social worker? Psychiatrist? Marriage and family specialist? Drug and alcohol specialist? Others?

What is my role of helper in this relationship?

What kinds of things do I see as important variables in the helping process?

What kind of behavior (thoughts, feelings, actions) do I expect of the client both in and outside of the therapy setting?

What kind of commitment do I expect of the client in terms of time, work, and responsibility?

What about confidentiality in the setting in which I work?

What legal, ethical, and moral considerations must be considered before working with this client? (p. 46)

These critical questions asked by the helper/therapist, coupled with printed client concerns, can serve as valuable assets and aid in the structuring of clinical interviews in the counseling/therapy process.

In summary, structuring the relationship entails defining for the client the nature, purpose, and goals within the therapeutic relationship. Critical to the structuring process is the therapist's ability to create an atmosphere that enables the client to know that the therapist is genuine, sincere, and empathic in his/her desire to assist the client. Attending skills and facilitative therapeutic techniques are employed by the therapist in the process of preparing the client for data gathering and assessment activities.

Remember that interviewing the client and having the client engage in other assessment procedures are only part of the overall assessment process in counseling and psychotherapy. Equally important are the therapist's own mental and covert actions that go on during the process. The therapist typically gathers great amounts of information from clients during this stage of counseling/therapy. However, data are of little value or useless unless the therapist can integrate and synthesize data.

The counselor's/therapist's task during the assessment process includes knowing what information to obtain and how to obtain it, putting it together in some meaningful way, and using it to generate clinical hunches, or hypotheses about

client's problems, hunches that lead to tentative ideas for treatment planning. (Cormier & Cormier, 1985, p. 147)

ASSESSMENT ACTIVITIES

The following is a description and format of typical assessment activities occurring prior to and in the initial stages of counseling/therapy.

Obtaining Authorizations

The first step in the process of counseling and psychotherapy is obtaining the appropriate authorizations prior to the start of therapy. Examples of authorization forms are included for this purpose: *Parental Release Form* to counsel a child (Form 4.1) and *Client Release Form* to initiate counseling (Form 4.2). These forms should be adapted for use by the practicum student or intern according to the field site requirements.

Obtaining Information from Client and Others

A practical step in obtaining client information from others (parents, therapists, teachers) is to develop a form that focuses upon the specific information to be obtained. For example, *Initial Intake Form* (Clinical) (Form 4.3) tends to include more medical, psychological, and psychiatric data that focus upon the history and outcomes of treatment. Similarly, background and developmental data are obtained for the purpose of assessing the acuteness or chronicity of current complaints. In contrast, *School Counseling Referral Forms* (Forms 4.4 and 4.5) tend to include more data regarding the academic history of the student and his/her behavior and demeanor in school. Aptitude, attitude, and interest toward school typically are stressed.

The *Initial Intake Form* (Clinical) (Form 4.3) is designed to provide the counselor/therapist with initial identifying data about the client. Data about the client are obtained directly from the client at the initial interview.

The elementary and secondary *School Counseling Referral Forms* (Forms 4.4 and 4.5) are designed to obtain appropriate precounseling data from sources other than the client. Typically, the professional making a referral of a school-age child for counseling/therapy is asked to describe and comment on his/her perceptions and knowledge of the pupil's current academic and social standing.

Assessing Client's Mental Status

To gain insight into the client's presenting condition, the client's mental status may need to be assessed. The mental status examination is, therefore, designed to provide the therapist with signs that indicate the "functional" nature of the person's psychiatric condition. In addition, the mental status examination can be used to provide the therapist with a current view of the client's mental capabilities and deficits prior to and during the course of treatment and is beneficial to the beginning therapist who lacks the clinical experience to quickly assess the client's mental status.

Many formats can be used to obtain a client's mental status. However, all formats have common areas that are routinely assessed. The following is an example of items fairly typically covered, with an explanation of material generally included. A copy of a *Mental Checklist* is presented as Form 4.6.

Appearance and Behavior: This consists of data gathered throughout the interview so that the person reading the narrative has a "photograph" of the client during the interview. Data is gathered by direct observation of the client. Questions: Is the client's appearance age appropriate? Does the client appear to be his/her stated age? Is the client's behavior appropriate to the surroundings? Is the behavior overactive/underactive? Is the behavior agitated/ retarded? Is speech pressured? Retarded? Logical? Clear? What is the content of speech?

Attention/Alertness: Is the client aware of his/her surroundings? Can the client focus attention on the therapist? Is the client highly distractible? Is the client scanning the environment? Is he/she hypervigilant?

Affect/Mood: What is the quality of the client's affect? Is the client's affect expressive? Expansive? Blunted? Flat? Agitated? Fearful? Is the client's affect appropriate to the current situation?

Perception/Thought: Does the client have false ideas/delusions? Does the client experience his/her own thoughts as being controlled? Does the client experience people putting thoughts in his/her head? Does the client experience his/her own thoughts being

withdrawn/taken away? Does the client feel that people are watching him/her? Out to get him/her? Does the client experience grandiose or bizarre delusions?

Sensory Perception: Does the client hallucinate? Does the client experience visual, auditory, tactile, or gustatory false perceptions?

Orientation: Is the client oriented to person, place, and time? Does the client know with whom he/she is dealing? Where he/she is? What day and time it is?

Judgment: Can the client act appropriately to typical social, personal, and occupational situations? Can the client show good judgment in conducting his/her own life?

Attention/Concentration: Does the client have any memory disturbance? *Recent Memory:* Can the client remember information given a few minutes ago (for example, give the client three or four things to remember and ask him/her to repeat back after several minutes). *Long-term memory:* Can the client remember/recall information from yesterday? Childhood? Can the client concentrate on facts given to him/her?

Abstract Ability: Can the client recognize and handle similarities? Absurdities? Proverbs?

Insight: Is the client aware that he/she has a problem? Possible Causes? Possible Solutions?

Recording Psychosocial History

The use of a Psychosocial History form such as is shown in Form 4.7 is a part of the pretherapy assessment procedures employed by most community mental health agencies. The psychosocial history provides the therapist with a comprehensive view of the client over time. In most instances, the pychosocial history provides more data than the initial intake and is invaluable in examining the acuteness or chronicity of the client's problem. Specific attention is directed toward the milestones or benchmarks in the client's developmental history that have implications for the treatment strategies to be employed in therapy.

MONITORING AND EVALUATING THE CLIENT'S PROGRESS

Monitoring of the client in therapy is a continuous process, beginning with the initial contact with the client and ending with therapy termination. Monitoring is an invaluable asset to providing the therapist with an understanding of goals and objectives, as well as the direction and progress taking place during therapy.

An adaptation of Kanfer and Schefft's (1988) discussion of monitoring and evaluating client progress suggests doing the following:

• Monitoring and evaluating session to session client's behavior and environment;

• Assessing improvement in coping skills by noting the client's use of the skills in relation to behavior and other activities;

• Evaluating any change in the client's status or in his/her relationship to significant others that resulted from treatment;

• Utilizing available data to review progress, to strengthen gains, and to maintain the client's motivation for completing the change process;

• Negotiating new treatment objectives or changes in methods or the rate of progress, if the evidence suggests the need for such changes; and

• Attending to new conditions that have been created by the client's change and that may promote or defeat further change efforts. (pp. 255–256)

Further, Kanfer and Schefft (1988), in examining treatment effectiveness, suggested asking yourself the following questions:

• Are the treatment interventions working? Noting the progress in the therapeutic objectives as compared with baseline data gathered at the beginning of treatment (initial assessment).

• Have other treatment targets been overlooked? By monitoring other changes and emergent problems, the therapist obtain the cues for the necessity of renegotiating treatment objectives or treatment methods.

• Is the therapeutic process on course? Individuals differ with regard to their rate of progress; plateaus may occur at various phases of therapy, and these need to be scrutinized.

• Are subsidiary methods needed to enhance progress or to handle newly emerged problems? Are there gaps in the client's basic skill level needed to execute the program?

• Are the client's problems and the treatment program being formulated effectively? Monitoring and evaluating the therapist in the process is key to successful treatment. Consultation with other professionals/colleagues is recommended. (pp. 257–258)

Building a Client Folder

A valuable adjunct to the monitoring process is the building of a folder for the client. When carefully and properly developed and organized, the file folder serves as a quick reference to review session-by-session developments and is used to assist in the summarization and evaluation of the course of treatment.

Additionally, practicum students and interns also will be responsible for contributing to the file folder maintained by the agency, institution, or school in which the counseling sessions are held. Each student needs to understand the format employed, the kinds of information desired, and the kinds of information to be added to the folder. Knowledge of the security procedures to be followed in the agency or school must be understood. Procedures to be followed will depend upon the procedures and policies of the agency, institution, or school.

The practicum/internship course objectives, in addition to those held by the agency, institution, or school in which the counseling is done, may necessitate a separate folder for the university supervisor. This folder would be maintained by the counselor and his/her school/agency site supervisor and be available for review.

The purposes for having a separate folder for each client may include the following:

• to teach the student counselor the procedures for building a folder for each client similar to what will be required on the job,

• to foster organizational skills in the managing of critical client data,

(Continued on p. 113)

PARENTAL RELEASE FORM

Parent's Name: _____

Address: _____

_____

Phone: _____ (Home) _____ (Office)

The Graduate Department of Counseling and Psychology at _____ College/University conducts a Counseling Practicum Course each semester at the College/University. The Counseling Practicum Course is an advanced course in counseling required of all Degree Candidates in the Counseling Program at _____ College/University. Students are required to audio and/or video tape counseling sessions as part of their course and degree requirements.

Student's Name: _____ would like to work with your son/daughter, a student at _____ School.

The counseling sessions conducted with your child will be audio and/or video taped and will be reviewed by the Student's Supervisor (Name): _____ . All audio and video tapes made will be erased at the completion of your child's involvement in the program.

We hope that you will take the opportunity to have your child become involved in the Counseling Program. If you are interested in having your child participate, please sign the form where indicated.

Thank you for your cooperation.

Parent's Signature: _____

Date: _____

CLIENT RELEASE FORM

Graduate Department of Counseling and Psychology

_____

(Name of college/university)

I _____ agree to be counseled by a practicum/intern in the Department of Counseling and Psychology at _____ College/University. I further understand that I will participate in counseling interviews that will be audio taped, video taped, and/or viewed by practicum/intern students through the use of one way observation windows. I understand that I will be counseled by a graduate student who has completed advanced course work in counseling/therapy. I understand that the student will be supervised by a faculty member or site supervisor.

Client's Signature _____

Age _____   Date _____

Counselor's Signature _____

                                            Date _____

Form 4.2, p. 1 of 1, Copy 1

INITIAL INTAKE FORM (Clinical)

Name: _____ Date: _____

Address: _____ City: _____ State: _____ Zip code: _____

Telephone (Home): _____ (Work): _____

Therapist Name: _____ Date: _____

Identifying Information

Age: _____ Date of Birth: ___/___/___ Place: _____

Sex: Male _____ Female _____ Height: _____ ft., _____ in. Weight: _____ lbs.

Race: white _____ black _____ Asian _____ Hispanic _____ other _____

Marital Status: M _____ S _____ D _____ W _____ SEP _____

If Married, Spouse's Name: _____ Age _____

Occupation: _____ Employer: _____

Occupation (Spouse): _____ Employer _____

Referral Source: Self _____ Other _____

Name of Referral Source: _____

Address of Referral Source: _____

Treatment History (General)

Are you currently taking medication? Yes _____ No _____

If yes, name(s) of the medication(s): _____

Dosage of medication(s): _____

Provider of medication(s): _____

Have you received previous psychiatric/psychological treatment? Yes _____ No _____

If yes, name of provider: _____

Date(s) of service: _____ Location: _____

Reason(s) for termination of treatment: _____

Presenting problem or condition (current): _____

Presenting factors (contributors): _____

Symptoms (describe): _____

_____

Acute: _____ Chronic: _____

Family History (General)

Father's Name: _____ Age: _____ Living _____ Deceased _____

Occupation: _____ full-time _____ part-time _____

Mother's Name: _____ Age: _____ Living _____ Deceased _____

Occupation: _____ full-time _____ part-time _____

Brother(s)/Sister(s)
Name: _____ Age: _____ Living _____ Deceased _____

Name: _____ Age: _____ Living _____ Deceased _____

Name: _____ Age: _____ Living _____ Deceased _____

Educational History (General)

	Name of Institution	Location	Dates	Degree
Secondary:				
College:				
Trade:				
Graduate:				

Employment History (General)

Title/Description (from when to when) full- or part-time

_____

_____

_____

Form 4.3, p. 2 of 2, Copy 1

INITIAL INTAKE FORM (Clinical)

Name: _____ Date: _____

Address: _____ City: _____ State: _____ Zip code: _____

Telephone (Home): _____ (Work): _____

Therapist Name: _____ Date: _____

Identifying Information

Age: _____ Date of Birth: ___/___/___ Place: _____

Sex: Male _____ Female _____ Height: _____ ft., _____ in. Weight: _____ lbs.

Race: white _____ black _____ Asian _____ Hispanic _____ other _____

Marital Status: M _____ S _____ D _____ W _____ SEP _____

If Married, Spouse's Name: _____ Age _____

Occupation: _____ Employer: _____

Occupation (Spouse): _____ Employer _____

Referral Source: Self _____ Other _____

Name of Referral Source: _____

Address of Referral Source: _____

Treatment History (General)

Are you currently taking medication? Yes _____ No _____

If yes, name(s) of the medication(s): _____

Dosage of medication(s): _____

Provider of medication(s): _____

Have you received previous psychiatric/psychological treatment? Yes _____ No _____

If yes, name of provider: _____

Date(s) of service: _____ Location: _____

Reason(s) for termination of treatment: _____

Presenting problem or condition (current): _____

Presenting factors (contributors): _____

Symptoms (describe): _____

_____

Acute: _____   Chronic: _____

Family History (General)

Father's Name: _____ Age: _____ Living _____ Deceased _____

Occupation: _____ full-time _____ part-time _____

Mother's Name: _____ Age: _____ Living _____ Deceased _____

Occupation: _____ full-time _____ part-time _____

Brother(s)/Sister(s)
Name: _____ Age: _____ Living _____ Deceased _____

Name: _____ Age: _____ Living _____ Deceased _____

Name: _____ Age: _____ Living _____ Deceased _____

Educational History (General)

	Name of Institution	Location	Dates	Degree
Secondary:				
College:				
Trade:				
Graduate:				

Employment History (General)

Title/Description   (from when to when)   full- or part-time

_____

_____

_____

INITIAL INTAKE FORM (Clinical)

Name: _____ Date: _____

Address: _____ City: _____ State: _____ Zip code: _____

Telephone (Home): _____ (Work): _____

Therapist Name: _____ Date: _____

Identifying Information

Age: _____ Date of Birth: ___/___/___ Place: _____

Sex: Male _____ Female _____   Height: _____ ft., _____ in.   Weight: _____ lbs.

Race: white _____ black _____ Asian _____ Hispanic _____ other _____

Marital Status: M _____ S _____ D _____ W _____ SEP _____

If Married, Spouse's Name: _____ Age _____

Occupation: _____ Employer: _____

Occupation (Spouse): _____ Employer _____

Referral Source: Self _____ Other _____

Name of Referral Source: _____

Address of Referral Source: _____   _____

Treatment History (General)

Are you currently taking medication?   Yes _____ No _____

If yes, name(s) of the medication(s): _____

Dosage of medication(s): _____

Provider of medication(s): _____

Have you received previous psychiatric/psychological treatment?   Yes _____ No _____

If yes, name of provider: _____

Date(s) of service: _____ Location: _____

Reason(s) for termination of treatment: _____

Presenting problem or condition (current): _____

Form 4.3, p. 1 of 2, Copy 3

Presenting factors (contributors): _____

Symptoms (describe): _____

_____

Acute: _____   Chronic: _____

Family History (General)

Father's Name: _____   Age: _____   Living _____ Deceased _____

Occupation: _____   full-time _____ part-time _____

Mother's Name: _____   Age: _____   Living _____ Deceased _____

Occupation: _____   full-time _____ part-time _____

Brother(s)/Sister(s)
Name: _____   Age: _____   Living _____ Deceased _____

Name: _____   Age: _____   Living _____ Deceased _____

Name: _____   Age: _____   Living _____ Deceased _____

Educational History (General)

	Name of Institution	Location	Dates	Degree
Secondary:				
College:				
Trade:				
Graduate:				

Employment History (General)

Title/Description	(from when to when)	full- or part-time

Form 4.3, p. 2 of 2, Copy 3

INITIAL INTAKE FORM (Clinical)

Name: _____ Date: _____

Address: _____ City: _____ State: _____ Zip code: _____

Telephone (Home): _____ (Work): _____

Therapist Name: _____ Date: _____

Identifying Information

Age: _____ Date of Birth: ___/___/___ Place: _____

Sex: Male _____ Female _____   Height: _____ ft., _____ in.   Weight: _____ lbs.

Race: white _____ black _____ Asian _____ Hispanic _____ other _____

Marital Status: M _____ S _____ D _____ W _____ SEP _____

If Married, Spouse's Name: _____ Age _____

Occupation: _____ Employer: _____

Occupation (Spouse): _____ Employer _____

Referral Source: Self _____ Other _____

Name of Referral Source: _____

Address of Referral Source: _____

Treatment History (General)

Are you currently taking medication?   Yes _____ No _____

If yes, name(s) of the medication(s): _____

Dosage of medication(s): _____

Provider of medication(s): _____

Have you received previous psychiatric/psychological treatment?   Yes _____ No _____

If yes, name of provider: _____

Date(s) of service: _____ Location: _____

Reason(s) for termination of treatment: _____

Presenting problem or condition (current): _____

Presenting factors (contributors): _____

Symptoms (describe): _____

_____

Acute: _____ Chronic: _____

Family History (General)

Father's Name: _____ Age: _____ Living _____ Deceased _____

Occupation: _____ full-time _____ part-time _____

Mother's Name: _____ Age: _____ Living _____ Deceased _____

Occupation: _____ full-time _____ part-time _____

Brother(s)/Sister(s)
Name: _____ Age: _____ Living _____ Deceased _____

Name: _____ Age: _____ Living _____ Deceased _____

Name: _____ Age: _____ Living _____ Deceased _____

Educational History (General)

	Name of Institution	Location	Dates	Degree
Secondary:				
College:				
Trade:				
Graduate:				

Employment History (General)

Title/Description	(from when to when)	full- or part-time

INITIAL INTAKE FORM (Clinical)

Name: _____ Date: _____

Address: _____ City: _____ State: _____ Zip code: _____

Telephone (Home): _____ (Work): _____

Therapist Name: _____ Date: _____

Identifying Information

Age: _____ Date of Birth: ___/___/___ Place: _____

Sex: Male _____ Female _____ Height: _____ ft., _____ in. Weight: _____ lbs.

Race: white _____ black _____ Asian _____ Hispanic _____ other _____

Marital Status: M _____ S _____ D _____ W _____ SEP _____

If Married, Spouse's Name: _____ Age _____

Occupation: _____ Employer: _____

Occupation (Spouse): _____ Employer _____

Referral Source: Self _____ Other _____

Name of Referral Source: _____

Address of Referral Source: _____

Treatment History (General)

Are you currently taking medication? Yes _____ No _____

If yes, name(s) of the medication(s): _____

Dosage of medication(s): _____

Provider of medication(s): _____

Have you received previous psychiatric/psychological treatment? Yes _____ No _____

If yes, name of provider: _____

Date(s) of service: _____ Location: _____

Reason(s) for termination of treatment: _____

Presenting problem or condition (current): _____

Presenting factors (contributors): _____

Symptoms (describe): _____

_____

Acute: _____ Chronic: _____

Family History (General)

Father's Name: _____ Age: _____ Living _____ Deceased _____

Occupation: _____ full-time _____ part-time _____

Mother's Name: _____ Age: _____ Living _____ Deceased _____

Occupation: _____ full-time _____ part-time _____

Brother(s)/Sister(s)
Name: _____ Age: _____ Living _____ Deceased _____

Name: _____ Age: _____ Living _____ Deceased _____

Name: _____ Age: _____ Living _____ Deceased _____

Educational History (General)

	Name of Institution	Location	Dates	Degree
Secondary:				
College:				
Trade:				
Graduate:				

Employment History (General)

Title/Description   (from when to when)   full- or part-time

_____

_____

_____

ELEMENTARY SCHOOL COUNSELING REFERRAL FORM*

(confidential information to be supplied
by teacher or counselor)

Date Referral Received: _____

Teacher's Name: _____ Date: _____

Principal's Name: _____ School: _____

Child's Name: _____

Grade: _____ Section: _____ Date of Birth: _____ Age: _____

TEST RESULTS

IQ: _____ Present Grade Level: _____ _____

Group: _____ Individual: _____ Math: _____ Reading: _____

If the child has ever been retained, indicate grade: _____

Father's Name: _____ Mother's Name: _____

Address: _____ Address: _____

Phone Number: _____ Phone Number: _____

_____

*Form developed by Dale Malecki, Elementary Counselor, Abington Heights School District, Clarks Summit, PA. Used with permission.

Have you had discussion with the child's parent(s) regarding this referral?   Yes _____ No _____

Was the parent receptive to you referring the child for counseling?

Positive _____   Neutral _____   Negative _____

To your knowledge, has the child received counseling services in the school or out of school?

Yes _____   No _____   If yes, please supply name.

Counselor's or Agency Name: _____

Does the child presently qualify or receive any special education services? Yes _____ No _____

(If so, give dates): _____

Have the child's parents requested counseling?   Yes _____ No _____

Have you discussed your concerns about the child with the building principal?   Yes _____ No _____

Have you discussed your concerns about the child with the multidisciplinary team (child study team)?

Yes _____ No _____

Form 4.4, p. 2 of 4, Copy 1

Student's Present Functioning
(as you perceive it)

	Excellent	Above Average	Average	Below Average	Poor
Reading					
Mathematics					
Language Arts					
Social Studies					
General Learning Rate					
On-task Behavior					
Self-directed Learner					
Follows Directions (oral)					
Follows Directions (written)					
Attention Span					
Completes Assignments					
Returns Homework					
Works Well with Others					
Obeys Classroom Rules					
Motor Coordination					
Self-image Development					
Adult Relationships					
Peer Relationships					
Attitude toward School					
Shows Enthusiasm for Learning					
Participates in Class					

Possible Evidence of
(check if appropriate)

Daydreams _____   Worries _____

Easily Distracted _____   Lacks Assertiveness _____

Absenteeism _____   Impulsive Behavior _____

Withdrawn _____   Poorly Motivated _____

Family Problems _____   Inappropriate Academic Placement _____

Preoccupied _____

Form 4.4, p. 3 of 4, Copy 1

Other Variables
(check if applicable)

Vision _____   Stature _____

Hearing _____   Hygiene _____

Speech _____   Other (please specify) _____

Special skills, talents or competencies child has: _____

_____

Reason for referral (based on your observations): _____

_____

What strategies or techniques have you tried with this child? _____

_____

Comments and recommendations: _____

_____

Please indicate a time(s) which will be convenient for you to have a conference with me.

Monday	Period	Time
Tuesday	Period	Time
Wednesday	Period	Time
Thursday	Period	Time
Friday	Period	Time

Thank you for taking your time to share this information with me.

Date: _____

Signature: _____
              (Elementary Counselor)

ELEMENTARY SCHOOL COUNSELING REFERRAL FORM*

(confidential information to be supplied
by teacher or counselor)

Date Referral Received: _____

Teacher's Name: _____   Date: _____

Principal's Name: _____   School: _____

Child's Name: _____

Grade: _____   Section: _____   Date of Birth: _____   Age: _____

TEST RESULTS

IQ: _____   Present Grade Level: _____

Group: _____   Individual: _____   Math: _____   Reading: _____

If the child has ever been retained, indicate grade: _____

Father's Name: _____   Mother's Name: _____

Address: _____   Address: _____

Phone Number: _____   Phone Number: _____

---

*Form developed by Dale Malecki, Elementary Counselor, Abington Heights School District, Clarks Summit, PA. Used with permission.

Have you had discussion with the child's parent(s) regarding this referral?   Yes _____ No _____

Was the parent receptive to you referring the child for counseling?

Positive _____ Neutral _____ Negative _____

To your knowledge, has the child received counseling services in the school or out of school?

Yes _____ No _____ If yes, please supply name.

Counselor's or Agency Name: _____

Does the child presently qualify or receive any special education services? Yes _____ No _____

(If so, give dates): _____

Have the child's parents requested counseling?   Yes _____ No _____

Have you discussed your concerns about the child with the building principal?   Yes _____ No _____

Have you discussed your concerns about the child with the multidisciplinary team (child study team)?

Yes _____ No _____

Form 4.4, p. 2 of 4, Copy 2

Student's Present Functioning
(as you perceive it)

	Excellent	Above Average	Average	Below Average	Poor
Reading					
Mathematics					
Language Arts					
Social Studies					
General Learning Rate					
On-task Behavior					
Self-directed Learner					
Follows Directions (oral)					
Follows Directions (written)					
Attention Span					
Completes Assignments					
Returns Homework					
Works Well with Others					
Obeys Classroom Rules					
Motor Coordination					
Self-image Development					
Adult Relationships					
Peer Relationships					
Attitude toward School					
Shows Enthusiasm for Learning					
Participates in Class					

Possible Evidence of
(check if appropriate)

Daydreams _____   Worries _____

Easily Distracted _____   Lacks Assertiveness _____

Absenteeism _____   Impulsive Behavior _____

Withdrawn _____   Poorly Motivated _____

Family Problems _____   Inappropriate Academic Placement _____

Preoccupied _____

Other Variables
(check if applicable)

Vision _____   Stature _____

Hearing _____   Hygiene _____

Speech _____   Other (please specify) _____

Special skills, talents or competencies child has: _____

_____

Reason for referral (based on your observations): _____

_____

What strategies or techniques have you tried with this child? _____

_____

Comments and recommendations: _____

_____

Please indicate a time(s) which will be convenient for you to have a conference with me.

Monday	Period	Time
Tuesday	Period	Time
Wednesday	Period	Time
Thursday	Period	Time
Friday	Period	Time

Thank you for taking your time to share this information with me.

Date: _____

Signature: _____
                    (Elementary Counselor)

Form 4.4, p. 4 of 4, Copy 2

SECONDARY SCHOOL COUNSELING REFERRAL FORM

(confidential information to be supplied
by teacher or counselor)

Date Referral Received: _____

Teacher's Name: _____ Date: _____

(form completed by teacher)

Principal's Name: _____ School: _____

Child's Name: _____

Grade: _____ Date of Birth: _____

TEST RESULTS

I.Q. _____ Group _____ Individual _____

If the child has ever been retained, indicate grade: _____

Father's Name: _____ Mother's Name: _____

Address: _____ Address: _____

Phone Number: _____ Phone Number: _____

Have you had discussion with the child's parent(s) regarding this referral?   Yes _____ No _____

Was the parent receptive to you referring the child for counseling?

Positive _____ Neutral _____ Negative _____

To your knowledge, has the student received counseling services in school or out of school?

Yes _____ No _____ If yes, please supply name.
Counselor or Agency Name: _____

Does the student presently qualify or receive any special education services?   Yes _____ No _____

If so, specify: _____

Has the student had a psychoeducational assessment done?   Yes: _____ No: _____

If so, give date: _____

Have the student's parents requested counseling?   Yes _____ No _____

Have you discussed your concerns about the child with your supervisor/principal?   Yes _____ No _____

Form 4.5, p. 1 of 2, Copy 1

Student's Present Functioning
(as you perceive it)

	Excellent	Above Average	Average	Below Average	Poor
Self-directed learner	_____	_____	_____	_____	_____
Attention Span	_____	_____	_____	_____	_____
Quality of Writer Assessment	_____	_____	_____	_____	_____
Quality of Oral Assessment	_____	_____	_____	_____	_____
Self-image	_____	_____	_____	_____	_____
Attitude Toward Authority	_____	_____	_____	_____	_____
Peer Relationships	_____	_____	_____	_____	_____
Works Well with Others	_____	_____	_____	_____	_____
Completes Assignments	_____	_____	_____	_____	_____
Follows Classroom Rules	_____	_____	_____	_____	_____

Please Check
(If appropriate)

Aggressive _____   Personable _____   Engaging _____

Assertive _____   Shy _____   Ambitious _____

Noncompliant _____   Dependent _____   Impulsive _____

Disregard for Rights _____   Depressed _____   Preoccupied _____

Self-confident _____   Avoidant _____   Motivated _____

Withdrawn _____   Friendly _____   Distractible _____

Argumentative _____   Social _____

Special skills, talents, competencies student has: _____

_____

Reason for referral (based upon your observations): _____

_____

What interventions have you tried with this student? _____

_____

Comments and recommendations: _____

_____

Date: _____   Signed _____

Position: _____

Form 4.5, p. 2 of 2, Copy 1

SECONDARY SCHOOL COUNSELING REFERRAL FORM

(confidential information to be supplied
by teacher or counselor)

Date Referral Received: _____

Teacher's Name: _____ Date: _____
(form completed by teacher)

Principal's Name: _____ School: _____

Child's Name: _____

Grade: _____ Date of Birth: _____

TEST RESULTS

I.Q. _____ Group _____ Individual _____

If the child has ever been retained, indicate grade: _____

Father's Name: _____ Mother's Name: _____

Address: _____ Address: _____

Phone Number: _____ Phone Number: _____

Have you had discussion with the child's parent(s) regarding this referral?   Yes _____ No _____

Was the parent receptive to you referring the child for counseling?

Positive _____ Neutral _____ Negative _____

To your knowledge, has the student received counseling services in school or out of school?

Yes _____ No _____ If yes, please supply name.
Counselor or Agency Name: _____

Does the student presently qualify or receive any special education services?   Yes _____ No _____

If so, specify: _____

Has the student had a psychoeducational assessment done?   Yes: _____ No: _____

If so, give date: _____

Have the student's parents requested counseling?   Yes _____ No _____

Have you discussed your concerns about the child with your supervisor/principal?   Yes _____ No _____

Form 4.5, p. 1 of 2, Copy 2

Student's Present Functioning
(as you perceive it)

	Excellent	Above Average	Average	Below Average	Poor
Self-directed learner	_____	_____	_____	_____	_____
Attention Span	_____	_____	_____	_____	_____
Quality of Writer Assessment	_____	_____	_____	_____	_____
Quality of Oral Assessment	_____	_____	_____	_____	_____
Self-image	_____	_____	_____	_____	_____
Attitude Toward Authority	_____	_____	_____	_____	_____
Peer Relationships	_____	_____	_____	_____	_____
Works Well with Others	_____	_____	_____	_____	_____
Completes Assignments	_____	_____	_____	_____	_____
Follows Classroom Rules	_____	_____	_____	_____	_____

Please Check
(If appropriate)

Aggressive _____	Personable _____	Engaging _____
Assertive _____	Shy _____	Ambitious _____
Noncompliant _____	Dependent _____	Impulsive _____
Disregard for Rights _____	Depressed _____	Preoccupied _____
Self-confident _____	Avoidant _____	Motivated _____
Withdrawn _____	Friendly _____	Distractible _____
Argumentative _____	Social _____	

Special skills, talents, competencies student has: _____

_____

Reason for referral (based upon your observations): _____

_____

What interventions have you tried with this student? _____

_____

Comments and recommendations: _____

_____

Date: _____   Signed _____

Position: _____

Form 4.5, p. 2 of 2, Copy 2

MENTAL STATUS CHECKLIST

Appearance and Behavior

	Check	Circle	Therapist Comments
1. Posture	normal _____	limp, rigid, ill at ease	
2. Gestures	normal _____	agitated, tics, twitches	
3. Grooming	neat _____	well-groomed, disheveled, meticulous	
4. Dress	appropriate ___ casual _____ formal _____	dirty, careless, inappropriate, seductive	
5. Facial Expression	appropriate ___	poor eye contact, dazed, staring	
6. Speech			
a. pace	normal _____	retarded, pressured, blocking	
b. volume	normal _____	soft, very loud, monotone	
c. form	logical _____ rational _____	illogical, rambling, incoherent, coherent	
d. clarity	normal _____	garbled, slurred	
e. content	normal _____	loose associations, rhyming, obscene	

Attention/Affect/Mood

	Check	Circle	Therapist Comments
1. Attention	normal _____ alert _____	short span, hyper, alert, distractible	
2. Mood	normal _____	elated, euphoric, agitated, fearful, hostile, sad	
3. Affect	appropriate ___	inappropriate, shallow, flat, intense	

Form 4.6, p. 1 of 2, Copy 1

Perception and Thought Content

                    Check   Description
1. Hallucinations   _____
   a. auditory   _____   _____
   b. visual   _____   _____
   c. tactile   _____   _____
   d. gustatory   _____   _____
   e. olfactory   _____   _____

2. Delusions
   a. paranoid   _____   b. persecutory   _____
   c. grandiose   _____   d. reference   _____
   e. control   _____   f. thought   _____
   g. insertion   _____   h. broadcasting _____
   i. thought
      withdrawal   _____

3. Illusions
   a. visual   _____
   b. auditory   _____
   Describe   _____
   _____

4. Other Derealization
   a. phobias   _____   b. obsessions   _____
   c. compulsions   _____   d. ruminations   _____
   Describe   _____
   _____

5. Suicide/Homicide
   ideation _____   plans _____
   Describe _____
   _____

Orientation   oriented × 3 _____
    disoriented to: time _____   place _____   person _____
Judgment   intact _____   impaired _____
    Describe _____
    _____

Concentration/Memory
1. Memory   intact _____   impaired _____
2. Immediate recall   good _____   poor _____
3. Reversals   good _____   poor _____
4. Concentration   good _____   poor _____

Abstract Ability
1. Similarities   good _____   poor _____   bizarre _____
2. Absurdities   recognized _____   not recognized _____
3. Proverbs   appropriate _____   literal _____   concrete _____   bizarre _____
Insight   good _____   fair _____   poor _____   absent _____

Form 4.6, p. 2 of 2, Copy 1

MENTAL STATUS CHECKLIST

Appearance and Behavior

	Check	Circle	Therapist Comments
1. Posture	normal _____	limp, rigid, ill at ease	
2. Gestures	normal _____	agitated, tics, twitches	
3. Grooming	neat _____	well-groomed, disheveled, meticulous	
4. Dress	appropriate ___ casual _____ formal _____	dirty, careless, inappropriate, seductive	
5. Facial Expression	appropriate ___	poor eye contact, dazed, staring	
6. Speech			
a. pace	normal _____	retarded, pressured, blocking	
b. volume	normal _____	soft, very loud, monotone	
c. form	logical _____ rational _____	illogical, rambling, incoherent, coherent	
d. clarity	normal _____	garbled, slurred	
e. content	normal _____	loose associations, rhyming, obscene	

Attention/Affect/Mood

	Check	Circle	Therapist Comments
1. Attention	normal _____ alert _____	short span, hyper, alert, distractible	
2. Mood	normal _____	elated, euphoric, agitated, fearful, hostile, sad	
3. Affect	appropriate ___	inappropriate, shallow, flat, intense	

Form 4.6, p. 1 of 2, Copy 2

Perception and Thought Content

	Check	Description
1. Hallucinations		
a. auditory	_____	_____
b. visual	_____	_____
c. tactile	_____	_____
d. gustatory	_____	_____
e. olfactory	_____	_____

2. Delusions
   - a. paranoid _____   b. persecutory _____
   - c. grandiose _____   d. reference _____
   - e. control _____   f. thought _____
   - g. insertion _____   h. broadcasting _____
   - i. thought
      withdrawal _____

3. Illusions
   - a. visual _____
   - b. auditory _____
   - Describe _____

4. Other Derealization
   - a. phobias _____   b. obsessions _____
   - c. compulsions _____   d. ruminations _____
   - Describe _____

5. Suicide/Homicide
   - ideation _____   plans _____
   - Describe _____

Orientation   oriented × 3 _____
   disoriented to: time _____   place _____   person _____
Judgment   intact _____   impaired _____
   Describe _____

Concentration/Memory
1. Memory   intact _____   impaired _____
2. Immediate recall   good _____   poor _____
3. Reversals   good _____   poor _____
4. Concentration   good _____   poor _____

Abstract Ability
1. Similarities   good _____   poor _____   bizarre _____
2. Absurdities   recognized _____   not recognized _____
3. Proverbs   appropriate _____   literal _____   concrete _____   bizarre _____
Insight   good _____   fair _____   poor _____   absent _____

- to assist the student counselor in gathering pertinent data applicable to the treatment of the client,

- to provide a vehicle for reviewing client progress made during the course of treatment,

- to summarize the therapeutic activities that have been performed by the counselor and client,

- to serve as a format for the preparation and dissemination of summative data of all counseling activities that have taken place prior to and during treatment, and

- to provide essential information when writing a termination report regarding the client.

Thus, the development of a client folder, whether for meeting overall professional development or for continuing information to the agency, is an invaluable asset to the practicum/internship student.

—————— ★ ★ ★ ——————

PROCESSING INTERVIEW NOTES*
Joseph W. Hollis

During or following each counseling/therapy session, the student counselor or therapist will make notes of what occurred and comments regarding future plans for therapy.

With the large number of clients seen in therapy and seen over an extended period of time, the notes taken following therapy (*Therapy Notes,* Form 4.8) are an invaluable asset to the therapist. Therapy notes can serve various purposes.

1. The record of the interview can reacquaint the therapist with what previously had transpired in the contacts as well as with his/her initial impressions of the therapeutic process.

2. Notes may serve as valuable aids in helping a different therapist (who may take over therapy)

understand the developmental nature of the previous contacts and gain knowledge of the kind of treatment or methods employed in therapy.

3. Of great importance is the value that therapy notes have as a self-learning device. Notes can help us check ourselves against the tendencies to be restricted, preoccupied, or sterile in our contacts. Notes have a decided utility in promoting a greater psychological understanding of behavior as displayed by a variety of clients. Much of this understanding can be accomplished by attempting to put into words our impressions and our feelings about the client that too often have been implicitly assumed.

4. Therapy notes can be utilized in research and evaluation. They can aid in acquiring more ideas regarding the process itself and movement by the individual when certain techniques are used.

5. Notes serve to keep each helping professional in contact with the work and methods of other professional workers in the same settings. The knowledge gained from what others are doing may serve to help one become more flexible and productive in therapy.

6. Notes may serve as a type of protection for professionals because reference to these notes clarifies what actually occurred during the course of therapy.

————— ■ ■ ■ —————

————— ★ ★ ★ —————

A FORMAT FOR INDIVIDUAL PSYCHOTHERAPY SESSION NOTES*
Nan R. Presser and Karen S. Pfost

This article describes a format for individual case notes. The Individual Psychotherapy Session Notes (IPSN) form was designed to focus the clinician's attention on certain relevant aspects of the psychotherapy process and to facilitate the formation of inferences and hypotheses on the basis of clinical data. The form also encourages the therapist to examine his/her own behavior in sessions as well as to observe the therapist-client interaction. The form is designed to be used flexibly, in accordance with the practitioner's needs at different points during therapy. The implications of the IPSN form for training and supervision also are discussed.

* This material appeared in a chapter entitled "Counseling Techniques and Processes," pp. 77–174, in K. Dimick and F. Krause, *Practicum Manual for Counseling and Psychotherapy,* 1980, Muncie, IN: Accelerated Development. Reprinted with permission. (Edited to have terminology consistent with *Practicum and Internship Textbook for Counseling and Psychotherapy* (2nd ed.).

* This article appeared in *Professional Psychology: Research and Practice,* 1985, Vol. 16, No. 1, 11–16. Reprinted with permission.

The writing of case notes, although a necessary task, is one for which therapists often receive little or no training. Yet case notes can enhance the therapeutic process by enabling the clinician to assess the validity of conceptualization, to monitor progress toward goals, and to note patterns within and across sessions. In training institutions, case notes can serve an additional function: they provide the supervisor with another source of data regarding the supervisee, the client, and the client-therapist relationship. They provide a molar view of therapy that is a valuable precedent to a molecular analysis of events within a session. Case notes also indicate to the supervisor which aspects of therapy are both most salient and most recordable to the supervisee; omissions may serve as cues to focus on areas in supervision, either because they are problematic or inadequately conceptualized. Thus, thorough case notes can enhance both the supervisory process and the quality of services delivered and can serve as a safeguard for the supervisor as well.

In our experience, trainees' case notes were typically unfocused narratives of events within a session. Such notes often communicated little regarding the process and taught the trainee very little. The *Individual Psychotherapy Session Notes* (IPSN) form was developed for use within a training program. It was designed to focus the trainees' attention on important aspects of therapy sessions and to provide relevant information to the supervisor. Although the IPSN format is especially useful for fledgling clinicians, it is also appropriate for use by more experienced professionals. Its primary emphasis is on process, in contradistinction to the problem focus of other case note formats, most notably the *Problem Oriented Medical Record* (POMR) (Weed, 1968).

The development of the IPSN form was based on three principals. First, the form encourages therapists to attend to several specific, relevant aspects of the therapeutic process. Second, the form is, to the extent possible, atheoretical so that it can be adopted for use by therapists adhering to most theoretical positions. This is especially important for supervisors, who often train clinicians with various theoretical orientations. Third, it was important that the form not be excessively complex, cumbersome, or time-consuming to complete, so that after it has been learned it can be used easily after each session.

The initial version of this form was tested over the course of a year by master's-level clinical and counseling psychology trainees, and by doctoral-level psychology interns. They used the form to record several hundred client sessions occurring in a variety of settings. Systematic feedback from these trainees was used to determine the IPSN's usefulness and to make modifications.

Description of the IPSN Form

Each of the eight sections of the IPSN form is described below. (See Figure 4.1 for a replication of the form with sample notes.) What follows is a description of each section of the form.

I. Brief Summary of Session

This section allows for a narrative overview of the session. Although it is perhaps the least noteworthy section, it allows for the kind of case notes with which many practitioners are familiar and with which they may not be ready to dispense. Entries in this section are most likely to be in the form of a sequential account of major events within the session. Its relative brevity necessitates discrimination among the session's events.

II. Client

This section (and the following two) forces a clear distinction between data base and inference. The first subsection is provided for the recording of observations of the client's verbal and nonverbal behavior. Objectivity is the key to completion of this subsection, because it is important to resist the temptation to make inferences prior to specification of one's data base. The therapist's hypotheses and inferences are listed in the second subsection. The labeling of this subsection (interpretations and hypotheses) stresses both the speculative nature of such inferences as well as the desirability of further testing of hypotheses.

III. Therapist

This section encourages the clinician to examine his/her own behavior, retaining the distinction between data base and inferences. Such information is frequently not a part of traditional case notes. The use of this category appears likely to increase the therapist's awareness of his/her own behavior and to alter the therapist's perspective so that he/she is both subject and object. The underlying assumption, that the behavior of both parties can be observed and interpreted in a similar manner, discourages the clinician from making attributions regarding his/her own behavior differently from attributions regarding the client's behavior (e.g., situational vs. dispositional). Information in this section also provides a basis for an evaluation of the internal consistency of a therapist's behavior, correspondence to a theoretical stance, and the evolution of a therapist's own style. Data regarding the therapist's reaction to the client can also provide diagnostic information; with experience, the therapist learns to recognize his/her typical responses to persons who display various kinds of behavior.

IV. Therapist-Client Interaction

This section marks a shift in focus from intra- to interpersonal dynamics. The assumption of reciprocal influence that underlies this section encourages an interactional point of view. Because of the process orientation, this section can be extremely valuable in its illumination of dynamics. It is especially helpful in assisting the therapist to conceptualize both parties' behavior patterns and the degree to which these are specific or nonspecific to this relationship. The novice therapist may tend to underutilize this section of the form, a manifestation of the tendency at that stage to focus on persons (especially the client) rather than on the interaction between the client and the therapist. This section also tends to be used more as the therapeutic relationship develops and as behaviors that were formerly noted in the first or second section as independent come to be viewed in the context of an interaction.

V. Problems Addressed

Some clinicians, especially those who work in medical settings, are accustomed to the problem orientation exemplified in the POMR. This section differs from the POMR in that it refers specifically to problems that were addressed within the session. This is consistent with the form's focus on the analysis of events with a single session, but it links these events within the subsequent section.

VI. Progress Made

The assumption behind this section is a rather apparent one—that the client's progress is the ulti- mate criterion by which therapy must be assessed. The focus on progress highlights the need for movement within therapy, and is also consistent with the American Psychological Association's ethical standards (APA, 1977), which mandate that the basis for continuation of a therapeutic relationship must be its beneficial impact on the client.

VII. Plans

At this point, attention is shifted from a present to a future focus in order to provide continuity from one session to subsequent ones. This section encourages the clinician to plan therapeutic alternatives and conceptualize issues with which the client will most likely need to deal in future sessions. Practical strategies may also be noted here.

VIII. Other

This is a category for the information that needs to be recorded but that does not logically belong in any of the previous sections (e.g., test data, relevant correspondence). This section could also be termed as an "overflow" section.

The IPSN's Use in Supervision

The authors found the IPSN format to be useful in helping fledgling therapists learn concepts and skills requisite for effective therapy. It is rarely possible or desirable to describe everything that occurred in a session. The IPSN assists the novice in learning the necessary discrimination skills by prompting him/her to consider and examine those events and observations that are important and why.

Another skill the trainee needs to develop is that of regularly forming hypotheses about a client's behavior, the clinician's own behavior, and the interactions between these two people. Simply noting or observing the client will not lead to effective treatment unless the therapist can put these observations into a theoretical perspective that can eventuate in interventions with potential for producing changes in the client. The form assists the student in forming the habit of relating observations to conceptualizations, conceptualizations to treatment plans, and treatment plans to progress.

This form also can help the trainee to develop higher order observational skills. A trainee needs to learn not only to observe the client's verbal and

<table>
<tr><td colspan="2" align="center">**INDIVIDUAL PSYCHOTHERAPY NOTES**</td><td>CLIENT: Jane Doe
DATE: 1/14/85
SESSION: 6</td></tr>
</table>

I. BRIEF SUMMARY OF SESSION

Recent argument with her parents regarding lack of progress in finding another job led into discussion of pervasive feelings of inadequacy and hopelessness. She feels incapable of attaining the standards which her parents have set for her, but still she refuses to acknowledge any anger toward them. She appears more depressed and reports increased incidence of self-destructive behaviors. Does not appear to be suicidal at this time.

THERAPIST OBSERVATIONS OF:	THERAPIST'S INTERPRETATIONS AND HYPOTHESES:
II. CLIENT: At the beginning of session, pt. talked softly with infrequent pauses; slumped in chair; rarely made eye contact. Later, many self-depreciating statements as she discussed parents' expectations. Raised voice when discussing those, but denied anger. Reported drinking and contact with ex-boyfriend. Hinted re suicide, but denied intent.	Appears moderately depressed: turning anger inward? May be exacerbated by drinking. Seems threatened by suggestion that she might feel anger toward parents. Over-idealization of them is impediment. Presents self as victim and seems stuck in this role; assumes it with ex-boyfriend and parents. Could hints about suicide and drinking be to elicit rescuing by therapist?
III. THERAPIST Early in session felt tired, looked at watch frequently. Interventions primarily reflective and clarifying. Tone of voice gentle, soothing.	Initially impatient and bored. Am I becoming tired of her helplessness? Approach is relatively client-centered, with only mild confrontations. Is this avoidance of confrontation my issue (helpless behavior annoys me) or is it due to wanting to avoid recapitualization of victimization?
IV. THERAPIST-CLIENT INTERACTION: When pt. appears helpless or distressed, therapist is still responding supportively rather than confronting. Pt. asked if therapist was disappointed in her lack of progress and reported surprise at the negative reply: this was discussed vis-a-vis her father.	Does pt. typically elicit rescuing, or at times the opposite (frustration and alienating others with her helplessness)? Relationship with therapist is beginning to parallel relationship with father, particularly re projection of negative evaluation onto therapist and expectation of criticism.

Figure 4.1. Sample notes using a replication of the *Individual Psychotherapy Session Notes* form. (For the sake of clarity, these notes, which are usually handwritten, have been typeset.)

V. PROBLEMS ADDRESSED

1. Pt.'s feelings of unworthiness and despair re attaining the standards which she has injected.
2. Relationship with parents
3. Expectations of negative evaluations.

VI. PROGRESS MADE

Displays more insight into the connection between internalized standards and her depression.

Beginning to express some of the anger that she has heretofore turned inward.

Her expectation that therapist would also judge her negatively was examined.

Therapeutic alliance solidified by discussion of her reaction to therapist.

VII. PLANS

In supervision, bring up my reaction to her helplessness and consider reacting differently (first explore if this is my issue and, if not, how best to respond to her.)

Look for more signs of anger and point these out as they occur.

Explore idealization of parents.

Continue to monitor suicidal ideation.

VIII. OTHER

Will soon need to discuss my absence due to vacation.

Figure 4.1 continued. Sample notes using a replication of the *Individual Psychotherapy Session Notes* form.

nonverbal behavior but also the therapeutic process while he/she participates in it. Thus one learns to become simultaneously a participant and an observer during a session in order to ensure control of the session, to understand the therapeutic process on an ongoing basis, and to develop the ability to select appropriate interventions rather than to respond unsystematically. In this respect, the therapist learns to function much like a supervisor who does not participate in a session but observes the client, the therapist, and their interaction.

It has been our experience that the developmental stage of the trainee is reflected in how the individual completes the IPSN form. Early in training, therapists typically are able to complete only Sections I, V, VI, and VII comfortably and/or in-depth. The novice tends to focus attention primarily on the client, perhaps as a way of understanding the ambiguity and complexity of psychotherapeutic situations. It is not until later that most trainees seem able to observe and interpret their own behavior in therapy sessions. The ability to perceive, comprehend, and use interactional patterns is an even higher order therapeutic skill. For supervisors, the IPSN may

therefore provide a means of assessing their trainees' level of skills and monitoring progress in the trainees' development as therapists.

References

American Psychological Association. (1977). *Standards for providers of psychological services.* Washington, DC: Author.

Weed, L. (1968). Medical records that guide and teach. *New England Journal of Medicine, 278,* 595–600, 652–657.

CASE SUMMARY OUTLINE*
Joseph W. Hollis

Case summaries are essential to synthesize information and to provide baseline data for the counseling process. Summaries enable one to an-

* This material appeared in a chapter entitled "Counseling Techniques and Processes," pp. 77–174, in K. Dimick and F. Krause, *Practicum Manual for Counseling and Psychotherapy,* 1980, Muncie, IN: Accelerated Development. Reprinted with permission. (Wording has been modified to update for this edition.)

alyze whether or not all essential data regarding the planning and treatment of the client have been considered. In addition, summaries cause one to identify potential problems, directions for action with the client, and possible guidelines for determining whether or not satisfactory progress is being made during the series of therapy sessions.

A case summary also may be written prior to the initial interview. As such, the summary serves as a base for integrating what is known, as a baseline for comparison of future information, and as a springboard of what might be done when the individual is seen in therapy.

In addition, a case summary may be written at various times during the interval over which several therapy sessions were held. The summary may be for the counselor's benefit and as benchmarks for comparisons at a later date. Similarly, a summary may be needed to send to a referral person or to someone the client identifies as needing information about his/her status and/or progress. With those clients being seen within legal conditions (court cases, detention homes, penal institutions), periodic case summaries may be required. The length of the case summary is dependent upon its purpose and the amount and type of information available. One to three pages, single spaced, typewritten or computer generated generally are sufficient. When appropriate, copies of test data can be incorporated into or attached to the case summary.

A typical time for writing a case summary is after termination with the client. The summary will be a vehicle for the review of pertinent information if and when it is needed. The summary is placed in the client's folder and maintained along with other pertinent information gathered during the course of therapy.

Items to include in the case summary will be determined by such factors as purpose of the summary, who will use it, and professional expertise of users of the information. Even though items to be included in the case summary will vary form report to report, and outline of topics to be considered is beneficial (see Sample 5).

★ ★ ★

REPORTING THERAPEUTIC PROGRESS*
Joseph W. Hollis and Patsy A. Donn

The practicum student or intern frequently may receive requests from others to provide diagnostic information and reports of therapeutic progress, and to make recommendations regarding a client.

The format for reporting data will vary according to the specific requests that are made. Each progress report needs to be prepared in keeping with the request, the client, and the person to whom the report is sent. Qualitative and quantitative differences will be based upon the professional preparation of the person requesting the data, and the orientation and training of the individual preparing the report.

Requests for diagnostic information oftentimes are used by the agency or institution for the purpose of assisting in the development of treatment plans, for placement of clients into appropriate programs, and for providing information for the final disposition of a therapy case. Knowledge of the purpose for which the request is made is invaluable in assisting in the writing of a progress report that specifically addresses the request.

A request for treatment recommendations is a vital part of most progress reports. In some instances, the total report consists basically of treatment recommendations. The specific purpose of this report may be simply to communicate recommendations to someone else who must make a disposition of the case.

Requests for report of the client's therapeutic progress oftentimes are requested by the referring professional. Other professionals who have made previous referrals of any kind of the client are appreciative of reports on progress even if reports are not requested formally. In addition, others who are working concurrently with the client find progress reports invaluable in fulfilling their profes-

* This material appeared in a chapter entitled "Developing Reports in Response to Requests from Others," pp. 201–208, in J.W. Hollis and P.A. Donn, *Psychological Report Writing: Theory and Practice,* 1979, Muncie, IN: Accelerated Development. Reprinted with permission. (Edited to have terminology consistent with this book.)

CASE SUMMARY
(Topical Outline)

1. IDENTIFYING DATA
    The name, date, address, and telephone number of the client. Includes agency or school coding (client number, client file, social security number). The background (highest level attained).
2. REASON FOR THE REPORT
    A statement as to the purpose of the current report. Examples include: Interim progress reports of therapy, background information gathered prior to the initial session with the client, referral report to another agency or school, and termination report with the client.
3. SOURCE OF INFORMATION
    The source and the manner in which data were obtained in the preparation of this report.
4. STATEMENT OF THE PROBLEM
    A succinct statement of the presenting problem in therapy. May include a statement of reflecting the chronicity and acuteness of symptomatology.
5. FAMILY AND HOME BACKGROUND
    Identifying information about parents and siblings (names, ages, occupations, etc.). Client's perceptions of the home environment and relationships within the family. Critical family incidents may be included.
6. EDUCATIONAL HISTORY
    Description of pertinent information in relation to educational background including academic achievement, school instances that were significant for understanding the individual, and the client's attitude toward education.
7. PHYSICAL HEALTH HISTORY
    A statement of the client's significant health history, current treatment and medications, familial medical history that may impact upon the client, and current treatments.
8. SOCIAL INTERACTIONS
    Client's perception of the quality of his social interactions and interpersonal relationships.
9. PSYCHOLOGICAL DEVELOPMENT
    Statement of critical benchmarks in the client's psychological development, initial and current clinical impressions.
10. TESTING ASSESSMENT
    Inclusion of the name, form, and other identifying information about each test administered to the client and about the tests administered previously by others and the results utilized during the therapy sessions. Scores obtained and identification of norms used in reporting percentiles or other test scores. Interpretation of results.
11. OCCUPATIONAL HISTORY
    Chronology of the client's work history, when pertinent, jobs held, and reason for change. Quality of work satisfaction and interest.
12. HOBBIES, RECREATIONAL ACTIVITIES
    Interests and self-expressive uses of time.
13. SEXUAL ADJUSTMENT
    Current status, significant problems or disturbances in functioning, alternate lifestyles.
14. SUMMARY STATEMENT
    Summative statement concerning the client's current disposition and status.
15. DIAGNOSIS/ PROGNOSIS
    Statement of client's DSM IV diagnosis and clinical prognosis.
16. TREATMENT
    Description of current treatment and/or recommendations for follow-up treatment.
17. RECOMMENDATIONS

Sample 5. Topical outline for case summary format.

sional roles. Teachers, administrators, parents, and physicians can find an appropriately prepared progress report from a fellow professional an important source of assistance.

A *Therapeutic Progress Report* (Form 4.9), therefore, needs to include pertinent data about the method of treatment employed as well as the client's current status. Treatment recommendations are especially helpful to those who must make a final disposition of the case.

_____ ■ ■ ■ _____

CHAPTER REFERENCES

Cormier, W.H., & Cormier, L.S. (1985). *Interviewing strategies for helpers.* Monterey, CA: Brooks/Cole.

Dimick, K., & Krause, F. (1980). *Practicum manual for counseling and psychotherapy.* Muncie, IN: Accelerated Development.

Hutchins, D.E., & Cole, C.G. (1992). *Helping relationships and strategies* (second edition). Monterey, CA: Brooks/Cole.

Kanfer, F.H., & Schefft, B.K. (1988). *Guiding the process of therapeutic change.* Champaign, IL: Research Press.

Presser, N.B., & Pfost, K.S. (1985). A format for individual psychotherapy session notes. *Professional Psychology: Research and Practice, 16*(1), 11–16.

Weinrach, S.G. (1989). Guidelines for clients of private practitioners: Committing the structure to print. *Journal of Counseling and Development, 67,* 299–300.

PSYCHOSOCIAL HISTORY

Directions: The Practicum/Internship students should complete the form prior to the initiation of therapy and after completion of Initial Intake.

I.   IDENTIFYING INFORMATION

Name: _____   Age: _____

Address: _____   Date of Birth: _____

Phone: _____   Marital Status: _____

II.   PRESENTING PROBLEM/COMPLAINT

Nature of chief complaint: _____

_____

When did the problem begin (date of onset)? _____

How often does it occur? _____

How does it affect your daily functioning? _____

_____

Are there events, situations, and person that precipitate it? _____

_____

Symptoms:

Acute: _____   _____
          (Describe)

_____

Chronic: _____
          (Describe)

_____

Previous treatment (If yes, by whom? Outcome and reason for termination of treatment): _____

_____

_____

Form 4.7, p. 1 of 4, Copy 1

Medical:

Physician's Name: _____

Treatment dates from _____ to _____

Describe: _____

_____

Psychiatric:

Therapists's Name: _____

Treatment dates from _____ to _____

Describe: _____

_____

Prescription Drugs: _____

Substance Usage: _____

Description/Frequency/Amount: _____

_____

_____

III. DEVELOPMENTAL HISTORY

Pregnancy: _____

Delivery: _____

Infancy (Developmental Milestones): _____

_____

Middle Childhood (Developmental Milestones): _____

_____

Adolescence (Developmental Milestones): _____

_____

Young Adulthood, Middle Adulthood, Late Adulthood (Developmental Milestones): _____

_____

_____

IV. FAMILY HISTORY

Parents (Names, Ages, Occupations): _____

_____

_____

Parental Description (Personality/Attitude toward client): _____

_____

_____

Siblings/significant others (Name, Ages): _____

_____

_____

Personality/attitude toward the client: _____

_____

_____

V. EDUCATIONAL/OCCUPATIONAL HISTORY

Education (highest grade achieved; school performance/special classes/special needs):

_____

_____

_____

Occupational (job status, kinds of jobs, length of employment, vocational interests):

_____

_____

_____

VI. HEALTH HISTORY

Childhood disease, prior illnesses, surgery, etc.: _____

_____

_____

_____

Current Health (description of Clinic): _____

_____

_____

Family Health (grandparents, children): _____

_____

_____

Current Medications (prescribed and over the counter): _____

_____

_____

VII. MARITAL HISTORY

Current Status—years married, number of children (problems, stressors, enjoyment):

_____

_____

_____

Client's description of the current relationship with spouse: _____

_____

_____

_____

Client's perception of sexual relationship (attitudes/behavior): _____

_____

_____

_____

PSYCHOSOCIAL HISTORY

Directions: The Practicum/Internship students should complete the form prior to the initiation of therapy and after completion of Initial Intake.

I.   IDENTIFYING INFORMATION

Name: _____   Age: _____

Address: _____   Date of Birth: _____

Phone: _____   Marital Status: _____

II.   PRESENTING PROBLEM/COMPLAINT

Nature of chief complaint: _____

_____

When did the problem begin (date of onset)? _____

How often does it occur? _____

How does it affect your daily functioning? _____

_____

Are there events, situations, and person that precipitate it? _____

_____

Symptoms:

  Acute: _____
        (Describe)

_____

  Chronic: _____
         (Describe)

_____

Previous treatment (If yes, by whom? Outcome and reason for termination of treatment): _____

_____

_____

Medical:

 Physician's Name: _____

 Treatment dates from _____ to _____

 Describe: _____

 _____

Psychiatric:

 Therapists's Name: _____

 Treatment dates from _____ to _____

 Describe: _____

 _____

Prescription Drugs: _____

Substance Usage: _____

Description/Frequency/Amount: _____

_____

_____

III. DEVELOPMENTAL HISTORY

Pregnancy: _____

Delivery: _____

Infancy (Developmental Milestones): _____

_____

Middle Childhood (Developmental Milestones): _____

_____

Adolescence (Developmental Milestones): _____

_____

Young Adulthood, Middle Adulthood, Late Adulthood (Developmental Milestones): _____

_____

_____

IV. FAMILY HISTORY

Parents (Names, Ages, Occupations): _____

_____

_____

Parental Description (Personality/Attitude toward client): _____

_____

_____

Siblings/significant others (Name, Ages): _____

_____

_____

Personality/attitude toward the client: _____

_____

_____

V. EDUCATIONAL/OCCUPATIONAL HISTORY

Education (highest grade achieved; school performance/special classes/special needs):

_____

_____

_____

Occupational (job status, kinds of jobs, length of employment, vocational interests):

_____

_____

_____

VI. HEALTH HISTORY

Childhood disease, prior illnesses, surgery, etc.: _____

_____

_____

_____

Current Health (description of Clinic): _____

_____

_____

Family Health (grandparents, children): _____

_____

_____

Current Medications (prescribed and over the counter): _____

_____

_____

VII. MARITAL HISTORY

Current Status—years married, number of children (problems, stressors, enjoyment):

_____

_____

_____

Client's description of the current relationship with spouse: _____

_____

_____

_____

Client's perception of sexual relationship (attitudes/behavior): _____

_____

_____

_____

THERAPY NOTES

Therapist Name: _____ Agency/School: _____

Therapist Phone: _____

CLIENT IDENTIFYING DATA

Client Name: _____ Age: _____ Sex: _____

Date of Session: _____ Session Number: _____

Taping: Audio _____ Video _____

Presenting/Current Concern:

Key issues addressed:

Summary of the Session:

Diagnostic Impression(s):

Treatment Plan/Objectives:

Therapist's Comments:

Supervisor's Comments:

Date: _____ Therapist's Signature: _____

Date: _____ Supervisor's Signature: _____

THERAPY NOTES

Therapist Name: _____ Agency/School: _____

Therapist Phone: _____

CLIENT IDENTIFYING DATA

Client Name: _____ Age: _____ Sex: _____

Date of Session: _____ Session Number: _____

Taping: Audio _____ Video _____

Presenting/Current Concern:

Key issues addressed:

Summary of the Session:

Diagnostic Impression(s):

Treatment Plan/Objectives:

Therapist's Comments:

Supervisor's Comments:

Date: _____ Therapist's Signature: _____

Date: _____ Supervisor's Signature: _____

THERAPY NOTES

Therapist Name: _____   Agency/School: _____

Therapist Phone: _____

CLIENT IDENTIFYING DATA

Client Name: _____   Age: _____   Sex: _____

Date of Session: _____   Session Number: _____

Taping: Audio _____   Video _____

Presenting/Current Concern:

Key issues addressed:

Summary of the Session:

Diagnostic Impression(s):

Treatment Plan/Objectives:

Therapist's Comments:

Supervisor's Comments:

Date: _____   Therapist's Signature: _____

Date: _____   Supervisor's Signature: _____

THERAPY NOTES

Therapist Name: _____ Agency/School: _____

Therapist Phone: _____

CLIENT IDENTIFYING DATA

Client Name: _____ Age: _____ Sex: _____

Date of Session: _____ Session Number: _____

Taping: Audio _____ Video _____

Presenting/Current Concern:

Key issues addressed:

Summary of the Session:

Form 4.8, p. 1 of 2, Copy 4

Diagnostic Impression(s):

Treatment Plan/Objectives:

Therapist's Comments:

Supervisor's Comments:

Date: _____   Therapist's Signature: _____

Date: _____   Supervisor's Signature: _____

Form 4.8, p. 2 of 2, Copy 4

THERAPY NOTES

Therapist Name: _____ Agency/School: _____

Therapist Phone: _____

CLIENT IDENTIFYING DATA

Client Name: _____ Age: _____ Sex: _____

Date of Session: _____ Session Number: _____

Taping: Audio _____   Video _____

Presenting/Current Concern:

Key issues addressed:

Summary of the Session:

Diagnostic Impression(s):

Treatment Plan/Objectives:

Therapist's Comments:

Supervisor's Comments:

Date: _____ Therapist's Signature: _____

Date: _____ Supervisor's Signature: _____

Form 4.8, p. 2 of 2, Copy 5

THERAPY NOTES

Therapist Name: _____ Agency/School: _____

Therapist Phone: _____

CLIENT IDENTIFYING DATA

Client Name: _____ Age: _____ Sex: _____

Date of Session: _____ Session Number: _____

Taping: Audio _____ Video _____

Presenting/Current Concern:

Key issues addressed:

Summary of the Session:

Diagnostic Impression(s):

Treatment Plan/Objectives:

Therapist's Comments:

Supervisor's Comments:

Date: _____ Therapist's Signature: _____

Date: _____ Supervisor's Signature: _____

Form 4.8, p. 2 of 2, Copy 6

THERAPY NOTES

Therapist Name: _____ Agency/School: _____

Therapist Phone: _____

CLIENT IDENTIFYING DATA

Client Name: _____ Age: _____ Sex: _____

Date of Session: _____ Session Number: _____

Taping: Audio _____ Video _____

Presenting/Current Concern:

Key issues addressed:

Summary of the Session:

Diagnostic Impression(s):

Treatment Plan/Objectives:

Therapist's Comments:

Supervisor's Comments:

Date: _____ Therapist's Signature: _____

Date: _____ Supervisor's Signature: _____

Form 4.8, p. 2 of 2, Copy 7

THERAPY NOTES

Therapist Name: _____ Agency/School: _____

Therapist Phone: _____

CLIENT IDENTIFYING DATA

Client Name: _____ Age: _____ Sex: _____

Date of Session: _____ Session Number: _____

Taping: Audio _____ Video _____

Presenting/Current Concern:

Key issues addressed:

Summary of the Session:

Diagnostic Impression(s):

Treatment Plan/Objectives:

Therapist's Comments:

Supervisor's Comments:

Date: _____ Therapist's Signature: _____

Date: _____ Supervisor's Signature: _____

Form 4.8, p. 2 of 2, Copy 8

THERAPY NOTES

Therapist Name: _____ Agency/School: _____

Therapist Phone: _____

CLIENT IDENTIFYING DATA

Client Name: _____ Age: _____ Sex: _____

Date of Session: _____ Session Number: _____

Taping: Audio _____ Video _____

Presenting/Current Concern:

Key issues addressed:

Summary of the Session:

Diagnostic Impression(s):

Treatment Plan/Objectives:

Therapist's Comments:

Supervisor's Comments:

Date: _____   Therapist's Signature: _____

Date: _____   Supervisor's Signature: _____

Form 4.8, p. 2 of 2, Copy 9

THERAPY NOTES

Therapist Name: _____ Agency/School: _____

Therapist Phone: _____

CLIENT IDENTIFYING DATA

Client Name: _____ Age: _____ Sex: _____

Date of Session: _____ Session Number: _____

Taping: Audio _____ Video _____

Presenting/Current Concern:

Key issues addressed:

Summary of the Session:

Diagnostic Impression(s):

Treatment Plan/Objectives:

Therapist's Comments:

Supervisor's Comments:

Date: _____ Therapist's Signature: _____

Date: _____ Supervisor's Signature: _____

Form 4.8, p. 2 of 2, Copy 10

THERAPY NOTES

Therapist Name: _____ Agency/School: _____

Therapist Phone: _____

CLIENT IDENTIFYING DATA

Client Name: _____ Age: _____ Sex: _____

Date of Session: _____ Session Number: _____

Taping: Audio _____ Video _____

Presenting/Current Concern:

Key issues addressed:

Summary of the Session:

Diagnostic Impression(s):

Treatment Plan/Objectives:

Therapist's Comments:

Supervisor's Comments:

Date: _____ Therapist's Signature: _____

Date: _____ Supervisor's Signature: _____

Form 4.8, p. 2 of 2, Copy 11

THERAPY NOTES

Therapist Name: _____ Agency/School: _____

Therapist Phone: _____

CLIENT IDENTIFYING DATA

Client Name: _____ Age: _____ Sex: _____

Date of Session: _____ Session Number: _____

Taping: Audio _____ Video _____

Presenting/Current Concern:

Key issues addressed:

Summary of the Session:

Diagnostic Impression(s):

Treatment Plan/Objectives:

Therapist's Comments:

Supervisor's Comments:

Date: _____   Therapist's Signature: _____

Date: _____   Supervisor's Signature: _____

Form 4.8, p. 2 of 2, Copy 12

THERAPY NOTES

Therapist Name: _____ Agency/School: _____

Therapist Phone: _____

CLIENT IDENTIFYING DATA

Client Name: _____ Age: _____ Sex: _____

Date of Session: _____ Session Number: _____

Taping: Audio _____ Video _____

Presenting/Current Concern:

Key issues addressed:

Summary of the Session:

Diagnostic Impression(s):

Treatment Plan/Objectives:

Therapist's Comments:

Supervisor's Comments:

Date: _____   Therapist's Signature: _____

Date: _____   Supervisor's Signature: _____

Form 4.8, p. 2 of 2, Copy 13

THERAPY NOTES

Therapist Name: _____ Agency/School: _____

Therapist Phone: _____

CLIENT IDENTIFYING DATA

Client Name: _____ Age: _____ Sex: _____

Date of Session: _____ Session Number: _____

Taping: Audio _____ Video _____

Presenting/Current Concern:

Key issues addressed:

Summary of the Session:

Diagnostic Impression(s):

Treatment Plan/Objectives:

Therapist's Comments:

Supervisor's Comments:

Date: _____ Therapist's Signature: _____

Date: _____ Supervisor's Signature: _____

Form 4.8, p. 2 of 2, Copy 14

THERAPY NOTES

Therapist Name: _____ Agency/School: _____

Therapist Phone: _____

CLIENT IDENTIFYING DATA

Client Name: _____ Age: _____ Sex: _____

Date of Session: _____ Session Number: _____

Taping: Audio _____ Video _____

Presenting/Current Concern:

Key issues addressed:

Summary of the Session:

Diagnostic Impression(s):

Treatment Plan/Objectives:

Therapist's Comments:

Supervisor's Comments:

Date: _____ Therapist's Signature: _____

Date: _____ Supervisor's Signature: _____

Form 4.8, p. 2 of 2, Copy 15

THERAPY NOTES

Therapist Name: _____ Agency/School: _____

Therapist Phone: _____

CLIENT IDENTIFYING DATA

Client Name: _____ Age: _____ Sex: _____

Date of Session: _____ Session Number: _____

Taping: Audio _____ Video _____

Presenting/Current Concern:

Key issues addressed:

Summary of the Session:

Diagnostic Impression(s):

Treatment Plan/Objectives:

Therapist's Comments:

Supervisor's Comments:

Date: _____ Therapist's Signature: _____

Date: _____ Supervisor's Signature: _____

THERAPY NOTES

Therapist Name: _____ Agency/School: _____

Therapist Phone: _____

CLIENT IDENTIFYING DATA

Client Name: _____ Age: _____ Sex: _____

Date of Session: _____ Session Number: _____

Taping: Audio _____ Video _____

Presenting/Current Concern:

Key issues addressed:

Summary of the Session:

Diagnostic Impression(s):

Treatment Plan/Objectives:

Therapist's Comments:

Supervisor's Comments:

Date: _____ Therapist's Signature: _____

Date: _____ Supervisor's Signature: _____

Form 4.8, p. 2 of 2, Copy 17

THERAPY NOTES

Therapist Name: _____ Agency/School: _____

Therapist Phone: _____

CLIENT IDENTIFYING DATA

Client Name: _____ Age: _____ Sex: _____

Date of Session: _____ Session Number: _____

Taping: Audio _____ Video _____

Presenting/Current Concern:

Key issues addressed:

Summary of the Session:

Diagnostic Impression(s):

Treatment Plan/Objectives:

Therapist's Comments:

Supervisor's Comments:

Date: _____ Therapist's Signature: _____

Date: _____ Supervisor's Signature: _____

Form 4.8, p. 2 of 2, Copy 18

THERAPY NOTES

Therapist Name: _____ Agency/School: _____

Therapist Phone: _____

CLIENT IDENTIFYING DATA

Client Name: _____ Age: _____ Sex: _____

Date of Session: _____ Session Number: _____

Taping: Audio _____ Video _____

Presenting/Current Concern:

Key issues addressed:

Summary of the Session:

Diagnostic Impression(s):

Treatment Plan/Objectives:

Therapist's Comments:

Supervisor's Comments:

Date: _____ Therapist's Signature: _____

Date: _____ Supervisor's Signature: _____

Form 4.8, p. 2 of 2, Copy 19

THERAPY NOTES

Therapist Name: _____ Agency/School: _____

Therapist Phone: _____

CLIENT IDENTIFYING DATA

Client Name: _____ Age: _____ Sex: _____

Date of Session: _____ Session Number: _____

Taping: Audio _____ Video _____

Presenting/Current Concern:

Key issues addressed:

Summary of the Session:

Diagnostic Impression(s):

Treatment Plan/Objectives:

Therapist's Comments:

Supervisor's Comments:

Date: _____ Therapist's Signature: _____

Date: _____ Supervisor's Signature: _____

Form 4.8, p. 2 of 2, Copy 20

THERAPEUTIC PROGRESS REPORT

Date: _____

Therapist's Name: _____   Client's Name: _____

Therapist's Phone: _____   Client's Age: _____ Sex: _____

Sessions to date with client (_____)
                                                    Number

Client's Presenting Complaint: _____

_____

_____

Therapeutic Summary: _____

_____

_____

Method(s) of Treatment: _____

_____

_____

Duration of Treatment: _____

_____

_____

Current Status: _____

_____

_____

Treatment Recommendations: _____

_____

_____

_____
Therapist's Signature

_____
Supervisor's Signature

Form 4.9, p. 1 of 1, Copy 1

THERAPEUTIC PROGRESS REPORT

Date: _____

Therapist's Name: _____ Client's Name: _____

Therapist's Phone: _____ Client's Age: _____ Sex: _____

Sessions to date with client (_____)

Number

Client's Presenting Complaint: _____

_____

_____

Therapeutic Summary: _____

_____

_____

Method(s) of Treatment: _____

_____

_____

Duration of Treatment: _____

_____

_____

Current Status: _____

_____

_____

Treatment Recommendations: _____

_____

_____

_____

Therapist's Signature

_____

Supervisor's Signature

Form 4.9, p. 1 of 1, Copy 2

THERAPEUTIC PROGRESS REPORT

Date: _____

Therapist's Name: _____ Client's Name: _____

Therapist's Phone: _____ Client's Age: _____ Sex: _____

Sessions to date with client (_____)

                                                 Number

Client's Presenting Complaint: _____

_____

_____

Therapeutic Summary: _____

_____

_____

Method(s) of Treatment: _____

_____

_____

Duration of Treatment: _____

_____

_____

Current Status: _____

_____

_____

Treatment Recommendations: _____

_____

_____

_____
Therapist's Signature

_____
Supervisor's Signature

Form 4.9, p. 1 of 1, Copy 3

THERAPEUTIC PROGRESS REPORT

Date: _____

Therapist's Name: _____ Client's Name: _____

Therapist's Phone: _____ Client's Age: _____ Sex: _____

Sessions to date with client (_____)
                                                      Number

Client's Presenting Complaint: _____

_____

_____

Therapeutic Summary: _____

_____

_____

Method(s) of Treatment: _____

_____

_____

Duration of Treatment: _____

_____

_____

Current Status: _____

_____

_____

Treatment Recommendations: _____

_____

_____

_____
Therapist's Signature

_____
Supervisor's Signature

Chapter 5

MONITORING THE PROFESSIONAL DEVELOPMENT OF PRACTICUM STUDENTS AND INTERNS

Judith Scott, Ph.D.

Supervision of the counselor or psychologist in training is the primary mode by which field-based professional development is facilitated and monitored. The term "monitored" has been chosen specifically because it implies a steady but unobtrusive action to guide the student, over time, toward higher levels of role mastery. Supervision is the cornerstone of practicum and internship experiences and provides the opportunity for training, data gathering, and feedback regarding the full range of counselor or psychologist professional role activities. Individual supervision, group supervision, peer supervision, and self-supervision are the several modalities of supervision that have been identified in the literature (Hart & Falvey, 1987). Individual and group supervision are the modalities that are required specifically by CACREP and APA accreditation guidelines for both practicum and internship experiences.

In order to utilize the various modalities effectively in an integrated manner, a comprehensive framework for defining counselor/therapist skills is necessary. Categories for assessing professional development of counselors have been outlined in the *Handbook of Counseling Supervision* (Borders & Leddick, 1987). These categories—Counseling Performance Skills, Cognitive Counseling Skills, and Developmental Level—will be used as the framework for professional development in this chapter.

ROLE AND FUNCTION OF THE SUPERVISOR IN PRACTICUM AND INTERNSHIP

The role of the supervisor in practicum and internship is "(1) facilitation of the counselor's per-

sonal and professional development, (2) promotion of counselor competencies, and (3) promotion of accountable counseling and guidance services and programs" (Bradley, 1989, p. 8). Supervisors are considered to be master practitioners who, because of their special clinical abilities and experience, have been identified by the field site to monitor and oversee the professional activities of trainees. University supervisors share a similar role of promoting applied learning skills but have an indirect or liaison relationship to the field site.

The functions of the supervisor have been variously described. Kadushin (1976) outlined supervisory functions in the field of social work as encompassing administration, education, and support. Counselor education literature identifies supervisory functions as consultation, counseling, training, evaluation, and research (Borders & Leddick, 1987; Bradley, 1989). In the specialization area of professional psychology, the supervisor is viewed as functioning as therapist, teacher, and administrator (Eckstein, 1972).

The area of supervision that has perhaps the most controversy lies in the contrast between clinical supervision functions and administrative supervision functions. *Clinical supervision functions* emphasize counseling, consultation, and training related to the direct service provided to clients by the trainee. *Administrative supervision functions* emphasize work assignment, work review, evaluation, and institutional accountability in services and programs. For example, when clinical supervision is the emphasis, the trainee's development of clinical skills is the focus of the supervisor-supervisee interaction. Feedback is related to professional standards and clinical literature. In contrast, when administrative supervision is the focus, issues such as keeping certain hours, meeting deadlines, following policy and procedures, and making a judgment about whether work is being accomplished at a minimally acceptable level are emphasized. Feedback is related to institutional standards.

A survey conducted by the North Atlantic Region Association for Counselor Education and Supervision (Hart & Falvey, 1987) showed that trainees received equivalent amounts of clinical and administrative supervision each week and that the same person provided clinical and administrative supervision in the majority of responding agencies. Ideally, recommendations are that the same person should not provide both administrative and clinical supervision. If this is not possible, then separate meetings should be scheduled for clinical supervision. This strategy reduces authority and trust conflicts and ensures that reflection on clinical work will not be avoided by focusing on administrative issues (Falvey, 1987).

A trainee can expect to experience both emphases of supervision and feedback. The relative emphasis in this chapter, however, will be on clinical supervision and the intervention, assessment, and evaluation techniques related to a clinical emphasis. The trainee may wish to reflect on the proportion of clinical to administrative supervision he/she is receiving in practicum or internship.

SUPERVISOR-SUPERVISEE RELATIONSHIP

Direct supervision of clinical work is perhaps the most important element in the training of a counselor or psychotherapist. Supervision is more than a didactic experience. It includes intensive interpersonal interaction with all of the potential complications that such relationships can include. Research has documented the importance of the supervisor-supervisee relationship. Several studies have related success in supervision to the quality of the relationship between the supervisor and supervisee (Cohen & DeBetz, 1977; Nash, 1975). A study examining supervisees' positive and negative experiences in supervision (Hutt, Scott, & King, 1983) indicated that effective supervision integrates both task- and person-oriented behavior. Relationship qualities of warmth, acceptance, trust, and under-

standing are defined as fundamental to positive supervision. Good supervision must integrate both task- and relationship-oriented behavior. In positive supervision experiences, a critical balance exists between relationship and task focus. In negative supervision experiences, the total emotional focus is on the relationship with its intensely negative focus.

The supervisee enters into the supervisory relationship with a number of predictable anxieties. Common sources of supervisee anxiety are: "the supervisee's questions, fears, and uncertainties relative to starting in a training position; irrational thoughts pertaining to whether he/she will be competent and gain others' approval; and the concerns stemming from being in a subordinate role to the supervisor" (Deck & Morrow, 1989, pp. 41–42). Performance and approval anxieties can result in defensive strategies by the supervisee, which include inappropriate silences, intellectualization, catastrophizing, or dropping out of training. Dominance anxieties on the part of the supervisee that are related to the supervisor's dominant position in the relationship can lead to retaliatory strategies identified by Ricoh (1980). These include pointing out errors in supervision, reporting that the supervisor's suggestions did not work, or acting passive and uninvolved in supervision.

A study examining conflict and conflict resolution within the supervisory relationship outlined three types of conflict (Moskowitz & Rupert, 1983):

> The first category consisted of conflicts that were due primarily to differences between supervisor and trainee in theoretical orientation or views on appropriate therapeutic approach or techniques. . . .
>
> The second category consisted of conflicts that involved primarily the supervisor's style of supervision. Many of these conflicts involved dissatisfaction with the amounts of direction or support provided by the supervisor. . . .
>
> The third category consisted of conflicts that . . . reflected a personality clash or personal issues on the part of the trainee or supervisor. . . . (p. 636)

Also reported in the study was that "in most cases, these conflicts were discussed and resolved so that the supervisory relationship became a productive one" (p. 639). Even though trainees would have preferred that the supervisor initiated discussion regarding the conflict, such discussions were reported to be initiated by the trainee.

Scott (1976) emphasized the importance of establishing a collegial relationship within the supervisor-supervisee interaction. The relationship is characterized by balance and a shared responsibility for understanding the counseling process. Disruption of the balance or the inability to establish collegiality should be an open area of discussion in order to identify learning problems. A general rule is that disruptions in the supervisor-supervisee relationship that occur within the supervisory work always take precedence.

The literature cited in this section may provide the practicum student or intern with sufficient rationale and motivation to consider the supervisor-supervisee relationship as an important area to address during supervision. Relational concerns and conflicts clearly detract from the amount of learning in supervision.

APPROACHES IN SUPERVISION

The practicum student or intern often approaches clinical supervision with mixed feelings. On the positive side, supervision can be regarded as a helpful supportive interaction where the work will focus on validating some practices, improving others, and learning new techniques and insights about the counseling process. On the negative side, supervision can be regarded as an interaction that will expose inadequacies and leave the student with even more feelings of incompetence. Both sets of expectations coexist as the student approaches supervision. The tendency, particularly in the early stages of supervision, is for the student to work at proving himself/herself as a counselor so that the negative inadequate feelings will diminish. This is a natural and understandable tendency. However, giving full reign to this tendency would lead the supervision away from the ambiguous aspects of the counseling that require clarification and could lead to avoidance or defensiveness about aspects of the counseling that need improvement. Generally, the initial phases of supervision are spent on establishing a working alliance between the supervisor and supervisee. This holds true across the several approaches to supervision that might be implemented. To reduce the practicum student's or intern's anxieties about supervision and facilitate establishing a working alliance, a preview of how supervision could be implemented is in order. A review of the

various practices in counseling supervision has resulted in the identification and explication of five major approaches to supervision (Bradley, 1989).

Psychotherapeutic Approaches to Supervision

This approach revolves around increasing awareness, understanding, and use of interpersonal and intrapersonal dynamics. The supervisee can expect that awareness of his/her own dynamics will be a focus. Techniques associated with this approach are *interpersonal process recall* (IPR) and unstructured and intensive therapeutic supervision. The IPR technique requires the supervisee to listen to or view an audiotape or videotape of a session with a client. The recall supervisor uses inductive questioning to direct the counselor's attention to the interpersonal and intrapersonal dynamics in the interaction. The unstructured technique requires that the counselor bring something to the supervisor for discussion. This may be a tape of a session, a professional problem, or a consulting concern. If the concern involves any human interaction, the dynamics of the interaction can receive focus. The role of the supervisor is to focus on the dynamics and respond so that the supervisee can give attention to the dynamics involved (Bradley, 1989, pp. 65–124).

Behavioral Approaches to Supervision

This approach focuses on the skill behaviors of the counselor. Included in skill behaviors are the feelings, thoughts, and acts of the counselor. The goal of behavioral supervision is to develop and refine skill behaviors appropriate to counseling. In order to set supervision goals, skill analysis and assessment must be done. Any one of several models that identify skill dimensions of counseling competency, as the supervisor's own repertoire of identified counseling competencies, may be used. Skill behavior analysis is best implemented when the purpose of the skill and the process sequence of the skill are identified and understood. After supervisory goals are set, strategies to accomplish the goals are constructed and implemented (Bradley, 1989, pp. 125–189).

Integrative Approaches to Supervision

This approach combines methods and techniques from several supervisory approaches and represents the usual practice of a large number of supervisors. The *Carkhuff Training Model* and the

Psychobehavioral Model are two integrative approaches identified by Bradley (1989). In the Carkhuff Training Model, the practicum student or intern can expect that the supervisor will model facilitative interpersonal skills as well as action oriented skills. While the supervisor offers psychologically facilitative conditions, the supervisee is directed through a three-stage program of learning activities: *discrimination training to recognize and differentiate between high levels and low levels of facilitative conditions, communication training to develop and demonstrate competence in responding, and developing courses of action where intervention strategies are taught and practiced.*

In the psychobehavioral model, a blend of insight counseling and action oriented counseling is utilized. The practicum student or intern can expect to proceed through three stages of supervision:

1. the initial stage—exploration of anxieties and expectations and experiences focusing on interpersonal and intrapersonal dynamics are combined with skill development activities;

2. the intermediate stage—a more confrontational supervision that examines dynamic patterns and provides therapeutic feedback from the supervisor is utilized; and

3. the terminal stage—the supervisor functions more as a consultant, and training activities are minimal (Bradley, 1989, pp. 201–203).

Systems Approach to Supervision

In this approach, systems technology is applied to the supervisory function. The trainee and his/her performance are viewed in the context of the helping services the counselor is responsible for delivering. The supervisor is a consultant who collaborates with trainees in conceptualizing the counseling activities in terms of broad goals and performance objectives within the total counseling or helping service program. The practicum student or intern can expect to meet with the supervisor to review an activity plan to determine how realistic it may be and how likely it is to reach intended goals and objectives (Bradley, 1989, pp. 229–256).

Person-Process Model of Supervision (PPM): A Developmental Approach to Supervision

In this approach, developmental theory is applied to the supervisory process. Loevinger's work on ego and development provides the theory base for the first component of PPM, entitled "Understanding the Personal Meaning Making System of the Supervisee." Supervisees proceed through the preconformist level, which coincides with the impulsive and self protective stages of Loevinger's developmental model. Persons at this level think very simply and concretely. The conformist level, in which supervisees have a genuine concern about what others think of them, follows. Supervisees at this level are receptive to act on criticisms and recommendations made by a supervisor or coworker. The third level of personal meaning making is the self-aware/postconformist level. Supervisees at this level demonstrate greater cognitive complexity in the way they approach their work (D'Andrea, 1989, pp. 257–296).

The second component of the PPM model attends to the supervision process and is derived from the work of Hess and Erikson. Stages identified are the inception stage, where trust is established and goals assessed; the exploration stage, where autonomy and the development of broader based professional competencies are emphasized; and the consolidation and mutuality stage, where professional identity is established and higher order competencies demonstrated (D'Andrea, 1989).

The five approaches to supervision that have been reviewed are those that are most likely to be experienced by the practicum student or intern. Because the trainee probably will have more than one supervisor during his/her field experiences, the probability is that he/she may be working with a university supervisor who utilizes the behavioral approach to supervision at the same time he/she may be working with a field site supervisor who utilizes a systems approach to supervision. The trainee is advised to be open to any one of the approaches to supervision by recognizing goals and advantages inherent in each of the approaches.

ASSESSING PROFESSIONAL DEVELOPMENT

A comprehensive framework for defining skills categories for the counselor-in-training has been

(Continued on p. 181.)

SELF-ASSESSMENT OF BASIC HELPING SKILLS AND PROCEDURAL SKILLS

Purposes:

1. To provide the trainee with an opportunity to review levels of competency in the performance skill areas of basic helping skills and procedural skills.

2. To provide the trainee with a basis for identifying areas of emphasis within supervision.

Directions:

Circle a number next to each item to indicate your perceived level of competence: continuum is from 1, which is poor, to 5, which is good.

Basic Helping Skills	**Poor**		**Average**		**Good**
1. Ability to demonstrate active attending behavior.	1	2	3	4	5
2. Ability to listen to and understand nonverbal behavior.	1	2	3	4	5
3. Ability to listen to what client says verbally, noticing mix of experiences, behaviors and feelings.	1	2	3	4	5
4. Ability to understand accurately the client's point of view.	1	2	3	4	5
5. Ability to identify themes in client's story.	1	2	3	4	5
6. Ability to identify inconsistencies between client's story and reality.	1	2	3	4	5
7. Ability to respond with accurate empathy.	1	2	3	4	5
8. Ability to ask open-ended questions.	1	2	3	4	5
9. Ability to help clients clarify and focus.	1	2	3	4	5
10. Ability to balance empathic response, clarification, and probing.	1	2	3	4	5
11. Ability to assess accurately severity of client's problems.	1	2	3	4	5
12. Ability to establish a collaborative working relationship with client.	1	2	3	4	5
13. Ability to assess and activate client's strengths and resources in problem solving.	1	2	3	4	5
14. Ability to identify and challenge unhealthy or distorted thinking or behaving.	1	2	3	4	5
15. Ability to use advanced empathy to deepen client's understanding of problems and solutions.	1	2	3	4	5

Form 5.1, p. 1 of 2, Copy 1

		Poor		Average		Good
16.	Ability to explore the counselor-client relationship.	1	2	3	4	5
17.	Ability to share constructively some of own experiences, behaviors, and feelings with clients.	1	2	3	4	5
18.	Ability to summarize.	1	2	3	4	5
19.	Ability to share information appropriately.	1	2	3	4	5
20.	Ability to understand and facilitate decision making.	1	2	3	4	5
21.	Ability to help clients set goals and move toward action in problem solving.	1	2	3	4	5
22.	Ability to recognize and manage client reluctance and resistance.	1	2	3	4	5
23.	Ability to help clients explore consequences of the goals they set.	1	2	3	4	5
24.	Ability to help clients sustain action in direction of goals.	1	2	3	4	5
25.	Ability to help clients review and revise or recommit to goals based on new experiences.	1	2	3	4	5

Procedural Skills

		Poor		Average		Good
26.	Ability to open the session smoothly.	1	2	3	4	5
27.	Ability to collaborate with client to identify important concerns for the session.	1	2	3	4	5
28.	Ability to establish continuity from session to session.	1	2	3	4	5
29.	Knowledge of policy and procedures of educational or agency setting regarding harm to self and others, substance abuse, and child abuse.	1	2	3	4	5
30.	Ability to keep appropriate records related to counseling process.	1	2	3	4	5
31.	Ability to end session smoothly.	1	2	3	4	5

_____ (Trainee Signature)   _____ (Supervisor Signature)

_____ (date)

Form 5.1, p. 2 of 2, Copy 1

SELF-ASSESSMENT OF BASIC HELPING SKILLS AND PROCEDURAL SKILLS

Purposes:

1. To provide the trainee with an opportunity to review levels of competency in the performance skill areas of basic helping skills and procedural skills.

2. To provide the trainee with a basis for identifying areas of emphasis within supervision.

Directions:

Circle a number next to each item to indicate your perceived level of competence: continuum is from 1, which is poor, to 5, which is good.

Basic Helping Skills	Poor		Average		Good
1. Ability to demonstrate active attending behavior.	1	2	3	4	5
2. Ability to listen to and understand nonverbal behavior.	1	2	3	4	5
3. Ability to listen to what client says verbally, noticing mix of experiences, behaviors and feelings.	1	2	3	4	5
4. Ability to understand accurately the client's point of view.	1	2	3	4	5
5. Ability to identify themes in client's story.	1	2	3	4	5
6. Ability to identify inconsistencies between client's story and reality.	1	2	3	4	5
7. Ability to respond with accurate empathy.	1	2	3	4	5
8. Ability to ask open-ended questions.	1	2	3	4	5
9. Ability to help clients clarify and focus.	1	2	3	4	5
10. Ability to balance empathic response, clarification, and probing.	1	2	3	4	5
11. Ability to assess accurately severity of client's problems.	1	2	3	4	5
12. Ability to establish a collaborative working relationship with client.	1	2	3	4	5
13. Ability to assess and activate client's strengths and resources in problem solving.	1	2	3	4	5
14. Ability to identify and challenge unhealthy or distorted thinking or behaving.	1	2	3	4	5
15. Ability to use advanced empathy to deepen client's understanding of problems and solutions.	1	2	3	4	5

Form 5.1, p. 1 of 2, Copy 2

		Poor		**Average**		**Good**
16.	Ability to explore the counselor-client relationship.	1	2	3	4	5
17.	Ability to share constructively some of own experiences, behaviors, and feelings with clients.	1	2	3	4	5
18.	Ability to summarize.	1	2	3	4	5
19.	Ability to share information appropriately.	1	2	3	4	5
20.	Ability to understand and facilitate decision making.	1	2	3	4	5
21.	Ability to help clients set goals and move toward action in problem solving.	1	2	3	4	5
22.	Ability to recognize and manage client reluctance and resistance.	1	2	3	4	5
23.	Ability to help clients explore consequences of the goals they set.	1	2	3	4	5
24.	Ability to help clients sustain action in direction of goals.	1	2	3	4	5
25.	Ability to help clients review and revise or recommit to goals based on new experiences.	1	2	3	4	5

Procedural Skills

		Poor		**Average**		**Good**
26.	Ability to open the session smoothly.	1	2	3	4	5
27.	Ability to collaborate with client to identify important concerns for the session.	1	2	3	4	5
28.	Ability to establish continuity from session to session.	1	2	3	4	5
29.	Knowledge of policy and procedures of educational or agency setting regarding harm to self and others, substance abuse, and child abuse.	1	2	3	4	5
30.	Ability to keep appropriate records related to counseling process.	1	2	3	4	5
31.	Ability to end session smoothly.	1	2	3	4	5

_____ (Trainee Signature)   _____ (Supervisor Signature)

_____ (date)

Form 5.1, p. 2 of 2, Copy 2

proposed in the *Handbook of Counseling Supervision* (Borders & Leddick, 1987). Three broad skill categories have been identified as those within which self-assessment, supervisor assessment, goal identification, and evaluation can be implemented.

The first skill category is *counseling performance skills*. Counseling performance skills refer to "what the counselor does during a session or his counseling behaviors" (p. 14). This includes (1) the basic helping skills such as attending behaviors, primary and advanced empathy, concreteness, and effective self-disclosure; (2) theory-based techniques such as challenging irrational beliefs or relaxation training; and (3) procedural skills such as opening or closing an interview or managing special issues such as suicide.

The second skill category is *cognitive counseling skills*. This refers to "how the counselor thinks about the client and chooses interventions" (p. 16). This is an area of professional development that has received relatively less attention than the performance skill categories. Nevertheless, this area is integral to the mastery of the counselor or psychologist professional role. Trainees need to be able to discriminate important client data from less important client data. They must be able to sort through and synthesize information in order to identify underlying patterns and themes, which helps in the understanding of client problems. And finally, they must be able to formulate clinical hypotheses in order to be planful about interventions and recommendations. This skill category most likely will be emphasized at the more advanced levels of field experience. However, awareness of important information and the ability to discriminate between important and unimportant information is part of early training.

A third skill category is the *developmental level*. This refers to the degree to which trainees are able to internalize the role of counselor and achieve a peer-like collegial relationship with the supervisor. Assessment and evaluation in this category can help identify the personal and professional issues the trainee is facing. For example, the trainee might be described as functioning at a dependent and primarily imitative level. The trainee might be described as lacking awareness of his/her own personal needs and motivations. At higher developmental levels, the trainee might be described as able to understand his/her own strengths and weaknesses. This is often a difficult area in which to self-assess and will require some dialogue with the supervisor in order to be specific in identifying personal and professional concerns.

We suggest that the trainee spend time early in the supervisory relationship discussing and clarifying the three skill categories. This discussion will facilitate the self-assessment process for the trainee. At the early phases, of practicum. the possibility may be that the counselor performance skills area will be targeted for work while the areas of cognitive counseling skills and developmental level may be more background and have primarily awareness level goals. At the advanced phases of internship, the possibility may be that the counselor performance skills area is background and cognitive counseling skills and developmental level areas are targeted for work. (See Figure 5.1.) The framework suggested here can be adapted to the individual needs of the trainee at various stages of experiences.

MONITORING COUNSELING PERFORMANCE SKILLS

Self-assessment of Counseling Performance Skills: Setting Goals for Supervision

Several kinds of assessment are utilized throughout the practicum and internship experience. These include self-assessment, peer assessment, and supervisor assessment. Initially, a self-assessment is recommended so that the trainee can enter into supervision activities with peers and supervisors with a clearer idea of the performance skill areas that may need validated and reinforced, and the performance skill areas that represent new techniques or skills that need to be developed. We recommend that the trainee begin the supervisory process by reflecting on all the previous experiences that he/she brings to the current field training situation. These would include educational preparation, related work experience, volunteer activities, paraprofessional counseling activities, and previous supervision related to counseling. When entering into supervisory interactions, the trainee can be expected to provide peers and supervisors with his/her perceptions of the performance skill area in which he/she is well grounded

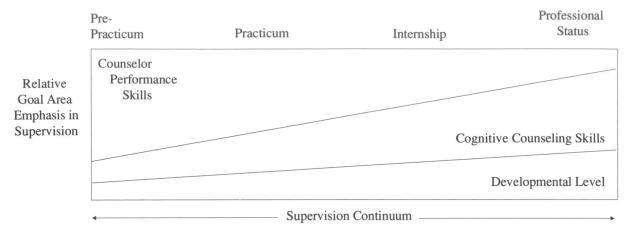

Figure 5.1. Schematic representation of relative goal emphasis in supervision and the shift in goal emphasis as the student progresses from pre-practicum to completion of internship.

and also of perceptions of the areas that need more development.

Counseling performance skills include the basic helping skills, theory-based techniques, and procedural skills. The basic helping skills include such techniques as responding with basic empathy, asking open-ended questions, using advanced empathy and confrontation, and setting goals. Theory-based counseling performance skills include techniques that are related to a particular theoretical orientation such as relaxation training or identifying automatic thoughts or interpretation of transference. Procedural skills include such techniques as beginning and ending sessions or handling "red flag" situations such as harm to self or others or child abuse.

Two self-assessment activities have been included to assist the student/intern in evaluating his/her counseling performance skills. The first self-assessment activity (Form 5.1) focuses on basic counseling skills and procedural skills. The second self-assessment activity, which can be used prior to meeting with peer supervisors or a new supervisor, is completion of the *Counseling Techniques List,* which is presented in the section entitled "Techniques used in Counseling and Psychotherapy" by Joseph Hollis.

After completing Form 5.1 and the *Counseling Techniques List,* the student/intern should write a brief statement concerning his/her needs in supervision that are related to counseling performance skills. For example, he/she may decide that skills

related to challenging and achieving a balance between empathy, probing, and clarification responses are in need of development. Or he/she may decide to focus on how he/she ends sessions and establishes continuity from session to session. Another possible self-assessment may be to extend knowledge and skill in cognitive therapy techniques. The statements regarding needs related to counseling performance skills can be used to focus peer review of audiotapes (Form 5.3) and to establish short-term and long-term goals (Form 5.4) in the contract between supervisor and trainee.

(Continued on p. 187.)

TECHNIQUES USED IN COUNSELING AND PSYCHOTHERAPY*
Joseph W. Hollis

Major growth has occurred in counseling and psychotherapy professions in recent years. Different philosophical positions have given rise to new theories, which in turn have produced a search for additional approaches. The number of counselors, therapists, and clinicians has increased, while also expanding the scope of individuals with whom counseling services have been available.

---

* The material was taken from chapter entitled "Counseling Techniques and Processes," pp. 77–174, in K. Dimick and F. Krause (Eds.), *Practicum Manual for Counseling and Psychotherapy.* Muncie, IN: Accelerated Development, 1980. Reprinted with permission.

Because no one counseling technique is appropriate for all clients or is flexible enough to use at the various depths required in counseling, additional counseling techniques have become a necessity. Research and experimentation have led to new techniques and to an identification of which techniques are most appropriate when using a specific theoretical base with a client in the remedial, preventive, or developmental area. Thus, the counseling profession has developed to the stage where each counselor can select techniques according to his/her own philosophical base and according to the client's needs. When the counselor recognizes his/her own limitations in using a wide range of techniques, this knowledge enables the counselor to refer certain clients, seek consultation when working with some clients, request that a cocounselor or cotherapist to work with specific clients, or limit one's practice to clients who can be assisted with the competencies of the counselor.

The following list of counseling and psychotherapy techniques is not all-inclusive but does represent techniques used by a broad spectrum of philosophical bases. The number of counseling techniques used by any one counselor varies. By a counselor reviewing his/her tape recordings from several sessions with different clients, 10 to 15 techniques may be identified that were used frequently with competence. An additional 10 to 15 may be identified that were used but used less frequently or, in some cases, with less professional competency.

Suggestions for using the following techniques list are dependent upon one's professional development. Students in my courses used the list primarily in two ways:

1. to check out and expand their knowledge about counseling techniques and

2. to introspect into their own counseling, philosophical bases, and treatment approaches.

Directions for Use of the Techniques List

First, examine the techniques listed in column one. Then, technique by technique, decide the extent to which you do or would be competent to use each. Indicate the extent of use or competency by circling the appropriate letter in column two. If you do not know the technique, then mark an "X" through the "N" for an indication that the technique is unknown. Space is available at the end of the techniques in column one to add other techniques.

Second, after completing examination of the list and indicating your extent of use or competency, then go through the techniques list again and mark in the third column the theory or theories with which each technique is appropriate. The third column, of course, can be marked only for the techniques with which you have knowledge.

The third task is to become more knowledgeable about techniques that you do not know—the ones marked with "X." As you gain knowledge relating to each technique, you can decide whether or not you will use it and, if so, with which kinds of clients and under what conditions.

The fourth task is to review columns two and three and determine whether or not techniques in which you have competencies are within one or two theories. If so, are these theories the ones that best reflect your self concept? Do those techniques marked reflect those most appropriate, as revealed in the literature, for the clients with whom you want to work?

——————————— ■ ■ ■ ———————————

COUNSELING TECHNIQUES LIST
Joseph W. Hollis

(Read the above material before proceeding.)

Extent of Use or Competency		Theories With Which Technique Is Most Appropriate	
N	= None	Be	= Behavioral Modification (Wolpe)
M	= Minimal	Cl	= Client Center (Rogers)

Technique

| A | = | Average |
| E | = | Extensive |

Circle one to represent extent

Mark X across the N if technique is unknown.

Co	=	Conjoint Family (Satir)
Ex	=	Existential (May)
Ge	=	Gestalt (Perls)
Lo	=	Logo (Frankl)
Ps	=	Psychoanalytic (Freud)
RE	=	Rational Emotive Therapy (Ellis)
TA	=	Transactional Analysis (Berne)
TF	=	Trait Factor (Williamson)
CT	=	Cognitive Therapy (Beck)

Circle one or more

acceptance . . . . N   M   A   E . . . . Be Cl Co Ex GE Lo Ps RE TA TF CT
active imagination . . . . N   M   A   E . . . . Be Cl Co Ex GE Lo Ps RE TA TF CT
active listening . . . . N   M   A   E . . . . Be Cl Co Ex GE Lo Ps RE TA TF CT
advice giving . . . . N   M   A   E . . . . Be Cl Co Ex GE Lo Ps RE TA TF CT
alter-ego . . . . N   M   A   E . . . . Be Cl Co Ex GE Lo Ps RE TA TF CT
analyzing symbols . . . . N   M   A   E . . . . Be Cl Co Ex GE Lo Ps RE TA TF CT
analysis . . . . N   M   A   E . . . . Be Cl Co Ex GE Lo Ps RE TA TF CT
assertive training . . . . N   M   A   E . . . . Be Cl Co Ex GE Lo Ps RE TA TF CT
audiotape recorded models . . . . N   M   A   E . . . . Be Cl Co Ex GE Lo Ps RE TA TF CT
authoritarian approach . . . . N   M   A   E . . . . Be Cl Co Ex GE Lo Ps RE TA TF CT
aversion-aversive conditioning . . . . . N   M   A   E . . . . Be Cl Co Ex GE Lo Ps RE TA TF CT

behavior modification . . . . N   M   A   E . . . . Be Cl Co Ex GE Lo Ps RE TA TF CT
bibliotherapy . . . . N   M   A   E . . . . Be Cl Co Ex GE Lo Ps RE TA TF CT
break-in, break-out . . . . N   M   A   E . . . . Be Cl Co Ex GE Lo Ps RE TA TF CT
bumping in a circle . . . . N   M   A   E . . . . Be Cl Co Ex GE Lo Ps RE TA TF CT

cajoling . . . . N   M   A   E . . . . Be Cl Co Ex GE Lo Ps RE TA TF CT
case history . . . . N   M   A   E . . . . Be Cl Co Ex GE Lo Ps RE TA TF CT
catharsis . . . . N   M   A   E . . . . Be Cl Co Ex GE Lo Ps RE TA TF CT
chemotherapy . . . . N   M   A   E . . . . Be Cl Co Ex GE Lo Ps RE TA TF CT
clarifying feelings . . . . N   M   A   E . . . . Be Cl Co Ex GE Lo Ps RE TA TF CT
cognitive restructure . . . . N   M   A   E . . . . Be Cl Co Ex GE Lo Ps RE TA TF CT
commitment . . . . N   M   A   E . . . . Be Cl Co Ex GE Lo Ps RE TA TF CT
conditioning techniques . . . . N   M   A   E . . . . Ex Cl Co Ex GE Lo Ps RE TA TF CT
confession . . . . N   M   A   E . . . . Be Cl Co Ex GE Lo Ps RE TA TF CT
confrontation . . . . N   M   A   E . . . . Be Cl Co Ex GE Lo Ps RE TA TF CT
congruence . . . . N   M   A   E . . . . Be Cl Co Ex GE Lo Ps RE TA TF CT
contractual agreements . . . . N   M   A   E . . . . Be Cl Co Ex GE Lo Ps RE TA TF CT
cotherapist . . . . N   M   A   E . . . . Be Cl Co Ex GE Lo Ps RE TA TF CT
counter propaganda . . . . N   M   A   E . . . . Be Cl Co Ex GE Lo Ps RE TA TF CT
countertransference . . . . N   M   A   E . . . . Be Cl Co Ex GE Lo Ps RE TA TF CT
crying . . . . N   M   A   E . . . . Be Cl Co Ex GE Lo Ps RE TA TF CT

decision making . . . . N   M   A   E . . . . Be Cl Co Ex GE Lo Ps RE TA TF CT
democratic . . . . N   M   A   E . . . . Be Cl Co Ex GE Lo Ps RE TA TF CT
desensitization . . . . N   M   A   E . . . . Be Cl Co Ex GE Lo Ps RE TA TF CT
detailed inquiry . . . . N   M   A   E . . . . Be Cl Co Ex GE Lo Ps RE TA TF CT
diagnosing . . . . N   M   A   E . . . . Be Cl Co Ex GE Lo Ps RE TA TF CT

doubling . . . . N M A E . . . . Be Cl Co Ex GE Lo Ps RE TA TF CT
dream interpretation . . . . N M A E . . . . Be Cl Co Ex GE Lo Ps RE TA TF CT
dreaming . . . . N M A E . . . . Be Cl Co Ex GE Lo Ps RE TA TF CT
drugs . . . . N M A E . . . . Be Cl Co Ex GE Lo Ps RE TA TF CT

empathy . . . . N M A E . . . . Be Cl Co Ex GE Lo Ps RE TA TF CT
encouragement . . . . N M A E . . . . Be Cl Co Ex GE Lo Ps RE TA TF CT
environmental manipulation . . . . . . N M A E . . . . Be Cl Co Ex GE Lo Ps RE TA TF CT
explaining . . . . N M A E . . . . Be Cl Co Ex GE Lo Ps RE TA TF CT

fading . . . . N M A E . . . . Be Cl Co Ex GE Lo Ps RE TA TF CT
family chronology . . . . N M A E . . . . Be Cl Co Ex GE Lo Ps RE TA TF CT
family group counseling . . . . N M A E . . . . Be Cl Co Ex GE Lo Ps RE TA TF CT
fantasizing . . . . N M A E . . . . Be Cl Co Ex GE Lo Ps RE TA TF CT
feedback . . . . N M A E . . . . Be Cl Co Ex GE Lo Ps RE TA TF CT
filmed models . . . . N M A E . . . . Be Cl Co Ex GE Lo Ps RE TA TF CT
first memory . . . . N M A E . . . . Be Cl Co Ex GE Lo Ps RE TA TF CT
free association . . . . N M A E . . . . Be Cl Co Ex GE Lo Ps RE TA TF CT
frustration . . . . N M A E . . . . Be Cl Co Ex GE Lo Ps RE TA TF CT

game theory techniques . . . . N M A E . . . . Be Cl Co Ex GE Lo Ps RE TA TF CT
group centered . . . . N M A E . . . . Be Cl Co Ex GE Lo Ps RE TA TF CT
group play . . . . N M A E . . . . Be Cl Co Ex GE Lo Ps RE TA TF CT

homework . . . . N M A E . . . . Be Cl Co Ex GE Lo Ps RE TA TF CT
hot seat . . . . N M A E . . . . Be Cl Co Ex GE Lo Ps RE TA TF CT

identification of an animal,
    defend it . . . . N M A E . . . . Be Cl Co Ex GE Lo Ps RE TA TF CT
identification of self as
    great personage . . . . N M A E . . . . Be Cl Co Ex GE Lo Ps RE TA TF CT
imagery . . . . N M A E . . . . Be Cl Co Ex GE Lo Ps RE TA TF CT
inception inquiry . . . . N M A E . . . . Be Cl Co Ex GE Lo Ps RE TA TF CT
informativity . . . . N M A E . . . . Be Cl Co Ex GE Lo Ps RE TA TF CT
interpersonal process recall—IPR . . . N M A E . . . . Be Cl Co Ex GE Lo Ps RE TA TF CT
interpretation . . . . N M A E . . . . Be Cl Co Ex GE Lo Ps RE TA TF CT
irrational behavior identification . . . . N M A E . . . . Be Cl Co Ex GE Lo Ps RE TA TF CT

laissez faire groups . . . . N M A E . . . . Be Cl Co Ex GE Lo Ps RE TA TF CT
life space . . . . N M A E . . . . Be Cl Co Ex GE Lo Ps RE TA TF CT
live models . . . . N M A E . . . . Be Cl Co Ex GE Lo Ps RE TA TF CT

magic mirror . . . . N M A E . . . . Be Cl Co Ex GE Lo Ps RE TA TF CT
misinterpretation, deliberately . . . . . . N M A E . . . . Be Cl Co Ex GE Lo Ps RE TA TF CT
modeling . . . . N M A E . . . . Be Cl Co Ex GE Lo Ps RE TA TF CT
multiple counseling . . . . N M A E . . . . Be Cl Co Ex GE Lo Ps RE TA TF CT

natural consequences . . . . N M A E . . . . Be Cl Co Ex GE Lo Ps RE TA TF CT
negative practice . . . . N M A E . . . . Be Cl Co Ex GE Lo Ps RE TA TF CT
negative reinforcement . . . . N M A E . . . . Be Cl Co Ex GE Lo Ps RE TA TF CT

orientative . . . . N M A E . . . . Be Cl Co Ex GE Lo Ps RE TA TF CT

paradoxical intention . . . . .N   M   A   E   . . . . .Be   Cl   Co   Ex   GE   Lo   Ps   RE   TA   TF   CT
play therapy . . . . .N   M   A   E   . . . . .Be   Cl   Co   Ex   GE   Lo   Ps   RE   TA   TF   CT
positive regard . . . . .N   M   A   E   . . . . .Be   Cl   Co   Ex   GE   Lo   Ps   RE   TA   TF   CT
positive reinforcement . . . . .N   M   A   E   . . . . .Be   Cl   Co   Ex   GE   Lo   Ps   RE   TA   TF   CT
predicting . . . . .N   M   A   E   . . . . .Be   Cl   Co   Ex   GE   Lo   Ps   RE   TA   TF   CT
probing . . . . .N   M   A   E   . . . . .Be   Cl   Co   Ex   GE   Lo   Ps   RE   TA   TF   CT
problem solving . . . . .N   M   A   E   . . . . .Be   Cl   Co   Ex   GE   Lo   Ps   RE   TA   TF   CT
processing . . . . .N   M   A   E   . . . . .Be   Cl   Co   Ex   GE   Lo   Ps   RE   TA   TF   CT
prognosing . . . . .N   M   A   E   . . . . .Be   Cl   Co   Ex   GE   Lo   Ps   RE   TA   TF   CT
progressive relaxation . . . . .N   M   A   E   . . . . .Be   Cl   Co   Ex   GE   Lo   Ps   RE   TA   TF   CT
projection . . . . .N   M   A   E   . . . . .Be   Cl   Co   Ex   GE   Lo   Ps   RE   TA   TF   CT
psychodrama . . . . .N   M   A   E   . . . . .Be   Cl   Co   Ex   GE   Lo   Ps   RE   TA   TF   CT
punishment . . . . .N   M   A   E   . . . . .Be   Cl   Co   Ex   GE   Lo   Ps   RE   TA   TF   CT

questioning . . . . .N   M   A   E   . . . . .Be   Cl   Co   Ex   GE   Lo   Ps   RE   TA   TF   CT

rational . . . . .N   M   A   E   . . . . .Be   Cl   Co   Ex   GE   Lo   Ps   RE   TA   TF   CT
reality testing .N   M   A   E   . . . . .Be   Cl   Co   Ex   GE   Lo   Ps   RE   TA   TF   CT
reassurance . . . . .N   M   A   E   . . . . .Be   Cl   Co   Ex   GE   Lo   Ps   RE   TA   TF   CT
recall . . . . .N   M   A   E   . . . . .Be   Cl   Co   Ex   GE   Lo   Ps   RE   TA   TF   CT
reciprocity of affect . . . . .N   M   A   E   . . . . .Be   Cl   Co   Ex   GE   Lo   Ps   RE   TA   TF   CT
reconscience . . . . .N   M   A   E   . . . . .Be   Cl   Co   Ex   GE   Lo   Ps   RE   TA   TF   CT
re-education . . . . .N   M   A   E   . . . . .Be   Cl   Co   Ex   GE   Lo   Ps   RE   TA   TF   CT
reflection . . . . .N   M   A   E   . . . . .Be   Cl   Co   Ex   GE   Lo   Ps   RE   TA   TF   CT
regression . . . . .N   M   A   E   . . . . .Be   Cl   Co   Ex   GE   Lo   Ps   RE   TA   TF   CT
reinforcement .N   M   A   E   . . . . .Be   Cl   Co   Ex   GE   Lo   Ps   RE   TA   TF   CT
relaxation . . . . .N   M   A   E   . . . . .Be   Cl   Co   Ex   GE   Lo   Ps   RE   TA   TF   CT
release therapy . . . . .N   M   A   E   . . . . .Be   Cl   Co   Ex   GE   Lo   Ps   RE   TA   TF   CT
restatement of content . . . . .N   M   A   E   . . . . .Be   Cl   Co   Ex   GE   Lo   Ps   RE   TA   TF   CT
reward . . . . .N   M   A   E   . . . . .Be   Cl   Co   Ex   GE   Lo   Ps   RE   TA   TF   CT
rocking or cradling above
    head trust .N   M   A   E   . . . . .Be   Cl   Co   Ex   GE   Lo   Ps   RE   TA   TF   CT
role-playing . . . . .N   M   A   E   . . . . .Be   Cl   Co   Ex   GE   Lo   Ps   RE   TA   TF   CT
role reversal . . . . .N   M   A   E   . . . . .Be   Cl   Co   Ex   GE   Lo   Ps   RE   TA   TF   CT

self-modeling .N   M   A   E   . . . . .Be   Cl   Co   Ex   GE   Lo   Ps   RE   TA   TF   CT
sensitivity exercises . . . . .N   M   A   E   . . . . .Be   Cl   Co   Ex   GE   Lo   Ps   RE   TA   TF   CT
sensitivity training . . . . .N   M   A   E   . . . . .Be   Cl   Co   Ex   GE   Lo   Ps   RE   TA   TF   CT
shaping . . . . .N   M   A   E   . . . . .Be   Cl   Co   Ex   GE   Lo   Ps   RE   TA   TF   CT
silence . . . . .N   M   A   E   . . . . .Be   Cl   Co   Ex   GE   Lo   Ps   RE   TA   TF   CT
simulation . . . . .N   M   A   E   . . . . .Be   Cl   Co   Ex   GE   Lo   Ps   RE   TA   TF   CT
sociodrama . . . . .N   M   A   E   . . . . .Be   Cl   Co   Ex   GE   Lo   Ps   RE   TA   TF   CT
sociometrics . . . . .N   M   A   E   . . . . .Be   Cl   Co   Ex   GE   Lo   Ps   RE   TA   TF   CT
stimulation . . . . .N   M   A   E   . . . . .Be   Cl   Co   Ex   GE   Lo   Ps   RE   TA   TF   CT
structuring . . . . .N   M   A   E   . . . . .Be   Cl   Co   Ex   GE   Lo   Ps   RE   TA   TF   CT
SUD (Subjective Unit of
    Discomfort) . . . . .N   M   A   E   . . . . .Be   Cl   Co   Ex   GE   Lo   Ps   RE   TA   TF   CT
summarization . . . . .N   M   A   E   . . . . .Be   Cl   Co   Ex   GE   Lo   Ps   RE   TA   TF   CT
supporting . . . . .N   M   A   E   . . . . .Be   Cl   Co   Ex   GE   Lo   Ps   RE   TA   TF   CT
systematic desensitization . . . . .N   M   A   E   . . . . .Be   Cl   Co   Ex   GE   Lo   Ps   RE   TA   TF   CT

termination . . . . .N   M   A   E   . . . . .Be   Cl   Co   Ex   GE   Lo   Ps   RE   TA   TF   CT

transference . . . . N M A E . . . . Be Cl Co Ex GE Lo Ps RE TA TF CT
transparency . . . . N M A E . . . . Be Cl Co Ex GE Lo Ps RE TA TF CT
trust walk . . . . N M A E . . . . Be Cl Co Ex GE Lo Ps RE TA TF CT

urging . . . . N M A E . . . . Be Cl Co Ex GE Lo Ps RE TA TF CT

value clarification . . . . N M A E . . . . Be Cl Co Ex GE Lo Ps RE TA TF CT
value development . . . . N M A E . . . . Be Cl Co Ex GE Lo Ps RE TA TF CT
verbal shock . . . . N M A E . . . . Be Cl Co Ex GE Lo Ps RE TA TF CT
vicarious learning . . . . N M A E . . . . Be Cl Co Ex GE Lo Ps RE TA TF CT

warmth . . . . N M A E . . . . Be Cl Co Ex GE Lo Ps RE TA TF CT

ADD YOUR OWN

. . . . N M A E . . . . Be Cl Co Ex GE Lo Ps RE TA TF CT
. . . . N M A E . . . . Be Cl Co Ex GE Lo Ps RE TA TF CT
. . . . N M A E . . . . Be Cl Co Ex GE Lo Ps RE TA TF CT

ONGOING SELF-ASSESSMENT

Continuing reflection upon and assessment of one's counseling practices are integral parts of the practicum and internship experiences. This ongoing self-assessment occurs while transcribing interview notes, reviewing tapes of counseling sessions, preparing material to take to supervision, and keeping journals of personal feelings and attitudes about counseling practice. A number of different forms and directed activities can assist the trainee with organizing and focusing these self-assessment activities. We suggest that the trainee keep a file of all self-assessment activities as a record of his/her professional development.

Two forms that have appeared in other sections of this manual are aids for focusing self-assessment. The *Tape Critique Form* (Chapter 2, Form 2.4) provides a systematic approach to reviewing and assessing sessions that have been audiotaped or videotaped. The *Therapy Notes* (Chapter 4, Form 4.8) and the *Case Summary* (Chapter 4, Sample 5) provide an organization for written review of counseling sessions and can demonstrate cognitive counseling skills and developmental level of the trainee. An additional aid for self-assessment is also included here—a Self Rating form (Form 5.2) to be used after a therapy session.

PEER ASSESSMENT OF COUNSELING PERFORMANCE SKILLS

Peer supervision and assessment has been identified as a valuable aid in the supervision process. This modality is recommended with some precautions. Peer supervision should be used only as a supplement to regular supervision and seems best utilized within the behavioral skills training areas. The peer supervisor can promote skill awareness through ratings and shared perceptions, but an important procedure to follow is to make sure that if the peer supervision activities are initiated, they occur after group supervision has provided sufficient training and practice (Boyd, 1978). After a particular counseling skill has been introduced, modeled, and practiced within the group context, peer rating of counseling tapes can be implemented. We suggest that the peer critique of tapes be structured to focus on the rating of specific skills. For instance, the target skills might be identified as one or more of the facilitative skills such as basic empathy, asking open-ended questions, or concreteness. Other targeted skills could be the recognition and handling of positive or negative affect, or the effective use of probes. Form 5.3, Peer Rating Form, has been included here to structure the use of peer rating activities.

Another approach to improving the use of functional basic skills is to teach students to identify their dysfunctional counseling behaviors and then minimize those behaviors (Collins, 1990). Instead of rating functional skills, peer reviewers can measure the incidence of dysfunctional skills such as premature problem solving or excessive questioning in their review of counseling tapes. The goal would be for the counselor to decrease or eliminate dysfunctional counseling behaviors in their sessions. Collins (1990), in a study of the occurrence of dysfunctional counseling behaviors in both role-play and real client interviews of social work students, identified the following as dysfunctional behaviors:

> Poor beginning statements: Session starts with casual talk or chitchatting instead of engagement skills.
>
> Utterances: Utterances are counselor responses consisting of short utterances or one word responses such as "uh-huh," "yeah," "okay," "sure"; two different types of utterance responses rated were: utterances (alone) and utterances (preceding a statement).
>
> Closed questions: Questions that require one-word answers by clients, like yes/no, their age, number of children.
>
> Why questions: A statement starting with the word "why."
>
> Excessive questioning: Three questions in a row without any clear reflective component to the question. Reflective component refers to restating content the client has expressed in his/her statement to the counselor.
>
> Premature advice or premature problem solving: Counselor gives advice that is considered premature; i.e., in first ten minutes of session, first interview, judgmental statement, or counselor is doing work for the client.
>
> Minimization: Down-playing the problem, glib responses, inappropriate comments, i.e., "Life can't be all that bad." (p. 70)

Carmichael (1992) has developed a *Peer Supervision Rating Sheet,* which was developed for use in group supervision. Items included on the rating sheet were drawn from the work of Wittmer and Myrick (1974), Ivey and Gluckstern (1974), Egan (1986) and Cormier and Hockney (1987). Consistent with the previously mentioned precautions regarding the use of peer supervisors, this rating sheet was intended to keep the peer supervisor focused during observations and to reinforce the learning of counseling skills. Prior to using the rating sheet, each element in the rating sheet was discussed and students generated examples of what would be a level 1, 3, and 5 rating. Although this rating sheet was developed and used to rate student role-played counseling sessions, it also could be used to rate real counseling session tapes.

Elements included on the *Peer Supervision Rating Sheet* (each rated on a continuum from 1, which is poor, to 5, which is good) were as follows:

1. Establishes rapport
2. Keeps focus
3. Explores problem
4. Reflects feeling
5. Makes open-ended statements
6. Communicates clearly
7. Does not use questions
8. Congruent non-verbal and verbal behavior
9. Problem-solving model evident
10. Closure
11. Summarizes
12. Clarifies
13. Generates alternatives
14. Confronts
15. Uses humor appropriately (p. 61)

MONITORING COGNITIVE SKILLS

The case conceptualization approach is a primary modality included in individual and group supervision that addresses the skill category of cognitive counseling skills. The goals of using the case presentation approach in supervision are to assist the "trainee to have a basic understanding of the client's underlying psychological dynamics and behavior," (Loganbill & Stoltenberg, 1983, p. 235); to "enhance participant's cognitive complexity," (McAuliffe, 1992, p. 164); and to "improve supervised conceptualization skills through development of complex and integrated thinking skills," (Biggs, 1988, p. 242). Case conceptualization formats have been suggested that primarily emphasize the understanding of client dynamics (Loganbill & Stoltenberg, 1983), that emphasize the relationship between the client's condition and choice of intervention (Biggs, 1988; McAuliffe, 1992), and that emphasize the complete understanding of a theoretical perspective (Murdock, 1991). Each of these approaches can be useful in assisting the trainee to move toward higher levels of understanding and effectiveness in the practice of counseling and psychotherapy.

Biggs (1988), applying Perry's (1970) framework of intellectual development, characterized the supervisee as moving from a Dualistic position in cognitive development where he/she may demand the correct answer from the supervisor; to a multiplistic position where no particular approach to dealing with clients is more correct than any other; to a commitment-in-relativism position where the counselor can defend particular clinical decisions while recognizing the tentativeness and uncertainty of a choice. The task for the supervisor is to promote divergent thinking and problem-finding in the counselor by using skillful probes, discussing cognitive conflicts among group members, and supporting the reasoning process. Three major tasks are included in the case conceptualization format:

> a.) identifying how observations and inferences are used to provide evidence for clinical judgments; b.) describing and discussing major dimensions of the counseling relationship, and c.) describing assumptions regarding client's personality, problem condition, and choice of treatment." (Biggs, 1988, p. 243)

An alternate case presentation format has been proposed by McAuliffe (1992). Similar guidelines are incorporated regarding the goal of moving toward cognitive complexity and the role of the supervisor in promoting critical thinking. Supervisees also are expected to present evidence for their judgments in the case presentation format. The suggested format uses the acronym SOAP. The *Subjective* portion (or S) asks the counselor to describe reasons for presenting the case, including a description of the client's presenting problem. The second part, *Objective* (or O), includes background information including test results, previous work in therapy, and summary of present work as it relates to the presenting problem. In the *Assessment* (or A) segment, the counselor gives a tentative 5-axis DSM-IV diagnostic impression. The final portion, the *Plan* (or P), contains a summary of work done to date and a treatment plan. Group dialogue then follows and can include discussion of how treatment may vary based on theoretical perspective used (McAuliffe, 1992).

A case conceptualization format that emphasizes a complete understanding of a theoretical perspective is presented in the following article by Nancy L. Murdock.

CASE CONCEPTUALIZATION: APPLYING THEORY TO INDIVIDUALS*
Nancy L. Murdock

A model of case conceptualization is presented that can be used with any theoretical approach to counseling. Issues surrounding the use of this model are discussed.

Over the course of training, counseling students are taught numerous counseling theories, yet little systematic attention is directed toward using these theories to understand and help individual clients. In many counseling texts, students are directed to construct their own perspective in working with clients (Corsini & Wedding, 1989; Gilliland, James, & Bowman 1989; Ivey & Simek-Downing, 1980; Pietrofesa, Hoffman, & Splete, 1984), a stance that seems to encourage a flexible eclecticism. Other writers argue for the adoption of a single theoretical perspective in counseling practice (Patterson, 1985; Russell, 1986). Regardless of which path the student takes (it is not my intent to enter this debate), it seems that the learning process prior to this choice could be enhanced by increased emphasis on applying the various theories students are taught in the course of their training.

Theoretical case conceptualization is a difficult process, but it also may be one of the most effective routes to complete understanding of a theoretical perspective. The process of conceptualization fosters a more thorough understanding of a theory because it requires complex types of learning (Bloom, Madaus, & Hastings, 1981). Bloom et al. identified six levels of learning. The first two, knowledge and comprehension, are achieved routinely in teaching theories of counseling. However, higher levels of learning—application, analysis, synthesis, and evaluation—are involved in applying theory if the application process involves critical evaluation of the approach in question. Case conceptualization should engage all of these learning processes. Conceptualization also should result in an awareness of the strengths and weaknesses of a particular approach. Some clients may present problems or issues that require extension of the theory beyond the

* This material appeared in *Counselor Education and Supervision*, Vol. 30, pp. 355–365, Copyright June, 1991 by the American Counseling Association. Reprinted with permission.

convenient examples provided in textbooks. For example, a client displaying a great deal of emotion presents a conceptual challenge for person-centered theory (Raskin & Rogers, 1989), because this theory traditionally has focused on helping clients who repress affect. Understanding the emotive client from this perspective requires more conceptual work and therefore a more complete understanding of person-centered theory.

Numerous calls have been made for counselor educators to teach the skills and processes of case conceptualization (Bernier, 1980; Borders & Leddick, 1987; Fuqua, Johnson, Anderson, & Newman, 1984; Holloway, 1988). Although various models of case conceptualization have been proposed (e.g., Biggs, 1988; Halgin, 1985; Held, 1984; Hulse & Jennings, 1984; Loganbill & Stoltenberg, 1983; Swensen, 1968), most of these do not emphasize the integrated application of a single theoretical perspective. Most efforts seem to specify categories of information that are essential to the counseling process, e.g., specific demographic information, interpersonal style, and personality dynamics (Hulse & Jennings, 1984; Loganbill & Stoltenberg, 1983), or they construct an integrative eclectic approach useful in conceptualizing cases (Halgin, 1985; Held, 1984; Swensen, 1968). Biggs (1988) discussed briefly how theory contributes to case conceptualization and detailed factors that influence the conceptualization process. Models that guide the systematic application of one theory that can be used with a wide range of theoretical approaches, however, seem scarce. This article presents a model that I find useful in teaching case conceptualization, in the supervision of practicum students, and in my own counseling practice. My primary purpose was to provide a structure that can be used with almost any well developed theory of counseling and that will help the student through this most difficult and complex process.

Theoretical Structure

Before applying a theory, the counselor must have a solid understanding of the theory in question. The counselor must know how the theory defines the healthy personality and psychological dysfunction. In order to help, counselors need to have some idea of where the client "should" be going and why the client has come to counseling. Linked to this theoretically based construction are the specific areas of the client's presentation that are considered most important. To give a rather simplistic example, a counselor adopting a behavioral approach that emphasizes operand learning (e.g., Kazdin, 1980) assumes that the client presented for help because of faulty learning (or the failure to learning a desired behavior). This therapist then is interested in a number of aspects of the client's life, including (a) the specific behavior to be modified, (b) the history of the behavior, (c) the type of learning that first produced the behavior, and (d) the stimuli that evoke the behavior. In contrast, psychoanalytic therapists (e.g., Arlow, 1989) would be interested in very different information because, from their theoretical base, the origins of dysfunction are found in conflicts that reside in the unconscious. Thus, psychoanalysts would be interested in issues such as (a) what the client remembers of early childhood, (b) past and current relationships with parental figures, (c) past and current relationships with siblings and other significant persons, (d) the client's character style as indicated by current relationships with siblings and other significant persons, and (e) the client's character style as indicated by current interactions.

The preceding types of issues are considered preliminary to the actual process of conceptualizing a client; they represent information that ensures the needed understanding of the theory before it is applied. Questions that help counselors obtain a sufficient level of understanding prior to application are the following:

1. What is the core motivation of human existence?

    Whether explicitly or implicitly, theories of counseling tend to emphasize one major theme that directs or governs individuals' lives. For example, classic psychoanalytic theory emphasizes the conflicts between the various mental structures. In contrast, Gestalt theorists (Perls, Hefferline, & Goodman, 1951) postulated that humans tend toward homeostasis.

2. How is the core motivation expressed in healthy ways? What are the characteristics of a healthy personality?

    Too often counselors find themselves focused on definitions of pathology. At least as important (and possibly more so) are definitions of health. Definitions of psychological health are theory-linked. Cognitive theorists (e.g., Beck & Weishaar, 1989) are interested in helping the client become healthy through the elimination of faulty thought processes. According to multigenerational family theorists (e.g., Kerr & Bowen, 1988), health is defined as a relatively clear differentiation from the family of origin. Thus, the counselor seeking to remain theory-consistent must recognize that the approach chosen specifies the most important characteristics that define psychological health.

Cross-cultural and gender-role issues are important factors to consider at this point. Because many theories were developed in a restricted cultural context (i.e., Western, White, male, middle to upper socioeconomic status), definitions of health and dysfunction are products of these cultures. The degree to which these definitions apply across cultures and to women is certainly not established, although the idea that human universals exist has not been disconfirmed entirely (Draguns, 1981). Therefore, great care must be taken by the practitioner in applying these definitions, and the degree to which the theory's definitions of health are inconsistent with the client's cultural definitions must be assessed carefully. For example, theories that advocate autonomy from one's family of origin may be in conflict with the cultural norms learned by a Japanese client (Sue & Zane, 1987). If confronted with this type of situation, the counselor must assess the impact of helping the client individuate. Deciding that individuation might do more harm than good, the counselor may simply attempt to help the client understand the effect of his/her family system. In this case, understanding of cultural norms may help the client devise ways to individuate that do not conflict seriously with important cultural rules. At times, however, the counselor may find that extension of a theory in an attempt to incorporate cultural concerns is impossible and may at this point consider adopting a theoretical structure more compatible with the client's cultural background.

3. How does the process of development get derailed or stuck? What are the factors that contribute to psychological dysfunction?

That complement of the question of psychological health is the issue of how individuals get "unhealthy." Theories are often better at specifying factors that lead to dysfunction than they are at describing psychological health. In considering these definitions, attention to cultural and gender-role issues is again critical. Classic psychoanalytic theory has been criticized, for example, because its definition of health for women is stereotypic, tending to support traditional roles and values. Therefore, a nontraditional female client may be judged to be dysfunctional under this system. A counselor aware of this bias could revise this definition but still remain theory-consistent by acknowledging the influence of sexual conflicts while avoiding interpretations that promote stereotypes.

4. What stages of the client's life are considered key in the developmental process?

Theorists clearly differ on developmental factors. Some theories incorporate almost no developmental theory (e.g., rational emotive therapy, Ellis, 1989), while others stipulate that development is crucial to the presenting problem (e.g., psychoanalytic theory).

5. Who are the critical individuals in the client's presentation? Does the theory restrict the focus to the individual, or does it extend to interactions with family and acquaintances or to multigenerational issues?

Most theories deal with social interaction in some form. Some theories conclude that internal processes are primary (e.g., cognitive theories), although they may affect relationship events. Other approaches postulate that relationships are the key to psychological functioning (i.e., interpersonal theory; Kiesler, 1983; Strong & Claiborn, 1982) and, therefore, place great emphasis on these factors in determining psychological health. Past relationships are significant for some approaches, even relationships generations removed (Kerr & Bowen, 1988).

6. What are the relative importance of affect, cognition, and behavior in this theory?

Theories place different emphases on the roles of affect, cognition, and behavior in determining psychological life. Some approaches identify emotional factors as primary (e.g., person centered, Gestalt, and psychoanalytic), others emphasize cognitive factors (cognitive therapy and rational emotive therapy), and still others target behavior (behavioral approaches). Regardless of the focus, the other two components usually are considered, so this postulate does not direct the counselor to ignore any of these domains. Neglect of any of these factors probably indicates a misunderstanding of the theory; rather, the point of this discussion is to understand the theoretical relationships of these components.

Gathering Information

Armed with a theoretical framework, the counselor attempting to apply theory must next understand the client as fully as possible. Two types of information are important in this process. First, the counselor probably will want general information that is not strongly theory-linked, such as demographics (age, sex, and ethnic origin), current living situation, and physical health. Although different theories might place different emphasis on this type of information, or ignore it altogether, a counselor attempting to understand fully his/her client generally collects these data. Demographics also help the counselor avoid misunderstandings due to cultural bias.

Second, the counselor seeks information that is theory-specific as determined by his/her understanding the basic issues emphasized by the theory. The six questions that help build theoretical structure (listed previously) can guide this information search.

Integration

Perhaps the most difficult aspect of case conceptualization is the process of fitting together in a coherent way the pieces of the puzzle presented by the client. The counselor must translate the specific presentation of the client into theoretical terms. This process requires the counselor to compare carefully the client's presentation to the theoretical structure to be used. Some questions to be considered are the following:

1. Do the details of the presenting problem fit the theory's postulates concerning psychological dysfunction?

If the elements of the client's presenting problem fit easily, the counselor can proceed to

treatment planning, keeping in mind that further information gained from the client may alter this conceptualization. Because clients rarely speak in theoretical terms, however, it is more likely that some, or many, elements seem to be outside of the theory's structure to at least some degree. In fact, the first difficulty in the process of conceptualization is that the counselor often is tempted to focus narrowly on the "presenting problem." For instance, clients often present with interpersonal problems that can be labeled as lack of assertiveness. Although this label might be useful at times, the counselor attempting to use theoretical conceptualization may get distracted by the label. At his point, the counselor usually reports that a particular theory says nothing about assertiveness and hence decides to use another theory instead. Instead of prematurely abandoning the theoretical approach, the counselor should consider why (in a theoretical sense) the client is nonassertive. To answer this question, the counselor must return to the core principles of the theoretical structure to focus on the underlying mechanisms that lead to the appearance of the "symptom." A cognitive counselor would therefore translate lack of assertion into behavior that is the result of distorted thinking and proceed to determine what irrational thoughts or beliefs the client holds. The process of going beyond "symptoms," therefore, involves translating them into theoretical terms that emphasize the links between client presentations and theoretical definitions of health and dysfunction.

The example of the person-centered therapist confronted with a highly emotive client also can illustrate this process. According to the procedure outlined previously, the therapist would consider how emotional outbursts could be understood through the construct of incongruence. For example, the counselor might see the affect as resulting from aspects of experience that are distorted and then denied, but which are then overtly expressed, because repressive processes are depleted by unusual levels of stress. Again, the general method is to first detach from the symptom to a more general understanding and then transfer back to the anomaly.

In rare cases, discrepancies between client presentation and theory may call for a change of perspective. I have not encountered this situation unless the client is of a different culture from that in which the theory originated. As previously noted in the case of the Japanese client (Sue & Zane, 1987), at times the core postulates may be in direct opposition to the norms of the client's culture. Therefore, the counselor must make a careful study of the multicultural counseling situation and may decide that modification to deal with cultural issues does not destroy the usefulness of the theory. Alternatively, the counselor may elect to shift perspectives to one that is more consistent with the client's culture. In instances in which hypothetical cases are in use (e.g., in practicing case conceptualization in theory classes), abandoning the original perspective should be considered a last resort as it may lead to a superficial understanding of the theory. In practicum, in which students are conceptualizing the clients they are counseling, consideration of alternative theoretical structures might be introduced more quickly than when hypothetical cases are in use because the risk of harm to the client is real.

Issues regarding gender bias seem more subtle. Most theoretical definitions of health do not seem blatantly biased (except perhaps for classic psychoanalytic theory, which in some interpretations emphasizes the acceptance of traditional aspects of the female role). Some of the major theories of counseling could be criticized for relying on a male-biased model of health in their emphasis on rational thought and consequent relative neglect of affective processes (e.g., rational emotive therapy, cognitive therapy, and cognitive-behavior modification). Likewise, the experiential theories (person-centered, Gestalt, and other existential approaches) could be criticized for being female-biased in their reliance on what is a stereotypically feminine process (affect). This bias, however, seems somehow less clear than cultural bias, and in many cases it seems likely that gender bias often resides in the application of the theory, not in its basic assumptions. For example, the personal attitudes of the counselor can lead the counselor to encourage a female client to adopt traditional behaviors regardless of what theory the counselor is applying (an analogous situation may occur in multicultural counseling). If the counselor determines that the source of gender bias lies in the central postulates of the theory, the counselor has the same options as those outlined for the situation in which cultural bias appears.

2. How do other aspects of the client's presentation fit with the postulates of the theory and the presenting problem?

Once the counselor has gained a theoretical understanding of the presenting problem, the counselor must integrate this knowledge with the rest of the client's presentation to obtain a coherent picture of the client. In the person-centered example, the therapist would look for other aspects of experience that are repressed, plus examine the conditions of worth held by the client and how they were learned. Also, the therapist would look for evidence of the client's self-actualizing tendencies that are sure to be at least faintly evident.

3. Based on this theory, where does the client need to go (i.e., what changes does the theory specify)?

Because the beginnings of intervention start with the understanding of the theory's definition of the healthy person, the therapist should establish how this client would appear as a healthy person. In the case of the emotive client, the person-centered therapist would want the client to be able to experience the volatile emotions in a meaningful, accepting way. Similarly, the Gestalt counselor would want the client to increase his/her awareness in all areas of experience.

4. How can I help the client get where he/she needs to go?

Interventions designed for the client should follow directly from the definitions of health developed for this individual. Some theorists are specific about productive interventions whereas others are less so. Rather than confining the therapist to theory-specified interventions, I agree with other authors (e.g., Lazarus, 1974) that many interventions could be employed to help a given client. An important point to add, however, is that these interventions should be undertaken with a theoretical goal in mind. The critical question becomes why this intervention now? I cannot count the times students have offered empty-chair interventions but have had no specific theoretical goal in mind. Another common problem is that students often equate intervention with technique. Techniques are understood easily because they are generally concrete, circumscribed actions taken by the counselor. Interventions (at least in my understanding) can be more general in nature (such as when the psychoanalytic counselor provides an ambiguous situation on which the client can project) and often are overlooked by students even though they are powerful change tools. Continuing the person-centered example, a major intervention is allowing the client to disclose to an accepting, empathic therapist. Instead, the student who must choose an intervention may identify a more concrete technique (such as having the client keep a self-talk log). Although such a specific technique may be helpful in this case, the student may bypass the simpler, broader intervention specified by person-centered theory.

5. How will I know when the client is better?

Although implicit in the specification of health as defined by theory, it should be emphasized that the specific criteria for health for the client be defined by the counselor through applying the basic concepts of the theory. This consideration brings up yet another important question: What about the client's input in this process? When conceptualizing from a theoretical base, are we ignoring the client's stated goals and wishes? Misguided use of theory could result in this rigid stance. Careful consideration, however, of the client's goals in light of the theory can integrate this aspect of the client's presentation into the theoretical structure. In my example, the client's stated wish to deal with her affective outbursts can be construed as the client's self-actualizing tendencies, encouraging her toward more authentic experiencing of her existence.

Uses of the Model

The case conceptualization model presented in this article can be used in several ways. Because this approach is only recently developed, I have no empirical outcome data to present, simply my impressions that are based on the comments of students who have used the model. As noted by previous writers in the area of case conceptualization (Bernier, 1980; Borders & Leddick, 1987; Fuqua et al., 1984; Holloway, 1988), cognitive style

and developmental issues need to be recognized in the training process. Therefore, the following suggestions for using this model are guided loosely by such concerns.

In beginning level (master's) theories courses, I have presented the model as a general outline to teach case conceptualization. Students at this stage are struggling to learn the various theories presented, and the six questions about theoretical structure seem to help them in organizing information. Application of theory seems to be most difficult at this level of learning, and these students have had little or no supervised counseling experience. Laboratory sections of several classes are devoted to case conceptualization, using the steps of the integration portion of the model as a guide. One case is assigned across small groups of students, and groups present and compare their conceptualizations.

In practicums, I ask students to present their theoretical perspectives by answering the six questions outlined under theoretical structure. This process helps students clarify the basic assumptions of their perspectives. Often, students find this process quite difficulty because they have devoted little systematic thought to organizing their perspectives. They are then asked to conceptualize cases based on the guidelines in the model. Students report that the structure gives direction to what is normally a rather ambiguous assignment. My observation is that their conceptualizations seem clearer and more organized than those done when students do not have guidelines to follow.

I currently am using this model in my advanced (doctoral) theories of counseling course. In this class, students spend the majority of class time presenting theoretical conceptualizations of clients they have previously counseled. Class members supply written case studies for class use. Each student is responsible for supplying readings on a major theoretical approach, and all students complete reaction papers on each theory studied. Students also are required to develop a research proposal that tests a well developed theory relevant to counseling. The first portion of each class meeting (approximately 45 minutes of a 2-hour and 40-minute total class time) is devoted to outlining each theory according to the six questions relevant to theoretical structure. For the remainder of the class, two class members present case conceptualizations (of different clients) developed according to the model as if they were proponents of the theory under discussion. The presenters attempt to integrate aspects of the client's presentation, set theory-based goals, and design theoretically consistent interventions. These presentations can be organized around the five integration questions specified by the model. The rest of the class challenges these conceptualizations, with particular attention paid to theoretical anomalies in the cases or in the presenters' theoretical explanations. Presenters are required to use only explanations that are consistent with the approaches they are advocating and are therefore not able to avoid aspects of the cases that are theoretically inconvenient by shifting to other perspectives. This case-intensive approach leads to active discussions that include cross-cultural and gender-role issues. Often, different theoretical approaches are pitted against one another and compared for their utilities in understanding the case in question. The case conceptualization model, therefore, guides students in all steps of the application process, and students report that this approach is quite helpful to them.

Conclusion

Given the lack of systematic guides for the process of case conceptualization, the model presented seems to be a step toward improved teaching in this area. As mentioned previously, however, the model is relatively untested because it has been evolving over the last several years. Further use of the model will demonstrate whether it achieves its purpose of leading to a clearer understanding of the counseling process, improved training of students, and thus, better services to our clients.

References

Arlow, J.A. (1989). Psychoanalysis. In R.J. Corsini & D. Wedding (Eds.), *Current psychotherapies* (pp. 19–62). Itasca, IL: Peacock.

Beck. A.T., & Weishaar, M.E. (1989). Cognitive therapy. In R.J. Corsini & D. Wedding (Eds.), *Current psychotherapies* (pp. 285–320). Itasca, IL: Peacock.

Bernier, J.E. (1980). Training and supervising counselors: Lessons learned from deliberate psychological education. *The Personnel and Guidance Journal, 59,* 15–20.

Biggs, D.A. (1988). The case presentation approach in clinical supervision. *Counselor Education and Supervision, 20,* 240–248.

Bloom, B.S., Madaus, G.F., & Hastings, J.T. (1981). *Evaluation to improve learning.* New York: McGraw-Hill.

Borders, L.D., & Leddick, G.R. (1987). *Handbook of counseling supervision.* Alexandria, VA: Association for Counselor Education and Supervision.

Corsini, R.J., & Wedding, D. (1989). *Current psychotherapies.* Itasca, IL: Peacock.

Draguns, J.G. (1981). Counseling across cultures: Common themes and distinct approaches. In P.P. Pedersen, J.G. Draguns, W.J. Lonner, & J.E. Trimble (Eds.), *Counseling across cultures* (pp. 3–21). Honolulu, HI: University Press of Hawaii.

Ellis, A. (1989). *Rational-emotive therapy.* In R.J. Corsini & D. Wedding (Eds.), Current psychotherapies (pp. 197–238). Itasca, IL: Peacock.

Fuqua, D.R., Johnson, A.W., Anderson, M.W., & Newman, J.L. (1984). Cognitive methods in counselor training. *Counselor Education and Supervision, 24,* 85–95.

Gilliland, B.E., James, R.K., & Bowman, J.T. (1989). *Theories and strategies in counseling and psychotherapy.* Englewood Cliffs, NJ: Prentice-Hall.

Halgin, R.P. (1985). Teaching integration of psychotherapy models to beginning therapists. *Psychotherapy, 22,* 555–563.

Held, B.S. (1984). Toward a strategic eclecticism: A proposal. *Psychotherapy, 21,* 232–241.

Holloway, E.L. (1988). Instruction beyond the facilitative conditions: A response to Biggs. *Counselor Education and Supervision, 27,* 252–258.

Hulse, D., & Jennings, M.A. (1984). Toward comprehensive case conceptualizations in counseling: A visual integrative technique. *Professional Psychology, 15,* 251–259.

Ivey, A.E., & Simek-Downing, L. (1980). *Counseling and psychotherapy: Skills, theories and practice.* Englewood Cliffs, NJ: Prentice-Hall.

Kazdin, A.E. (1980). *Behavior modification in applied settings.* Homewood, IL: Dorsey.

Kerr, M., & Bowen, M. (1988). *Family evaluation.* New York: Norton.

Kiesler, D.J. (1983). The 1983 Interpersonal Circle: A taxonomy for complementarity in human transactions. *Psychological Review, 90,* 185–214.

Lazarus, A.A. (1974). Multimodal behavior therapy: Treating the "basic id." In C.M. Franks & G.T. Wilson (Eds.), *Annual review of behavior therapy theory and practice.* New York: Brunner/Mazel.

Loganbill, C., & Stoltenberg, C. (1983). The case conceptualization format: A training device for practicum. *Counselor Education and Supervision, 22,* 235–241.

Patterson, C.H. (1985). New light for counseling theory. *Journal of Counseling and Development, 63,* 349–350.

Perls, F.S., Hefferline, R.F., & Goodman, P. (1951). *Gestalt therapy.* New York: Julian.

Perry, W.F. (1970). *Forms of intellectual and ethical development in the college years.* New York: Holt, Rinehart and Winston.

Pietrofesa, J.J., Hoffman, A., & Splete, H.H. (1984). *Counseling.* Boston: Houghton Mifflin.

Russell, R.L. (1986). The inadvisability of admixing psychoanalysis with other forms of psychotherapy. *Journal of Contemporary Psychotherapy, 16,* 76–86.

Strong, S.R., & Claiborn, C.D. (1982). *Change through infraction.* New York: Wiley.

Sue, D.W., & Zane, N. (1987). The role of culture and cultural techniques in psychotherapy. *American Psychologist, 42,* 37–45.

Swensen, C. (1968). *An approach to case conceptualization.* Boston: Houghton Mifflin.

■ ■ ■

MONITORING DEVELOPMENT LEVEL

Developmental level previously has been described as the degree to which counselor trainees are able to internalize the role of counselor and achieve a peer-like collegial relationship with the supervisor. A number of developmental models of supervisee growth have been proposed. Hogan (1964) was among the first to propose a four-stage model of supervisee development that described the trainee's progress while learning to function in a clinical setting. Level 1 trainees were described as anxious and dependent on the supervisor and more likely to function out of a recipe oriented or imitative approach to counseling. Level 2 trainees were less method-bound and move toward using and clarifying the use of their own personalities in the counseling work. At Level 3, the trainee has greater and more stable insight into professional and personal concerns, while at Level 4 the trainee approached the master level and functioned independently.

The Counselor Complexity Model proposed by Stoltenberg (1981) built upon the Hogan Model as well as Hunt's (1971) Conceptual Systems Theory to describe more fully the characteristics of the counselor at each level as well as the corresponding supervisory environments. Progress through the four levels varied from trainee to trainee. The Level 1 supervisee was described as dependent, uninsightful, and highly motivated. The corresponding supervisory level involved instruction, structure, and support. Level 2 supervisees struggled between dependency and autonomy and showed a beginning of insight. Continued supervisory support with less structure and instruction was indicated. Level 3 supervisees had increased confidence and could begin to differentiate between their healthy and neurotic motives. Supervision at this level could include sharing and confrontation. Level 4 supervisees were essentially independent with a secure professional identity, and supervision was consultative. An elaboration of the counselor complexity

model was proposed by Wiley and Ray (1986) and is presented in Tables 5.1 and 5.2. This elaboration forms the basis of the descriptive phrases used as items in the Supervision Level Scale (SLS).

An empirically derived model of counselor development by Hill, Charles, and Reed (1981) was similar to the theorizing of Hogan (1964). In the first stage, they described the trainees as self-conscious and attentive to their own internal experiences, sometimes to the exclusion of understanding the client's experience. During the second stage, supervisees adopted the counselor's role and used some standard approaches to counseling. Application of theory and technique was rigid. As unexplained exceptions occurred in their counseling work, they became uncertain about their theorizing, which gave rise to a third stage—usually in late practicum and through internship. The supervisee at this point usually resisted the original theory and moved toward eclecticism, although his/her own theory often was not articulated or could be contradictory or inconsistent. If the supervisees progressed beyond this stage, they articulated a reasonably clear personal theory of counseling and behaved according to this personal theory.

Freedman and Kaslow (1986) proposed six normative relationship stages for psychotherapists-in-training. They commented that the stages could overlap and that retrograde movement is inherent in the developmental process. Further, they assumed that the process of achieving a professional identity never takes less than four years and may take many more.

Deck and Morrow (1989) summarized their proposed stages as follows:

Stage 1: Excitement and Anticipatory Anxiety—the supervisee is aware of the prospect of learning to be therapeutic and experiences diffused anxiety

Stage 2: Dependency and Identification—the supervisee has high dependence due to lack of confidence and limited skill, has an idealized perception of supervisor, and imitates supervisor and/or is full of "how to" questions.

Stage 3: Activity and Continued Dependency—the supervisee fluctuates between more independence and dependency, can over- or

(Continued on p. 199)

Table 5.1. An Elaboration of the Counselor Complexity Model: Supervisee Levels

| Category | Supervisee level (P-level) | | | |
	1	2	3	4
Degree of confidence in present counseling skill	Usually lacks confidence in present counseling skills and is overwhelmed by own weaknesses (S)	Characteristically fluctuates between feeling confident and feeling very inadequate about present counseling skills (S)	Usually has a firm sense of confidence about his/her counseling skills, although he/she is shaken when challenged by clients, supervisors, and/or colleagues	Has a consistent and firm sense of confidence about his/her counseling skills even when challenged by clients, supervisors, and colleagues (S)
Insight about impact on clients	Has very little awareness of his/her strengths, weaknesses, motivations, neurotic needs, etc. and their impact on clients (S)	Is inconsistent in awarenesses, motivations, neurotic needs, etc. and their impact on clients (S)	Is consistently aware of his/her strengths, weaknesses, motivations, neurotic needs, etc. and their impact on clients, but is only beginning to develop the capacity to use them as resources during the counseling session	Is consistently aware of his/her strengths, weaknesses, motivations, neurotic needs, etc. and is able to use them as resources during counseling sessions (S)
Approach to a theoretical framework	Is prone to readily identify with a theoretical school or individual practitioner without thorough consideration (S)	Is beginning to view clients from a variety of perspectives and is becoming aware of a need to develop an internalized theoretical framework (S)	Views clients from a variety of rather thoroughly examined perspectives and is testing out the goodness of fit of an internalized theoretical framework (S)	Is committed to a theoretical framework or composite which is internalized, integrated with his/her counseling behavior, and can be articulated
Sense of professional identity	Nearly always looks to others for ideas about how he/she should behave as a counselor (S)	Is developing an inner sense of self as a counselor but frequently looks to others for ideas about how he/she should behave as a counselor (S)	Has a well developed sense of self as counselor but is only beginning to integrate it with his/her sense of self as a person (S)	Has essentially completed his/her sense of self as a counselor and integrated it with his/her sense of self as a person (S)
Awareness of limitation of counseling	Tends to regard counseling as all-powerful (S)	Sees counseling as a very powerful instrument but is becoming vaguely aware and uneasy about a few limitations of counseling, such as the inappropriateness of counseling for some clients and/or problems	Is clearly aware of a broad range of limitations of counseling, including the limits of counseling as a treatment per se, and is struggling to integrate this with his/her sense of self as a professional	Clearly understands a broad range of limitations of counseling, including the limits of counseling as a treatment per se, and essentially has completed integrating this knowledge into a firm sense of professional identity (S)

Note: Cells identified as (S) have been taken from "Approaching Supervision from a Developmental Perspective: The Counselor Complexity Model" by C. Stoltenberg, 1981, *Journal of Counseling Psychology 28,* p. 60. Copyright 1981 by the American Psychological Association, Inc. Taken from "Counseling Supervision by Developmental Level," by M. Wiley and P. Ray, 1986, *Journal of Counseling Psychology 33(4),* p. 441. Copyright 1986 by the American Psychological Associaion, Inc. Used by permission.

Table 5.2. An Elaboration of the Counselor Complexity Model: Optimal Supervision Environments

| Category | Supervision environment level (E-level) | | | |
	1	2	3	4
Role of supervisor	Supervisor most often serves as a directive instructor and model, providing readings, examples, opportunities for observation, and didactic instruction (S)	Supervisor's role is moving away from that of a directive instructor, encouraging supervisee to try out and expand the skills already developed (S)	Supervisor's role is that of mentor dealing with resolution of the personal and professional dilemmas of supervisee, and an instructor on rare occasions (S)	Supervisor is primarily a collegial consultant (S)
Affective focus of supervision	Supervisee is unaware of many of the feelings he/she has in counseling and supervision, and supervisor focuses on raising awareness of them (S)	Supervisor focuses heavily on helping supervises to clarify and deal with inner feelings and/or ambivalence toward both clients and supervisor (S)	Supervisor focuses on establishing supervisee's sense of confidence and dealing with the feelings surrounding the development of a professional style and/or identity (S)	Supervisor helps supervisee deal with the feelings involved in integrating and consolidating his/her already developed personal and professional identities
Cognitive/skills focus of supervision	Supervisor focuses on supervisee's applying skills and techniques learned in a classroom to a counseling situation (S)	Developing supervisee's basic skills in strategizing and independent decision making is one of the major objectives	Supervisor emphasizes supervisee's conceptualization of cases in relation to each other	The much more subtle aspects of counseling such as timing and orchestrating receive much attention
Dependency in supervision	Supervisee is almost always dependent for structure, advice, directions, and rules (S)	Supervisee fluctuates between being dependent and independent of supervisor consistently (S)	Supervisee is almost always completely independent, but on rare occasions such as emergencies he/she falls back into dependence on supervisor (S)	Supervisee is essentially a fully independent professional (S)
Role of support and confrontation	Supervisee is unable to handle much confrontation; hence, supervisor draws almost solely on supportive behaviors (S)	Supervisor merging confrontational behaviors with primarily supportive style	Supervisor uses relatively equal amounts of support and confrontation (S)	There is rarely a need to support or confront supervisee

Note: Cells identified as (S) have been taken from "Approaching Supervision from a Developmental Perspective: The Counselor Complexity Model" by C. Stoltenberg, 1981, *Journal of Counseling Psychology 28,* p. 60. Copyright 1981 by the American Psychological Association, Inc. Taken from "Counseling Supervision by Developmental Level," by M. Wiley & P. Ray, 1986, *Journal of Counseling Psychology 33(4),* p. 442. Copyright 1986 by the American Psychological Associaion, Inc. Used by permission.

underestimate his/her capacity to intervene with clients, is likely to use jargon, and is not clearly able to integrate information.

Stage 4: Exuberance and Taking Charge—supervisee is more appropriately self-confident, didactic and experiential facets of learning process come together, and supervisee can organize and synthesize information into personal style and framework.

Stage 5: Identity and Independence—the stage of separation and conflict with supervisor; the supervisee asserts independence by basing decisions on his/her clinical judgment and internalized frame of reference, and can reject or devalue the "less-than-perfect" supervisor.

Stage 6: Calm and Collegiality—the supervisee enters into peer collegiality, is less preoccupied with evaluation concerns, and seeks supervision for professional enhancement.

Any of the aforementioned models of developmental level may be referred to when discussing the perceived progress of the supervisee. The use of these stage models is intended to be descriptive rather than prescriptive. Dialogue between the supervisor and supervisee might best occur at the end of the practicum to allow the trainee to have a better sense of his/her own progress. This dialogue also can underscore and reinforce understandings of the process of achieving a professional identity.

SUPERVISOR MONITORING AND ASSESSMENT ACTIVITIES

Assessment is provided by the supervisor at various times throughout the practicum and internship experiences. The first assessment occurs at the onset of supervision to facilitate a working alliance between supervisor and supervisee and to establish mutually agreed upon goals. The supervisor is referred to the *Handbook on Clinical Supervision* (Borders & Leddick, 1987) for a review of standardized assessment and evaluation instruments that can be used for this purpose. The self-assessment format included earlier in this chapter (Form 5.1) has been

presented as one approach to the goal setting process. The supervisor reviews and discusses awareness, knowledge, and practice in the categories of counseling performance skills, cognitive counseling skills, and developmental level of the trainee. Based on this dialogue and the use of standardized measures (if preferred), short-term and long-term goal statements can be formulated. We suggest that the goal statements be developed within the categories of performance skills, cognitive skills, and developmental level. These goal statements then become the context within which the professional development of the practicum student and intern can be interpreted. Progress toward goals can be reviewed at the midpoint and completion of each term of practicum and internship. Goals also can be renegotiated at the midpoint review to adjust for any special circumstances. A sample of a goal statement agreement is provided here. (See Sample 6 and Form 5.4.)

Continuing assessment of the student's work occurs regularly during the weekly individual and/or group supervision sessions conducted at both field site and university settings. In internship the student may be a full-time intern in a location too far from campus for regular weekly meetings. However, the weekly or more often meetings with site supervisor will be held. An *Interview Rating Form* (Form 5.5) provides one approach to organizing and focusing the supervisor ratings of an individual session.

Two additional rating forms are included here to provide structured rating of the trainee at the midpoint and endpoint of practicum and/or internship. The *Site Supervisor's Evaluation of Student Counselor's Performance* (Form 5.6) is recommended for use at the midpoint of practicum/internship. This can be used as an adjunct to the *Goal Statement Agreement* (Form 5.4) review and can be interpreted within the goal statement categories. The more extensive *Counselor Competence Scale* (Form 5.7) is recommended for use at the endpoint of practicum/internship. This scale provides a broader array of performance and cognitive skills to be rated. We recommend use of this scale in addition to the final assessment of progress toward goal statement objectives.

GOAL STATEMENT AGREEMENT

Directions: The student completes the agreement in duplicate and submits one copy to the supervisor.

Student's Name: _____   Supervisor's Name: _____

Date submitted: _____

SHORT-TERM GOALS

COUNSELING PERFORMANCE SKILLS: Demonstrate application of facilitative and challenging skills in client interviews.

COGNITIVE COUNSELING SKILLS: Demonstrate awareness in important client information.

DEVELOPMENTAL LEVEL: Decrease anxiety concerning supervision.

LONG-TERM GOALS

COUNSELING PERFORMANCE SKILLS: Demonstrate ability to integrate and apply skills related to client self-exploration, goal setting, and action.

COGNITIVE COUNSELING SKILLS: Demonstrate ability to analyze client and counselor interaction from at least one theoretical frame of reference.

DEVELOPMENT LEVEL: Demonstrate ability to collaborate and discuss with supervisor regarding appropriate application of an identified counseling method.

Sample 6. An example of a completed Goal Statement Agreement appropriate for a practicum student.

CHAPTER REFERENCES

Biggs, D.A. (1988). The case presentation approach in clinical supervision. *Counselor Education and Supervision, 20,* 240–248.

Borders, L.D., & Leddick, G.R. (1987). *Handbook of counseling supervision.* Alexandria, VA: Association for Counselor Education and Supervision.

Boyd, J. (1978). The behavioral approach to counselor supervision. In J. Boyd (Ed.), *Counselor supervision* (pp. 89–132). Muncie, IN: Accelerated Development.

Bradley, L. (1989). *Counselor supervision: Principles, process and practice* (2nd ed.). Muncie, IN: Accelerated Development.

Carmichael, K. (1992). Peer rating form in counselor supervision. *Texas Association of Counseling and Development Journal, 20*(1), 57–61.

Cohen, R.J., & DeBetz, B. (1977). Responsive supervision of the psychiatric resident and clinical psychology intern. *American Journal of Psychoanalysis, 37,* 51–64.

Collins, D. (1990). Identifying dysfunctional counseling skills behaviors. *The Clinical Supervisor, 8*(1), 67–79.

Cormier, S., & Hockney, H. (1987). *The professional counselor: A process guide to helping.* Englewood, NJ: Prentice-Hall.

D'Andrea, M. (1989). Person-process model of supervision: A developmental approach. In L. Bradley (Ed.), *Counselor supervision: Principles, process, practice* (2nd ed.) (pp. 257–296). Muncie, IN: Accelerated Development.

Deck, M., & Morrow, J. (1989). Supervision: An interpersonal relationship. In L. Bradley (Ed.), *Counselor supervision: Principles, process, and practice* (2nd ed.) (pp. 35–62). Muncie, IN: Accelerated Development.

Eckstein, R. (1972). Supervision of psychotherapy. Is it teaching? Is it therapy? Or is it administration? In D.E. Hendrickson & F.H. Krause (Eds.), *Counseling and psychotherapy: Training and supervision.* Columbus, OH: Charles E. Merrill.

Egan, G. (1986). *The skilled helper: A systematic approach to effective helping.* Monterey, CA: Brooks/Cole Publishing.

Falvey, J.E. (1987). *Handbook of administrative supervision.* Alexandria, VA: Association for Counselor Education and Supervision.

Freedman, D., & Kaslow, N.J. (1986). The development of professional identity in psychotherapists: Six stages in the supervision process. In F.W. Kaslow (Ed.), *Supervision and training: Models, dilemmas, and challenges* (pp 29–49). New York: Haworth.

Hart, G., & Falvey, E. (1987, March). Field supervision of counselors in training: A survey of the North Atlantic Region. *Counselor Education and Supervision, 26,* 204–212.

Hill, C.E., Charles, D., & Reed, K.G. (1981). A longitudinal analysis of changes in counseling skills during doctoral training in counseling psychology. *Journal of Counseling Psychology, 23,* 254–258.

Hogan, R.A. (1964). Issues and approaches in supervision. *Psychotherapy: Theory, Research, and Practice, 1,* 139–141.

Hunt, D.E. (1971). *Matching models in education: The ordination of teaching methods with student characteristics.* Toronto: Ontario Institute for Studies in Education.

Hutt, C.H., Scott, J., & King, M. (1983, Spring). A phenomenological study of supervisee's positive and negative experiences in supervision. *Psychotherapy: Theory, Research, and Practice, 20,* 118–123.

Ivey, A., & Gluckstern, N. (1974). *Basic attending skills.* North Amherst, MA: Microtraining Associates.

Kadushin, A., (1976). *Supervision in social work.* New York: Columbia University Press.

Loganbill, C., & Stoltenberg, C. (1983). The case conceptualization format: A training device for practicum. *Counselor Education and Supervision, 22,* 235–241.

McAuliffe, G. (1992). A case presentation approach to group supervision for community college counselors. *Counselor Education and Supervision, 31,* 163–174.

Moskowitz, S., & Rupert, P. (1983). Conflict resolution within the supervisory relationship. Professional Psychology: Research and Practice, 14, 632–641.

Murdock, N. (1991). Case conceptualization: Applying theory to individuals. *Counselor Education and Supervision, 30,* 355–365.

Nash, V.C. (1975). The clinical supervision of psychotherapy. Dissertation Abstracts International, 36, 2480B-2481B. (University Microfilms No. 75-24, 581).

Ricoh, M.J. (1980). The dilemmas of supervision in dynamic psychotherapy. In A.K. Hess (Ed.), *Psychotherapy supervision: Theory, research, and practice* (pp. 68–76). New York: John Wiley.

Scott, J. (1976). Process supervision. In J. Scott (Ed.), *A monograph on training supervisors in the helping professions* (pp. 1–10). Continuation of Northeastern EPDA/PPS Center/Satellite Project, Award Number: OGG-070–2021(725).

Stoltenberg, C. (1981). Approaching supervision from a developmental perspective: The counselor complexity model. *Journal of Counseling Psychology, 28*(1), 59–65.

Wiley, M., & Ray, P.B. (1986). Counseling supervisions by developmental level. *Journal of Counseling Psychology, 33*(4), 439–445.

Wittmer, J., & Myrick, R. (1974). *Facilitative teaching: Theory and practice.* Santa Monica, CH: Goodyear Publishing.

SELF-RATING BY THE STUDENT COUNSELOR*

SUGGESTED USE: The student counselor may use this sheet as a self-evaluation after a therapy session.

Date: _____ Student Counselor Name: _____ Client Name: _____

DIRECTIONS: The student counselor following a therapy session is to answer each question. The questions serve as a self-rating initiator and may enable the student counselor to determine means for improvement in his/her counseling.

Preparation for the Interview

	YES	?	NO
1. Was I physically in good condition and mentally alert?			
2. Did I schedule sufficient time for the interview?			
3. Was provision made for privacy and reasonable freedom from interruption?			
4. Did I have the physical space arranged where we met so as to suggest welcome and an atmosphere conducive to counseling?			
5. Did I have a background of available data about the client that would help me to understand him/her better in the interview but would not prejudice me?			
6. Did I have and understand information so as to personalize information processes with the client?			
7. Had I previously established a reputation for seeing the client's point of view, being genuinely helpful, and not disclosing confidence?			

Comments:

Beginning the Interview

1. Was I sensitive to the client and did I use an appropriate approach?			
2. Was I able to create a psychological atmosphere in which the client was stimulated to take the responsibility of thinking through the situation?			
3. Was I successful in maintaining open communication between us?			

Comments:

---

* This material was taken from K. Dimick and F. Krause, *Practicum Manual for Counseling and Psychotherapy.* Muncie, IN: Accelerated Development Inc., 1980. Reprinted with permission.

Development of the Interview

	YES	?	NO
1. Did the client feel freedom to express negative feelings?	_____	_____	_____
2. Did the client have the opportunity to release tension?	_____	_____	_____
3. Was my attitude one of reflecting objectivity while expressing caring?	_____	_____	_____
4. Was I sincere and did I show genuine respect for the client?	_____	_____	_____
5. Was my own attitude, so far as I know, free from bias?	_____	_____	_____
6. Did I follow the leads suggested by the client?	_____	_____	_____
7. Did I help the client to clarify and expand positive feelings?	_____	_____	_____
8. Did the client establish a more forward looking, positive, hopeful attitude during the interview or series of interviews?	_____	_____	_____
9. Was I able to assist in information processing by the client?	_____	_____	_____
10. Was information provided in a manner which caused the client to move forward realistically in his/her thinking?	_____	_____	_____

Comments:

Planning for Next Session

	YES	?	NO
1. Was I able to identify areas with which to follow through for the next session?	_____	_____	_____
2. Was I able to help client gain a clear view of what might be done in the next one?	_____	_____	_____
3. Was I able to help client gain a clear view of what might be done in the next session?	_____	_____	_____
4. Did I establish with the client a definite meeting time and place for the next session?	_____	_____	_____
5. Have I identified techniques that might be considered for the next session?	_____	_____	_____
6. Have I identified the materials and/or preparation I will need for the next session?	_____	_____	_____

Comments:

Form 5.2, p. 2 of 2, Copy 1

SELF-RATING BY THE STUDENT COUNSELOR*

SUGGESTED USE: The student counselor may use this sheet as a self-evaluation after a therapy session.

Date: _____   Student Counselor Name: _____   Client Name: _____

DIRECTIONS: The student counselor following a therapy session is to answer each question. The questions serve as a self-rating initiator and may enable the student counselor to determine means for improvement in his/her counseling.

Preparation for the Interview

	YES	?	NO
1. Was I physically in good condition and mentally alert?	_____	_____	_____
2. Did I schedule sufficient time for the interview?	_____	_____	_____
3. Was provision made for privacy and reasonable freedom from interruption?	_____	_____	_____
4. Did I have the physical space arranged where we met so as to suggest welcome and an atmosphere conducive to counseling?	_____	_____	_____
5. Did I have a background of available data about the client that would help me to understand him/her better in the interview but would not prejudice me?	_____	_____	_____
6. Did I have and understand information so as to personalize information processes with the client?	_____	_____	_____
7. Had I previously established a reputation for seeing the client's point of view, being genuinely helpful, and not disclosing confidence?	_____	_____	_____

Comments:

Beginning the Interview

1. Was I sensitive to the client and did I use an appropriate approach?	_____	_____	_____
2. Was I able to create a psychological atmosphere in which the client was stimulated to take the responsibility of thinking through the situation?	_____	_____	_____
3. Was I successful in maintaining open communication between us?	_____	_____	_____

Comments:

---

* This material was taken from K. Dimick and F. Krause, *Practicum Manual for Counseling and Psychotherapy.* Muncie, IN: Accelerated Development Inc., 1980. Reprinted with permission.

Development of the Interview

	YES	?	NO
1. Did the client feel freedom to express negative feelings?	___	___	___
2. Did the client have the opportunity to release tension?	___	___	___
3. Was my attitude one of reflecting objectivity while expressing caring?	___	___	___
4. Was I sincere and did I show genuine respect for the client?	___	___	___
5. Was my own attitude, so far as I know, free from bias?	___	___	___
6. Did I follow the leads suggested by the client?	___	___	___
7. Did I help the client to clarify and expand positive feelings?	___	___	___
8. Did the client establish a more forward looking, positive, hopeful attitude during the interview or series of interviews?	___	___	___
9. Was I able to assist in information processing by the client?	___	___	___
10. Was information provided in a manner which caused the client to move forward realistically in his/her thinking?	___	___	___

Comments:

Planning for Next Session

1. Was I able to identify areas with which to follow through for the next session?	___	___	___
2. Was I able to help client gain a clear view of what might be done in the next one?	___	___	___
3. Was I able to help client gain a clear view of what might be done in the next session?	___	___	___
4. Did I establish with the client a definite meeting time and place for the next session?	___	___	___
5. Have I identified techniques that might be considered for the next session?	___	___	___
6. Have I identified the materials and/or preparation I will need for the next session?	___	___	___

Comments:

Form 5.2, p. 2 of 2, Copy 2

SELF-RATING BY THE STUDENT COUNSELOR*

SUGGESTED USE: The student counselor may use this sheet as a self-evaluation after a therapy session.

	Student Counselor		Client	
Date: _____	Name: _____		Name: _____

DIRECTIONS: The student counselor following a therapy session is to answer each question. The questions serve as a self-rating initiator and may enable the student counselor to determine means for improvement in his/her counseling.

Preparation for the Interview

	YES	?	NO

1. Was I physically in good condition and mentally alert? _____ _____ _____

2. Did I schedule sufficient time for the interview? _____ _____ _____

3. Was provision made for privacy and reasonable freedom from interruption? _____ _____ _____

4. Did I have the physical space arranged where we met so as to suggest welcome and an atmosphere conducive to counseling? _____ _____ _____

5. Did I have a background of available data about the client that would help me to understand him/her better in the interview but would not prejudice me? _____ _____ _____

6. Did I have and understand information so as to personalize information processes with the client? _____ _____ _____

7. Had I previously established a reputation for seeing the client's point of view, being genuinely helpful, and not disclosing confidence? _____ _____ _____

Comments:

Beginning the Interview

1. Was I sensitive to the client and did I use an appropriate approach? _____ _____ _____

2. Was I able to create a psychological atmosphere in which the client was stimulated to take the responsibility of thinking through the situation? _____ _____ _____

3. Was I successful in maintaining open communication between us? _____ _____ _____

Comments:

---

* This material was taken from K. Dimick and F. Krause, *Practicum Manual for Counseling and Psychotherapy.* Muncie, IN: Accelerated Development Inc., 1980. Reprinted with permission.

Form 5.2, p. 1 of 2, Copy 3

Development of the Interview

	YES	?	NO
1. Did the client feel freedom to express negative feelings?	____	____	____
2. Did the client have the opportunity to release tension?	____	____	____
3. Was my attitude one of reflecting objectivity while expressing caring?	____	____	____
4. Was I sincere and did I show genuine respect for the client?	____	____	____
5. Was my own attitude, so far as I know, free from bias?	____	____	____
6. Did I follow the leads suggested by the client?	____	____	____
7. Did I help the client to clarify and expand positive feelings?	____	____	____
8. Did the client establish a more forward looking, positive, hopeful attitude during the interview or series of interviews?	____	____	____
9. Was I able to assist in information processing by the client?	____	____	____
10. Was information provided in a manner which caused the client to move forward realistically in his/her thinking?	____	____	____

Comments:

Planning for Next Session

1. Was I able to identify areas with which to follow through for the next session?	____	____	____
2. Was I able to help client gain a clear view of what might be done in the next one?	____	____	____
3. Was I able to help client gain a clear view of what might be done in the next session?	____	____	____
4. Did I establish with the client a definite meeting time and place for the next session?	____	____	____
5. Have I identified techniques that might be considered for the next session?	____	____	____
6. Have I identified the materials and/or preparation I will need for the next session?	____	____	____

Comments:

Form 5.2, p. 2 of 2, Copy 3

PEER RATING FORM

Purposes: 1. To provide trainee with additional sources of feedback regarding skill development.
2. To provide rater with opportunity to increase knowledge and recognition of positive skill behavior.

Directions: 1. Trainee submits this sheet once a week to be completed by peer who reviews the trainee's tapes. The particular skills the counselor is working on are identified by the counselor trainee.
2. Peer writes remarks once a week on all tapes reviewed rating performance on the targeted skill behavior.
3. Information is cumulative to aid in review of progress.

Counselor's Name: _____

Targeted Skills (to be identified by counselor):

Remarks (based on all tapes reviewed during the week):

Signature of Rater: _____ Date: _____

- -

PEER RATING FORM

Purposes: 1. To provide trainee with additional sources of feedback regarding skill development.
2. To provide rater with opportunity to increase knowledge and recognition of positive skill behavior.

Directions: 1. Trainee submits this sheet once a week to be completed by peer who reviews the trainee's tapes. The particular skills the counselor is working on are identified by the counselor trainee.
2. Peer writes remarks once a week on all tapes reviewed rating performance on the targeted skill behavior.
3. Information is cumulative to aid in review of progress.

Counselor's Name: _____

Targeted Skills (to be identified by counselor):

Remarks (based on all tapes reviewed during the week):

Signature of Rater: _____ Date: _____

Form 5.3, p. 1 of 1, Copy 1 & 2

PEER RATING FORM

Purposes: 1. To provide trainee with additional sources of feedback regarding skill development.
            2. To provide rater with opportunity to increase knowledge and recognition of positive skill behavior.

Directions: 1. Trainee submits this sheet once a week to be completed by peer who reviews the trainee's tapes. The particular skills the counselor is working on are identified by the counselor trainee.
            2. Peer writes remarks once a week on all tapes reviewed rating performance on the targeted skill behavior.
            3. Information is cumulative to aid in review of progress.

Counselor's Name: _____

Targeted Skills (to be identified by counselor):

Remarks (based on all tapes reviewed during the week):

Signature of Rater: _____ Date: _____

- -

PEER RATING FORM

Purposes: 1. To provide trainee with additional sources of feedback regarding skill development.
            2. To provide rater with opportunity to increase knowledge and recognition of positive skill behavior.

Directions: 1. Trainee submits this sheet once a week to be completed by peer who reviews the trainee's tapes. The particular skills the counselor is working on are identified by the counselor trainee.
            2. Peer writes remarks once a week on all tapes reviewed rating performance on the targeted skill behavior.
            3. Information is cumulative to aid in review of progress.

Counselor's Name: _____

Targeted Skills (to be identified by counselor):

Remarks (based on all tapes reviewed during the week):

Signature of Rater: _____ Date: _____

Form 5.3, p. 1 of 1, Copy 3 & 4

GOAL STATEMENT AGREEMENT

Directions: The student completes the agreement in duplicate and submits one copy to the supervisor.

Student's Name: _____   Supervisor's Name: _____

Date submitted: _____

SHORT-TERM GOALS

COUNSELING PERFORMANCE SKILLS: _____

_____

_____

COGNITIVE COUNSELING SKILLS: _____

_____

_____

DEVELOPMENTAL LEVEL: _____

_____

_____

- -

GOAL STATEMENT AGREEMENT

Directions: The student completes the agreement in duplicate and submits one copy to the supervisor.

Student's Name: _____   Supervisor's Name: _____

Date submitted: _____

SHORT-TERM GOALS

COUNSELING PERFORMANCE SKILLS: _____

_____

_____

COGNITIVE COUNSELING SKILLS: _____

_____

_____

DEVELOPMENTAL LEVEL: _____

_____

_____

LONG-TERM GOALS

COUNSELING PERFORMANCE SKILLS: _____

_____

_____

COGNITIVE COUNSELING SKILLS: _____

_____

_____

DEVELOPMENTAL LEVEL: _____

_____

_____

- -

LONG-TERM GOALS

COUNSELING PERFORMANCE SKILLS: _____

_____

_____

COGNITIVE COUNSELING SKILLS: _____

_____

_____

DEVELOPMENTAL LEVEL: _____

_____

_____

Form 5.4, p. 2 of 2, Copy 1 & 2

GOAL STATEMENT AGREEMENT

Directions: The student completes the agreement in duplicate and submits one copy to the supervisor.

Student's Name: _____   Supervisor's Name: _____

Date submitted: _____

SHORT-TERM GOALS

COUNSELING PERFORMANCE SKILLS: _____

_____

_____

COGNITIVE COUNSELING SKILLS: _____

_____

_____

DEVELOPMENTAL LEVEL: _____

_____

_____

- -

GOAL STATEMENT AGREEMENT

Directions: The student completes the agreement in duplicate and submits one copy to the supervisor.

Student's Name: _____   Supervisor's Name: _____

Date submitted: _____

SHORT-TERM GOALS

COUNSELING PERFORMANCE SKILLS: _____

_____

COGNITIVE COUNSELING SKILLS: _____

_____

DEVELOPMENTAL LEVEL: _____

_____

_____

Form 5.4, p. 1 of 2, Copy 3 & 4

LONG-TERM GOALS

COUNSELING PERFORMANCE SKILLS: _____
_____
_____

COGNITIVE COUNSELING SKILLS: _____
_____
_____

DEVELOPMENTAL LEVEL: _____
_____
_____

- -

LONG-TERM GOALS

COUNSELING PERFORMANCE SKILLS: _____
_____
_____

COGNITIVE COUNSELING SKILLS: _____
_____
_____

DEVELOPMENTAL LEVEL: _____
_____
_____

Form 5.4, p. 2 of 2, Copy 3 & 4

INTERVIEW RATING FORM*
Rating of a Counseling Session Conducted by a Student Counselor

Gordon Poling

Client Name or
Identification: _____

Student
Counselor Name: _____

CHECK ONE
____ Audiotape
____ Videotape
____ Observation
____ Other (Specify) _____

Signature of
Supervisor or Observer: _____

Date of Interview: _____

DIRECTIONS: Supervisor or peer of the student counselor is to mark a rating for each item and as much as possible is to provide remarks that will help the student counselor in his/her development.

SPECIFIC CRITERIA	RATING (best to least)	REMARKS
1. OPENING: Was opening unstructured, friendly, and pleasant? Any role definition needed? Any introduction necessary?	5 4 3 2 1	
2. RAPPORT: Did student counselor establish good rapport with client? Was the stage set for a productive interview?	5 4 3 2 1	
3. INTERVIEW RESPONSIBILITY: If not assumed by the client, did student counselor assume appropriate level of responsibility for interview conduct? Did student counselor or client take initiative?	5 4 3 2 1	
4. INTERACTION: Were the client and student counselor really communicating in a meaning manner.	5 4 3 2 1	
5. ACCEPTANCE/PERMISSIVENESS: Was the student counselor accepting and permissive of client's emotions, feelings, and expressed thoughts?	5 4 3 2 1	
6. REFLECTIONS OF FEELINGS: Did student counselor reflect and react to feelings or did interview remain on an intellectual level?	5 4 3 2 1	

* This material was taken from chapter entitled "Evaluation of Student Counselors and Supervisors," pp. 265–314 in K. Dimick and F. Krause (Eds.), *Practicum Manual for Counseling and Psychotherapy*. Accelerated Development, 1980. Reprinted with permission from Gordon Poling, Professor, School of Education, University of South Dakota.

Form 5.5, p. 1 of 2, Copy 1

SPECIFIC CRITERIA	RATING (best to least)					REMARKS

7. STUDENT COUNSELOR RESPONSES: Were student counselor responses appropriate in view of what the client was expressing or were responses concerned with trivia and minutia? Meaningful questions? — 5 4 3 2 1

8. VALUE MANAGEMENT: How did the student counselor cope with values? Were attempts made to impose counselor values during the interview? — 5 4 3 2 1

9. COUNSELING RELATIONSHIP: Were student counselor-client relationships conducive to productive counseling? Was a counseling relationship established? — 5 4 3 2 1

10. CLOSING: Was closing student counselor or client initiated? Was it abrupt or brusque? Any follow-up or further interview scheduling accomplished? — 5 4 3 2 1

11. GENERAL TECHNIQUES: How well did the student counselor conduct the mechanics of the interview? — 5 4 3 2 1

  A. Duration of interview: Was the interview too long or too short? Should interview have been terminated sooner or later?

  B. Vocabulary level: Was student counselor vocabulary appropriate for the client?

  C. Mannerisms: Did the student counselor display any mannerism which might have conversely affected the interview or portions thereof?

  D. Verbosity: Did the student counselor dominate the interview, interrupt, override, or become too wordy?

  E. Silences: Were silences broken to meet student counselor needs or were they dealt with in an effectual manner?

COMMENTS FOR STUDENT COUNSELOR ASSISTANCE: Additional comments that might assist the student counselor in areas not covered by the preceding suggestions.

Form 5.5, p. 2 of 2, Copy 1

SITE SUPERVISOR'S EVALUATION OF STUDENT COUNSELOR'S PERFORMANCE

SUGGESTED USE: This form is to be used to check performances in counseling practicum. The form may be completed after each supervised counseling session or may cover several supervisions over a period of time. The form is appropriate for individual or group counseling.

ALTERNATE USE: The student counselor may ask a peer to observe a counseling session and mark the evaluation.

Name of Student Counselor: _____

Name or Identifying Code of Client: _____

Date of Supervision: _____ or Period Covered by the Evaluation: _____

DIRECTIONS: The supervisor following each counseling session that has been supervised or after several supervisions covering a period of time is to circle a number that best evaluates the student counselor on each performance at that point in time.

	General Supervision Comments	Poor	Adequate	Good
1.	Demonstrates a personal commitment in developing professional competencies	1 2	3 4	5 6
2.	Invests time and energy in becoming a counselor	1 2	3 4	5 6
3.	Accepts and uses constructive criticism to enhance self-development and counseling skills	1 2	3 4	5 6
4.	Engages in open, comfortable, and clear communication with peers and supervisors	1 2	3 4	5 6
5.	Recognizes own competencies and skills and shares these with peers and supervisors	1 2	3 4	5 6
6.	Recognizes own deficiencies and actively works to overcome them with peers and supervisors	1 2	3 4	5 6
7.	Completes case reports and records punctually and conscientiously	1 2	3 4	5 6
	The Counseling Process			
8.	Researches the referral prior to the first interview	1 2	3 4	5 6
9.	Keeps appointments on time	1 2	3 4	5 6
10.	Begins the interview smoothly	1 2	3 4	5 6
11.	Explains the nature and objectives of counseling when appropriate	1 2	3 4	5 6
12.	Is relaxed and comfortable in the interview	1 2	3 4	5 6
13.	Communicates interest in and acceptance of the client	1 2	3 4	5 6
14.	Facilitates client expression of concerns and feelings	1 2	3 4	5 6
15.	Focuses on the content of the client's problem	1 2	3 4	5 6
16.	Recognizes and resists manipulation by the client	1 2	3 4	5 6
17.	Recognizes and deals with positive affect of the client	1 2	3 4	5 6
18.	Recognizes and deals with negative affect of the client	1 2	3 4	5 6
19.	Is spontaneous in the interview	1 2	3 4	5 6
20.	Uses silence effectively in the interview	1 2	3 4	5 6
21.	Is aware of own feelings in the counseling session	1 2	3 4	5 6
22.	Communicates own feelings to the client when appropriate	1 2	3 4	5 6
23.	Recognizes and skillfully interprets the client's covert messages	1 2	3 4	5 6

Reprinted by permission from Dr. Harold Hackney, Assistant Professor, Purdue University. This form was designed by two graduate students based upon material from *Counseling Strategies and Objectives* by H. Hackney and S. Nye, Prentice-Hall, 1973. This material was taken from a chapter entitled "Evaluation of Student Counselors and Supervisors," pp. 265–274, in K. Dimick and F. Krause (Eds.), *Practicum Manual for Counseling and Psychotherapy*, Muncie, IN: Accelerated Development.

24.	Facilitates realistic goal setting with the client	1 2	3 4	5 6
25.	Encourages appropriate action-step planning with the client	1 2	3 4	5 6
26.	Enjoys judgment in the timing and use of different techniques	1 2	3 4	5 6
27.	Initiates periodic evaluation of goals, action-steps, and process during counseling	1 2	3 4	5 6
28.	Explains, administers, and interprets tests correctly	1 2	3 4	5 6
29.	Terminates the interview smoothly	1 2	3 4	5 6

The Conceptualization Process

30.	Focuses on specific behaviors and their consequences, implications, and contingencies	1 2	3 4	5 6
31.	Recognizes and pursues discrepancies and meaning of inconsistent information	1 2	3 4	5 6
32.	Uses relevant case data in planning both immediate and long-range goals	1 2	3 4	5 6
33.	Uses relevant case date in considering various strategies and their implications	1 2	3 4	5 6
34.	Bases decisions on a theoretically sound and consistent rationale of human behavior	1 2	3 4	5 6
35.	Is perceptive in evaluating the effects of own counseling techniques	1 2	3 4	5 6
36.	Demonstrates ethical behavior in the counseling activity and case management			

Additional Comments and/or Suggestions: _____

_____

_____

_____

_____

_____

_____

_____

_____

Date: _____   Signature of Supervisor: _____

or Peer: _____

My signature indicates that I have read the above report and have discussed the content with my site supervisor. It does not necessarily indicate that I agree with the report in part or in whole.

Date: _____ Signature of Student Counselor _____

COUNSELOR COMPETENCY SCALE*
For the Analysis And Assessment of Counselor Competencies

This scale is an altered version of the "Survey of Counselor Competencies" developed by Dennis B. Cogan, Department of Counselor Education, Arizona State University, Tempe, Arizona 85282.

COUNSELOR COMPETENCY	ANALYSIS Skill Value to Interview Non-Essential / Important / Critical			ASSESS-MENT Proficiency +	−
PERSONAL CHARACTERISTICS					
1. SOCIAL RESPONSIBILITY—the counselor states, and his/her past experiences show, that he/she is interested in social change.	___	___	___	___	___
2. PEOPLE ORIENTED—the counselor is people oriented as demonstrated by his/her past experiences and by his/her present social interactions.	___	___	___	___	___
3. FALLIBILITY—the counselor recognizes that he/she is not free from making errors.	___	___	___	___	___
4. PERSONAL PROBLEMS—the counselor's personal problems are kept out of the counseling session.	___	___	___	___	___
5. MODELING—the counselor models appropriate cognitive processes, behaviors, and feelings during the counseling session.	___	___	___	___	___
6. NONDEFENSIVE—the counselor gives and receives feedback to and from his/her clients, peers, and supervisor without making excuses or justifications.	___	___	___	___	___
Other: _____	___	___	___	___	___
Other: _____	___	___	___	___	___
Other: _____	___	___	___	___	___
7. EVALUATION—the counselor's theoretical frame of reference includes a means for describing the cognitive, behavioral and/or affective change(s) that take place in determining the effectiveness of the selected counseling strategy.	___	___	___	___	___
8. DIAGNOSIS—regardless of his/her theoretical orientation, the counselor can identify maladaptive symptomology consistent with his/her theoretical frame of reference.	___	___	___	___	___
9. THEORY—the counselor states his/her assumptions about human behavior, through which he/she will incorporate or abstract his/her empirical findings and through which he/she will make predictions concerning his/her client.	___	___	___	___	___

* This material was taken from Appendix A, pp. 482–490 in J. Boyd (Ed.), *Counselor Supervision,* Muncie, IN: Accelerated Development, 1978. Reprinted with permission.

	ANALYSIS Skill Value to Interview	ASSESS- MENT
COUNSELOR COMPETENCY	Non-Essential / Important / Critical	Proficiency + −

10. THEORY—the counselor explains human behavior from at least two theories of personality.

11. PRIORITIZING—the counselor decides on which problem, when presented with more than one, to deal with first according to his/her theoretical frame of reference.

12. INTERPRETATION—the counselor provides the client with a possible explanation for or relationships between certain behaviors, cognition's, and/or feelings.

13. PROGNOSIS—the counselor can make an evaluation of the client's potential for successful treatment consistent with theoretical frame of reference.

14. INTERACTIONS—the counselor describes the interactions that take place between the counselor and client consistent with his/her theoretical frame of reference.

15. DEFENSE MECHANISMS—the counselor is aware of the defense mechanisms used by the client, the purpose they serve, and can help the client substitute more appropriate ones.

16. CATHARSIS—the counselor understands the concept of catharsis.

17. NATURAL CONSEQUENCES—the counselor understands the concept of "natural consequences."

18. ENVIRONMENTAL MANIPULATION—the counselor under-stands the concept of environmental manipulation.

19. TEST SELECTION—the counselor selects an appropriate test(s) according to his/her theoretical frame of reference.

20. INFERENCES—the counselor provides an explanation for and the functional use of the client's behaviors, cognition's, and/or feelings consistent with his/her theoretical frame of reference and how they might influence the counseling process.

Other: _____

Other: _____

Other: _____

COUNSELOR COMPETENCY	ANALYSIS Skill Value to Interview			ASSESS-MENT Proficiency	
	Non-Essential Important Critical			+	−
COMMUNICATIONS					
21. OPEN-ENDED QUESTION—the counselor asks the client a question that cannot be answered by a yes or no, and the question does not provide the client with the answer.	____	____	____	____	____
22. MINIMAL VERBAL RESPONSE—the counselor uses "mmmh, oh, yes" to communicate to the client that he/she is listening without interrupting the client's train of thought or discourse.	____	____	____	____	____
23. GENUINENESS—the counselor's responses are sincere and appropriate.	____	____	____	____	____
24. POSITIVE REGARD—without interjecting his/her own values, the counselor communicates respect and concern for the client's feelings, experiences, and potentials.	____	____	____	____	____
25. LANGUAGE—the counselor uses terminology that is understood by the client.	____	____	____	____	____
26. CLARIFICATION—the counselor has the client clarify vague and ambiguous cognitions, behaviors, and/or feelings.	____	____	____	____	____
27. PARAPHRASING—without changing the meaning, the counselor states in fewer words what the client has previously stated.	____	____	____	____	____
28. SUMMARIZES—the counselor combines two or more of the client's cognition's, feelings, and/or behaviors into a general statement.	____	____	____	____	____
29. RESTATEMENT—the counselor conveys to the client that he/she has heard the content of the client's previous statement(s) by restating in exactly or near exact words, that which the client has just verbalized.	____	____	____	____	____
30. EMPATHIC UNDERSTANDING—the counselor's responses add noticeably to the expressions of the client in such a way as to express feelings at a level deeper than the client was able to express for himself/herself.	____	____	____	____	____
31. REFLECTION—from nonverbal cues the counselor accurately describes the client's affective state.	____	____	____	____	____
32. PERCEPTIONS—the counselor labeled his/her perceptions as perceptions.	____	____	____	____	____
33. CONFRONTATION—the counselor confronts the client by stating the possible consequences of his/her behaviors, cognition's, and/or feelings.	____	____	____	____	____

	ANALYSIS Skill Value to Interview			ASSESS- MENT Proficiency	
COUNSELOR COMPETENCY	Non-Essential Important Critical			+	−

34. SUPPORTIVE—the counselor makes statements that agree with the client's cognitions, accepts the client's behavior, and/or shares with the client that his/her feelings were not unusual.

35. PROBING—the counselor's statement results in the client providing additional information about his/her cognitions, behaviors, and/or feelings.

36. DISAPPROVAL—the counselor makes a statement that conveys disapproval of one or more of the client's cognitions, behaviors, and/or feelings.

37. ADVICE GIVING—the counselor shares with the client which alternative he/she would select if it were his/her decision to make.

Other: _____

Other: _____

Other: _____

COUNSELING SKILLS

38. VOICE—the counselor's tone of voice and rate of speech is appropriate to the client's present state and/or counseling session.

39. EYE CONTACT—the counselor maintains eye contact at a level that is comfortable for the client.

40. INITIAL CONTACT—the counselor greets the client in a warm and accepting manner through some accepted form of social greeting (handshake, nod of head, etc.)

41. ACTIVITY LEVEL—the counselor maintains a level of activity appropriate to the client during the counseling session.

42. PHYSIOLOGICAL PRESENCE—the counselor's body posture, facial expressions, and gestures are natural and congruent with those of the client's.

43. COUNSELOR DISCLOSURE—the counselor shares personal information and feelings when it is appropriate in facilitating the counseling process.

44. SILENCE—the counselor does not speak when appropriate in facilitating client movement.

Form 5.7, p. 4 of 9, Copy 1

COUNSELOR COMPETENCY	ANALYSIS Skill Value to Interview			ASSESS-MENT Proficiency	
	Non-Essential	Important	Critical	+	−
45. ACCENTING—from the client's previous statement, behavior, and/or feeling, the counselor repeats or accentuates the same, or has the client repeat or accentuate the statement, behavior, and/or feeling.	_____	_____	_____	_____	_____
46. OBJECTIVITY—the counselor has sufficient control over his/her feelings and does not impose his/her values on the client.	_____	_____	_____	_____	_____
47. PROBING—the counselor avoids bringing up or pursuing areas that are too threatening to the client.	_____	_____	_____	_____	_____
48. RESISTANCE—the counselor is able to work through the client's conscious and/or unconscious opposition to the counseling process.	_____	_____	_____	_____	_____
49. VERBOSITY—the counselor speaks when it is necessary, does not inappropriately interrupt the client or verbally dominate the counseling session.	_____	_____	_____	_____	_____
50. ATTENDING—the counselor's attention is with the client's cognitions, behaviors, and/or feelings during the counseling session in accord with his/her stated theoretical frame of reference.	_____	_____	_____	_____	_____
51. TRANSFERENCE—the counselor is able to work through feelings directed at him/her by the client which the client originally had for another object or person.	_____	_____	_____	_____	_____
52. COUNTER-TRANSFERENCE—the counselor is aware of and is able to correct his/her placing his/her own wishes on the client.	_____	_____	_____	_____	_____
53. MANIPULATION—the counselor recognizes the client's attempt at influencing the counselor for his/her own purpose.	_____	_____	_____	_____	_____
54. FACTORS—the counselor explores and is aware of socio-economic, cultural, and personal factors that might affect the client's progress.	_____	_____	_____	_____	_____
55. DEPENDENCY—the counselor encourages the client to be independent, does not make decisions for the client or accept responsibility for the client's behaviors, cognitions, and/or feelings.	_____	_____	_____	_____	_____
56. THEORY—the counselor can work with clients from at least two theories of counseling.	_____	_____	_____	_____	_____
57. ALTERNATIVE EXPLORATION—the counselor, with the client, examines the other options available and the possible consequences of each.	_____	_____	_____	_____	_____

COUNSELOR COMPETENCY	ANALYSIS Skill Value to Interview			ASSESS-MENT Proficiency	
	Non-Essential	Important	Critical	+	−
58. IMPLEMENTATION—the counselor helps the client put insight into action.	___	___	___	___	___
59. DISTORTIONS—the counselor explains to the client his/her previously distorted perceptions of self and the environment.	___	___	___	___	___

PERSONAL CHARACTERISTICS

COUNSELOR COMPETENCY	Non-Essential	Important	Critical	+	−
60. MOTIVATION—the counselor can verbally confront the client with his/her lack of goal directed behavior.	___	___	___	___	___
61. CASE HISTORY TAKING—the counselor obtains factual information from the client that will be helpful in developing a course of action for the client consistent with his/her theoretical frame of reference.	___	___	___	___	___
62. INSIGHT—the counselor helps the client become more aware of his/her cognitive, behavioral, affective, and spiritual domain.	___	___	___	___	___
63. STRUCTURE—the counselor structures the on-going counseling sessions so there is continuity from session to session.	___	___	___	___	___
64. INCONSISTENCIES—the counselor identifies and explores with the client contradictions within and/or between client behaviors, cognitions, and/or affect.	___	___	___	___	___
65. RE-FOCUSING—the counselor makes a statement or asks a question that redirects the client to a specific behavior, cognition, or feeling.	___	___	___	___	___
66. GOALS—the counselor, with the client, establishes short and long range goals which are congruent with societal goals and are within the client's potential.	___	___	___	___	___
67. REINFORCEMENT—the counselor identifies and uses reinforcers that facilitate the identified client goals.	___	___	___	___	___
68. FLEXIBILITY—the counselor changes long and short term goals within a specific session or during the overall counseling process as additional information becomes available.	___	___	___	___	___
69. BEHAVIORAL GAME—the counselor can develop specific plans, that can be observed and/or counted, for changing the client's behavior(s).	___	___	___	___	___
70. STRATEGY—the counselor's course of action is consistent with the counselor's stated theory of counseling.	___	___	___	___	___
71. TERMINATION—the counselor resolves the client's desire for premature termination.	___	___	___	___	___

Form 5.7, p. 6 of 9, Copy 1

COUNSELOR COMPETENCY	ANALYSIS Skill Value to Interview			ASSESS-MENT Proficiency	
	Non-Essential	Important	Critical	+	−
72. EMERGENCIES—the counselor can handle emergencies that arise with the client.	___	___	___	___	___
73. TERMINATION—the counselor ends each session and the counseling relationship on time or at a point at which the client is comfortable with the issues that have been explored.	___	___	___	___	___
74. TERMINATION—the counselor advises the client that he/she may return in the future.	___	___	___	___	___
75. PERIODIC EVALUATION—with the client, the counselor periodically evaluates the progress made toward the established goals.	___	___	___	___	___
76. FANTASY—the counselor has the client use his/her imagination to gain insight and/or move toward the client's established goals.	___	___	___	___	___
77. HOMEWORK—the counselor appropriately assigns work to the client that is to be completed outside the counseling session.	___	___	___	___	___
78. PROBLEM SOLVING—the counselor teachers the client a method for problem solving.	___	___	___	___	___
79. TEST INTERPRETATION—the counselor interprets test(s) according to the procedures outlined in the test manual.	___	___	___	___	___
80. ROLE PLAYING—the counselor helps the client achieve insight by acting out conflicts and/or situations unfamiliar to him/her.	___	___	___	___	___
81. DESENSITIZATION—the counselor can apply a purposeful technique to reduce the level of anxiety that the client is experiencing.	___	___	___	___	___
82. DREAMS—the counselor works with client's dreams in a manner consistent with his/her stated theoretical frame of reference.	___	___	___	___	___
83. CONTRACTS—the counselor makes a contractual agreement with the client.	___	___	___	___	___
Other: _____	___	___	___	___	___
Other: _____	___	___	___	___	___
Other: _____	___	___	___	___	___

COUNSELOR COMPETENCY	ANALYSIS Skill Value to Interview			ASSESS-MENT Proficiency	
	Non-Essential	Important	Critical	+	–

ADJUNCTIVE ACTIVITIES

84. CASE NOTES—the counselor is able to communicate in a clear and concise manner initial, ongoing, and summary case notes.

85. STAFFING—the counselor can staff a case in a clear and concise manner by presenting an objective description of the client, significant information, goals for the client, strategy to be used, and a prognosis for the client.

86. TEST ADMINISTRATION—the counselor can administer test(s) according to the procedures in the test manual.

87. DIAGNOSIS—the counselor identifies cognitions, behaviors, and/or feelings in the client important in making a diagnosis according to the Diagnostic and Statistical Manual of Mental Disorders II.

88. APPOINTMENTS—the counselor is on time for his/ her appointments with clients, peers, and supervisors.

89. INFORMS—the counselor provides the client with factual information.

90. ORGANIZED—the counselor effectively organizes and completes the assigned work within the prescribed time limits of the setting in which he/she is employed.

91. DRESS—the counselor's attire is appropriate to the client population and work setting being served.

92. RESPONSIBILITIES—the counselor can clarify the role and responsibilities he/she and the client have in the counseling relationship according to his/her theoretical frame of reference.

93. ATMOSPHERE—within the limits of his/her work setting, the counselor provides an atmosphere that is physically and psychologically comfortable for the client.

94. CANCELLATIONS—the counselor notifies the client as soon as possible when he/she will be unable to keep an appointment.

95. COMPETENCY—the counselor is aware of and does not go beyond his/her counseling abilities.

COUNSELOR COMPETENCY	ANALYSIS Skill Value to Interview			ASSESS-MENT Proficiency	
	Non-Essential	Important	Critical	+	−
Other: _____	___	___	___	___	___
Other: _____	___	___	___	___	___
Other: _____	___	___	___	___	___

ETHICAL STANDARDS

96. PROFESSIONALISM—the counselor maintains a professional relationship with the client in accord with APA and/or APGA ethical standards.

97. ETHICS—the counselor adheres to the ethical standards outlined by the APA and/or APGA.

98. CONFIDENTIALITY—the counselor adheres to the ethical standards of confidentiality as outlined by the APA and/or APGA.

Other: _____

Other: _____

Other: _____

Form 5.7, p. 9 of 9, Copy 1

ETHICAL AND LEGAL GUIDELINES

Patrick B. Malley, Ph.D.

In Chapter 6 are addressed the ethical and legal definitions of confidentiality, privileged communication, and informed consent. This chapter also apprises the practicum students and interns of the rapidly changing nature of these concepts due to new legal mandates. Representative ethical codes also are presented in this chapter. The practicum student and intern should refer to these codes when information is needed regarding the ethical issues encountered in their training.

CONFIDENTIALITY, PRIVILEGED COMMUNICATION, AND INFORMED CONSENT

Confidentiality has long been considered an integral part of the helping professional's role with his/her clients. Most therapists agree that maintaining a right to privacy is a basic ingredient to maintaining human dignity. Client's rights to confidentiality are reflected in all of the ethical codes, some of which are exemplified in the following:

Summary of Ethical Codes on Confidentiality as issued by American Counseling Association (ACA, 1988) formerly the American Association for Counseling and Development (as revised by AACD Governing Council, March 1988):

Members make provisions for maintaining confidentiality in the storage and disposal of records and follow an established record retention and disposition policy. The counseling relationship and information resulting therefrom must be kept confidential, consistent with the obligations of the member as a professional person. In a group counseling setting, the counselor must set a norm of confidentiality regarding all group participants' disclosures.

Ethical Principles of Psychologists and Code of Conduct (APA, 1992):

Psychologists have a primary obligation and take reasonable precautions to respect the confidentiality rights of those with whom they work or consult, recognizing that confidentiality may be established by law, institutional rules, or professional or scientific relationships.

The origins of confidentiality in the therapeutic relationship came initially from the physician-patient relationship (Denkowski & Denkowski, 1982). The state of New York in 1828 was the first to legislate that patients had a right to confidentiality (Slovenko, 1973). Through the next 100 years, most of the states came to this recognition also. Since psychiatrists were medical doctors, this confidential mandate also was extended to them in their therapeutic endeavors. Finally, therapists who were not medical doctors were included in the context of those who, by law and by ethical mandate, included confidentiality as part of the client/therapist contract. Today those in the helping professions regard confidentiality as primary constituent factor in the therapeutic relationship.

Confidentiality initially was defined as a professional ethic under which the client is protected from unauthorized disclosures by the professional without the consent of the client. Confidentiality is an explicit contract between the therapist and client to reveal nothing about the client except under conditions agreed to by the client (Siegel, 1979).

Initially many professionals believed that in order for counseling relationships to be beneficial, an absolute standard of confidentiality had to be adhered to (Hollander, 1965). As time progressed, viewing confidentiality as an absolute construct became increasingly more difficult both from an ethical and legal standpoint, and those in the helping professions began to view it as limited rather than absolute. Probably legal mandates provided the impetus for the change in the ethical codes. The primary legal constraints that have had influence on how confidentiality in therapeutic relationships is construed are as follows:

1. The *Tarasoff* Case. The California Supreme Court rules that therapists may need to break confiden-

tiality to protect others who are in eminent danger.

2. Law suits are brought against doctors and institutions for not providing adequate care for suicidal patients.

3. The enactment of child abuse laws requires professionals to report such cases. (The *Tarasoff* Case, suicide, and child abuse are reviewed in Chapter 8.)

In summary, the concept of confidentiality in professional relationships evolved over time. Initially, it generally was regarded as absolute. However, in recent years, changes in legal and ethical thinking have moved professionals to believe confidentiality in the therapeutic relationship is limited. Confidentiality should be broken given the manifestation of a certain criterion. The criterion for limited confidentiality is that the client presents a serious and imminent danger to the client or to others.

Privileged communication is a right granted by law to certain professionals not to testify in court regarding confidential information obtained within their professional relationship. Privileged communication originated in common law and has expanded over the years through legislative bodies. McDermott (1975) stated the reason for the existence of privileged communications.

> The nature of any particular physical or emotional anguish may be so intimate, suggestive or potentially injurious, that disclosure of the facts would subject the citizen to undue pain, loss of stature or injury to reputation. The citizen would be most reluctant to engage in helping relationships with the helping professionals if the intimacies of his private life were vulnerable to exposure on the entire public. (p. 25)

Privileged communication laws are construed strictly by the courts. Consequently, each practicum student and intern should be aware of what statutes exist in the state in which he/she is practicing. Care should be taken that the exact word of the law is taken. As an example, Virginia grants privileges to counselors, social workers, and psychologists in civil cases, not criminal cases. The law does not name school counselors or clerical workers who maintain school records (Hummel, Talbutt, & Alexander, 1985).

In contrast, Pennsylvania school counselors and school clerks are extended the privilege. The following is an example of Pennsylvania law regarding privileged communication:

Act 287 (1972)

Amending the act of March 10, 1949 (P.L.30), entitled "An act relating to the public school system, including certain provisions applicable as well to private and parochial schools; amending, revising, consolidating and changing the laws relating thereto," providing for confidentiality of student communications.

The General Assembly of the Commonwealth of Pennsylvania hereby enacts as follows:

Section 1. The act of March 10, 1949, P.L.30), known as the "Public School Code of 1949", is amended by adding after section 1318, a new section to read:

Section 1319. Confidentiality of Student Communications— No guidance counselor, school nurse or school psychologist in the public schools or in private or parochial schools or other educational institutions providing elementary or secondary education, including any clerical worker of such schools and institutions, who, while in the course of his/her professional duties for a guidance counselor, school nurse or school psychologist, has acquired information from a student in confidence shall be compelled or allowed, without the consent of the student, if the student is eighteen (18) years of age or over, if the student is under the age of eighteen (18) years, without the consent of his or her parent or legal guardian, to disclose that information in any legal proceeding, civil or criminal, trial, investigation before any grand, traverse, or petit jury, or any officer thereof, before the General Assembly or any committee thereof, or before any commission, department or bureau of this Commonwealth, or municipal body, officer of committee thereof. Notwithstanding the confidentiality provisions of this section, no such person shall be excused or prevented from complying with the act of August 14, 1967 (P.L. 239), entitled "An act relating to gross physical neglect of, or injury to, children under eighteen years of age; requiring reports in such cases by examining physicians or heads of institutions to county public child welfare agencies; imposing powers and duties on county public child welfare agencies based on such reports; and providing penalties." (p. 1335)

Given that the client has a right to privacy, then a valid procedure is to inform him/her if any limits exist to confidentiality that could possibly endanger that right. Some argue that to inform the clients of all the myriad right they have is a detriment to the therapeutic relationship, giving rise to fears that are nonexistent. On the other hand, others believe that a client should be given every opportunity to reflect on whether or not he/she wants to waive any rights and that if the therapist shows sensitivity to this issue, it will nurture a trusting relationship. Today many therapists, although not all, routinely inform their clients that if they present a serious harm to themselves or others, confidentiality may have to be broken. Ideally this should be done before therapy starts.

Many writers think that a client should be informed of other variables that possibly could influence his/her consent. Some of the variables are as follows:

1. What counseling techniques are going to be used?

2. Why are these techniques more appropriate to a particular client's presenting symptoms?

3. What other techniques have been found useful and beneficial to similar clients?

4. How long will the counseling/therapy take place?

5. What risks are involved in the treatment?

6. What are the professional background, credentials, and experience of the counselor/psychologist?

7. What are the resulting benefits of the treatment?

8. After the treatment has started, may questions be asked about the procedures being used?

9. When and with whom can the client review his/her records?

10. Can the client withdraw from the treatment at any time?

11. Will the sessions be supervised and, if so, by whom?

12. Will electronic systems such as audiotapes or videotapes be used? If so,

    a. Who will view and/or hear the tapes?

    b. How long will the tapes be kept?

13. Has the therapist been granted privileged communication?

_____ _____

ETHICAL PRINCIPLES OF PSYCHOLOGISTS AND CODE OF CONDUCT*

American Psychological Association

PREAMBLE

Psychologists work to develop a valid and reliable body of scientific knowledge based on research. They may apply that knowl-

_____

edge to human behavior in a variety of contexts. In doing so, they perform many roles, such as researcher, educator, diagnostician, therapist, supervisor, consultant, administrator, social interventionist, and expert witness. Their goal is to broaden knowledge of behavior and, where appropriate, to apply it pragmatically to improve the condition of both the individual and society. Psychologists respect the central importance of freedom of inquiry and expression in research, teaching, and publication. They also strive to help the public in developing informed judgments and choices concerning human behavior. This Ethics Code provides a common set of values upon which psychologists build their professional and scientific work.

This Code is intended to provide both the general principles and the decision rules to cover most situations encountered by psychologists. It has as its primary goal the welfare and protection of the individuals and groups with whom psychologists work. It is the individual responsibility of each psychologist to aspire to the highest possible standards of conduct. Psychologists respect and protect human and civil rights, and do not knowingly participate in or condone unfair discriminatory practices.

The development of a dynamic set of ethical standards for a psychologist's work-related conduct requires a personal commitment to a lifelong effort to act ethically; to encourage ethical behavior by students, supervisees, employees, and colleagues, as appropriate; and to consult with others, as needed, concerning ethical problems. Each psychologist supplements, but does not violate, the Ethics Code's values and rules on the basis of guidance drawn from personal values, culture, and experience.

GENERAL PRINCIPLES

Principle A: Competence

Psychologists strive to maintain high standards of competence in their work. They recognize the boundaries of their particular competencies and the limitations of their expertise. They provide only those services and use only those techniques for which they are qualified by education, training, or experience. Psychologists are cognizant of the fact that the competencies required in serving, teaching, and/or studying groups of people vary with the distinctive characteristics of those groups. In those areas in which recognized professional standards do not yet exist, psychologists exercise careful judgment and take appropriate precautions to protect the welfare of those with whom they work. They maintain knowledge of relevant scientific and professional information related to the services they render, and they recognize the need for ongoing education. Psychologists make appropriate use of scientific, professional, technical, and administrative resources.

Principle B: Integrity

Psychologists seek to promote integrity in the science, teaching, and practice of psychology. In these activities psychologists are honest, fair, and respectful of others. In describing or reporting their qualifications, services, products, fees, research, or teaching, they do not make statements that are false, misleading, or deceptive. Psychologists strive to be aware of their own belief systems, values, needs, and limitations and the effect of these on their work. To the extent feasible, they attempt to clarify for relevant parties the roles they are performing and to function appropriately in accordance with those roles. Psychologists avoid improper and potentially harmful dual relationships.

Principle C: Professional and Scientific Responsibility

Psychologists uphold professional standards of conduct, clarify their professional roles and obligations, accept appropriate responsibility for their behavior, and adapt their methods to the needs of different populations. Psychologists consult with, refer to, or cooperate with other professionals and institutions to the extent needed to serve the best interests of their patients, clients, or other recipients of their services. Psychologists' moral standards and conduct are personal matters to the same degree as is true for any other person, except as psychologists' conduct may compromise their professional responsibilities or reduce the public's trust in psychology and psychologists. Psychologists are concerned about the ethical compliance of their colleagues' scientific and professional conduct. When appropriate, they consult with colleagues in order to prevent or avoid unethical conduct.

Principle D: Respect for People's Rights and Dignity

Psychologists accord appropriate respect to the fundamental rights, dignity, and worth of all people. They respect the rights of individuals to privacy, confidentiality, self-determination, and autonomy, mindful that legal and other obligations may lead to inconsistency and conflict with the exercise of these rights. Psychologists are aware of cultural, individual, and role differences, including those due to age, gender, race, ethnicity, national origin, religion, sexual orientation, disability, language, and socioeconomic status. Psychologists try to eliminate the effect on their work of biases based on those factors, and they do not knowingly participate in or condone unfair discriminatory practices.

Principle E: Concern for Others' Welfare

Psychologists seek to contribute to the welfare of those with whom they interact professionally. In their professional actions, psychologists weigh the welfare and rights of their patients or clients, students, supervisees, human research participants, and other affected persons, and the welfare of animal subjects of research. When conflicts occur among psychologists' obligations or concerns, they attempt to resolve these conflicts and to perform their roles in a responsible fashion that avoids or minimizes harm. Psychologists are sensitive to real and ascribed differences in power between themselves and others, and they do not exploit or mislead other people during or after professional relationships.

Principle F: Social Responsibility

Psychologists are aware of their professional and scientific responsibilities to the community and the society in which they work and live. They apply and make public their knowledge of psychology in order to contribute to human welfare. Psychologist are concerned about and work to mitigate the causes of human suffering. When undertaking research, they strive to advance human welfare and the science of psychology. Psychologists try to avoid misuse of their work. Psychologists comply with the law and encourage the development of law and social policy that serve the interests of their patients and clients and the public. They are encouraged to contribute a portion of their professional time for little or no personal advantage.

ETHICAL STANDARDS

1.   General Standards

These General Standards are potentially applicable to the professional and scientific activities of all psychologists.

1.01   Applicability of the Ethics Code

The activity of a psychologist subject to the Ethics Code may be reviewed under these Ethical Standards only if the activity is part of his or her work-related functions or the activity is psychological in nature. Personal activities having no connection to or effect on psychological roles are not subject to the Ethics Code.

1.02   Relationship of Ethics and Law

If psychologists' ethical responsibilities conflict with law, psychologists make known their commitment to the Ethics Code and take steps to resolve the conflict in a responsible manner.

1.03   Professional and Scientific Relationship

Psychologists provide diagnostic, therapeutic, teaching, research, supervisory, consultative, or other psychological services only in the context of a defined professional or scientific relationship or role. (See also Standards 2.01. Evaluation, Diagnosis, and Interventions in Professional Context, and 7.02, Forensic Assessments.)

1.04   Boundaries of Competence

(a) Psychologists provide services, teach, and conduct research only within the boundaries of their competence, based on the education, training, supervised experience, or appropriate professional experience.

(b) Psychologists provide services, teach, or conduct research in new areas or involving new techniques only after first undertaking appropriate study, training, supervision, and/or consultation from persons who are competent in those areas or techniques.

(c) In those emerging areas in which generally recognized standards for preparatory training do not yet exist, psychologists nevertheless take reasonable steps to ensure the competence of their work and to protect patients, clients, students, research participants, and others from harm.

1.05   Maintaining Expertise

Psychologists who engage in assessment, therapy, teaching, research, organizational consulting, or other professional activities maintain a reasonable level of awareness of current scientific and professional information in their fields of activity, and undertake ongoing efforts to maintain competence in the skills they use.

1.06   Basis for Scientific and Professional Judgments

Psychologists rely on scientifically and professionally derived knowledge when making scientific or professional judgments or when engaging in scholarly or professional endeavors.

1.07   Describing the Nature and Results of Psychological Services

(a) When psychologists provide assessment, evaluation, treatment, counseling, supervision, teaching, consultation, research, or other psychological services to an individual, a group, or an organization, they provide, using language that is reasonably understandable to the recipient of those services, appropriate information beforehand about the nature of such services and appropriate information later about results and conclusions. (See also Standard 2.09, Explaining Assessment Results.)

(b) If psychologists will be precluded by law or by organizational roles from providing such information to particular individuals or groups, they so inform those individuals or groups at the outset of the service.

1.08   Human Differences

Where differences of age, gender, race, ethnicity, national origin, religion, sexual orientation, disability, language, or socioeconomic status significantly affect psychologists' work concerning particular individuals or groups, psychologists obtain the training, experience, consultation, or supervision necessary to ensure the competence of their services, or they make appropriate referrals.

1.09   Respecting Others

In their work-related activities, psychologists respect the rights of others to hold values, attitudes, and opinions that differ from their own.

1.10   Nondiscrimination

In their work-related activities, psychologists do not engage in unfair discrimination based on age, gender, race, ethnicity, national origin, religion, sexual orientation, disability, socioeconomic status, or any basis proscribed by law.

1.11   Sexual Harassment

(a) Psychologists do not engage in sexual harassment. Sexual harassment is sexual solicitation, physical advances, or verbal or non-verbal conduct that is sexual in nature, that occurs in connection with the psychologist's activities or roles as a psychologist, and that either; (a) is unwelcome, is offensive, or creates a hostile workplace environment, and the psychologist knows or is told this: or (2) is sufficiently severe or intense to be abusive to a reasonable person in the context. Sexual harassment can consist of a single intense or severe act or of multiple persistent or pervasive acts.

1.12   Other Harassment

Psychologists do not knowingly engage in behavior that is harassing or demeaning to persons with whom they interact in their work based on factors such as those persons' age, gender, race ethnicity, national origin, religion, sexual orientation, disability, language, or socioeconomic status.

1.13   Personal Problems and Conflicts

(a) Psychologists recognize that their personal problems and conflicts may interfere with their effectiveness. Accordingly, they refrain from undertaking an activity when they know or should know that their personal problems are likely to lead to harm to a patient, client, colleague, students, research participant, or other person to whom they may owe a professional or scientific obligation.

(b) In addition, psychologists have an obligation to be alert to signs of, and to obtain assistance for, their personal problems at an early stage, in order to prevent significantly impaired performance.

(c) When psychologists become aware of personal problems that may interfere with their performing work-related duties adequately, they take appropriate measures, such as obtaining professional consultation or assistance, and determine whether they should limit, suspend, or terminate their work-related duties.

1.14   Avoiding Harm

Psychologist take reasonable steps to avoid harming their patients or clients, research participants, students, and others with whom they work, and to minimize harm where it is foreseeable and unavoidable.

1.15   Misuse of Psychologists' Influence

Because psychologists' scientific and professional judgments and actions may affect the lives of others, they are alert to and guard against personal, financial, social, organizational, or political factors that might lead to misuse of their influence.

1.16   Misuse of Psychologists' Work

(a) Psychologists do not participate in activities in which it appears likely that their skills or data will be misused by others, unless corrective mechanisms are available. (See also Standard 7.04, Truthfulness and Candor.)

(b) If psychologists learn of misuse or misrepresentation of their work, they take reasonable steps to correct or minimize the misuse or misrepresentation.

1.17   Multiple Relationships

(a) In many communities and situations, it may not be feasible or reasonable for psychologists to avoid social or other nonprofessional contacts with persons such as patients, clients, students, supervisees, or research participants. Psychologists must always be sensitive to the potential harmful effects of other contacts on their work and on those persons with whom they deal. A psychologist refrains from entering into or promising another personal, scientific, professional, financial, or other relationship with such persons if it appears likely that such a relationship reasonably might impair the psychologist's objectivity or otherwise interfere with the psychologist's effectively performing his or her functions as a psychologist, or might harm or exploit the other party.

(b) Likewise, whenever feasible, a psychologist refrains from taking on professional or scientific obligations when preexisting relationships would create a risk of such harm.

(c) If a psychologist finds that, due to unforeseen factors, a potentially harmful multiple relationship has arisen, the psychologist attempts to resolve it with due regard for the best interests of the affected person and maximal compliance with the Ethics Code.

1.18   Barter (With Patients or Clients)

Psychologists ordinarily refrain from accepting goods, services, or other nonmonetary remuneration from patients or clients in return for psychological services because such arrangements create inherent potential for conflicts, exploitation, and distortion of the professional relationship. A psychologist may participate in bartering *only* if (1) it is not clinically contraindicated, *and* (2) the relationship is not exploitative. (See also Standards 1.17, Multiple Relationships, and 1.25, Fees and Financial Arrangements.)

1.19   Exploitative Relationships

(a) Psychologists do not exploit persons over whom they have supervisory, evaluative, or other authority such as students, supervisees, employees, research participants, and clients or patients. (See also Standards 4.05–4.07 regarding sexual involvement with clients or patients.)

(b) Psychologists do not engage in sexual relationships with students or supervisees in training over whom the psychologist has evaluative or direct authority, because such relationships are so likely to impair judgment or be exploitative.

1.20   Consultations and Referrals

(a) Psychologists arrange for appropriate consultations and referrals based principally on the best interests of their patients or clients, with appropriate consent, and subject to other relevant considerations, including applicable law and contractual obligations. (See also Standards 5.01, Discussing the Limits of Confidentiality, and 5.06, Consultations.)

(b) When indicated and professionally appropriate, psychologists cooperate with other professionals in order to serve their patients or clients effectively and appropriately.

(c) Psychologists' referral practices are consistent with law.

1.21   Third-Party Requests for Services

(a) When a psychologist agrees to provide services to a person or entity at the request of a third party, the psychologist clarifies to the extent feasible, at the outset of the service, the nature of the relationship with each party. This clarification includes the role of the psychologist (such as therapist, organizational consultant, diagnostician, or expert witness), the probable uses of the services provided or the information obtained, and the fact that there may be limits to confidentiality.

(b) If there is a foreseeable risk of the psychologist's being called upon to perform conflicting roles because of the involvement of a third part, the psychologist clarifies the nature and direction of his or her responsibilities, keeps all parties appropriately informed as matters develop, and resolves the situation in accordance with this Ethics Code.

1.22   Delegation to and Supervision of Subordinates

(a) Psychologists delegate to their employees, supervisees, and research assistants only those responsibilities that such persons can reasonably be expected to perform competently, on the basis of their education, training, or experience, either independently or with the level of supervision being provided.

(b) Psychologists provide proper training and supervision to their employees or supervisees and take reasonable steps to see that such persons perform services responsibly, competently, and ethically.

(c) If Institutional policies, procedures, or practices prevent fulfillment of this obligation, psychologists attempt to modify their role or to correct the situation to the extent feasible.

1.23   Documentation of Professional and Scientific Work

(a) Psychologists appropriately document their professional and scientific work in order to facilitate provision of services later by them or by other professionals, to ensure accountability, and to meet other requirements of institutions or the law.

(b) When psychologists have reason to believe that records of their professional services will be used in legal proceedings involving recipients of or participants in their work, they have a responsibility to create and maintain documentation in the kind of detail and quality that would be consistent with reasonable scrutiny in an adjudicative forum. (See also Standard 7.01, Professionalism, under Forensic Activities.)

1.24   Records and Data

Psychologists create, maintain, disseminate, store, retain, and dispose of records and data relating to their research, practice, and other work in accordance with law and in a manner that permits compliance with the requirements of this Ethics Code. (See also Standard 5.04, Maintenance of Records.)

1.25   Fees and Financial Arrangements

(a) As early as is feasible in a professional or scientific relationship, the psychologist and the patient, client, or other appropriate recipient of psychological services reach an agreement specifying the compensation and the billing arrangements.

(b) Psychologists do not exploit recipients of services or payors with respect to fees.

(c) Psychologists' fee practices are consistent with law.

(d) Psychologists do not misrepresent their fees.

(e) If limitations to services can be anticipated because of limitations in financing, this is discussed with the patient, client, or other appropriate recipient of services as early as is feasible. (See also Standard 4.08, Interruption of Services.)

(f) If the patient, client, or other recipient of services does not pay for services as agreed, and if the psychologist wishes to use collection agencies or legal measures to collect the fees, the psychologist first informs the person that such measures will be taken and provides that person an opportunity to make prompt payment. (See also Standard 5.11, Withholding Records for Nonpayment.)

1.26   Accuracy in Reports to Payors and Funding Sources

In their reports to payors for services or sources of research funding, psychologists accurately state that nature of the research or service provided, the fees or charges, and where applicable, the identity of the provider, the findings, and the diagnosis. (See also Standard 5.05, Disclosures.)

1.27 Referrals and Fees

When a psychologist pays, receives payment from, or divides fees with another professional other than in an employer-employee relationship, the payment to each is based on the services (clinical, consultative, administrative, or other provided and is not based on the referral itself.

2. Evaluation, Assessment, or Intervention

2.01 Evaluation, Diagnosis, and Interventions in Professional Context

(a) Psychologists perform evaluations, diagnostic services, or interventions only within the context of a defined professional relationship. (See also Standard 1.03, Professional and Scientific Relationship.)

(b) Psychologists' assessments, recommendations, reports, and psychological diagnostic or evaluative statements are based on information and techniques (including personal interviews of the individual when appropriate) sufficient to provide appropriate substantiation for their findings. (See also Standard 7.02, Forensic Assessments.)

2.02 Competence and Appropriate Use of Assessments and Interventions

(a) Psychologists who develop, administer, score, interpret, or use psychological assessment techniques, interventions, results, and interpretations and take reasonable steps to prevent others from misusing the information these techniques provide. This includes refraining from releasing raw test results or raw data to persons, other than to patients or clients as appropriate, who are not qualified to use such information. (See also Standards 1.02, Relationship of Ethics and Law, and 1.04, Boundaries of Competence.)

2.03 Test Construction

Psychologists who develop and conduct research with tests and other assessment techniques use scientific procedures and current professional knowledge for test design, standardization, validation, reduction or elimination of bias, and recommendations for use.

2.04 Use of Assessment in General and With Special Populations

(a) Psychologists who perform interventions or administer, score, interpret, or use assessment techniques are familiar with the reliability, validation, and related standardization or outcome studies of, and proper applications and uses of, the techniques they use.

(b) Psychologists recognize limits to the certainty with which diagnoses, judgments, or predictions can be made about individuals.

(c) Psychologists attempt to identify situations in which particular interventions or assessment techniques or norms may not be applicable or may require adjustment in administration or interpretation because of factors such as individuals' gender, age, race, ethnicity, national origin, religion, sexual orientation, disability, language, or socioeconomic status.

2.05 Interpreting Assessment Results

When interpreting assessment results, including automated interpretations, psychologists take into account the various test factors and characteristics of the person being assessed that might affect psychologists' judgments or reduce the accuracy of their interpretations. They indicate any significant reservations they have about the accuracy or limitations of their interpretations.

2.06 Unqualified Persons

Psychologists do not promote the use of psychological assessment techniques by unqualified persons. (See also Standard 1.22, Delegation to and Supervision of Subordinates.)

2.07 Obsolete Tests and Outdated Test Results

(a) Psychologists do not base their assessment or intervention decisions or recommendations on data or test results that are outdated for the current purpose.

(b) Similarly, psychologists do not base such decisions or recommendations on tests and measures that are obsolete and not useful for the current purpose.

2.08 Test Scoring and Interpretation Services

(a) Psychologists who offer assessment or scoring procedures to other professionals accurately describe the purpose, norms, validity, reliability, and applications of the procedures and any special qualifications applicable to their use.

(b) Psychologists select scoring and interpretation services (including automated services) on the basis of evidence of the validity of the program and procedures as well as on other appropriate considerations.

(c) Psychologists retain appropriate responsibility for the appropriate application, interpretation, and use of assessment instruments, whether they score and interpret such tests themselves or use automated or other services.

2.09 Explaining Assessment Results

Unless the nature of the relationship is clearly explained to the person being assessed in advance and precludes provision of an explanation of results (such as in some organizational consulting, preemployment or security screenings, and forensic evaluations), psychologists ensure that an explanation of the results is provided using language that is reasonably understandable to the person assessed or to another legally authorized person on behalf of the client. Regardless of whether the scoring and interpretation are done by the psychologist, by assistants, or by automated or other outside services, psychologists take reasonable steps to ensure the appropriate explanations of results are given.

2.10 Maintaining Test Security

Psychologists make reasonable efforts to maintain the integrity and security of tests and other assessment techniques consistent with law, contractual obligations, and in a manner that permits compliance with the requirements of this Ethics Code, (See also Standard 1.02, Relationship of Ethics and Law.)

3.   Advertising and Other Public Statements

3.01   Definition of Public Statements

Psychologists comply with this Ethics Code in public statements relating to their professional services, products, or publications or to the field of psychology. Public statements include but are not limited to paid or unpaid advertising, brochures, printed matter, director listings, personal resumes or curricula vitae, interview or comments for use in media, statements in legal proceedings, lectures and public oral presentations, and published materials.

3.02   Statements by Others

(a) Psychologists who engage others to create or place public statements that promote their professional practice, products, or activities retain professional responsibility for such statements.

(b) In addition, psychologists make reasonable efforts to prevent others whom they do not control (such as employers, publishers, sponsors, organizational clients, and representatives of the print or broadcast media) from making deceptive statements concerning psychologists' practice or professional or scientific activities.

(c) If psychologists learn of deceptive statements about their work made by others, psychologists make reasonable efforts to correct such statements.

(d) Psychologists do not compensate employees of press, radio, television, or other communication media in return for publicity in a news item.

(e) A paid advertisement relating to the psychologist's activities must be identified as such, unless it is already apparent from the context.

3.03   Avoidance of False or Deceptive Statements

(a) Psychologists do not make public statements that are false, deceptive, misleading, or fraudulent, either because of what they state, convey, or suggest or because of what they omit, concerning their research, practice, or other work activities or those of persons or organizations with which they are affiliated. As examples (and not in limitation) of this standard, psychologists do not make false or deceptive statements concerning (1) their training, experience, or competence; (2) their academic degrees; (3) their credentials; (4) their institutional or association affiliations; (5) their services; (6) the scientific or clinical basis for, or results or degree of success of, their services; (7) their fees; or (8) their publications or research findings. (See also Standards 6.15, Deception in Research, and 6.18, Providing Participants With Information About the Study.)

(b) Psychologists claim as credentials for their psychological work, only degrees that (1) were earned from a regionally accredited educational institution or (2) were the basis for psychology licensure by the state in which the practice.

3.04   Media Presentations

When psychologists provide advice or comment by means of public lectures, demonstrations, radio or television programs, prerecorded tapes, printed articles, mailed material, or other media, they take reasonable precautions to ensure that (1) the statements are based on appropriate psychological literature and practice, (2) the statements are otherwise consistent with this Ethics Code, and (3) the recipients of the information are not encouraged to infer that a relationship has been established with them personally.

3.05   Testimonials

Psychologists do not solicit testimonials from current psychotherapy clients or patients or other persons who because of their particular circumstances are vulnerable to undue influence.

3.06   In-Person Solicitation

Psychologists do not engage, directly or through agents, in uninvited in-person solicitation of business from actual or potential psychotherapy patients or clients or other person who because of their particular circumstances are vulnerable to undue influence. However, this does not preclude attempting to implement appropriate collateral contacts with significant others for the purpose of benefiting an already engaged therapy patient.

4.   Therapy

4.01   Structuring the Relationship

(a) Psychologists discuss with clients or patients as early as is feasible in the therapeutic relationship appropriate issues, such as the nature and anticipated course of therapy, fees, and confidentiality. (See also Standards 1.25, Fees and Financial Arrangements, and 5.01, Discussing the Limits of Confidentiality.)

(b) When the psychologist's work with clients or patients will be supervised, the above discussion includes that fact, and the name of the supervisor, when the supervisor has legal responsibility for the case.

(c) When the therapist is a student intern, the client or patient is informed of that fact.

(d) Psychologists make reasonable efforts to answer patients' questions and to avoid apparent misunderstandings about therapy. Whenever possible, psychologists provide oral and/or written information, using language that is reasonably understandable to the patient or client.

4.02   Informed Consent to Therapy

(a) Psychologists obtain appropriate informed consent to therapy or related procedures, using language that is reasonably understandable to participants. The content of informed consent will vary depending on many circumstances; however, informed consent generally implies that the person (1) has the capacity to consent, (2) has been informed of significant information concerning the procedure, (3) has freely and without undue influence expressed consent, and (4) consent has been appropriately documented.

(b) When persons are legally incapable of giving informed consent, psychologists obtain informed permission from a legally authorized person, if such substitute consent is permitted by law.

(c) In addition, psychologists (1) inform those persons who are legally incapable of giving informed consent about the proposed interventions in a manner commensurate with the persons' psychological capacities, (2) seek their assent to those interventions, and (3) consider such persons' preferences and best interests.

4.03   Couple and Family Relationships

(a) When a psychologist agrees to provide services to several persons who have a relationship (such as husband and wife or parents and children), the psychologist attempts to clarify at the outset (1) which of the individuals are patients or clients and (2) the relationship the psychologist will have with each person. This clarification includes the role of the psychologist and the probable uses of the services provided or the information obtained. (See also Standard 5.01, Discussing the Limits of Confidentiality.)

(b) As soon as it becomes apparent that the psychologist may be called on to perform potentially conflicting roles (such as marital counselor to husband and wife, and then witness for one party in a divorce proceeding), the psychologist attempts to clarify and adjust, or withdraw form, roles appropriately. (See also Standard 7.03, Clarification of Role, under Forensic Activities.)

4.04   Providing Mental Health Services to Those Served by Others

In deciding whether to offer or provide services to those already receiving mental health services elsewhere, psychologists carefully consider the treatment issues and the potential patient's or client's welfare. The psychologist discusses these issues with the patient or client, or another legally authorized person on behalf of the client, consults with the other service providers when appropriate, and proceeds with caution and sensitivity to the therapeutic issues.

4.05   Sexual Intimacies With Current Patients or Clients

Psychologists do not engage in sexual intimacies with current patients or clients.

4.06   Therapy With Former Sexual Partners

Psychologists do not accept as therapy patients or clients persons with whom they have engaged in sexual intimacies.

4.07   Sexual Intimacies With Former Therapy Patients

(a) Psychologists do not engage in sexual intimacies with a former therapy patient or client for at least two years after cessation or termination of professional services.

(b) Because sexual intimacies with a former therapy patient or client are so frequently harmful to the patient or client, and because such intimacies undermine public confidence in the psychology profession and thereby deter the public's use of needed services, psychologists do not engage in sexual intimacies with former therapy patients and clients even after a two-year interval except in the most unusual circumstances. The psychologist who engages in such activity after the two years following cessation or termination of treatment bears the burden of demonstrating that there has been no exploitation, in light of all relevant factors, including (1) the amount of time that has passed since therapy terminated, (2) the nature and duration of the therapy, (3) the circumstances of termination, (4) the patient's or client's per-

sonal history, (5) the patient's or client's current mental status, (6) the likelihood of adverse impact on the patient or client and others, and (7) any statements or actions made by the therapist during the course of therapy suggesting or inviting the possibility of a posttermination sexual or romantic relationship with the patient or client. (See also Standard 1.17, Multiple Relationships.)

4.08   Interruption of Services

(a) Psychologists make reasonable efforts to plan for facilitating care in the event that psychological services are interrupted by factors such as the psychologist's illness, death, unavailability, or relocation or by the client's relocation or financial limitations. (See also Standard 5.09, Preserving Records and Data.)

(b) When entering into employment or contractual relationships, psychologists provide for orderly and appropriate resolution of responsibility for patient client care in the event that the employment or contractual relationship ends, with paramount consideration given to the welfare of the patient or client.

4.09   Terminating the Professional Relationship

(a) Psychologists do not abandon patients or clients. (See also Standard 1.25e, under Fees and Financial Arrangements.)

(b) Psychologists terminate a professional relationship when it becomes reasonably clear that the patient or client no longer needs the service, is not benefiting, or is being harmed by continued service.

(c) Prior to termination for whatever reason, except where precluded by the patient's or client's conduct, the psychologist discusses the patient's or client's views and needs, provides appropriate predetermination counseling, suggests alternative service providers as appropriate, and takes other reasonable steps to facilitate transfer of responsibility to another provider if the patient or client needs one immediately.

5.   Privacy and Confidentiality

These Standards are potentially applicable to the professional and scientific activities of all psychologists.

5.01   Discussing the Limits of Confidentiality

(a) Psychologists discuss with persons and organizations with whom they establish a scientific or professional relationship (including, to the extent feasible, minors and their legal representatives) (1) the relevant limitations on confidentiality, including limitations where applicable in group, marital, and family therapy or in organizational consulting, and (2) the foreseeable uses of the information generated through their services.

(b) Unless it is not feasible or is contraindicated, the discussion of confidentiality occurs at the outset of the relationship and thereafter as new circumstances may warrant.

(c) Permission for electronic recording of interviews is secured from clients and patients.

5.02   Maintaining Confidentiality

Psychologists have a primary obligation and take reasonable precautions to respect the confidentiality rights of those with whom they work or consult, recognizing that confidentiality may be established by law, institutional rules, or professional or scientific relationships. (See also Standard Professional Reviewers.)

5.03   Minimizing Intrusions on Privacy

(a) In order to minimize intrusions on privacy, psychologists include in written and oral reports, consultations, and the like, only information germane to the purpose for which the communication is made.

(b) Psychologists discuss confidential information obtained in clinical or consulting relationships, or evaluative data concerning patients, individual or organizational clients, students, research participants, supervisees, and employees, only for appropriate scientific or professional purposes and only with persons clearly concerned with such matters.

5.04   Maintenance of Records

Psychologists maintain appropriate confidentiality in creating, storing, accessing, transferring, and disposing of records under their control, whether these are written, automated, or in any other medium. Psychologists maintain and dispose of records in accordance with law and in a manner that permits compliance with the requirements of this Ethics Code.

5.05   Disclosure

(a) Psychologists disclose confidential information without the consent of the individual only as mandated by law, or where permitted by law for a valid purpose, such as (1) to provide needed professional services to the patient or the individual or organizational client, (2) to obtain appropriate professional consultations, (3) to protect the patient or client or others from harm, or (4) to obtain payment for services, in which instance disclosure is limited to the minimum that is necessary to achieve the purpose.

(b) Psychologists also may disclose confidential information with the appropriate consent of the patient or the individual or organizational client (or of another legally authorized person on behalf of the patient or client), unless prohibited by law.

5.06   Consultations

When consulting with colleagues, (1) psychologists do not share confidential information that reasonably could lead to the identification of a patient, client, research participant, or other person or organization with whom they have a confidential relationship unless they have obtained the prior consent of the person or organization or the disclosure cannot be avoided, and (2) they share information only to the extent necessary to achieve the purposes of the consultation. (See also Standard 5.02, Maintaining Confidentiality.)

5.07   Confidential Information in Databases

(a) If confidential information concerning recipients of psychological services is to be entered into databases or systems of records available to persons whose access has not been consented to by the recipient, then psychologists use coding or other techniques to avoid the inclusion of personal identifiers.

(b) If a research protocol approved by an institutional review board or similar body requires the inclusion of personal identifiers, such identifiers are deleted before the information is made accessible to persons other than those of whom the subject was advised.

(c) If such deletion is not feasible, then before psychologists transfer such data to others or review such data collected by others, they take reasonable steps to determine that appropriate consent of personally identifiable individuals has been obtained.

5.08   Use of Confidential Information for Didactic or Other Purposes

(a) Psychologists do not disclose in their writings, lectures, or other public media, confidential, personally identifiable information concerning their patients, individual or organizational clients, students, research participants, or other recipients of their services that they obtained during the course of their work, unless the person or organization has consented in writing or unless there is other ethical or legal authorization for doing so.

(b) Ordinarily, in such scientific and professional presentations, psychologists disguise confidential information concerning such persons or organizations so that they are not individually identifiable to others and so that discussions do not cause harm to subjects who might identify themselves.

5.09   Preserving Records and Data

A psychologist makes plans in advance so that confidentiality of records and data is protected in the event of the psychologist's death, incapacity, or withdrawal from the position or practice.

5.10   Ownership of Records and Data

A psychologist makes plans in advance so that confidentiality of records and data is protected in the event of the psychologist's death, incapacity, or withdrawal from the position or practice.

5.11   Withholding Records for Nonpayment

Psychologists may not withhold records under their control that are requested and imminently needed for a patient's or client's treatment solely because payment has not been received, except as otherwise provided by law.

6.   Teaching, Training Supervision, Research, and Publishing

6.01   Design of Education and Training Programs

Psychologists who are responsible for education and training programs seek to ensure that the programs are competently designed, provide the proper experiences, and meet the requirements for licensure, certification, or other goals for which claims are made by the program.

6.02 Descriptions of Education and Training Programs

(a) Psychologists responsible for education and training programs seek to ensure that there is a current and accurate description of the program content, training goals and objectives, and requirements that must be met for satisfactory completion of the program. This information must be made readily available to all interested parties.

(b) Psychologists seek to ensure that statements concerning their course outlines are accurate and not misleading, particularly regarding the subject matters to be covered, bases for evaluating progress, and the nature of course experiences. (See also Standard 3.03, Avoidance of False or Deceptive Statements.)

(c) To the degree to which they exercise control, psychologists responsible for announcements, catalogs, brochures, or advertisements describing workshops, seminars, or other non-degree-granting educational programs ensure that they accurately describe the audience for which the program is intended, the educational objectives, the presenters, and the less involved.

6.03 Accuracy and Objectivity in Teaching

(a) When engaged in teaching or training, psychologists present psychological information accurately and with a reasonable degree of objectivity.

(b) When engaged in teaching or training, psychologists recognize the power they hold over students or supervisees and therefore make reasonable efforts to avoid engaging in conduct that is personally demeaning to students or supervisees. (See also Standards 1.09, Respecting Others, and 1.12, Other Harassment.)

6.04 Limitation on Teaching

Psychologists do not teach the use of techniques or procedures that require specialized training, licensure, or expertise, including but not limited to hypnosis, biofeedback, and projective techniques, to individuals who lack the prerequisite training, legal scope of practice, or expertise.

6.05 Assessing Student and Supervisee Performance

(a) In academic and supervisory relationships, psychologists establish an appropriate process for providing feedback to students and supervisees.

(b) Psychologists evaluate students and supervisees on the basis of their actual performance on relevant and established program requirements.

6.06 Planning Research

(a) Psychologists design, conduct, and report research in accordance with recognized standards of scientific competence and ethical research.

(b) Psychologists plan their research so as to minimize the possibility that result will be misleading.

(c) In planning research, psychologists consider its ethical acceptability under the Ethics Code. If an ethical issue is unclear, psychologists seek to resolve the issue through consultation with institutional review boards, animal care and use committees, peer consultations, or other proper mechanisms.

(d) Psychologists take reasonable steps to implement appropriate protections for the rights and welfare of human participants, other persons affected by the research, and the welfare of animal subjects.

6.07 Responsibility

(a) Psychologists conduct research competently and with due concern for the dignity and welfare of the participants.

(b) Psychologists are responsible for the ethical conduct of research conducted by them or by others under their supervision or control.

(c) Researchers and assistants are permitted to perform only those tasks for which they are appropriately trained and prepared.

(d) As part of the process of development and implementation of research projects, psychologists consult those with expertise concerning any special population under investigation or most likely to be affected.

6.08 Compliance With Law and Standards

Psychologists plan and conduct research in a manner consistent with federal and state law and regulations, as well as professional standards governing the conduct of research, and particularly those standards governing research with human participants and animal subjects.

6.09 Institutional Approval

Psychologists obtain from host institutions or organizations appropriate approval prior to conducting research, and they provide accurate information about their research proposals. They conduct the research in accordance with the approved research protocol.

6.10 Research Responsibilities

Prior to conducting research (except research involving only anonymous surveys, naturalistic observations, or similar research), psychologists enter into an agreement with participants that clarifies the nature of the research and the responsibilities of each party.

6.11 Informed Consent to Research

(a) Psychologists use language that is reasonably understandable to research participants in obtaining their appropriate informed consent (except as provided in Standard 6.12, Dispensing With Informed Consent). Such informed consent is appropriately documented.

(b) Using language that is reasonably understandable to participants, psychologists inform participants of the nature of the research; they inform participants that they are free to participate or to decline to participate or to withdraw from the research; they explain the foreseeable consequences of declining or withdrawing; they inform participants of significant factors that may be expected to influence their willingness to participate (such as risks, discomfort, adverse effects, or limitations on confidentiality, except as provided in Standard 6.15, Deception in Research); and they explain other aspects about which the prospective participants inquire.

(c) When psychologists conduct research with individuals such as students or subordinates, psychologists take special care to protect the prospective participants from adverse consequences of declining or withdrawing from participation.

(d) When research participation is a course requirement or opportunity for extra credit, the prospective participant is given the choice of equitable alternative activities.

(e) For persons who are legally incapable of given informed consent, psychologists nevertheless (1) provide an appropriate explanation, (2) obtain the participant's assent, and (3) obtain appropriate permission from a legally authorized person, if such substitute consent is permitted by law.

6.12   Dispensing With Informed Consent

Before determining that planned research (such as research involving only anonymous questionnaires, naturalistic observations, or certain kinds of archival research) does not require the informed consent of research participants, psychologists consider applicable regulations and institutional review board requirements, and they consult with colleagues as appropriate.

6.13   Informed Consent in Research Filming or Recording

Psychologists obtain informed consent from research participants prior to filming or recording them in any form, unless the research involves simply naturalistic observations in public places and it is not anticipated that the recording will be used in a manner that could cause personal identification or harm.

6.14   Offering Inducements for Research Participants

(a) In offering professional services as an inducement to obtain research participants, psychologists make clear the nature of the services, as well as the risks, obligations, and limitations. (See also Standard 1.18, Barter [With Patients or Clients].)

(b) Psychologists do not offer excessive or inappropriate financial or other inducements to obtain research participants, particularly when it might tend to coerce participation.

6.15   Deception in Research

(a) Psychologists do not conduct a study involving deception unless they have determined that the use of deceptive techniques is justified by the study's prospective scientific, educational, or applied value and that equally effective alternative procedures that do not use deception are not feasible.

(b) Psychologists never deceive research participants about significant aspects that would affect their willingness to participate, such as physical risks, discomfort, or unpleasant emotional experiences.

(c) Any other deception that is an integral feature of the design and conduct of an experiment must be explained to participants as early as is feasible, preferably at the conclusion of their participation, but no later than at the conclusion of the research. (See also Standard 6.18, Providing Participants With Information About the Study.)

6.16   Sharing and Utilizing Data

Psychologists inform research participants of their anticipated sharing or further use of personally identifiable research data an. of the possibility of unanticipated future uses.

6.17   Minimizing Invasiveness

In conducting research, psychologists interfere with the participants or milieu from which data are collected only in a manner that is warranted by an appropriate research design and that is consistent with psychologists' roles as scientific investigators.

6.18   Providing Participants With Information About the Study

(a) Psychologists provide a prompt opportunity for participants to obtain appropriate information about the nature, results, and conclusions of the research, and psychologists attempt to correct any misconceptions that participants may have.

(b) If scientific or humane values justify delaying or withholding this information, psychologists take reasonable measures to reduce the risk of harm.

6.19   Honoring Commitments

Psychologists take reasonable measures to honor all commitments they have made to research participants.

6.20   Care and Use of Animals in Research

(a) Psychologists who conduct research involving animals treat them humanely.

(b) Psychologists acquire, care for, use, and dispose of animals in compliance with current federal, state, and local laws and regulations, and with professional standards.

(c) Psychologists trained in research methods and experienced in the care of laboratory animals supervise all procedures involving animals and are responsible for ensuring appropriate consideration of their comfort, health, and humane treatment.

(d) Psychologists ensure that all individuals using animals under their supervision have received instruction in research methods and in the care, maintenance, and handling of the species being used, to the extent appropriate to their role.

(e) Responsibilities and activities of individuals assisting in a research project are consistent with their respective competencies.

(f) Psychologists make reasonable efforts to minimize the discomfort, infection, illness, and pain of animal subjects.

(g) A procedure subjecting animals to pain, stress, or privation is used only when an alternative procedure is unavailable and the goal is justified by its prospective scientific, educational, or applied value.

(h) Surgical procedures are performed under appropriate anesthesia; techniques to avoid infection and minimize pain are followed during and after surgery.

(i) When it is appropriate that the animal's life be terminated, it is done rapidly, with an effort to minimize pain, and in accordance with accepted procedures.

6.21 Reporting of Results

(a) Psychologists do not fabricate data or falsify results in their publications.

(b) If psychologists discover significant errors in their published data, they take reasonable steps to correct such errors in a correction, retraction, erratum, or other appropriate publication means.

6.22 Plagiarism

Psychologists do not present substantial portions or elements of another's work or data as their own, even if the other work or data source is cited occasionally.

6.23 Publication Credit

(a) Psychologists take responsibility and credit, including authorship credit, only for work they have actually performed or to which they have contributed.

(b) Principal authorship and other publication credits accurately reflect the relative scientific or professional contributions of the individuals involved, regardless of their relative status. Mere possession of an institutional position, such as Department Chair, does not justify authorship credit. Minor contributions to the research or to the writing for publications are appropriately acknowledged, such as in footnotes or in an introductory statement.

(c) A student is usually listed as principal author on any multiple-authored article that is substantially based on the student's dissertation or thesis.

6.24 Duplicate Publication of Data

Psychologists do not publish, as original data, data that have been previously published. This does not preclude republishing data when they are accompanied by proper acknowledgment.

6.25 Sharing Data

After research results are published, psychologists do not withhold the data on which their conclusions are based from other competent professionals who seek to verify the substantive claims through reanalysis and who intend to use such data only for that purpose, provided that the confidentiality of the participants can be protected and unless legal rights concerning proprietary data preclude their release.

6.26 Professional Reviewers

Psychologists who review material submitted for publication, grant, or other research proposal review respect the confidentiality of and the proprietary rights in such information of those who submitted it.

7. Forensic Activities

7.01 Professionalism

Psychologists who perform forensic functions, such as assessments, interviews, consultations, reports, or expert testimony, must comply with all other provisions of this Ethics Code to the extent that they apply to such activities. In addition, psychologists base their forensic work on appropriate knowledge of and competence in the areas underlying such work, including specialized knowledged concerning special populations. (See also Standards 1.06, Basis for Scientific and Professional Judgments; 1.08, Human Differences; 1.15, Misuse of Psychologists' Influence; and 1.23, Documentation of Professional and Scientific Work.)

7.02 Forensic Assessments

(a) Psychologists' forensic assessments, recommendations, and reports are based on information and techniques (including personal interviews of the individual, when appropriate) sufficient to provide appropriate substantiation for their findings. (See also Standards 1.03, Professional and Scientific Relationship; 1.23, Documentation of Professional and Scientific Work; 2.01, Evaluation, Diagnosis, and Interventions in Professional Context; and 2.05, Interpreting Assessment Results.)

(b) Except as noted in (c), below, psychologists provide written or oral forensic reports or testimony of the psychological characteristics of an individual only after they have conducted an examination of the individual adequate to support their statements or conclusions.

(c) When, despite reasonable efforts, such an examination is not feasible, psychologists clarify the impact of their limited information on the reliability and validity of their reports and testimony, and they appropriately limit the nature and extent of their conclusions or recommendations.

7.03 Clarification of Role

In most circumstances, psychologists avoid performing multiple and potentially conflicting roles in forensic matters. When psychologists may be called on to serve in more than one role in a legal proceeding—for example, as consultant or expert for one party or for the court and as a fact witness—they clarify role expectations and the extent of confidentiality in advance to the extent feasible, and thereafter as changes occur, in order to avoid compromising their professional judgment and objectivity and in order to avoid misleading others regarding their role.

7.04 Truthfulness and Candor

(a) In forensic testimony and reports, psychologists testify truthfully, honestly, and candidly and, consistent with applicable legal procedures, describe fairly the bases for their testimony and conclusions.

(b) Whenever necessary to avoid misleading, psychologists acknowledge the limits of their data or conclusions.

7.05 Prior Relationships

A prior professional relationship with a party does not preclude psychologists from testifying as fact witnesses or from testifying to their services to the extent permitted by applicable law. Psychologists appropriately take into account ways in which the prior relationship might affect their professional objectivity or opinions and disclose the potential conflict to the relevant parties.

7.06　Compliance With Law and Rules

In performing forensic roles, psychologists are reasonably familiar with the rules governing their roles. Psychologists are aware of the occasionally competing demands placed upon them by these principles and the requirements of the court system, and attempt to resolve these conflicts by making known their commitment to this Ethics Code and taking steps to resolve the conflict in a responsible manner. (See also Standard 1.02, Relationship of Ethics and Law.)

8.　Resolving Ethical Issues

8.01　Familiarity With Ethics Code

Psychologists have an obligation to be familiar with this Ethics Code, other applicable ethics codes, and their application to psychologists' work. lack of awareness or misunderstanding of an ethical standard is not itself a defense to a charge of unethical conduct.

8.02　Confronting Ethical Issues

When a psychologist is uncertain whether a particular situation or course of action would violate this Ethics Code, the psychologist ordinarily consults with other psychologists knowledgeable about ethical issues, with state or national psychology ethics committees, or with other appropriate authorities in order to choose a proper response.

8.03　Conflicts Between Ethics and Organizational Demands

If the demands of an organization with which psychologists are affiliated conflict with this Ethics. Code, psychologists clarify the nature of the conflict, make known their commitment to the Ethics Code, and to the extent feasible, seek to resolve the conflict in a way that premise the fullest adherence to the Ethics Code.

8.04　Informal Resolution of Ethical Violations

When psychologists believe that there may have been an ethical violation by another psychologist, they attempt to resolve the issue by bringing it to the attention of that individual if an informal resolution appears appropriate and the intervention does not violate any confidentiality rights that may be involved.

8.05　Reporting Ethical Violations

If an apparent ethical violation is not appropriate for informal resolution under Standard 8.04 or is not resolved properly in that fashion, psychologists take further action appropriate to the situation, unless such action conflicts with confidentiality rights in ways that cannot be resolved. Such action might include referral to state or national committees on professional ethics or to state licensing boards.

8.06　Cooperating With Ethics Committees

Psychologists cooperate in ethics investigations, proceedings, and resulting requirements of the APA or any affiliated state psychological association to which they belong. In doing so, they make

reasonable efforts to resolve any issues as to confidentiality. Failure to cooperate is itself an ethics violation.

8.07　Improper Complaints

Psychologists do not file or encourage the filing of ethics complaints that are frivolous and are intended to harm the respondent rather than to protect the public.

ETHICAL STANDARDS*
American Counseling Association
(As Revised by AACD Governing Council, March 1988)

PREAMBLE

The Association is an educational, scientific, and professional organization whose members are dedicated to the enhancement of the work, dignity, potential, and uniqueness of each individual and that to the service of society.

The Association recognizes that the role definitions and work settings of its members include a wide variety of academic disciplines, levels of academic preparation, and agency services. This diversity reflects the breath of the Association's interest and influence. It also poses challenging complexities in efforts to set standards for the performance of members, desired requisite preparation or practice, and supporting social, legal, and ethical controls.

The specification of ethical standards enables the Association to clarify to present and future members and to characterized by members the nature of ethical responsibilities held in common by its members.

The existence of such standards serves to stimulate greater concern by members, for their own professional functioning and for the conduct of fellow professionals such as counselors, guidance and student personnel workers, and others in the helping professions. As the ethical code of the Association, this document establishes principles that define the ethical behavior of Association members. Additional ethical guidelines developed by the Association's Divisions for their specialty areas may further define a member's ethical behavior.

Section A: General

1. The member influences the development of the profession by continuous efforts to improve professional practices, teaching, services, and research. Professional growth if continuous throughout the member's career and is exemplified by the development of a philosophy that explains why and how a member functions in the helping relationship. Members must gather data on their effectiveness and be guided by the findings. Members recognize the need for continuing education to ensure competent service.

2. The member has a responsibility both to the individual who is served and to the institution within which the service is performed to maintain high

---

standards of professional conduct. The member strives to maintain the highest levels of professional services offered to the individuals to be served. The member also strives to assist the agency, organization, or institution in providing the highest caliber of professional services. The acceptance of employment in an institution implies that the member is in agreement with the general policies and principles of the institution. Therefore the professional activities of the member are also in accord with the objectives of the institution. If, despite concerned efforts, the member cannot reach agreement with the employer as to acceptable students of conduct that allow for changes. In institutional policy conducive to the positive growth and development of client, then terminating the affiliation should be seriously considered.

3. Ethical behavior among professional associates, both members and nonmembers, must be expected at all times. When information is possessed that raises doubt as to the ethical behavior of professional colleagues, whether Association members or not, the member must take action in attempt to rectify such a condition. Such action shall use the institution's channels first and than use procedures established by the Association.

4. The member neither claims not implies professionals qualifications exceeding those possessed and it responsible for correcting any misrepresentations of these qualification by others.

5. In established fees for professional counseling services, members must consider the financial status of clients and locality. In the event that the established fee structure is inappropriate for client, assistance must be provided in finding comparable services of acceptable cost.

6. When members provide information to the public or to subordinates, peers, or supervisors, they have a responsibility to ensure that the contents is general unidentified client information that is accurate, unbiased, and consists of objective, actual data.

7. Members recognize their boundaries of competence and provide only those services and use only those techniques for which they may qualified by training or experience. Members should only accept those positions for which they are professionally qualified.

8. In the counseling relationship, the counselor is aware of the intimacy of the relationship and maintains respect for the effect and avoids engaging in activities that seek to meet the counselor's personnel needs at the expense of that client.

9. Members do not condom or engage in sexual harassment which is defined as deliberate or repeated comments, gestures, or physical contacts of a sexual nature.

10. The member avoids bringing personal issues into the counseling relationship, especially if the potential for harm is presented. Through awareness of the negative impact of both social and sexual stereotyping and discrimination, the counselor guards the individual rights and personal dignity of the client in the counseling relationship.

11. Product or services provided by the member by means of classroom instruction, public lectures, demonstrations, written articles, radio or television programs, or other types of media must meet the criteria cited in these standards.

Section B: Counseling Relationships

This section refers to practices and procedures of individual and/or group counseling relationships.

The member must recognize the need for client freedom of choice. Under those circumstances where this is not possible, the member must apprise clients of restrictions that may limit their freedom of choice.

1. The member's primary obligation is to respect the integrity and promote the welfare of the client(s), whether the client(s) is (and) assisted individually or in a group relationship. In a group seeking, the member is also responsible for taking reasonable precautions to protect individuals from physical and/or psychological trauma resulting from interaction within the group.

2. Members make provisions for maintaining confidentiality in the storage and disposal of records and follow an established record retention and disposition policy. The counseling relationship and information resulting therefrom must be kept confidential, consistent with the obligations of the member as a professional person. In a group counseling setting, the counselor must set a norm of confidentiality regarding all group participants' disclosures.

3. If an individual is already in a counseling relationship with another professional person, the member does not cater into a counseling relationship without first contacting and receiving the approval of that other professional. If the member discover that the client is in another counseling relationship after the counseling relationship begins, the member must gain the consent of the other professional or terminate the relationship, unless the client elects to terminate the other relationship.

4. When the client's condition indicates that there is clear and imminent danger to the client or others, the member must take reasonable personal action or inform responsible authorities. Consultation with other professionals must be used where possible. The assumption of responsibility for the client's(s') behavior must be taken only after careful deliberation. The client must be involved in the resumption of responsibility as quickly is possible.

5. Records of the counseling relationship, including interview notes, test data, correspondence, tape recordings, electronic data storage, and other documents are to be considered professional information for use in counseling, and they should not be considered a part of the records of the institution of agency in which the counselor is employed unless specified by some statute or regulation. Revision to others of counseling material must occur only upon the expressed consent of the client.

6. In view of the extensive data storage and protesting capacities of the computer, the member must ensure that data initialized on a computer is: (a) limited to information that is appropriate and necessary for the services being provided; (b) destroyed after it is determined that the information is no longer of any value in providing services; and (c) restricted in terms of access to appropriate staff members involved in the provision of services by using the best computer security methods available.

7. Use of data derived from a counseling relationship for purposes of counselor training or research shall be confined to content that can be disguised to ensure full protection of the identity of the subject client.

8. The member must inform the client of the purposes, goals, techniques, rules, of procedure, and limitations that may affect the relationship at or before the time that the counseling relationship is

entered. When working with minors or persons who are unable to give consent, the member protects these clients' best interests.

9. In view of common misconceptions related to the perceived validity of computer-generated data and comparative reports, the member must ensure that the client is provided with information as part of the counseling relationship that adequately explains the limitations of computer technology.

10. The member must screen prospective group participants, especially when the emphasis is on self-understanding and growth through self disclosure. The member must maintain an awareness of the group participants' compatibility throughout the life of the group.

11. The member may choose to consult with any other professionally competent person about a client. In choosing a consultant, the member must avoid placing the consultant in a conflict of interest situation that would preclude the consultant's being a proper party to the member's efforts to help the client.

12. If the member determines an inability to be of professional assistance to the client, the member must either avoid initialing the counseling relationship or immediately terminate that relationship or immediately terminate that relationship. In either event, the member must suggest appropriate alternatives. (The member must be knowledgeable about referral resources so that a satisfactory referral can be initiated.) In the event the client declines the suggested referral, the member is not obligated to continue the relationship.

13. When the member has other relationships, particularly of an administrative, supervisory, and/or evaluative mature with an individual seeking counseling services, the member must not serve as the counselor but should refer the individual to another professional. Only in instances where such a alternative is unavailable and where the individual's situation warrants counseling intervention should the member enter into and/or maintain a counseling relationship. Dual relationships with clients that might impair the member's objectivity and professional judgment (e.g., and with close friends or relatives), must be avoided and/or the counseling relationship terminated through referral to another competent professional.

14. The member will avoid any type of sexual intimates with clients. Sexual relationships with clients are unethical.

15. All experimental methods of treatment must be clearly indicated to prospective recipients, and safety presentations are to be adhered to by the member.

16. When computer applications are used as a component of counseling services, the member must ensure that (a) the client is intellectually, emotionally, and physically capable of using the computer applicator; (b) the computer application is appropriate for the needs of the client; (c) the client understands that purpose and operation of the computer application; and (d) a follow-up of client use of a computer application is provided to both correct possible problems (misconceptions or inappropriate use) and assess subsequent needs.

17. When the member is engaged in short-term group treatment/training programs (e.g., marathons and other encountertype or growth groups), the member ensures that there is professional assistance available during and following the group experience.

18. Should the member be engaged in a work setting that calls for any variation from the above statements, the member is obligated to consult with other professionals whenever possible to consider justifiable alternatives.

19. The member must ensure that members of various ethnic, racial, religious, disability, and socioeconomic groups have equal access to computer applications used to support counseling services and that the content of available computer applications does not discriminate against the groups described above.

20. When computer applications are developed by the member for use by the general public as self-help/stand-alone computer software the member must ensure that: (a) self-help computer applications are designed from the beginning to function in a stand-alone manner, as opposed to modifying software that was originally designed to require support from a counselor; (b) self-help computer applications will include within the program statements regarding intended user outcomes, suggestions for using the software, a description of the conditions under which self-help computer applications might not be appropriate, and a description for when and how counseling services might be beneficial; (c) the manual for such applications will include the qualifications of the developer, the development process, validation data, and operating procedures.

Section C: Measurement & Evaluation

The primary purpose of educational and psychological testing is to provide descriptive measures that are objective and interpretable in either comparative or absolute terms. The member must recognize the need to interpret the statements that follow as applying to the whole range of appraisal techniques including test and nontest data. Test results constitute only one of a variety of pertinent sources of information for personnel, guidance, and counseling decisions.

1. The member must provide specific orientation or information to the examinee(s) prior to and following the test administration so that the results of testing may be placed in proper perspective with other relevant factors. In so doing, the member must recognize the effects of socioeconomic, ethnic, and cultural factors on test scores. It is the member's professional responsibility to use additional invalidated information carefully in modifying interpretation of the test results.

2. In selecting tests for use in a given situation or with a particular client, the member must consider carefully the specific validity, reliability, and appropriateness of the test(s). General validity, reliability, and related issues may be questioned legally as well as ethically when tests we used for vocational and educational selection, placement, or counseling.

3. When making any statements to the public about tests and testing the member must give accurate information and avoid false claims or misconceptions. Special efforts are often required to avoid unwarranted connotations of such termed as IQ and grade equivalent scores.

4. Different tests demand different level of competence for administration scoring and interpretation. Members must recognize the limits of their competence and perform only those functions for which they are prepared. In particular, members using computer-based test interpretations must be trained in the construct being measured and the specific instrument being used prior to using this type of computer applications.

5. In situations where a computer is used for test administration and scoring, the member is responsible for ensuring that administration and scoring programs function properly to provide clients with accurate test results.

6. Tests must be administered under the same conditions that were established in their standardization. When tests are not administered under standard conditions or when unusual behavior or occur during the testing session, those conditions must be noted and the results designated as invalid or of questionable validity. Unsupervised or inadequately supervised test-taking, such as the use of tests through the mails, is considered unethical. On the other had, the use of instruments that are so designed or standardized to be self-administrated and self-scored, such as interest inventories, is to encouraged.

7. The meaningfulness of test results used is personnel, guidance, and counseling functions general depends on the examinee's unfamiliarity with the specific issues on the test. Any prior coaching or discrimination of the test material can invalidate test results. Therefore, test security is one of the professional obligations of the member. Conditions that produce most favorable test results must be made known to the examinee.

8. The purpose of testing had the explicit use of the result must be made known to the examinee prior to testing. The counselor must ensure that instrument limitations are not exceeded and that periodic review and/or retesting are made to prevent client stereotyping.

9. The examinee's welfare and explicit prior understanding must be the criteria for determining the recipients of the test results. The member must see that specific interpretation accompanies any release of individual or group test data. The interpretation of test data must be related to the examinee's particular concerns.

10. Members responsible for making decisions based on test results have an understanding of educational and psychological measurement, validation criteria, and test results.

11. The member must be cautious when interpreting the results of research instruments possessing insufficient technical data. The specific purposes for the use of such instruments must be stated explicitly to examinees.

12. The member must proceed with caution when attempting to evaluate and interpret the performance of minority group members or other persons who are not represented in the norm group on which the instrument was standardized.

13. When computer-based test interpretations are developed by the member to support the assessment process, the member must ensure that the validity of such interpretations is established prior to the commercial distribution of such a computer application.

14. The member recognizes that test results may become obsolete. The member will avoid and prevent the misuse of obsolete test results.

15. The member must guard against the appropriation, reproduction, or modification of published tests or parts thereof without acknowledgment and permission from the previous publisher.

16. Regarding the preparation, publications, and distribution of tests, reference should be made to:

a. "Standards for Educational and Psychological Testing," revised edition, 1985, published by the American Psychological Association on behalf of itself, the American Psychological Association on behalf of itself, the American Educational Research Association and the National Counsel of Measurement in Education.

b. "The Responsible Use of Tests: A Position Paper of AMEG, APGA, and NCME," *Measurement and Evaluation In Guidance,* 1972, *5,* 385–388.

c. "Responsibilities of Users of Standardized Tests," APGA, *Guidepost,* October 5, 1978, pp. 5–8.

Section D: Research and Publication

1. Guidelines on research with human subjects should be adhered to, such as:

a. *Ethical Principles in the conduct of Research with Human Participants,* Washington, D.C.: American Psychological Association, Inc., 1982.

b. Code of Federal Regulation, Title 45, Subtitle A, Plan 46, as correctly issued.

c. *Ethical Principles of Psychologists,* American Psychological Association, Principle 49; Research with Human Participants.

d. Family Education Rights and Privacy Act (the Buckley Amendment).

e. Current federal regulations and various state rights privacy acts.

2. In planning any research activity dealing with human subjects, the member must be warn of and responsive to till pertinent ethical principles and ensure that the research problem, design, and execution are in full compliance with them.

3. Responsibility for ethical research practice lies with the principal researcher while others involved in the research activities share ethical obligation and full responsibility for their own actions.

4. In research with human subjects, research are responsible for the subjects' welfare throughout the experiment, and they must take all responsible precautions to avoid causing injurious psychological, physical, or social effects on their subjects.

5. All research subjects must be informed of the purpose of the study except when withholding information or providing misinformation to them is essential to the investigation. In such research the member must be responsible for corrective action as soon as possible following completion of the research.

6. Participation in research must be voluntary. Involuntary participations is appropriate only when it can be demonstrated that participation will have no harmful effects on subjects and it essential to the investigation.

7. When reporting research results, explicit mention must be made of all variables and conditions known to the investigator that might affect the outcome of the investigation or the interpretation of the data.

8. The member must be responsible for conducting and reporting investigations in a manner that minimized the possibility that results will be misleading.

9. The member has no obligation to make available sufficient original research data to qualified others who may wish to replicate the study.

10. When supplying data, aiding in the research of another person, reporting research results, or making original data available, due care must be taken to disguise the identity of the subjects in the absence of specific authorization from such subjects to do otherwise.

11. When conducting and reporting research, the member must be familiar with and give recognition to previous work, on the topic, as well as to observe all copyright laws and follow the principles of giving full credit to all to whom credit is due.

12. The member must give due credit through joint authorship, acknowledgments, footnote statements, or other appropriate means to those who have contributed significantly to the research and/or publication. In accordance with such contributions.

13. The member must communicate to other members the results of my research judged to be of professional or scientific value. Results reflecting unfavorably on institutions, programs, services, or vested interests must not be with held for such reasons.

14. If members agree to cooperate with another individual in research and/or publication, they incur on obligation to cooperate at promised in terms of punctuality of performance and with full regard to the completeness and accuracy of the information required.

15. Ethical practice requires that authors not submit the same manuscript or essentially similar in consent for simultaneous publication consideration by two or more journals. In addition, manuscripts published in whole or in substantial part in another journal or published work should not be submitted for publication without acknowledgment and permission from the previous publications.

Section E: Consulting

Consultation refers to a voluntary relationship between a professional helper and help-needing individual, group, or social unit in which the consultant is providing help to the client(s) in defining and solving a work-related problem or potential problem which a client or client system.

1. The member acting as consultant must have a high degree of self-awareness of his/her own values, knowledge, skills, limitations, and needs in entering a helping relationship that involves human and/or organizational change and that the focus of the relationship be on the issues to be resolved and not on the person(s) presenting the problem.

2. There must be understanding and agreement between member and client for the problems definitions, change of goals, and prediction of interventions selected.

3. The member must be reasonably certain that she/he or the organization represented has the necessary competencies and resources for giving the kind of help that is needed now or may be needed later and that appropriate referral are available to be consultant.

4. The consulting relationship must be one in which client adaptability and growth toward self-direction are encouraged and cultivated. The member must maintain this role consistently and not become a decision maker for the client or create a future dependency on the consultant.

5. When announcing consultant availability for services, the member conscientiously adheres to the Association's Ethical Standards.

6. The member refuse a private fee or other remuneration for consultation with persons who are entitled to there services through the member's employing institution or agency. The policies of a particular agency may make explicit provisions for private practice with agency clients by members of its staff. In such instances, the clients must be apprised of other opinions open to them should they seek private counseling services.

Section F: Private Practice

1. The members should assist the profession by facilitating the availability of counseling services in private as well as public settings.

2. In advertising services as a private practitioner, the member must advertise the services in a manner that accurately informs the public of professional services, expertise and techniques of counseling available. A member who assumes an executive leadership role in the organization shall not permit his/her home to be used in professional notices during periods when he/she is not actively engaged in the private practice of counseling.

3. The member may list the following: highest relevant degree, type and level of certification and/or license, address, telephone number, office hours, type and/or description of services and other relevant information. Such information must not contain false, inaccurate, mistaking, partial, out-of-context, or deceptive material or statements.

4. Members do not present their affiliation with any organization in such a way that would imply inaccurate sponsorship or certification by that organization.

5. Members may join in partnership/corporation with other members and/or other professionals provided that each member of the partnership or cooperation makes clear the separate specialties by name in compliance with the regulations of the locality.

6. A member has an obligation to withdraw from a counseling relationship if it is believed that employment will result in violation of the Ethical Standards. If the mental or physical condition of the member renders it difficult to carry out an effective professional relationship or if the member is discharged by the client because the counseling relationship is no longer productive for the client, then the member is obligated to terminated the counseling relationship.

7. A member must adhere to the regulation for private practice of the locality where the services are offered.

8. It is unethical to use one's institutional affiliation to recruit clients for one's private practice.

Section G: Personnel Administration

It is recognized that most members are employed in public or quasi-public institutions. The functioning of a member within no institution must contribute to the goals of the institution and vice versa if either is to accomplish their respective goals or objectives. It is therefore essential that the member and the institution fusion in ways to: (a) make the institutional goals specific, and public; (b) make the member's contribution to institutional goals specific; and (c) foster manual accountability for goal achievement.

To accomplish these objectives, it is recognized that the member and the employer must share responsibilities in the formulation and implementation of personal policies.

1. Members must define and describe the and levels of their professional competency.

2. Members must establish interpersonal relations and working agreements with supervisors and subordinates regarding counseling or clinical relationships, confidentiality, distinction between public and private material, maintenance and dissemination of recorded information, workload, and accountability. Working agreements in each instance must be specified and made known to those concerned.

3. Members must alert their employers to conditions that may be potentially disruptive or damaging.

4. Members must inform employers of conditions that may limit their effectiveness.

5. Members must submit regularly to professional review and evaluations.

6. Members must be responsible for inservice development of self and/or staff.

7. Members must inform their staff of goals and programs.

8. Members must provide personnel practices that guarantee and enhance the rights and welfare of each recipient of their service.

9. Members must select competent persons and assign responsibilities compatible with their skills and experiences.

10. The member, of the onset of a counseling relationship, will inform the client of the member's intended use of supervisors regarding the disclosure of information concerning this case. The member will clearly inform the client of the of confidentiality in the relationship.

11. Members, as either employers or employees, do not engage in or condom practices that are inhuman, illegal, or unjustifiable (such as considerations based on sex, handicap, age, race) in hiring, promotion, or training.

Section H: Preparation Standards

Members who are responsible for training others must be guided by the preparation standards of the Association and relevant Division(s). The members who functions in the capacity of trainer assumes unique ethical responsibilities that frequently go beyond that of the member who does not function in a training capacity. These ethical responsibilities are out-lined as follows:

1. Members must orient students to program expectations, basic skills development, and employment prospects prior to admission to the program.

2. Members in charge of learning experiences must establish programs that integrate academic study and supervised practice.

3. Members must establish a program directed toward developing students' skills, knowledge and self-understanding stated whenever possible in competency or performance terms.

4. Members must identify the level of competencies of their students in compliance with relevant Division standards. These competencies must accommodate the paraprofessional as well as the professional.

5. Members, through continual student evaluation and appraisal, must be aware of the personal limitation of the learner in securing remedial assistance but who screen from the program those individuals who are unable to provide competent services.

6. Members must provide a program that includes training in research with levels of role functioning. Paraprofessional and technician-level personnel must be trained as consumers of research. In addition, personnel must learn how to evaluate their own and their program's effectiveness. Graduate training, especially at the doctoral level, would include preparation for original research by the member.

7. Members must make students aware of the ethical responsibilities and standards of the profession.

8. Preparatory programs must encourages students to value the ideals of service to individuals and to society. In this regard, direct financial remuneration or lack thereof must not be allowed to overshadow professional and humanities needs.

9. Members responsible for educational programs must be skilled as teacher and practitioners.

10. Members must present thoroughly varied theoretical positions so that students may make comparisons and have the opportunity to select a position.

11. Members must develop clear polities within their educational institutions regarding field placement and the roles of the student and the instructor in such placement.

12. Members must ensure that forms of learning focusing on self-understanding or growth are voluntary, or it required as part of the educational program, are made known to prospective students prior to entering the programs. When the educational program offers a growth experience with an emphasis on self-disclosure or other relatively interments or personal involvement, the member must have no administrative, supervisory, or evaluating authority regarding the participant.

13. The member will at all times provide students with clear and equally acceptable alternatives for self-understanding or growth experiences. The member will assure students that they have a right to accept these alternatives without prejudice or penalty.

14. Members must conduct an educational program in keeping with the current relevant guidelines of the Association.

POLICIES AND PROCEDURES FOR PROCESSING COMPLAINTS OF ETHICAL VIOLATIONS

American Counseling Association
(As approved March, 1990 —
Amended December, 1991)

Section A: General

1. The American Counseling Association, hereinafter referred to as the "Association" or "ACA", an educational, scientific, and charitable organization, is dedicated to enhancing the worth, dignity, potential, and uniqueness of each individual and rendering service to society.

2. The Association in furthering its objectives, administers. Ethical Standards that have been developed and approved by the ACA Governing Council.

3. The purpose of this document is to facilitate the work of the ACA Ethics Committee by specifying the procedures for processing cases of alleged violations of the ACA Ethical Standards, codifying options for sanctioning members, and stating appeal procedures. The intent of the Association is to monitor the professional conduct of its member to ensure sound ethical practices.

Section B: Ethics Committee Members

1. The Ethics Committee is a standing committee of the Association. The Committee consists of six (6) appointed members, including the Chairperson. The editor of the *Ethical Standards Casebook* serves as an *ex officio* member of this Committee without voice. Two members are appointed annually for a three (3) year term by the president-elect, appointments are subject to confirmation by the ACA Governing Council. Any vacancy according on the Committee will be filled by the President in the same manner, and the person appointed shall serve the inexpert term of the member whose place he or she took. Committee members may be reappointed to not more than one (1) additional consecutive term.

2. The Chairperson of the Committee is appointed annually by the incumbent President-Elect, subject to confirmation by the ACA Governing Council. A chairperson may be reappointed to one additional term during any three (3) year period.

Section C: Role and Function

1. The role of the Ethics Committee of the Association is to assist in the contribution and conciliation of conflicts among members of the Association, except where appropriate client concerns may be expressed. The Committee also is responsible for:

A. Educating the membership as to the Association's Ethical Standards.

B. Periodically reviewing and recommending changes in the Ethical Standards of the Association as well as the Policies and Procedures for Processing Complaints of Ethical Violations.

C. Receiving and processing complaints of alleged violations of the Ethical Standards of the Association, and

D. Receiving and processing questions.

2. In processing complaints about alleged ethical misconduct, the Committee will compile in objective, factual account of the dispute in question and make the best possible recommendation for the resolution of the case. The Committee, in taking any action, shall do so only for cause, shall only take the degree of disciplinary action that it reasonable, shall utilize these procedures with objectively and fairness, and is general shall act only to further the interests and objectives of the Association and its membership.

3. The ACA Ethics Committee itself will not initiate any ethical violation charges against an ACA member.

4. Of the six (6) voting members of the Committee, a vote of four (4) if necessary to conduct business. In the event the Chair or any other member of the Committee had a personal interest in the case, he or she shall withdraw from reviewing the case. A unanimous vote of those members of the Committee who reviewed the case is necessary to expel a member from the Association.

5. The Chairperson of the ACA Ethics Committee and/or the ACA legal counsel of any time.

Section D: Responsibilities of Committee Members

1. The members of the Ethics Committee must be conscious that their position in extremely important and sensitive and that their decisions involve the rights of many individuals, the reputation of the counseling and human development community, and the careers of the members. The Committee members have the obligation to act in an unbiased manner, to work expeditiously, to safeguard the confidentiality of the Committee's activities, and to follow procedures that protect the rights of all individuals involved.

Section E: Responsibilities of the Chairperson

1. In addition to the above guidelines for members of the Committee, the Chairperson, in conjunction with Headquarters staff, has the responsibilities of:

A. Receiving (vis ACA Headquarters) complaints that have been certified for membership status of the accused,

B. Notifying the compliment and the accused of receipt of the case,

C. Notifying the members of the Ethics Committee of the case,

D. Presiding over the meetings of the Committee,

E. Preparing and sending (by certified mail) communications to the complainant and accused member on the recommendations and decisions of the Committee, and

F. Arranging for legal advice with assistance and Financial approval of the ACA Executive Director.

Section F: Complaints

1. All correspondence, records, and activities of the ACA Ethics Committee will remain confidential.

2. The ACA Ethics Committee will not act on unanimous complaints, nor will it act on complaints currently under civil or critical litigation.

3. The ACA Ethics Committee will not only on those cases where the secured is a current member of ACA or was a member of ACA at the time of the alleged violation. State Division and State Branch Ethics Committees may act only on those cases where the accused is a member of the State Division or State Branch and not a member of ACA.

Section G: Submitting Complaints— Procedures for ACA Members

1. The procedures for submission of complaints to the Ethics Committee are as follows:

A. If feasible, the compliment should discuss with utmost confidentiality the nature of the complaint with a colleague to see if he or she views the situation as an ethical violation.

B. Whenever feasible, the compliment is to approach the accused directly to discuss and resolve the complaint.

C. In cases where a resolution is not forthcoming at the personal level, the complaint shall prepare a formal written submit it to the ACA Ethics Committee, Action or consideration by he ACA Ethics Committee may not be introduced until this requirement is satisfied.

D. Formal written complaints must include a statement indicating the behavior(s) that constituted the alleged violation(s), and the date(s) of the alleged violation(s). The written statement must also contain the accord member's full name and complete address. Any relevant supporting documentation may be included with the complaint.

E. All complaints that are directed to the ACA Ethics Committee should be mailed to the Ethics Committee, c/o The Executive Director, American Counseling Association, 5999 Stevenson Avenue, Alexandria, Virginia 22304. The envelope must be marked "CONFIDENTIAL." This procedure is necessary to ensure the confidentiality of the person submitting the complaint and the person accused in the complaint.

Section H: Submitting Complaints— Procedures for Non-members

1. The ACA Ethics Committee recognizes the rights of non-ACA members to file grievances concurring a member. Ordinarily this non-member will be a client or student of an ACA member who believes that the ACA member has acted unethically.

2. In such cases, the compliment shall contact the ACA Executive Director (or his/her designee) and outline, in writing, those behaviors he or she feels were unethical in nature. Headquarters staff will delineate the complaint process to the compliment.

Section I: Processing Complaints

1. When complaints are received a Headquarters, the ACA Executive Director (or his/her designer) shall: (a) check on the membership status of the accused (b) acknowledge receipt of the complaint within ten (10) working days after it is received in ACA Headquarters, and (c) consult with the Chairperson of the ACA Ethics Committee within ten (10) working days after the complaint is received in ACA Headquarters to determine whether it is appropriate to proceed with the complaint. If the Director (or designee) and Chairperson determine it is inappropriate to proceed, the compliment shall be so notified. If the Director (or designee) and Chairperson determine it is appropriate to proceed with the complaint, they will identify which Ethical Standard(s) are applicable to the alleged violation. A formal statement containing the Ethical Standard(s) that were alleged violated will be forwarded to the compliment for his/her signature. This signed formal statement will then become a part of the formal complaint.

2. Once the formal complaint has been compiled (as indicated above), the Chairperson of the ACA Ethics Committee shall do the following:

A. Inform the compliment in writing that the accused member has been notified of the charges.

B. Direct a letter to the accused member informing the member of accusation lodged against him or her, including copies of all materials submitted by the complainant, asking for a response, and requesting that relevant information be submitted to the Chairperson within thirty (30) working days.

3. The accused is under no duty to respond to the allegations, but the Committee will not be obligated to delay or postpone its review of the case unless the accused so requests, with good cause, in advance. Failure of the accused to respond should not be viewed by the Committee as sufficient ground for taking disciplinary action.

4. Once the Chairperson has received the accused member's response or the thirty (30) days have elapsed, then the Chairperson shall forward to the members of the ACA Ethics Committee legal counsel's opinion (if applicable), staff verification membership status, allegations, and responses, and direct the Committee to review the case and make recommendations for this disposition within two (2) weeks of receipt of the case.

5. The ACA Ethics Committee will review the case and make recommendations for its disposition and/or resolution within two hundred (200) working days following its receipts.

6. The ACA Ethics Committee Chairperson may ask the President of ACA to appoint an investigating committee at the local or state level to gather and submit relevant information concerning the case to the Committee.

Section J: Options Available to the Ethics Committee

1. After reviewing the information forwarded by the Chairperson the Ethics Committee shall have the power so:

A. Dismiss the charges, find that no violation has occurred and dismiss the complaint, or

B. Find that the practice(s) in which the member engages that is (are) the subject of the complaint, is (are) unethical, notify the accused of this determination, and request the member to voluntarily cease and desist in the practice(s) without impositions of further stanchions, or

C. Find that the practice(s) in which the member engages, that is (are) the subject of the complaints, is (are) unethical, notify the accused of this determination and impose sanctions.

Section K: Appropriate Sanctions

1. The Committee may consider extenuating circumstances before deciding on the penalty to be imposed. If the Committee finds the accused has violated the Ethical Standards and decides to impose sanctions, the Committee may take any o the following actions:

A. Issue a reprimand with recommendations for corrective action, subject to review by the Committee, or

B. Place the member on probation for a specified period of time, subject to review by the Committee, or

C. Suspend eligibility for membership in ACA for a specified period of time, subject to review by the Committee, or

D. Expel the member from ACA permanently.

Section L: Consequences of Sanctions

1. Both a reprimand and probation carry with it no loss of membership rights or privileges.

2. A suspended member forfeits the rights and privileges of membership only for the period of his or her suspension.

3. In the event a member is expelled from ACA membership, he or she shall lose all rights and privileges of membership in ACA and its divisions permanently. The expelled member shall not be entitled to a refund of dues already paid.

4. If the member is suspended or expelled, and after any right to appeal has been exhausted, the Committee will notify the appropriate state licensing board(s) of the disciplined member's status with ACA. Notice also will be given to the National Board for Certified Counselors, the ACA Divisions of which the disciplined party is a member, the State Branch of ACA in which the member resides, the members of ACA, the compliment, and other organizations as the Committee deems necessary. Such notice shall only state the sanctions imposed and the sections of the ACA Ethical Standards that were violated. Further elaboration shall not be disclosed.

5. Should a member resign from the Association after a complaint has been brought against him or her and before the Ethics Committee has completed its deliberations, that member is considered to have been expelled from the Association for failure to respond in a timely and complete manner to the Ethics Committee.

Section M: Hearing

1. At the discretion of the Ethics Committee, a hearing may be conducted when the results of the Ethics Committee's preliminary determination indicate that additional information is needed. The Chairperson shall schedule a formal hearing on the case and notify both the and the accused of their right to attend.

2. The hearing will be held before apparel made up of the Ethics Committee and if the accused member chooses, a representative of the

accused member's primary Division. This representative will be identified by the Division President and will have voting privileges.

Section N: Recommended Hearing Procedures

1. Purposes of Hearings. The purpose for which hearings shall be conducted are: (a) to determine whether a breach of the Ethical standards of ACA has occurred, and (b) if so, to determine what disciplinary action should be taken by the ACA. If a hearing is held, no disciplinary action will be taken by ACA until after the accused member has been given reasonable notice of the hearing and the specific charges raised against him or her and has had the opportunity to be heard and to present evidence in his or her behalf. The hearings will be formally conducted. The committee will be guided in its deliberations by principles of basic fairness and professionalism, and will keep its deliberations as confidential as possible, except as provided herein.

2. Notice. At least forty-five (45) working days before the hearing, the accused member should be advised in writing of the time and place of the hearing and of the charges involved. Notice shall be given either personally or by certified or registered mail and shall be signed by the Committee Chair. The action should be addressed to the accused member at his or her address as it appears in the membership records of the ACA. The notice should include a brief statement of the complaints lodged against him or her, and should be supported by the evidence. The accused is under no duty to respond to the notice, but the Committee will, not be obligated to delay or postpone in hearing unless the accused in requests in writing with good cause, in advance. Failure of the accused to appear at the hearing should not be viewed by the Committee as sufficient ground for taking disciplinary action.

3. Conduct of the Hearing.

A. Accommodations. The Committee shall provide a private room to conduct the hearings, and no observers shall be permitted. The location of the hearing shall be determined at the discretion of the Committee, taking into consideration the convenience of the Committee and the parties involved.

B. Presiding Officer. The Chair of the Ethics Committee shall preside over the hearing and deliberations of the Committee. In the event the Chair or any other member of the Committee has a personal interest in the case, be or she shall withdraw from the hearing and deliberations and shall not participate therein. The Committee shall select from among its members a presiding officer for any case where the Chair has excused himself or herself. At the conclusion of the hearing and deliberation of the Committee, the Chair shall promptly notify the accused and complainant of the Committee's decision in writing.

C. Record. A record of the hearing shall be made and preserved, together with any documents presented as evidence, at the ACA. Headquarters for a period of three (3) years following the hearing decision. The record may consist of a summary of testimony received, or a verbatim transcript, at the discretion of the Committee.

D. Right to Counsel. The parties shall be entitled to have counsel present to advise them throughout the hearing, but they may not participate beyond advising. Legal Counsel for ACA shall also be present at the hearing to advise the Committee and shall have the privilege of the floor.

E. Witnesses. Either party shall have the right to call witnesses to substitutes his or her version of the case. The Committee shall also have the right to call witnesses it believes may provide further insight into the matter before the Committee. Witnesses shall not be present during the hearings except when they are called soon to testify. The presiding officers shall allow questions to be asked of any witness by the opposition or members of the Committee and shall ensure that questions and testimony are relevant to the issues to the case. Should the hearing be disturbed by disturbed by disparaging or irrelevant testimony or by the flare-up of tempers, the presiding officer shall call a brief recess until order can be restored. Witnesses shall be excused upon completion of their testimony. All expenses associated with witnesses or counsel on behalf of the parties shall be born by the respective parties.

F. Presentation of Evidence.

(1) A member of the Committee shall be called upon first to present the charge(s) made against the accused and to briefly describe the evidence supporting the charge(s).

(2) The complainant or a member of the Committee shall then be called upon to present the case against the accused. Witnesses who can substantiate the case shall be called upon to testify and anger questions of the accused and the Committee.

(3) If the accused has exercised the right to be present at the hearing, he or she shall be called upon last to present any evidence which refuses the charges against him or her. This includes the presentation of witnesses as in Subsection (E) above. The accused member has the right to refuse to make a statement in his or her behalf. The accused will not be found guilty simply for refusing to testify. Once the accused chooses to testify, however, he or she may be cross-examined by members of the Committee or the complainant.

(4) The Committee will endeavor to conclude the hearing within a period of approximately three (3) hours. The parties will be requested to be considerate of this time frame in planning their testimony. Testimony that is merely cumulative or repetitions may, of the discretion of the presiding officer, be excluded.

(5) The accused has the right to be present at all times during the hearing and to challenge all of the evidence presented against him or her.

G. Relevancy of Evidence. The Hearing Committee is not a court of law and to not required to observe the rules of evidence that apply in the trial of lawsuit. Consequently, evidence that would be admissible is the hearing before the Committee, if it is relevant to the case. That is, if the evidences offered tends to explain, clarify, or refuse any of the important facts of the case, it should generally be considered. The Committee will not receive evidence or testimony for the purpose of supporting any charge that was not set forth in the notice of the hearing or that is not relevant to the issues of the case.

4. Burden of Proof. The burden of proving a violation of the Ethical Standards is on the compliment, and/or the Committee. It is not up to the accused to prove his or her innocence of say wrong-doing. Although the charge(s) need not be proved "beyond a reasonable doubt," the Committee will not find the accused guilty in the absence of substantial, objective, and believable evidence to sustain the charge(s).

5. Deliberation of the Committee. After the hearing with the parties is completed, the Committee shall meet in a closed session in review the evidence presented and reach a conclusion. The Committee shall be the sole tries of fact and shall weigh the evidence presented and judge the creditability of the willingness. The act of a majority of the members of the Committee shall be the decision of the Committee and only those members of the Committee who were present throughout the entire hearing shall be eligible to voice.

6. Decision of the Committee. The Committee will first resolve the issue of the guilt of innocence of the accused. Applying the burden of proof in paragraph 4 above, the Committee will voice by screen ballot, unless the members of the Committee consent to an oral voice. In the event a majority of the members of the Committee do not find the accused guilty, the charges shall be dismissed and the parties notified. If the Committee finds the accused has violated the Ethical Standards, it must then determine what sanctions to impose in accord with Section K: Appropriate Sanctions.

Section O: Appeal Procedures

1. Appeals will be heard only in such cases wherein the appellant presents evidence that the sanction imposed by the Committee has been arbitrary or capricious or that the procedures outlined in the "Policy Document" have not been followed.

2. The complainant and accused shall be advised of the appeal procedures by the Chairperson of the ACA Ethics Committee. The following procedures shall govern appeals:

A. A three (3) member review committee composed of the Executive Director of the ACA the President of the ACA Division with which the accused member is most closely identified, and the immediate Past President of ACA. The ACA attorney shall serve as legal advisor and have the privilege of the floor.

B. The appeal with supporting documentation must be made in writing within sixty (60) working days by certified mail to the ACA Executive Director and indicate the basic upon which it is made. If the member requires a time extension, he or she must request it in writing by certified mail within thirty (30) working days of receiving the decision by the ACA Ethics Committee. The extension will consist of ninety (90) working days beginning from that request.

C. The review committee shall review all materials considered by the ACA Ethics Committee.

D. Within thirty (30) working days of this review, the members on the review committee shall submit to the President of the ACA a written statement giving their opinion regarding the decision of the Ethics Committee. Each member shall concur with or dissent from the decision of the Ethics Committee.

E. Within fifteen (15) working days of receiving this opinion, the President of ACA will reach a decision based on the considered opinions of the review committee from the following alternatives:

(1) support the decision of the Ethics Committee, or

(2) reverse the decision of the Ethics Committee,

3. The parties to the appeal shall be advised of the actions in writing.

Section P: Records

1. Records of the ACA Ethics Committee and the review committee shall remain at the ACA Headquarters.

Section Q: Procedures for Submitting and Interpreting Questions of Ethical Conduct

1. The procedures for submitting questions to the Ethics Committee are as follows:

A. Whenever possible, the questioner is first advised to consult other colleagues socking information of questions.

B. If a national level resolution is deceived appropriate, the questioner shall prepare a written statement, which details the conduct in question. Subscripts should include the section or sections of the Ethical Standards to be interpreted relative to the conduct in question. All questions that and directed to the Ethics Committee should be mailed to: Ethics Committee, c/o ACA Executive Director.

C. The ACA Ethics Committee Chairperson or his/her designee:

(1) may confer with legal counsel, and

(2) shall direct a letter to the questioner acknowledging receipt of the question, informing the member that the questions will be interpreted by the Committee, and outlining the procedures to be involved in the interpretation.

D. The Ethics Committee will review and interpret the question and if requested by the questioner, make recommendations for conduct.

■ ■ ■

CHAPTER REFERENCES

American Counseling Association (ACA). *Ethical standards of the American Counseling Association, formerly the American Association for Counseling and Development (as revised by AACD Governing Council, March 1988).* Alexandria, VA: Author.

American Psychological Association (APA). (1992). *Ethical principles of psychologists and code of conduct.* Washington, DC: Author.

Denkowski, K.M., & Denkowski, G.C. (1982). Client counselor confidentiality: An update of rationale, legal status, and implications. *The Personnel and Guidance Journal,* 371–375.

Hollander, M.H. (1965). Privileged communications and confidentiality. *Diseases of the Nervous System, 26,* 169–175.

Hummel, D.L., Talbutt, L.D., & Alexander, M.D. (1985). *Law and ethics in counseling.* New York: Van Nostrand Reinhold.

Laws of Pennsylvania. (1949). Volume I. Call #P.A.Y1.6–949.

McDermott, P.A. (1975). Law, liability, and the school psychologist: System of law, privileged communication and access to records. *Journal of Psychology, 10,* 299–305.

Siegel, M. (1979). Privacy, ethics and confidentiality. *Professional Psychology, 10,* 249–258.

Slovenko, R. (1973). *Psychiatry and the law.* Boston: Little, Brown.

Tarasoff II, Vacating Cal. 3rd. 117,529 P.2d 553, 118, Cal. Rptr. 129. (1974). (Tarasoff I).

Chapter 7

CONSULTATION IN SCHOOLS AND MENTAL HEALTH AGENCIES: MODELS AND METHODS

John C. Boylan, Ph.D.

Consultation is one of the most sought after services rendered by counselors and psychologists. During the last decade and with the passage of the Community Mental Health Act of 1963, consultation has become recognized as a more broadly defined helping process (Kurpius, 1978). Kurpius suggested that the intent of this early legislation was to urge helping professionals to move from individual and small group remedial activities as the primary care-giving intervention toward more developmental and preventative approaches.

DEFINITION

With the growth of consultation, a diversity of opinion has developed with regard to the definition of consultation. A review of the literature by Alpert and Meyers (1983) fails to provide an agreed upon definition of consultation. Ohlsen (1983) defined consultation as an activity in which a professional helps another person in regard to a third person or party. Caplan (1970) viewed consultation as a collaborative process between two professionals who each has his/her own area of expertise. Albee (1982) defined consultation in terms of a preventative approach to service delivery in mental health. Kirby (1985, p. 9) defined consultation in terms of four relationship conditions: (1) the relationship is voluntary, (2) the focus of attention is on the problem situation as articulated by the consultee(s), (3) the consultant is not functioning as a part of the structural hierarchy, and (4) the power that resides in consultant's expertise is sufficient to facilitate change. Dinkmeyer, Carlson, and Dinkmeyer (1994) defined consultation as follows: "Consultation is when the main focus of the relationship is a third person

(often a student) and when the relationship is characterized by collaboration on ways to help this third person" (pp. 89–90). For purpose of clarity, the definition provided by Meyers, Parsons, and Martin (1979) will be used in this chapter.

> Consultation is a helping or problem solving process occurring between a professional help giver and help seeker who has responsibility for the welfare of another person. It is a voluntary relationship in which the help giver and a help seeker share in solving a current problem of the help seeker. The help seeker profits from the relationship in such a way that future problems may be handled more positively and skillfully. (p. 4)

Similarly, authors disagree with reference to the focus of consolidation. Alpert (1977) suggested that consultation is a direct service provided by counselors and psychologists. Caplan (1970) viewed direct service as a part of the overall process of consultation. Meyers, Parsons, and Martin (1979) suggested that consultation and direct service should be viewed as being on opposite ends of a continuum.

The important point to note is that traditionally, counselors and psychologists have been involved in providing *direct service* to clients. Direct service implies that the focus of consultation is on the individual client and the intrapersonal factors affecting him/her. Typically taking the form of crisis intervention, direct service is thought to consist of psychodiagnosis and counseling as the primary remedial activities of the counselor/therapist.

More recently, attention has been focused upon the counselor and psychologist providing preventative approaches to service delivery (Conyne, 1987). The *indirect service* approach stresses the consultation efforts directed to understanding the environment of the client, with interventions aimed at assisting the professional who has responsibility for a caretaker role with the individual.

With the development of indirect service approaches, the counselor/psychologist must ensure that role confusion does not hamper the delivery of mental health services. An important point to assure is that counseling and consultation are seen as different but complimentary forms of intervention. Bloom (1977) suggested that consultation differs from counseling/ therapy in that the consultant does not assume the full responsibility for the final outcome of consultation. The consultant's role is to develop and enhance the work of the consultee rather than as in counseling where the focus is upon the personal improvement of the client. Thus, the consultant must remember that the relationship established with the consultee is not primarily therapeutic in nature. Rather, the consultant serves in the capacity of collaborator and facilitator, to assist the consultee in performing his/her duties and responsibilities in a more productive and effective manner (p. 156).

Bloom (1977) recognized the importance of distinguishing consultation from other forms of mental health activities. He stated that consultation is different form supervision on the grounds that (1) the consultant may not be of the same professional specialty as the consultee, (2) the consultant has no administrative responsibility for the work of the consultee, (3) consultation may be more irregular than continuous in character, and (4) the consultant is not in a position of power with respect to the consultee. Similarly, Bloom (1977) differentiated consultation from counseling because in the process of counseling a clear contractual relationship exists between an individual designated as client and another individual designated as counselor. Also, the goal of consultation is improved work performance, whereas in counseling the goal is personal adjustment (p. 156).

The remainder of this chapter provides an overview and discussion of mental health consultation and school consultation models that are applicable to the practicum student and intern in counseling and psychology.

MENTAL HEALTH CONSULTATION

Mental health consultation has been widely influenced by the writing of Gerald Caplan. With the writing of the book entitled *The Theory and Practice of Mental Health Consultation* in 1970, Caplan identified four consultation types that are employed in mental health settings.

The four types of consultation are summarized here to provide the practicum student and intern with an overview of the mental health models.

- **Client Centered Case Consultation**—A consultee has difficulty in dealing with the mental health aspects of one of his/her clients and calls in a specialist to investigate and advise on the nature of the difficulties and on what the consultee's work difficulty relates to the management of a particular case or group of cases. The consultant makes an assessment of the client's problem and recommends how the consultee should proceed.

- **Program Centered Administrative Consultation**—The consultant is invited by an administrator to help with a current problem of program development, with some predicament in the organization of an institution, or with planning and implementation of organizational policies, including personal policies. The consultant is expected to provide feedback to the organization in the form of a written report.

- **Consultee Centered Case Consultation**— The consultee's work problem relates to the management of a particular client, and he/she invokes the consultant's help in order to improve handling of the case. The consultant's primary focus is upon clarifying and remedying the shortcomings in the consultee's professional functioning that are responsible for his/ her difficulties with the case about which he/she is seeking help.

- **Consultee Centered Administrative Consultation**—The consultant helps the administrative staff of an organization deal with current problems in organizational planning, program development, or organizational policies. The focus of attention is the consultee's work difficulties and attempting to help improve his/her problem solving skills. (Caplan, 1970, pp. 109–50)

Caplan further described what he considered to be the characteristics of mental health consultation.

A summary of Caplan's characteristics are presented to give the student a clear understanding of the consultation model in mental health settings.

1. Mental health consultation is a method for use between two professionals in respect to a lay client or a program of such clients.

2. The consultee's work problem must be defined by him/her as being in the mental health area—relating to (a) mental disorder or personality idiosyncrasies of the client, (b) promotion of mental health in the client, or (c) interpersonal aspects of the work situation.

3. The consultant has no administrative responsibility for the consultee's work or professional responsibility for the outcome of the client's case.

4. The consultee is under no compulsion to accept the consultant's ideas or suggestions.

5. The basic relationship between the two is coordinate. No built-in hierarchial authority tension exists.

6. The coordinate relationship is fostered by the consultant's usually being a member of another profession and coming briefly into the consultee's institution from the outside.

7. Consultation is usually given as a short series of interviews—which take place intermittently in response to the consultee's awareness of current need for help with the work problem.

8. Consultation is expected to continue indefinitely.

9. A consultant has not predetermined a body of information that he/she intends to impart on a particular consultee.

10. The twin goals of consultation are to help the consultee improve his/her handling or understanding of the current work difficulty and to increase his/her capacity to master future problems of a similar type.

11. The aim is to improve the consultee's job performance and not his/her sense of well-being.

12. Consultation does not focus overtly on personal problems and feelings of the consultee.

13. This doesn't mean that the consultant does not pay attention to the feelings of the consultee. He/she is particularly sensitive to these and to the disturbance of task functioning produced by personal problems.

14. Consultation is usually only one of the professional functions of a specialist, even if he/she is formally entitled "consultant."

15. Finally, mental health consultation is a method of communication between a mental health specialist and other professionals. (pp. 28–30)

The understanding of stages and types of consultation and the characteristics of mental health counseling enable the student to begin to conceptualize an approach to consultation in light of his/her own needs as well as the needs of the consultee. The necessity of understanding a wide range of theoretical perspectives in consultation is stressed by Jacobson, Ravlin, and Cooper (1983). These authors conceptualized mental health consultation as a multilinear model. The first step in the model is the development and implementation of a formal intervention plan requiring the consultant to have summarized the available information into a useful systems assessment. The second step is entry into the system, which denotes the first formal contact between the two systems regarding the current consultation. Entry must be seen in the context of the agency's history. The third step, relationship building, is a long-term process that transcends the time constraints of a particular consultation agreement—thus it is conceptualized as an ongoing process. In the fourth step, formal interventions follow the mediation of a consultation agreement. In the fifth step, though the agreement often is negotiated earlier in the consultation process, the agreement generally undergoes repeated modification in the course of the intervention process based upon the ongoing system assessment and program evaluation. The sixth step, conclusion of the services provided by specific consultation, is often the precursor to subsequent cycling of the consultative process. Consequently, the termination of a consultative agreement rarely is as final as it is in clinical interventions (Jacobson, Ravlin, & Cooper, 1983, pp. 58–60).

SCHOOL CONSULTATION

Current interest in school consultation is part of a broader professional trend emphasizing preventative mental health, indirect service delivery, community interventions, and new sources of mental health manpower (Meyers, Parsons, & Martin, 1979).

Historically, consultation in schools has its roots in disciplines other than education. The fields of psychiatry, group dynamics, psychology, and organizational development have all contributed to the development of models of school consultation. Likewise, authors such as Caplan (1970) and Sarason (1971) have focused attention on the need for a coordinated sharing of expertise by professionals in the schools. The writings of these individuals have changed the focus of consultation from advice giving in the early years to a more coordinate, expertise-sharing process. They also have augmented the consultant's knowledge of the school as a culture and as an organization. Finally, they have contributed to a variety of techniques other than in-service education and case feedback, including group dynamics exercises, applied research techniques themes, interference reduction, organizational development techniques, and conflict resolution procedures (Meyers, Parsons & Martin, 1979, pp. 35–36).

Dinkmeyer, Carlson, and Dinkmeyer (1994), in writing about consultation by counselors psychologists, and other mental health professionals in schools, wrote

> Consultation relationships have the following four characteristics:
>
> 1. Information, observations, and concerns about a problem are *shared* between the consultant and the consultee.
>
> 2. *Tentative hypotheses* are developed to change the situation.
>
> 3. Joint *planning and collaboration* occur between the consultant and consultee.
>
> 4. The hypotheses, or recommendations, *reflect* and *respect* the uniqueness of the child, the teacher, and the setting. (p. 16)

Similar to mental health consultation, school consultation has generated a number of models of intervention in the schools, Parsons and Meyers (1984) discussed a model of school consultation with a focus on primary and secondary prevention. In the model are defined four categories of consultation in the schools.

> **Direct Service to the Client:** Consultation seeks to modify the behavior, attitudes, or feeling of a particular client or clients who present a problem or problems. Data about the client are gathered directly by the consultant using individual testing, interviewing, and behavioral observation of the client.
>
> **Indirect Service to the Client:** Consultation aims to change the behavior attitude, or feelings of the client(s). In contrast, data are not gathered directly by the consultant. Instead the consultee gathers the necessary data to be shared with the consultant.
>
> **Service to the Consultee:** The target for service is the consultee rather than the consultee's client. The goal is to change the behavior, attitudes, or feelings of the consultee.
>
> **Service to the System:** The target for service is to improve the organizational functioning of the system as a whole. This result should lead to improved mental health for both clients and individual consultees in the organization. (pp. 5–6)

Lambert (1983) discussed consultation in the schools as an interaction between a teacher and a school district employee from a mental health dis-

cipline. Although this model assumes that the consultant is school-based, nevertheless the steps in the process are the same for consultants brought in from outside the system. Lambert (1983) suggested that the process of consultation is initiated (1) when a teacher requests help, (2) when a consultant offers to assist a teacher or pupil, or (3) when a principal requests help for a teacher or for himself/herself. The objectives of school-based consultation may be a change in pupil behavior or a change in teacher behavior or both (p. 31). Lambert further elaborated what are considered to be the phases involved in school consultation. *The first phase* is identified as the relationship building-role clarification phase in which the consultant defuses teacher anxiety about being analyzed, exposed, and evaluated, and during which time the consultant interacts so as to be seen as a helpful, nonjudgmental, and knowledgeable person. *The second phase,* which follows several weeks later, consists of problem identification and the generation of intervention strategies. During this time, teachers and consultants are actively discussing cases, successfully sharing information from each of their professional perspectives, and developing alternative interventions to be considered and tried. *The third and final phase* occurs when the teacher and consultant each understand the other's role, and the teacher knows how to ask questions and can use the interaction to explore, propose, and rule out solutions. The relationship becomes one in which two professional peers can use one another effectively in exploration and discussion of matters of mutual concern (pp. 32–33).

In a similar fashion, Dustin and Ehly's (1984) model for school consultation asserts that consultation is indirect helping in which the consultant works with a second person (consultee) to help a third party (the client). This five-stage model includes the following: (1) Phasing In: to establish trust levels and to have the consultant employ such skills as active listening, understanding, empathy, and self-disclosure to assure relationship building between the consultant and teacher. (2) Problem Identification: to clarify the main problems being experienced by the client and to employ the skills of focusing, paraphrasing, and restatement in order to determine whether the focus of consultation is the consultee or the third party (the client). (3) Implementation: to assist the consultee in devising alternative change strategies. This stage is marked by consultant feedback empathy to assist the consultee in dealing with possible negative feelings associated with the process of narrowing down available strategies to the one that will be implemented. (4) Evaluation: to involve formation evaluation and the monitoring, implementing, and evaluating of change strategies. Consultant openness and flexibility is essential. (5) Termination: to bring closure to consultation arrangements and review the positive as well as negative outcomes derived from the change strategies that were implemented. The model stresses the importance of using counseling skills as they apply to the consulting process (pp. 23–28).

★ ★ ★

HELPFUL THEORIES TO GUIDE COUNSELORS' PRACTICE OF SCHOOL-BASED CONSULTATION*

William P. Erchul
Collie W. Conoley

Whenever you choose among several possible ways of handling a troubled youngster, an overwhelmed parent, or a demanding principal, you are using some theory of human behavior to guide your actions. Nonetheless, many human service professionals (including counselors) often believe that theories have little value because they rarely tell us exactly what to do. After all, theories deal with the theoretical not practical! (At least this is what we hear from some of our students.) We, on the other hand, believe that a theory can be very helpful, especially if one understands possible applications of that theory.

An increasingly important role for the school counselor is that of consultant (Humes & Hohenshil, 1987). As consultant, the counselor works directly with teachers, administrators, or parents who in turn work directly with children. This is quite different than someone who counsels individual students, a role familiar to most school counselors. Consulting requires a different set of skills, such as working effectively with other adults (Conoley & Gutkin, 1986). Unfortunately, not all school counselors receive formal training in consultation while in graduate school (Brown, Spano, & Schulte, 1988). This situation is likely to change, however, in that the Council for Accreditation of Counseling and

* This article appeared in *Elementary School Counseling and Guidance*, 1991, February, Vol. 25. Reprinted with permission.

Related Educational Program's standards require consultation experiences for trainees enrolled in accredited programs (American Association for Counseling and Development, 1983).

The purpose of this article is to present an introduction to, as well as some practical aspects of, two consultation theories to help school counselors improve their current approach to this important activity. We begin by defining consultation.

Consultation Defined

There is no universal agreement as to what exactly the term "consultation" means. Most agree, however, that it is a helping process that involves a consultant (e.g., counselor), "consultee" (e.g., teacher), and client (e.g., student). Brown, Pryzwansky and Schulte (1987) reviewed and integrated various writers' definitions and have offered the following list of key elements of consultation:

1. Initiated by either consultee or consultant.

2. Relationship is characterized by authentic communication.

3. Consultees may be professionals or nonprofessionals (e.g., parents).

4. Consultant provides indirect services to third-party clients.

5. Consultant provides direct services to consultees, assisting them to develop coping skills that ultimately make them independent of consultant.

6. Types of problems considered are work related when the concept of work is broadly conceived.

7. Consultant's role varies with consultees' needs.

8. Consultant may be based within consultee's organization or outside of it.

9. All communication between consultant and consultee is confidential. (Brown et al., 1987, p. 9)

There are three major theoretical perspectives in school-based consultation. These are mental health consultation (Caplan, 1970), behavioral consultation (Bergan, 1977), and process consultation (Schein, 1969). Overviews of mental health consultation and behavioral consultation models are presented.

Mental Health Consultation. To some degree, all consultation approaches are based on Caplan's (1970) mental health model. Caplan, a psychodynamically trained psychiatrist, proposed that a consultee's procession effectiveness could be improved through a process of case discussion and problem solving with a consultant. He saw this as involving a relationship between equals, meaning the consultant should have no direct-line authority over the consultee and should try to balance out whatever social power differences might exist between consultant and consultee. In a similar way, Caplan explained that consultation is different from collaboration in that the consultee must retain full responsibility for the outcome of the case. He also urged consultants to examine such elements as an organization's strengths, weaknesses, and capabilities as well as to consider the importance of relationships among people in the organization. Although Caplan's model also contains client-centered approaches, he is best known for his consultee-centered approaches.

Caplan viewed consultee difficulties as arising from deficits in skills, knowledge, confidence, or professional objectivity. Of these four, he believed that lack of objectivity accounted for the greater number of cases of lowered consultee effectiveness. In particular, *theme inference* is a term he used to illustrate a consultee's unconscious connection with a particular client case, a connection that produces short-term ineffectiveness on the job. For example, a classroom teacher may harbor a theme that states, "Boys from single-parent homes are always behavior problems in the classroom." Suppose further that a boy named Tom has recently entered this teacher's classroom. Tom lives at home with his mother, a divorced single parent. Given these issues, the teacher may falsely conclude that Tom is (or has a great potential to become) a disruptive student. Thus, this teacher may not accurately perceive or interpret Tom's actions in the classroom. Using Caplan's technique of theme inference reduction, the counselor-consultant may try to restore the teacher-consultee's objectivity by indicating to the teacher, through indirect confrontation, that not all boys who live with one parent turn out to be disruptive students.

Aside from theme inference reduction, there are at least three other strategies mental health consultants use to combat a consultee's lack of objectivity. First, the consultant may attempt persuading the consultee that the current problem is different from the past one. Using the aforementioned example, the consultant may try to show that Tom really doesn't live in a single-parent home, perhaps by indicating

to the consultee that Tom's mother was considering remarriage or that Tom had frequent contact with both parents through a joint custody arrangement. Second, the consultant may introduce a *parable,* a real of fictitious anecdote that parallels the consultee's current situation and resolves itself in a constructive way. Third, the consultant may provide a *nonverbal focus* on the case or the consultant relationship. Here, in addition to words, the consultant may respond to the consultee in a calm, respectful manner that suggests the latter is handling the situation as a competent professional.

The four strategies above clearly illustrate Caplan's psychodynamic orientation, including the importance of dealing with consultee themes at the unconscious level through indirect means. According to Caplan, directly confronting a consultee's theme destroys both the consultee's ego defenses and the coordinate, nonhierarchical relationship that is the cornerstone of the mental health consultation model. Others, such as Meyers (1981), have argued that direct confrontation is not only appropriate but is also advisable in many instances. Given the time-limited nature of the typical consultation and the corresponding need for direct communication, we support Meyer's position.

Of course, not all consultee difficulties may be attributed to a loss of objectivity. If a consultee lacks some knowledge relevant to a case, the consultant may be in a position to provide it to him or her. Caplan indicated, however, that the consultant should offer this knowledge within the spirit of a peer-professional relationship rather that a teacher-student relationship. If a consultee lacks certain skills, the consultant, again, may be in a position to assist. There are instances, however, when the skills needed by the consultee are not possessed by the consultant. (The fact that the consultant and consultee nearly always represent different professional disciplines contributes to this claim.) In these instances, the consultant is advised to defer to the consultee's supervisor whose background is more appropriate for the anticipated training.

Consultee difficulties also may stem from a lack of confidence. Because consulting is not the same as counseling, consultants need to keep these two roles separate. That is, whereas consultation involves an equal relationship between professionals engaging in solving work-related issues, counseling often involves an unequal relationship between two individuals in which the primary focus is on the client's personal issues. Caplan recommended that a counselor-consultant who works with a consultee having low self-confidence should offer much encouragement and support but ultimately should center discussions on problems in the workplace. Caplan believed that turning a consultation relationship into a personal counseling relationship was a grave mistake. Instead, he suggested that the consultation connect the consultee to other sources of support within the organization.

Gaining the school-wide support for conducting mental health consultation may pose problems. By this, we mean that in this age of accountability, it may be difficult for an administrator to endorse an approach that uses somewhat vague techniques (indirect confrontation, support, theme inference reduction) and offers no firm time frame for improved consultee functioning. Nevertheless, administrators often understand that some teachers' problems with students are because of teacher difficulties. In addition, explaining mental health consultation to teachers may be difficult because, although many teachers realize their contributions to children's failures to learn, for them to admit to their contributions is very threatening. Thus, mental health consultation must be explained to teacher-consultees in a sensitive, caring manner that reduces this threat. A strong commitment to confidentiality may be an excellent way for a counselor to transform a potentially threatening situation into one involving high levels of respect and trust. We continue next with behavioral consultation.

Behavioral Consultation. Behavioral consultation, like mental health consultation, is a problem solving process that seeks to improve the functioning of both consultees and children. In contrast with mental health consultation, however, behavioral consultation is based on behavioral and social learning theory and, thus, views observable behaviors (skills, knowledge) rather than unconscious themes as most important in determining a consultee's success (Bergan,1977). Behavioral consultants use a variety of behavior modification strategies drawn from behavioral and social learning theory. Because most counselors are familiar with many of these strategies, we do not review them here. Instead, we now examine the stages and tasks of behavioral consultation (Bergan, 1977).

Although there are various models of working with teachers using behavioral principles (e.g., Bauer & Sapona, 1988), perhaps the most well known of these was developed by Bergan (1977). Bergan conceptualized behavior consultation as involving four stages. The first stage is *problem identification,* which involves specifying the problems to be resolved as a result of consultation. Problem identification is accomplished through a problem identification interview (p. 11) between the consultant and consultee. The consultant must meet the following six objectives to define problems presented in consultation adequately:

1. Consultation must target the problems to be solved as a result of consultation. This generally involves asking the teacher about goals and expectations.

2. Each target problem must be described in behavioral terms rather than with medical model labels so that the exact nature of the problem as well as the course of problem solving can be agreed upon.

3. The environmental conditions surrounding each target behavior must be identified. Consultants accomplish this through questioning the teacher with regard to what events come before (antecedents), occur during (sequential), and follow (consequents) the problem behavior.

4. The consultant must ask the teacher to estimate the frequency, intensity, and/or duration of each target behavior to determine the severity of the problem and the extent of baseline (pretreatment) data collection procedures.

5. The consultant and teacher must agree on the type of data collection procedures that will be used and who will collect the data.

6. A date for the next interview must be arranged. It is important that an adequate sampling of baseline behavior be obtained before the next interview takes place.

The second stage of behavioral consultation is problem analysis. This is achieved through a problem analysis interview (PAI) during which each problem is examined further and a plan is designed to solve it. The PAI has four objectives:

1. The existence of each target problem must be documented by reviewing baseline data with the

teacher. Also, the difference between existing and desired performance of the child must be determined.

2. The antecedent, sequential, and consequent conditions surrounding the problem behavior must be specified and analyzed further.

3. An intervention plan must be devised.

4. A date for the next interview must be arranged. Also, the consultant should make plans to monitor the teacher's implementation of the plan and make arrangements for training the teacher (if necessary) in the application of the procedures agreed upon in the PAI.

The third stage of behavioral consultation is *plan implementation.* One aspect that distinguishes this stage from the three others is that in plan implementation there is no formal interview between the consultant and the teacher. Plan implementation has three objectives:

1. Whether or not the teacher has the necessary skills to implement the plan must be determined. If the teacher lacks the appropriate skills, the consultant must decide whether to train the teacher or select an easier procedure.

2. The consultant must monitor the teacher's data collection and plan operations.

3. The need for plan revisions must be determined. If the plan is not working, the consultant and the teacher must revise it to increase the probability of success.

The fourth and final stage of behavioral consultation is *problem evaluation,* in which the extent of the problem solution and plan effectiveness is determined. Problem evaluation is accomplished through a problem evaluation interview (PEI). The PEI has the following four objectives:

1. The extent to which the goals of consultation have been achieved must be determined. Different steps must be taken if goal attainment is complete, partial, or nonexistent.

2. The effectiveness of the intervention plan must be determined.

3. Strategies regarding the continuation, modification, or withdrawal of the intervention plan must be discussed.

4. Additional interviews (if needed) must be scheduled, or consultation on the problems(s) should be formally terminated (Bergan, 1977).

There is a considerable body of research that supports the utility of Bergan's model. This research also has revealed a very important implication for the practice of consultation. Specifically, Bergan and Tombari (1976) found that the single best predictor of whether a consultee would implement an intervention plan was successful problem identification during the problem identification interview (p. 11). The implication for the counselor-consultant is very clear—if you want to see positive results in consultation, make sure that during the initial interview you and your consultee specify in a concrete, observable way the problem to be solved.

Behavioral consultation, as compared with mental health consultation, is likely to be more easily accepted and implemented in schools. The focus of behavioral consultation is more easily understood as the client and his or her problem, thus making it less threatening to the consultee. Counselors who engage in behavioral consultation are able to tell consultees how the consultation will proceed, cite research in support of their interventions, and even indicate ahead of time what types of problems are more likely to improve as a result of the approach. The major problem, however, involved in introducing behavioral consultation to school personnel relates to the "bad name" associated with behavior modification. We have seen behavior modification techniques develop a poor reputation in some schools because, at times, behavioral consultants (a) enthusiastically use behavioral techniques regardless of consultee preference for or comfort with them, (b) become so involved with the techniques that they forgot to monitor their relationship with the consultee, and perhaps then suggest interventions that are unreasonable for the consultee to implement, and (c) use jargon (i.e., target behavior, generalization) that turns off consultees. In the last case, counselor-consultants are advised to speak "plain English" if teachers seem uneasy with the technical terminology, but to use the terminology freely with those teachers who use it themselves.

Conclusion

Research has shown consultation to be an effective method of improving the educational process and mental health of clients as well as the professional functioning of consultees (Medway & Updyke, 1985). This article has presented a definition of consultation and an overview of two theories of consultation—mental health and behavioral. A complex assortment of factors may influence a counselor's choice of one consultation approach over another, such as the sex of the consultee, type of consultee (e.g., teacher vs. administrator), setting in which the consultation occurs, consultant's comfort with a particular approach, type of client problem, target of consultation (e.g., client vs. consultee), and undoubtedly many others (Conoley & Conoley, 1981). For more information on the practice of consultation, readers are referred to Brown et al. (1987), Conoley (1981), Conoley and Conoley (1981), Gallessich (1982), and Parsons and Meyers (1984).

References

American Association for Counseling and Development. (1983). *Accreditation procedures manual and application for counseling and related educational programs.* Alexandria, VA: Author.

Bauer, A.M., & Sapona, R.H. (1988). Facilitation and problem solving: A framework for collaboration between counselors and teachers. *Elementary School Guidance & Counseling, 23,* 5–9.

Bergan, J.R. (1977). *Behavioral consultation.* Columbus, OH: Charles E. Merrill.

Bergan, J., & Tombari, M.L. (1976). Consultant skill and efficiency and the implementation and outcomes of consultation. *Journal of School Psychology, 14,* 3–13.

Brown, D., Pryzwansky, W.B., & Schulte, A.C. (1987). *Psychological consultation: Introduction to theory and practice.* Boston: Allyn & Bacon.

Brown, D., Spano, D., & Schulte, A.C. (1988). Consultation training in master's level counselor education programs. *Counselor Education and Supervision, 27,* 323–330.

Caplan, G. (1970). *The theory and practice of mental health consultation.* New York: Basic Books.

Conoley, J.C. (Ed.). (1981). *Consultation in schools: Theory, research, procedures.* New York: Academic Press.

Conoley, J.C., & Conoley, C.W. (1981). Toward prescriptive consultation. In J.C. Conoley (Ed.), *Consultation in schools: Theory, research, procedures* (pp. 265–294). New York: Academic Press.

Conoley, J.C., & Conoley, C.W. (1991). *School consultation* (2nd ed.). New York: Pergamon.

Conoley, J.C., & Gutkin, T.B. (1986). School psychology: A reconceptualization of service delivery realities. In S.N. Elliot & J.C. Witt (Eds.), *The delivery of psychological services in schools: Concepts, processes, and issues* (pp. 393–424). Hillsdale, NJ: Erlbaum.

Gallessich, J. (1982). *The profession and practice of consultation.* San Francisco: Jossey-Bass.

Humes, C.W., & Hohenshil, T.H. (1987). Elementary counselors, school psychologists, social workers: Who does what? *Elementary School Guidance & Counseling, 22,* 37–45.

Medway, F.J., & Updyke, J.F. (1985). Meta-analysis of consultation outcome studies. *American Journal of Community Psychology, 13,* 489–505.

Meyers, J. (1981). Mental health consultation. In J.C. Conoley (Ed.), *Consultation in schools: Theory, research, procedures* (pp. 35–58). New York: Academic Press.

Parsons, R.D., & Meyers, J. (1984). *Developing consultation skills.* San Francisco: Jossey-Bass.

Schein, E.H. (1969). *Process consultation: Its role in organization development.* Reading, MA: Addison-Wesley.

■ ■ ■

GUIDELINES FOR SCHOOL AND MENTAL HEALTH CONSULTATION

The stages of consultation outlined by Meyers, Parsons, and Martin (1979), and Kurpius, Fuqua, and Rozecki (1993) have been adapted here and serve as guidelines for the development of the consultation plan.

Pre-entry is considered part of the consultation process because it enables the consultant to assess the degree to which he/she is the proper "fit" for the consultation situation. According to Kurpius et al. (1993) pre-entry is the preliminary stage when the consultant forms a conceptual foundation to work from and through the process of self-assessment and is able to articulate to self and others who he/she is and the services he/she can provide. Kurpius et al. suggested that through this self-assessment and reflective process, consultants should understand their beliefs and values, understanding how individuals, families, programs, organizations, or systems cause, solve or avoid problems (p.601).

Further, Kurpius et al. (1993) maintained that the pre-entry stage is essential for consultants to conceptualize the meaning and operation of consultation to themselves and be ready to do the same with their consultees or consultee system. To this end, the following questions are oftentimes helpful:

- What models, processes, theories, and paradigms do you draw on to conceptualize your model of helping?

- How do you define consultation to the consultee or consultee system?

- Do you see it as triadic (consultant, consultee, client) or didactic (consultant and client)?

- When is visionary, looking into the future, and planning a better intervention better than cause and effect problem solving?

- What about acting as judge and evaluator of your consultees?

Enter into the System

The consultant's entry into the system is a crucial step in determining the success or failure of consultation efforts. Gallessich (1982) delineated several steps in the process of formal entry into the system. For the external consultant, entry usually begins with the exploration of the match between the organization's needs and the consultant's skill. Discussions between the consultant and members of the organization center around descriptive information about the organization, its needs, and desired outcomes. The consultant's skill, style of consultation, and a plan of how consultation efforts can be implemented in the setting are discussed and negotiated. Once the parties have agreed that consultation is indeed needed, the process proceeds to the negotiation of an informal or formal contract. The formulation of a contract follows the consultant having defined his/her function and role in the system. A clear understanding of the specific duties and functions of the consultant must be presented to personnel involved in the consultation effort. Negotiating a contract with key personnel serves to insure that the highest level of administrators as well as subordinates participate in the consultation process. Involvement of all personnel provides a smooth transition into the system and lessens the amount of resistance that can be encountered.

The formal discussion of the contract should include

- Goals or intended outcomes of consultation

- Identity of the consultees

- Confidentiality of service and limits of confidentiality

- Time frame—how long will the service be provided to the organization? To the individual consultee?

- Time(s) the consultant will be available

- Procedures for requesting to work with the consultant

- How to contact the consultant if needed

- Possibility of contract renegotiation if change is needed

- Fees, if relevant

- Consultant's access to different sources and types of information within the organization

- Person to whom the consultant is responsible (Brown, Pryzwansky, & Schulte, 1987, p. 137)

Orientation to Consultation

Orientation to consultation requires the consultant to communicate directly with key personnel in the system. Personnel need to know what to expect from the consultant and the consultant relationship. Initially, the consultant, in establishing a working relationship, must discuss roles the consultant and consultees will play in the process. This enables all parties to share in the expression of their needs and preferences and creates an atmosphere of open discussion and communication. Typical questions addressed in the orientation include the following:

- What are the consultant's expectations about consultation?

- What role will the consultant and consultee assume in the consultative effort?

- What are the parameters of the consultant's interventions?

- What are the ethical concerns of the consultee? The consultant?

- What are the parameters of confidentiality?

- How long with the consultation take?

- What are the procedures governing the gathering of data?

- What are the guidelines for the giving and receiving of feedback?

- What are the procedures used in the assessment of the consultation plan?

Problem Identification

Once the consultant and consultee have oriented themselves to the process of consultation, the consultant needs to identify the problem(s) to be addressed. A first step in problem identification is to meet with the consultee to gather appropriate data. Problem identification begins with establishing goals and objectives to be accomplished in consultation. Specific outcomes to be expected and the format for assessing outcomes is discussed. For example, questions to be considered might include the following:

- What are your general concerns about the problem?

- What needs to be accomplished to overcome your concerns?

- What role will the consultee play in overcoming the problem?

- What aspects of the consultee's problem are most distressing?

Consultation Interventions

Having defined the problem and reviewed the data gathered with the consultee, the consultant proceeds with the development of a specific intervention plan. The plan will include the establishment of objectives, the selection of strategies to be implemented, and the assessment procedures to be followed. Bergan (1977) suggested the following four-point outline as part of implementing a consultation plan:

1. Make sure that the consultee and consultant agree upon the nature of the problem.

Problem identification during the consultation process is critical to the overall success of consultation and sets the stage for the establishment of the consultant-consultee relationship. During the process, the consultant's main priority is to assist the consultee in identifying and clarifying the main problem that is experienced by the client. According to Dustin and Ehly (1984), the skills and techniques of focusing, paraphrasing, goal setting, empathy, and genuineness are particularly valuable at this problem identification stage. These skills assist in the development of a plan based upon authenticity and collaborative commitment between the consultant and consultee. According to Meyers, Parsons, and Martin (1979), a major task of the consultant is to determine which of four levels of consultation is most appropriate in conceptualizing the problem. The specific consultative techniques will vary depending upon whether the consultant chooses to respond with direct service to the client (level 1), indirect service to the child (level 2), direct service to the teacher (level 3), or direct service to the organization (level 4). Regardless of the level to be addressed, the consultant and consultee must agree upon the nature and scope of the problem.

2. Complete either the setting and intrapersonal analysis or skills analysis.

One role of the consultant is to assist the consultee to accurately estimate the importance of situations, as well as to develop self-efficacy expectations regarding performance. Once performance of a productive behavior has been completed, self-evaluation based on reasonable standards must occur. These processes can be facilitated through modeling and feedback to the consultee. Often the consultee's motivation can be enhanced by cueing the consultee in regard to the possible positive outcomes of consultation, assisting him/her to set goals that correspond with his/her own standards, and develop situations that will enhance consultee confidence that he/she can perform the skills needed to solve the problem (Brown, Pryzwansky, & Schulte, 1987, p. 284).

3. Design a plan to deal with the identified problem: (a) establish objectives, (b) select interventions, (c) consider barriers to implementation, and (d) select appropriate procedures.

Once the problem has been identified, the consultant and consultee work to establish realistic goals—the objectives of the consortium effort. Setting realistic expectations for the outcomes of consultation implies communication about and knowledge of environmental consultee constraints. Further, Bardon (1977) asserted that successful consultation requires consultees who are knowledgeable of the consultation process. Without this, understanding discordant expectations between consultant and consultee frequently will lead to resistance (Piersel & Gutkin, 1983). Gutkin and Curtis (1982) asserted that unless consultees actively contribute during consultation interactions, they often will be frustrated by recommendations that are inconsistent with their own thinking, feel little psychological ownership of treatment plans, and fail to expand their own professional skills. This agreement and acceptance of objectives of the consultation plan must be assured before consultation interventions can be planned.

The selection of intervention strategies should rest with the consultee (Bergan, 1977). The consultee involvement in the selection process will raise the client's awareness of the problem and should enhance motivation by engaging clients in goal setting and evaluation.

The major issue in selecting intervention strategies is their appropriateness to the setting and the amount of time needed to monitor strategies. Brown (1985), in his discussion of the training of consultants, suggested that the following questions be asked.

1. Is the intervention technically correct?

2. Why was the intervention selected over others?

3. How much work and change will this intervention cause for the consultee, or if the consultee involves the organization, what structure must change and what are the sources of resistance to this change?

4. How will the process and outcomes of the intervention be monitored?

5. If this fails what is proposed? (pp. 421–422)

Reimers, Wacker, and Keppl (1987) suggested that a number of factors influence the selection of interventions. In general, the more severe the problem, the higher the acceptance level of all proposed treatments.

4. Make arrangements for follow-up sessions with the consultee.

Successful termination of consultation includes the need on the part of the consultant to express an openness to work with the consultee again with other presenting problems. In addition, the collecting of data from the consultee on the outcomes of change efforts can document effective consultation and justify its use in professional practice (Dustin & Ehly, 1984).

Assessing the Impact of Consultation

The success or failure of consultation interventions is determined by assessing the degree to which the results are congruent with the specific objectives. Data for making this determination comes from the observations that began during the entry process and have continued throughout the consultation process. Brown et al. (1987) suggested that steps in the evaluation process are as follows:

Determine the Purpose(s) of the Evaluation—The extent to which consultees provide or gather data affects their involvement at this point. The opportunity to make choices that will affect the time that needs to be directed to evaluation as well as the types of information that are collected will contribute to the ownership of the evaluation. A major issue to be considered is the confidentiality of the information to be presented.

Agree on Measurements to Be Made—The consultant and consultee must agree on methods and procedures of measurement. Measures must specifically address the objectives and goals of the intervention plan.

Identify Data Gathering Techniques—The major goal here is to place the measures in a context which allows for their interpretation. Data gathering techniques include systematic observations, standardized tests, questionnaires, and feedback forms.

Set a Data Collection Schedule—The consultant and consultee agree upon a formalized calendar of data collection. The method of collection, the tasks assigned to each party, and the method for summarizing and reporting data are discussed.

Develop a Dissemination Plan—The dissemination plan, which includes the format in which data is reported, needs to be carefully considered by both parties. Issues surrounding the reporting of data; the individuals to whom data are reported; and the confidentiality of the data are agreed upon and follow a predetermined plan of action.

Concluding Consultation—The termination of the consultation process is as important as the initial entry into the system. An imperative step is for the consultant to provide the consultee with an open invitation to seek further assistance as the need arises. Follow-up of consultation activities insures that the consultant and consultee have the opportunity to measure the effects of the process over time. The degree to which the termination process is perceived as a smooth transition can determine whether consultation services will be sought in the future (pp. 243–244).

The *Consultation Rating Form* (Form 7.1) is provided for use by site supervisor and university supervisor to evaluate consultation activities carried out by the counseling or psychology intern. The form can be used as an interim or final evaluation.

Process and Content Models of Consultation

The writings of Schein (1969, 1990) focused upon the need for the helper/consultant to understand the basic assumptions he/she brings to the consultation relationship. Rockwood (1993), in a special issue of the *Journal of Counseling and Development,* discussed Schein's consultation models—examining content versus process components of problems and problem solving. The basic components and major assumptions of the Purchase-of-Expertise Model, Doctor-Patient Model, and Process Consultation Model are outlined here for your consideration.

The Purchase-of-Expertise Model makes the following assumptions:

1. The client has to have made a correct diagnosis of what the real problem is.

2. The client has identified the consultants capabilities to solve the problem.

3. The client must communicate what the problem is.

4. The client has thought through and accepted all the implications of the help that will take place (Schein, 1978).

The Purchase-of-Expertise Model, a content oriented approach, enables clients to remove themselves from the problem, relying on the skills and expertise of the consultant to "fix" the problem.

The Doctor-Patient Model also focuses upon content and assumes that the diagnosis and prescription for the problem solution rest solely in the hands of the consultant.

1. The client has correctly interpreted the organizational assumptions and knows where the sickness is.

2. The client can trust the diagnosis.

3. The person or group defined as such will provide the necessary information to make the diagnosis.

4. The client will understand and accept the diagnosis, implement the prescription, and think through and accept the consequences.

5. The client will be able to remain healthy after the consultant leaves (Schein, 1978).

The Process Consultation Model focuses upon how problems are solved in a collaborative effort.

1. The nature of the problem is such that the client not only needs help in making a diagnosis but would also benefit from participating in making of the diagnosis.

2. The client has constructive intent and some problem solving abilities.

3. Ultimately, the client is the one who knows what form of intervention or solution will work best in the organization.

4. When the client engages in the diagnosis and then selects and implements interventions, there will be an increase in his/her future problem solving abilities (Schein, 1979).

Process consultation is systematic in that it accepts the goals and values of the organization as a whole and attempts to work with the client within those values and goals to jointly find solutions that will fit within the organizational system (Rockwood, 1993).

Resistance to Consultation

Resistance in consultative relationships is defined as "What occurs when the consultant is unsuccessful in influencing the consultee to engage actively in the problem solving process (Piersel & Gutkin, 1983). Berlin (1979) identified four types of resistance to consultation: inertia, active opposition, planned ineptitude, and feared loss of power. Similarly, Parsons and Meyers (1984) discussed four types of organizational resistance: (1) The desire for systems maintenance—the entrance of the consultant into the system requires the system to adapt to new input that drains energy and threatens the system. To avoid this pitfall, Parsons and Meyers (1984) suggested that the consultant should be careful not to threaten existing roles or challenge others' jobs or role definitions. The simpler the consultant's entry and the less change in structure, tone, process, or product it entails, the easier it will be for the consultant to avoid resistance based upon system maintenance (p. 102). (2) The consultant as the outsider—the consultant often is viewed as an alien in the organization and is treated with suspicion and resistance. The consultant should become familiar with the institution's history, mission, philosophy, and procedures and increase his/her availability to and contact with the staff to reduce this outsider status. (3) The desire to reject the new as non-normative—the desire to maintain status quo by conforming to existing norms in the organization. The consultant must guard against tampering with "time honored" programs, processes, and procedures. Consultant sensitivity to organizational vulnerability is essential. (4) The desire to protect one's turf or vested interests—the consultant must recognize that his/her presence is often viewed as an intrusion on consultee's area of interest or professional responsibility. Involving the consultee in the process would tend to lessen the resistance (pp. 102–106).

Similarly, a number of authors have identified specific variables that increase resistance to consultation. Lin and Zaltsman (1973) suggested that the more complex and involved the intervention, the more likely it will be subject to resistance. Kast and Rosenweig (1974) suggested that resistance is tied to the ability of change agents to accurately communicate the nature of interventions to consultees. Reimers, Wacker, and Keppl (1987) suggested that the less time and resources needed to implement interventions, the greater the acceptance. Bardon

(1977) asserted that successful consultative interactions require consultees who are knowledgeable of consultation processes. Piersel and Gutkin (1983) maintained that discordant expectations between consultant and consultees frequently will lead to resistance.

The following article is presented to provide an overview and understanding of the sources, types, and management of methods used in dealing with resistance.

THE SOURCES AND MANAGEMENT OF RESISTANCE TO CONSULTATION*

A. Michael Dougherty
Leslie P. Dougherty
Diane Purcell

School counselors are increasingly being called on to provide consultation to other school personnel as well as to parents (Leonard & Gottsdanker-Willenkens, 1987; Rose, Friend, & Farnum, 1988). School counselors consult with teachers, administrators, and parents because these are among the adult "significant others" in the lives of children and adolescents (Aubrey, 1978). As it pertains to school counselors working with teachers and administrators, consultation can be defined as a process in which the school counselor assists a "consultee" (e.g., teacher, administrator) with a work-related problem (e.g., misbehavior in the classroom) with a client system (e.g., student, group of students) with a goal of helping both the client system and the consultee in some way (Dougherty, 1990). As this definition implies, consultation is typified by a problem-solving orientation (Carrington, Cleveland, & Ketterman, 1978; Osterweil, 1987) in which counselors consult with teachers and administrators concerning problems they are encountering with students. The following examples illustrate the problem-solving nature of the school counselor's consulting services:

- A school counselor assists a teacher in determining some ways to bolster the self-esteem of

(Continued on p. 269.)

* This article appeared in *School Counselor,* 1991, January, Vol. 38, pp. 179–186. Reprinted with permission.

CONSULTATION RATING FORM
John C. Boylan, Ph.D.

DIRECTIONS: For each of the following questions, please rate the degree to which you feel consultation was successful: 1. Highly Successful, 2. Moderately Successful, 3. Neutral, 4. Not Successful.

The consultant clearly defined his/her role to the staff.   _____

The consultant emphasized the importance of the services offered on a request or voluntary basis.   _____

The consultant stressed the importance of the services offered on a request or voluntary basis.   _____

The consultant explained the rationale for his/her consultative approach.   _____

The consultant encouraged open discussion of any problem or observations about the process of consultation.   _____

The consultant was open to suggestions and recommendations from the consultee.   _____

The consultant explained and described the steps in the consultation process.   _____

The consultant spent time carefully gathering data from the consultee.   _____

The consultant intervened with direct services to the consultee.   _____

The consultant intervened with indirect services to the consultee   _____

The consultant was successful in identifying the problem.   _____

The consultant defined the problem in terms of the person in the environment.,   _____

The consultant defined the problem in terms of lack of skill, lack of knowledge.,   _____

The consultant defined the problem in terms of broader organizational problems or issues.   _____

The consultant made specific recommendations for change.   _____

The consultant provided a variety of interventions and strategies in problem solving.   _____

The consultant evaluated the impact of his/her consultation efforts in a formal manner.   _____

The consultant provided feedback to the consultee about the assessment of the consultation process.   _____

The consultant encouraged follow-up of the consultation relationship.   _____

The consultant encouraged independent problem solving by the consultee.   _____

CONSULTATION RATING FORM
John C. Boylan, Ph.D.

DIRECTIONS: For each of the following questions, please rate the degree to which you feel consultation was successful: 1. Highly Successful, 2. Moderately Successful, 3. Neutral, 4. Not Successful.

The consultant clearly defined his/her role to the staff.   _____

The consultant emphasized the importance of the services offered on a request or voluntary basis.   _____

The consultant stressed the importance of the services offered on a request or voluntary basis.   _____

The consultant explained the rationale for his/her consultative approach.   _____

The consultant encouraged open discussion of any problem or observations about the process of consultation.   _____

The consultant was open to suggestions and recommendations from the consultee.   _____

The consultant explained and described the steps in the consultation process.   _____

The consultant spent time carefully gathering data from the consultee.   _____

The consultant intervened with direct services to the consultee.   _____

The consultant intervened with indirect services to the consultee.   _____

The consultant was successful in identifying the problem.   _____

The consultant defined the problem in terms of the person in the environment.,   _____

The consultant defined the problem in terms of lack of skill, lack of knowledge.,   _____

The consultant defined the problem in terms of broader organizational problems or issues.   _____

The consultant made specific recommendations for change.   _____

The consultant provided a variety of interventions and strategies in problem solving.   _____

The consultant evaluated the impact of his/her consultation efforts in a formal manner.   _____

The consultant provided feedback to the consultee about the assessment of the consultation process.   _____

The consultant encouraged follow-up of the consultation relationship.   _____

The consultant encouraged independent problem solving by the consultee.   _____

a group of students so that they can become more effective learners.

- A school counselor collaborates with a principal in developing a plan to keep a student from dropping out of school.

- A school counselor trains a group of teachers in understanding the multicultural issues inherent in teaching ethnic minorities so that such students will learn more.

As these examples suggest, consultation has as its goal a positive change in both the client system (e.g., student, group of students) and the consultee (e.g., teacher, administrator).

The very act of providing consultative services conveys a message that change is going to occur. To help students change effectively may imply that teachers or administrators themselves must also change their own behaviors. Therefore, as school counselors engage in consultation to bring about positive change, it is very common for teachers and administrators to demonstrate resistance to the consultation process because of the implication that they themselves must change in order to assist the students to change (Dougherty, 1990). Resistance can be defined as the failure of a consultee (e.g., teacher, administrator) to participate constructively in the consultation process. More specifically, resistance is any behavior that thwarts the probability of a successful process or outcome (Cormier & Cormier, 1985). Although there is some literature related to the skills necessary for school counselors to consult effectively (e.g., Dustin & Ehly, 1984), little has been written on the types of resistance. Furthermore, as Randolph and Graun (1988) noted, many counselors have not received adequate training in recognizing and dealing with consultee resistance to consultation.

The purpose of this article is to discuss the sources of consultee resistance and some things school counselors can do to minimize and manage that resistance. It is hoped that such a discussion will assist practicing school counselors in enhancing their ability to recognize and deal with resistance to consultation. The scope of this article is restricted to resistance of individual consultees and does not deal with resistance on the part of the entire school (i.e., organizational resistance).

Consultee Resistance

One of the most common sources of resistance is the *misconception* on the part of administrators and teachers of the counselor's consultation role. Administrators and teachers may not know what consultation is, how the counselor implements the role of consultant, or even that consultation is a legitimate role for the counselor to take on. Such lack of information might make it more difficult for administrators and teachers to take part in consultation.

Consultee resistance can be indicative of a *dysfunction within the consulting relationship* (Parsons & Meyers, 1984). This dysfunction may or may not be a product of the psychological concerns of the consultee. A necessary question to address is whether the consultee's resistance is due to the natural tendency of administrators or teachers to maintain their perceived roles in the school and resist change or whether the resistance is due to one of their psychological concerns. For example, resistance can occur when there are differences between what the school counselor views as the major problem on which the consulting relationship should focus and what the teacher or administrator views as the major problem (Parsons & Meyers, 1984). In effect, this type of resistance tells the counselor that there is a need for further exploration of the focus of consultation. If, on the other hand, a teacher with some disruptive students resists within the consultation relationship because of burnout, then the counselor needs to determine if consultation is a feasible choice in helping the students.

Consultees can be resistant due to *fear of discomfort*. This form of resistance is due to anxiety. It is a wish to maintain familiar patterns of behavior. The very fact that consultation is occurring implies the possible need for change and therefore causes discomfort. Consultees may try to remain comfortable even at their own professional expense (Ellis, 1985). For example, a teacher may feel anxious about trying alternative discipline techniques to control a student's behavior even though tried-and-true techniques are not working.

Another reason that consultation resistance can occur is *fear of disclosure and shame*. Teachers or administrators may fear that by sharing information during consultation with the counselor their imperfections may be revealed. The revelation that they may not always "have it together" professionally may cause shame (Ellis, 1985). For example, an administrator may feel inadequate in relating that he or she does not know how to handle an overly aggressive student.

Feelings of hopelessness can be a reason for resistance (Ellis, 1985). A consultee may feel that a student is "beyond help" and that consultation will not do any good. A teacher may feel, for example, that a potential dropout is a hopeless case and wish to "give up" on the student. Such a view may lead the teacher to suffer from lack of professional objectivity about the possibility of helping the student (see Caplan, 1970).

Some consultees may resist because they *fear success* (Ellis, 1985). That is, they are afraid that if they are successful they may be given students or responsibilities within the school that they cannot handle. For example, a teacher who has the ability for effectively handling "rough" classes may resist consultation services out of fear of being identified as the teacher who should always have such classes.

Resistance might be motivated by *rebelliousness*. When consultees perceive the consultive behavior of the counselor as being obtrusive on their freedom, they may act with rebellion. Consultees resisting in this way may well feel that the counselor is inappropriately attempting to control them. For example, a teacher balks at any consultation intervention made by the counselor with the statement, "I have the freedom to close my classroom door and do whatever I please."

Cognitive distortions can be a source of resistance in individual teachers and administrators. Cognitive distortions are misinterpretations of reality that can lead to defensiveness. All people engage in cognitive distortions at one time or another. There are several cognitive distortions (McKay, Davis, & Fanning, 1981) the individuals can engage in, such as overgeneralizing (e.g., "*All* seventh graders are promiscuous") and "catastrophizing" (e.g., "It's the students' fault that I can't teach them"), which promote resistance. Consultees (as well as consultants) might engage in these distortions as ways to diminish anxiety and fear about issues within the consultation process. In addition, because they lead to fallacious interpretations of reality (e.g., over-

generalization), cognitive distortions can cause misunderstandings that encourage consultee resistance. By understanding the cognitive distortions of consultees, the counselor can determine best how to diminish the resistance these cognitive distortions engender. For example, a counselor consultant with a teacher who perceives that all the children of the same family at the school "are all alike" may have the teacher compare and contrast the various children's behaviors at school. Although it is not the job of counselors to provide psychotherapy concerning cognitive distortions to teachers or administrators, it is certainly appropriate for consultants to assist their consultees in examining the logic of their ideas that lead to such distortions. "By examining the evidence" of their logic, consultees can learn to distort less and be even more cooperative in the consultation process. When counselors perceive extreme cases of cognitive distortions in their consultees, they need to reexamine whether or not consultation is feasible.

Dealing Effectively with Resistance

Given the sources of resistance, how does the school counselor effectively deal with resistance? Because of the variety of sources of resistance, perhaps the best method of dealing with resistance is to attempt to prevent its occurrence in the first place.

Resistance can often be minimized by affecting the consultees' perceptions of the consultant and the consulting process. It is what they *think* about the consultant's behavior, not the actual behavior itself, that is critical. When delivering consultation services, therefore, the school counselor should be concerned about creating positive expectations in teachers and administrators about the experience and the outcomes of consultation (Brown, Pryzwansky, & Schulte, 1987). Factors related to consultees' perceptions and positive expectations that counselors should examine include the following:

1. Maintaining objectivity

2. Getting appropriate support for consultation within the school

3. Making the counselor's role as a consultant explicit

4. Being aware of the organizational dynamics and the ways in which persons relate

5. Using social influence

6. Emphasizing the peer nature of the relationship

Maintaining Objectivity. In terms of objectivity, the consultee should perceive that the counselor's attempts to consult are collaborative, not a manipulative "tool" of the school's formal or informal power structure and not based on politics, friendships, or hidden agendas (Kurpius & Robinson, 1978). The consultee should in no way feel left out, overlooked, or insignificant regarding the process of consultation. Specificity is another critical factor in preempting the occurrence of resistance. Consultees need to perceive that the counselor is attempting to deal with them as unique individuals with idiosyncratic concerns. Consultees who are aware that the counselor is attempting to consult with them from a generic model may be resistant because they believe that general procedures are not necessarily applicable to their unique situations (Leibowitz, Farren, & Kaye, 1985) and may create the perception that consultation will not be effective. The use of multiple approaches in performing consultation can be related to meeting the perceived needs of the consultee. Resistance, particularly that due to cognitive distortions, can be minimized if counselors are flexible and able to proceed with consultation in a variety or ways.

Getting Appropriate Support for Consultation. Obtaining sanctioning of their consultation role by the chief administrator of the school is a politically savvy way for consultants to minimize resistance. The fact that the school counselor is sanctioned to provide consultation by the administration of the school implies that current ways of functioning in the school are inadequate to handle its concerns (Parsons & Meyers, 1984). Sanctioning of consultation makes change on the part of consultees legitimate and reduces the threat of trying new ways of behaving. In addition, this sanctioning provides the counselor with some leverage in ensuring that adequate time is allocated for consultation, thus minimizing the time and energy expenditure and the interference with the consultee's regular work schedule (Cohen, 1985).

In obtaining necessary support from within the school, the consultant should ensure that sanctions from the midlevel administration (e.g., assistant principals) and affected personnel have been se-cured. The informal power structure within the school must also sanction the consultant's activities. Midlevel administrators must be contacted by the counselor and sanction the consulting activities so that consultees who work closely with them will not perceive a possible forced choice of loyalty to either the counselor or the midlevel administrator (Cohen, 1985). Strong interactive relationships with relevant midlevel administrators build trust and provide for both their input into and understanding of the consulting process.

Making the Role of Consultant Explicit. The perceptions of teachers and administrators of the counselor's role early on in the consulting process are often unclear. In addition, the role and function of school counselors are frequently not well understood by other school personnel (see, for example, Wilgus & Shelley, 1988). Therefore, some resistance can be preempted by providing a clear picture of what consultation is and what the school counselor does when providing consultation (Fuchs, 1975). Such a statement of purpose can diminish resistance by making it clear to consultees that the counselor's main goal in consultation is to help them and the school and that their own performance is not under scrutiny (Cohen, 1985). Thus, fear of the unknown and fear of evaluation are minimized. For example, the term *consultation* may become a less threatening term to teachers because they come to view the implication of change on their part as an aspect of normal professional development.

Even if counselors are school-based, their role varies so much from that of other school personnel that they are frequently not seen as part of the mainstream of school life. Resistance to consultation can be minimized when counselors are viewed as "insiders" or "one of us" by consultees. When counselors are accepted as part of the system, their consulting activities are viewed by consultees more as attempts to help than as intrusions by an ill-informed outsider. There are several methods school counselors can employ to minimize their being viewed as outsiders. These methods include becoming familiar with the "ins and outs" of the entire school before attempting to provide consulting services. In terms of understanding the dynamics of the school, it is important for the counselor to take on the frame of reference of the typical consultee within that school (Meyers, Parsons, & Martin, 1979). This frame of reference can prevent the counselor from inadvertently creating stressful situations for the consultee during the consulting process. Other ways that can minimize resistance include associating frequently with school personnel, participating fully in several school wide activities during the year, creating rapport with members of both the formal and informal power structures, obtaining public sanctioning from the administration for consulting services, and creating a reward system for participating consultees.

Being Aware of Organizational Dynamics. As organizations, schools take time to develop normative behavior. Consultees may be aware of their own work-related problems but may feel secure with the degree to which they are dealing with these problems (Gallessich, 1982). In effect, the consultees have reached a sense of equilibrium and do not perceive a strong need to change. Therefore, it is normal for them to be slow to change and assimilate new norms that result from consultation. By being patient and planning for the long haul as far as expectations about change are concerned, the counselor can prevent the view of consultation as intrusive and counterproductive to "what is going on already." This patience can be interpreted as support and encouragement and thus can minimize resistance.

A related method of minimizing resistance involves the complexity of the counselor's consultative interventions. The more complex the interventions, the more likely significant changes will occur in the consultee as well as others directly or indirectly affected by consultation. These changes make demands on school personnel that may exacerbate concerns about the quality of their job performance (Brown, Pryzwansky, & Schulte, 1987). Resistance can be minimized by creating the conditions in which the total amount of change required by consultees is reduced. These conditions are best accomplished by the use of existing structures (e.g., rules and regulations) and procedures (e.g., communication channels) of the school.

Using Social Influence. Social influence is a primary skill for the consultant to possess. Social influence can be built in several ways. Personal orientations to what consultation is all about can put the elements of fear and uncertainty to rest (Fuchs, 1975). The use of effective communication skills helps develop strong working relationships (Brown,

Pryzwansky, & Schulte, 1987). Referent and expert power can also diffuse resistance (Meyers, Parsons, & Martin, 1979). Referent power is power based on perceived similarity. Expert power is power based on the knowledge and skills of another. Direct confrontation of the resistance by the consultant, although risky, can reduce consultee resistance (Meyers, 1981).

Emphasizing the Peer Nature of the Relationship. The school counselor can preempt a great deal of resistance by emphasizing the peer nature of consultation. By maintaining a nonjudgmental attitude toward the consultee and continually emphasizing a collaborative stance, the counselor behaviorally demonstrates lack of evaluation and criticism of the consultee. Because teachers and administrators typically develop a sense of autonomy and independence in their jobs, a peer orientation to consultation by the school counselor will not threaten the existing sense of independence, autonomy, and power of consultees. Two general ways of promoting a peer orientation to consultation are understanding and involvement (Kelley, 1981). Understanding refers to the ability of the consultant to comprehend and appreciate the consultee's views of events. Involvement refers to the use of a collaborative approach by the consultant whenever possible. Collaboration assists in preventing the counselor from overpowering the consultee. Understanding and involvement can reduce resistance because they focus on listening and learning.

Conclusion

Consultation is more than a craft, more than an art, more than a science—it is all of these along with commitment to oneself, commitment to those with whom one consults, and commitment to the ever-challenging tasks of getting ideas and concepts out of the mind of the consultant and into the mind of the consultee (Dougherty, 1990). Resistance to consultation is more than a craft, more than an art, more than a science—it is all of these along with commitment to preserve the status quo, commitment to avoid the anxiety of change, and commitment to the ever-challenging task of blocking the attempts of the consultant to be of help.

What should the school counselor remember about resistance to consultation? We have discussed seven major points, summarized as follows:

1. Resistance to consultation is a natural phenomenon in the consultation process, and the school counselor needs to anticipate it. Such a perspective helps counselors take resistance less personally and often prevents anger toward the person who is resisting.

2. Resistance typically occurs due to fear of change experienced by school personnel in their work settings. By minimizing the severity of the changes that result from consultation, the counselor can minimize the "cost" of consultation to consultees and hence minimize resistance.

3. Fear of consultation by school personnel can be minimized through publicizing the nature of the consultation services and developing strong consultant-consultee relationships. The more explicitly counselors define their consulting roles, the more likely it is that the consultee will develop a positive attitude toward consultation.

4. The school counselor must learn to cope effectively with resistance to consultation so that positive progress can be made. Discussing a resistant consultee with a trusted colleague can lead to more effective coping by the counselor.

5. Minimizing resistance is highly related to the school counselor's ability to build collaborative, peer relationships with teachers and administrators. The more the need for consultation is owned by each party involved, the more likely consultation will reach a successful conclusion.

6. While the consultation relationship is collaborative in nature, the school counselor must take the lead in dealing with and minimizing resistance.

7. There are many ways for the school counselor to handle resistance effectively in consultation. Therefore, school counselors should review the literature on ways to approach resistance to consultation. Although there is limited literature in this area, the literature on resistance to counseling does have some application to resistance to consultation.

By understanding the sources for resistance and how to cope effectively when resistance is shown, school counselors can more easily accomplish the following outcomes:

1. sustained motivation to engage in consulting activities even in the face of resistance by teachers and administrators,

2. increased flexibility in the school itself and its personnel in terms of creating and adapting to change, and

3. increased opportunities for consultation with a greater proportion of the personnel in the school.

References

Aubrey, R.F. (1978). Consultation, school interventions, and the elementary counselor. *The Personnel and Guidance Journal, 56*(6), 351–354.

Brown, D., Pryzwansky, W.B., & Schulte, A.C. (1987). *Psychological consultation: Introduction to theory and practice.* Boston: Allyn and Bacon.

Caplan, G. (1970). *The theory and practice of mental health consultation.* New York: Basic Books.

Carrington, D., Cleveland, A., & Ketterman, C. (1978). Collaborative consultation in the secondary schools. *The Personnel and Guidance Journal, 56*(6), 355–358.

Cohen, W.A. (1985). *How to make it big as a consultant.* New York: AMACOM.

Cormier, W.H., & Cormier, L.S. (1985). *Interviewing strategies for helpers.* Monterey, CA: Brooks/Cole.

Dougherty, A.M. (1990). *Consultation: Practice and perspectives.* Pacific Grove, CA: Brooks/Cole.

Dustin, D., & Ehly, S. (1984). Skills for effective consultation. *The School Counselor, 32,* 23–29.

Ellis, A. (1985). *Overcoming resistance: Rational emotive therapy with different clients.* New York: Springer.

Fuchs, J. (1975). *Making the most of management consulting services.* New York: AMACOM.

Gallessich, J. (1982). *The profession and practice of consultation.* San Francisco: Jossey-Bass.

Kelley, R.E. (1981). *Consulting: The complete guide to a profitable career.* New York: Scribner's.

Kurpius, D.J., & Robinson, S.E. (1978). An overview of consultation. *The Personnel and Guidance Journal, 56*(6), 321–323.

Leibowitz, Z., Farren, C., & Kaye, B. (1985). The 12-fold path to enlightenment. *Training and Development Journal, 39*(4), 29–32.

Leonard, P.Y., & Gottsdanker-Willenkens, A.E. (1987). The elementary school counselor as consultant for self-concept enhancement. *The School Counselor, 34,* 245–255.

McKay, M., Davis, M., & Fanning, P. (1981). *Thoughts and feelings: The art of cognitive stress intervention.* Richmond, CA: New Harbinger Publications.

Meyers, J. (1981). Mental health consultation. In J.C. Conoley (Ed.), *Consultation in schools: Theory, research, procedures* (pp. 35–58). New York: Academic Press.

Meyers, J., Parsons, R.D., & Martin, R. (1979). *Mental health consultation in the schools.* San Francisco: Jossey-Bass.

Osterweil, Z.O. (1987). A structural process of problem definition in school consultation. *The School Counselor, 34,* 345–352.

Parsons, R.D., & Meyers, J. (1984). *Developing consultation skills.* San Francisco: Jossey-Bass.

Randolph, D.L., & Graun, K. (1988). Resistance to consultation: A synthesis for counselor-consultants. *Journal of Counseling and Development, 67,* 182–184.

Rose, E., Friend, M., & Farnum, M. (1988). Transition planning for mildly handicapped students: The secondary school counselor's role. *The School Counselor, 35,* 275–284.

Wilgus, E., & Shelley, E. (1988). The role of the elementary-school counselor: Teacher perceptions, expectations, and actual functions. *The School Counselor, 35,* 259–266.

■ ■ ■

CONTRACTING AND THE FORCES OF CHANGE IN THE ORGANIZATION

Kurpius, Fuqua, and Rozecki (1993) suggested that an understanding of the cycles of change and the forces of change within the organization are helpful in gaining a better understanding of problems and culture surrounding the problem in the organization. Stages of change include the following:

1. Development—needing help at an early stage of a new problem or program.

2. Maintenance—things are becoming stagnant and falling behind, needing help to improve. This shows signs of consultee desire and motivation for change.

3. Decline—things are worse and consultees recognize that they cannot solve the problem. Consultee may want a quick fix and have high expectations placed in the consultant.

4. Crisis—consultee or consultee system is desperate for help. The consultant may look for dependency first, but it is important that consultees understand that their situation and the investment needs to return to a stable state.

The forces of change within the system need to be understood for consultation to proceed. When the system is closed to change and internal forces vary between being for or against change, there is usually little opportunity for change to occur. When the system recognizes that change is needed but forces for and against change are balanced, progress is possible but slow moving. When the forces for change are external to the members who prefer not to change, one can expect a high degree of conflict and slow change. Finally, when the members recognize the need for help and all want help to improve, then the best chance for successful helping occurs (Kurpius et al., p. 602).

These models can serve as a test of the feasibility of the consultant's effort and the type of contract the consultant will implement. The formal discussion of the contract between the consultant and the consultee should include a number of critical questions to be answered before a contract is developed and implemented. According to Remley (1993), consultation contracts should do the following:

1. Clearly specify the work to be completed by the consultant.

2. Describe in detail any work products expected from the consultant.

3. Establish a time frame for the completion of the work.

4. Establish lines of authority and the person to whom the consultant is responsible.

5. Describe the compensation plan for the consultant and the method of payment.

6. Specify any special agreements or contingency plans agreed upon by the parties.

CHAPTER BIBLIOGRAPHY

Albee, G.W. (1982). The politics of nature and nurture. *American Journal of Community Psychology, 10,* 1–36.

Alpert, J.L. (1977). Some guidelines for school consultation. *Journal of School Psychology, 15,* 308–19.

Alpert, J.L., & Meyers, J. (1983). *Training in consultation: Prospectives from mental health, behavioral, and organizational consultation.* Springfield, IL: Charles C. Thomas.

Bardon, J.I. (1977). *The consultee in consultation: Preparation and training.* Paper presented at annual meeting, American Psychological Association, San Francisco.

Bergan, J.R., & Tombari, M.L. (1976). Consultant skill and efficiency and the implementation and outcomes of consultation. *Journal of School Psychology, 14,* 3–14.

Bergan, J. R. (1977). *Behavior consultation.* Monterey, CA: Brooks/Cole.

Berlin, L. (1979). Resistance to mental health consultation directed as change in public institutions. *Community Mental Health Journals, 15*(2), 119–128.

Bloom, B.L. (1977). *Community mental health: A general introduction.* Monterey, CA: Brooks /Cole.

Brown, D. (1985). The preservice training and supervision of consultants. *The Counseling Psychologist 13,* 410–425.

Brown, D., Pryzwansky, W.B., & Schulte, A.C. (1987). *Psychological consultation: Introduction to theory and practice.* Boston: Allyn and Bacon.

Caplan, G. (1970). *The theory and practice of mental health consultation.* New York: Basic Books.

Conyne, R.K. (1987). *Primary preventive counseling: Empowering people and systems.* Muncie, IN: Accelerated Development.

Cormier, W.H., & Cormier, L.S. (1985). *Interviewing strategies for helpers: Fundamental skills and cognitive behavioral interventions.* Monterey, CA: Brooks/Cole.

Dinkmeyer, D., Jr., Carlson, J., & Dinkmeyer, D., Sr. (1994). *Consultation: School mental health professionals as consultants.* Muncie, IN: Accelerated Development.

Dougherty, A.M., Dougherty, L.P., & Purcell, D. (1991, January). The sources and management of resistance to consultation. *The School Counselor, 38,* 179–186.

Dustin, D., & Ehly, S. (1984, September). Skills for effective consultation. *The School Counselor,* 25–28.

Erchul, W.P., & Conoley, C.W. (1991, February). Helpful theories to guide counselors' practice of school based consultation. *Elementary School Counseling and Guidance, 25.*

Hutchins, D.E., & Cole, C.G. (1992). *Helping relationships and strategies* (second edition). Monterey, CA: Brooks/Cole.

Gallessich, J. (1982). *The profession and practice of consultation.* San Francisco: Jossey-Bass.

Gutkin, T.B., & Curtis. (1982). School-based consultation: Theory and techniques. In C.R. Reynolds & T.B. Gutkin (Eds.), *The handbook of school psychology* (pp. 796–820). New York: Wiley.

Jacobson, E., Ravlin, M., & Cooper, S. (1983). Issues in training of mental health consultants in community mental health centers. In J.L. Alpert and J. Meyers (Eds.), *Training in consultation: Prospectives from mental helath, behavioral and organizational consultation.* Springfield IL: Charles C. Thomas.

Kast, F.E., & Rosenweig, J.E. (1974). *Organization and management: A systems approach* (2nd edition). New York: McGraw-Hill.

Kirby, J. (1985). *Consultation: Practice and practitioner.* Muncie, IN: Accelerated Development.

Kurpius, D. (1978). Consultation theory and process: An integrated model. *The Personnel and Guidance Journal, 56,* 335–378.

Kurpius, D., Fuqua, R., & Rozecki, T. (1993, July/August). The consulting process: A multidimensional approach. *Journal of Counseling and Development, 71,* 601–606.

Lambert, N.M. (1983). Prospectives on training school-based consultants. In J.L. Alpert and J, Meyers (Eds.), *Training in consultation: Prospectives from mental health, behavioral and organizational consultation.* Springfield, IL: Charles C. Thomas.

Lin, N., & Zaltsman, G. (1973). Dimensions and innovations. In G. Zaltsman (Ed.), *Processes and phenomenons of social change* (pp. 93–115). New York: Wiley and Sons.

Meyers, J., Parsons, R.D., & Martin, R. (1979). *Mental health consultation in the schools.* San Francisco: Jossey-Bass.

Ohlsen, M.M. (1983). *Introduction to counseling.* Itasca, IL: F. E. Peacock.

Parsons, R.D., & Meyers, J. (1984). *Developing consultation skills.* San Francisco: Jossey-Bass.

Piersel, W.C., & Gutkin, F.B. (1983). Resistance to school based consultation: A behavioral analysis of the problem. *Psychology in the Schools, 20,* 311–320.

Reimers, T.M., Wacker, D.P., & Keppl, G. (1987). Acceptability of behavioral interventions: A review of the literature. *School Psychology Review, 16,* 212–227.

Remley, T.P. (1993). Consultation contracts. *Journal for Counseling and Development, 72,* 157–158.

Rockwood, G.F. (1993, July/August). Edgar Schein's process versus content consultation models. *Journal of Counseling and Development, 71,* 636–638.

Sarason, S.B. (1971). *The culture of the school and the problem of change.* Boston: Allyn and Bacon.

Schein, E.H. (1969). *Process consultation.* Reading, MA: Addison Wesley.

Schein, E.H. (1978). The role of the consultant: Content expert or process facilitator? *The Personnel and Guidance Journal, 56,* 339–345.

Schein, E.H. (1990). Organizational culture. *American Psychologist, 45,* 109–119.

Weinrach, S.G. (1989). Guidelines for clients of privates practitioners: Committing the structure to print. *Journal of Counseling and Development, 67,* 289–300.

Chapter 8

RECOGNIZING AND MANAGING CRITICAL CLIENT PROBLEMS

Patrick B. Malley, Ph.D.

This chapter of the Practicum and Internship Textbook is organized to aid students in the recognition and management of critical client problems. The specific problems are as follows: (1) suicide, (2) teen suicide, (3) harm to others, (4) substance abuse, (5) child abuse, and (6) social phobia.

Practicum students and interns need to learn what specific symptoms are associated with each of these problem areas and what therapeutic techniques are most useful in solving the problem. Of equal importance in the learning process is the value of supervision. Students must be knowledgeable of how and when to seek supervision in these areas. Supervision is vital to the development of student competence. Also, supervision provides a vehicle whereby students can learn about their schools'/ agencies' policies regarding these issues.

In the material presented are the ethical/legal considerations related to each problem area. As conditions change, ethical and legal advancements occur and the commonly accepted system of practice changes. Practicum students and interns need to be aware of these changes and integrate them into their practice.

SUICIDE: A GUIDE FOR PRACTICUM STUDENTS AND INTERNS

Beauchamp (1985) defined suicide in the following manner:

1. that person intentionally brings about his or her own death;

2. others do not coerce him or her to do the actions; and

3. death is caused by conditions arranged by the person for the purpose of bringing about his or her own death.

Practicum students and interns frequently encounter suicidal clients in their counseling activities. Treating a suicidal client is an especially important task. What a student/intern does or does not do in this counseling process may have far-reaching effects on the client's ultimate behavior.

The following areas represent skills and knowledge practicum students and interns should obtain in order to counsel suicidal clients:

1. have awareness of their ethical mandates,

2. have awareness of their legal restrictions,

3. know what presenting symptoms are characteristic of those who attempt and succeed at suicide,

4. learn the skills and knowledge necessary to counsel suicidal clients,

5. know how and when to consult with their supervisors about suicidal clients, and

6. know the policies of their institutions regarding suicidal clients.

The Legal System and Suicide

Suicidal patients, by definition, contribute to their own death. Liability, however, is not lessened in suicidal cases. In suicide cases, responsibility is taken away from the client and placed into the hands of parties who have assumed care for the patient.

Consequently, psychotherapists or hospitals can be held to a standard of care in treating a patient, although they can never guarantee that suicide will be prevented (Slawson, Flinn, & Swartz, 1974).

What is a standard of care? How is the standard established? One way a court establishes a standard is to summon people who practice the same profession as the person accused of violating the standard of care. The court requires these professionals to testify if the behavior of the accused was what they, as prudent and reasonable members of the profession, would approve. If not, in the opinion of these expert witness, the accused may be found guilty of negligence and malpractice.

Note that, although many malpractice suits are brought against physicians, the need to establish a standard of care belongs to mental health professionals as well. The counseling relationship is a special one based on trust and faith, and the legal restraints on it are the same as the special relationship between the physician-patient (Knapp & Vandecreek, 1983).

Fujimura, Weis, and Cochran (1985), in their review of the literature, listed characteristics of potentially suicidal clients. These characteristics of lethality include the following:

1. **Previous suicide attempts.** This is the best single predictor of lethality. Attempts made by family members or close friends will exert an influence as well.

2. **Sleep disruption.** This can increase the intensity of depression. The person may be hallucinating, possibly from an excess of such drugs as stimulants and depressants.

3. **Definitiveness of plan.** The suicidal individual must be asked to talk about this, and he or she almost always will if asked. The more definitive the plan, the more serious the intent.

4. **Reversibility of plan.** Time span is an important consideration. Using a gun or jumping from a high place are irreversible methods most of the time. Taking pills is less lethal because there is a better chance for reversibility.

5. **Proximity of others.** A person who really does not want to die will rely on intervention from other people. A person truly intent on committing suicide will ensure that no one can intervene.

6. **Giving possessions away.** The suicidal individual is likely to give prized possessions away, finalize his or her business affairs, or revise his or her will.

7. **A history of severe alcohol or drug abuse.** An individual who is dependent on drugs or alcohol is a greater suicide risk.

8. **A history of previous psychiatric treatment or hospitalization.** The suicidal individual is likely to have received previous psychiatric treatment or to have been hospitalized.

9. **Availability of resource and support systems.** Does the suicidal person realize that these systems exist, and do these groups realize that they are the person's source of support?

10. **Willingness to use resource and support systems.** A suicidal person's not using these systems signifies a cutting off of communication and makes the intent more serious. (p. 613)

Intervening with the Suicidal Client

Some techniques generally recognized by therapists tend to facilitate the counseling process for suicidal clients. Some of these techniques are as follows:

1. Be sure to listen intelligently, sensitively, and carefully to your client.

2. Accept and understand your client's suicidal thoughts.

3. Don't give false assurances to your client. Don't say things like "everything is going to be all right."

4. Be supportive to your client.

5. Assure your client of your availability.

6. Be firm with your client, while at the same time caring.

7. Don't use euphemisms. Use words like "you would like to kill yourself" rather than vague expressions of the problem.

8. Bring out any ambivalence the client has. Try to increase his/her choices.

9. If your client is in crisis, don't leave him/her alone.

10. Intervene in a search for hopefulness rather than helpfulness.

11. Intervene to dispose of any weapons the client might have.

12. Tell others, those who would be concerned and can help. You have already informed your client of the limits of confidentiality.

SAMPLE SUICIDE CONTRACT

1. I _____ agree not to kill myself, attempt to kill myself, or cause harm to myself during the next period of time, from _____ to _____ , the time of my next appointment.

2. I agree to get enough sleep and eat well.

3. I agree to get rid of things I could use to kill myself—my guns and the pills.

4. I agree that if I have a bad time, and I feel I might hurt myself, I will call _____ _____ , my counselor, immediately at # _____ or the Crisis Center (or Suicide Prevention Center) at # _____ .

5. I agree these conditions are part of my counseling contract with _____ .

Signed: _____

Witnessed: _____

Sample 7. An example of a suicide contract. Based upon W.L. Get et al. (1985). In L.E. Fujimura, D.M. Weis, & J.R. Cochran (1985), Suicide: Dynamics and implications for counseling. *Journal of Counseling and Development, 63,* p. 614.

13. Help the client develop support systems.

14. Trust your own judgment.

15. Have available the suicide hot lines in your area.

16. Understand the procedures for commitment in your area.

17. Use available and appropriate scales for judging suicide risks.

18. Have the client sign a suicide contract.

If a determination is made that the client is possibly suicidal and will not consent to hospitalization, the practicum student or intern may use a written contract to help the client get through the time until the next appointment. An example of a suicide contract is presented in Sample 7.

At times an appropriate procedure is to have a client commit himself/herself to a hospital for treatment. If the client refuses, the case may be serious enough to warrant attempting an involuntary commitment to a treatment center. The procedures for commitment, whether voluntary or involuntary, vary a great deal from area to area. Also laws surrounding commitment procedures are quite different from state to state. For example, in Pennsylvania, a minor over the age of 14 can commit himself/herself to a hospital without parents' permission. The parents must be notified of the commitment and may demand the minor be released. In Ohio, a minor over the age 14 may not be committed to a hospital without parental consent. However, upon commitment the minor must sign a release form before his/her parent or guardian may have access to the counseling records.

Specific behaviors and other presenting symptoms of potentially suicidal clients are presented in this section. Some professionally advised counseling techniques also are detailed. If the practicum student or intern has reason to suspect that his/her client is suicidal, he/she should immediately consult his/her supervisor rather than waiting until the next regularly scheduled supervisory session.

In order to facilitate the supervisory process, the practicum student/intern may use the *Suicide Consultation Form* (Form 8.1) that has been developed and can be found at the conclusion of this section. The practicum student or intern should fill out most of the form before the supervision conference and have the supervisor sign it at the conclusion of the session. The form is intended to help the student present data germane to his/her client in an accurate and consistent manner. It also may aid in determining what the institutional policies are regarding practicum student or interns counseling suicidal clients. The practicum student or intern should keep a copy of the completed form in the clients' confidential records. This form provides documentation that appropriate ethical standards have been followed.

References

Beauchamp, T.L. (1985). Suicide: Matters of life and death. *Suicide and Life-Threatening Behavior, 24*(2), 190–195.

Fujimura, L.E., Weis, D.M., & Cochran, F.R. (1985). Suicide: Dynamics and implications for counseling. *Journal of Counseling and Development, 63*, 612–615.

Knapp, S., & Vandecreek, L. (1983). Malpractice risks with suicidal patients. *Psychotherapy: Theory, Research and Practice, 3*, 274–280.

Slawson, P.F., Flinn, D., & Swartz, D. (1974). Legal responsibility for suicide. *The Psychiatric Quarterly, 48*, 50–64.

★ ★ ★

TEEN SUICIDE: A GUIDE FOR PRACTICUM STUDENTS AND INTERNS

Roxanne J. Bogo
Nancy T. Malley
Patrick B. Malley

Suicide among American youth is now growing at an epidemic rate. It is currently the fastest growing cause of death among adolescents in American society (Sheeley & Herlihy, 1989). Suicide is the third leading, and in some states the second leading, cause of death among young people (Strother, 1986; Rosenberg, Smith, Davidson, & Conn, 1987). Although the number of adolescent suicides has in-

creased 300% during the past 30 years (Peach & Reddick, 1991), actual cases of adolescent suicide are considered to be underreported due to the tendency to disguise them as accidents (Capuzzi & Golden, 1988). In 1985, Ross stated that she believed suicides to be underreported by about 4:1 (Davis, 1985).

The tragedy of suicide is further complicated by a strong possibility that suicides can be prevented (Eisenberg, 1984). Professionals concur that most potential suicide victims want to be saved and very often manifest signals that reflect their need for help. Considering the magnitude of this problem, schools have been given a moral imperative to develop suicide prevention programs (Celotta, Golden, Keys, & Cannon, 1988). These programs are most effective when they are comprehensive and systematic (Kush, 1990) or, in short, proactive.

Given the enormity of the problem of youth suicide, schools have been notoriously slow in developing procedures to work with this situation. There are a variety of reasons for this procrastination. School personnel usually are not exposed to suicide training procedures as part of their normal in-education training. This lack of education is true regardless of whether they are administrators, teachers, counselors, or school psychologists. Also, school suicide proposals often are met with responses of fear, denial, and resistance (Poland, 1989). Some educators acknowledge the need for programs but express concerns about the limitations presented by school systems already overburdened (Grob, Klein, & Eisen, 1982; Wise, Smead, & Huebner, 1987; Sandoval, 1985).

There are also those who do not support active prevention efforts in the schools. In substance, their argument is that talking about the problem somehow causes it, much the same as sex education often is viewed. Some community members profess that suicide is not a significant problem and any recognition of it should be addressed in the church or at home (Barrett, 1985). Finally, some professionals resist building suicide prevention programs because there are many ethical/legal issues, and many states do not have laws that address the unique moral issues raised by youth suicide

(Continued on p. 289.)

SUICIDE CONSULTATION FORM

Directions: Student will complete this form when working with potentially suicidal client. The student will take this information to his/her supervisor for consultation, collaborate on a treatment plan, and place in client's file.

Part I

Name of Institution: _____

Intern's Name: _____ Supervisor's Name: _____

Supervisor's Professional Degree: _____

Supervisor is licensed in _____ Supervisor is certified in _____

Client's Name: _____ Client's Age: _____

If the client is a minor, has the parent signed a consent form? _____

When was the counseling initiated? Month _____ Day _____ Year _____

Where was counseling initiated? _____

Number of times you have seen this client: _____

Part II

Check the presenting symptoms often associated with this suicidal client.

Client is between the ages of 14 and 19. Yes _____ No _____

Client is depressed. Yes _____ No _____

If yes, include a description of the client's depressive behavior.

_____

_____

_____

_____

_____

_____

Has a previous attempt of suicide occurred?   Yes _____ No _____

If yes, how long ago was the attempt? _____

Is the client abusing alcohol?   Yes _____ No _____

If yes, how much does he/she drink? _____

_____

Form 8.1, p. 1 of 4, Copy 1

Is the client abusing some other substance? Yes _____ No _____

If yes, what other substance? _____

_____

Is rational thinking lost? Yes _____ No _____

If yes, explain how this behavior is manifested. _____

_____

_____

_____

_____

_____

Does the client have little social support? Yes _____ No _____

How does the client spend his/her time? _____

_____

_____

_____

_____

_____

_____

Does the client have an organized plan. Yes _____ No _____

If yes, what is this plan? _____

_____

_____

_____

_____

If a plan, does it seem irreversible, i.e., guns versus pills?   Yes _____ No _____

Is the client divorced, widowed, or separated?   Yes _____ No _____

Is the client physically sick?   Yes _____ No _____

If yes, describe the symptoms. _____

_____

_____

_____

Does the client have sleep disruption?   Yes _____ No _____

If yes, describe the disruption. _____

_____

_____

_____

_____

_____

_____

_____

_____

Has the client given his/her possessions away?   Yes _____ No _____

Does the client have a history of previous psychiatric treatment or hospitalization?   Yes _____ No _____

If yes, describe for what the client was hospitalized. _____

_____

_____

_____

_____

_____

_____

_____

_____

Does the client have any one near him/her to intervene? Yes _____ No _____

Part III

Describe and summarize your interactions with the client. What are his/her basic problems? What is your goal with the client? What techniques are you using?

_____

_____

_____

_____

_____

_____

_____

Describe your supervisor's reaction to the problem. _____

_____

_____

_____

_____

_____

_____

_____

_____

_____

_____

_____

_____

_____

_____

_____

_____

_____
Supervisor's Signature

What are your plans for the client? _____

_____

_____

_____

_____

_____

_____

_____

_____

_____

_____

_____

_____

_____

_____

_____

SUICIDE CONSULTATION FORM

Directions: Student will complete this form when working with potentially suicidal client. The student will take this information to his/her supervisor for consultation, collaborate on a treatment plan, and place in client's file.

Part I

Name of Institution: _____

Intern's Name: _____ Supervisor's Name: _____

Supervisor's Professional Degree: _____

Supervisor is licensed in _____ Supervisor is certified in _____

Client's Name: _____ Client's Age: _____

If the client is a minor, has the parent signed a consent form? _____

When was the counseling initiated? Month _____ Day _____ Year _____

Where was counseling initiated? _____

Number of times you have seen this client: _____

Part II

Check the presenting symptoms often associated with this suicidal client.

Client is between the ages of 14 and 19. Yes _____ No _____

Client is depressed. Yes _____ No _____

If yes, include a description of the client's depressive behavior.

_____

_____

_____

_____

_____

Has a previous attempt of suicide occurred? Yes _____ No _____

If yes, how long ago was the attempt? _____

Is the client abusing alcohol? Yes _____ No _____

If yes, how much does he/she drink? _____

Is the client abusing some other substance? Yes _____ No _____

If yes, what other substance? _____

_____

Is rational thinking lost? Yes _____ No _____

If yes, explain how this behavior is manifested. _____

_____

_____

_____

_____

_____

Does the client have little social support? Yes _____ No _____

How does the client spend his/her time? _____

_____

_____

_____

_____

_____

_____

Does the client have an organized plan. Yes _____ No _____

If yes, what is this plan? _____

_____

_____

_____

_____

If a plan, does it seem irreversible, i.e., guns versus pills?   Yes _____ No _____

Is the client divorced, widowed, or separated?   Yes _____ No _____

Is the client physically sick?   Yes _____ No _____

If yes, describe the symptoms. _____

_____

_____

_____

Form 8.1, p. 2 of 4, Copy 2

Does the client have sleep disruption?   Yes _____   No _____

If yes, describe the disruption. _____

_____

_____

_____

_____

_____

_____

_____

Has the client given his/her possessions away?   Yes _____   No _____

Does the client have a history of previous psychiatric treatment or hospitalization?   Yes _____   No _____

If yes, describe for what the client was hospitalized. _____

_____

_____

_____

_____

_____

_____

_____

_____

Does the client have any one near him/her to intervene? Yes _____   No _____

Part III

Describe and summarize your interactions with the client. What are his/her basic problems? What is your goal with the client? What techniques are you using?

_____

_____

_____

_____

_____

_____

_____

Describe your supervisor's reaction to the problem. _____

_____

_____

_____

_____

_____

_____

_____

_____

_____

_____

_____

_____

_____

_____

_____

_____

_____

_____

                                   _____
                                        Supervisor's Signature

What are your plans for the client? _____

_____

_____

_____

_____

_____

_____

_____

_____

_____

_____

_____

_____

_____

_____

(Celotta et al., 1988). For this reason, teenage suicide too often is viewed as a "hands-off" situation.

Assessment of Teen Lethality

We know that, because schools and colleges have an enormous amount of consistent and direct contact with a large population of adolescents, they are a strategic setting for the implementation of suicide prevention/intervention/postvention programs.

Practicum and internship students should be prepared to assess lethality because of professional and legal obligations. In relation to professional standards, the American Counseling Association (1988) stated in their *Ethical Standards*

> When the client's condition indicates that there is clear and imminent danger to the client or others, the member must take reasonable personal action or inform the responsible authorities. Consultation with other professionals must be used where possible. The assumption of responsibility for the client's(s') behavior must be taken only after careful deliberation. The client must be involved in the resumption of responsibility as quickly as possible.

Liability issues have been entering the court system in relation to suicidal clients and the responsibility of the counselor. The Maryland Court of Appeals has ruled that school counselors have a legal duty to prevent the suicide of a student client if the counselor foresees a danger of suicide (Pate, 1992). Appropriate intervention steps cannot be implemented, however, until the lethality is determined. The following process is outlined to be utilized as soon as a student is suspected as suicidal:

1. Make a direct inquiry during a session. Ask the student, without hesitation, if he/she is thinking about killing himself/herself. If the student claims that he/she has had suicidal ideation, the strength of the intent should be determined. Continue with this line of questioning.

2. Ask the student if he/she has ever attempted suicide before. If so, how many times has an attempt been made and when were they made? The more attempts and the more recent the attempts, the more serious this situation becomes.

3. Ask the student how the previous attempts were made. If the student took aspirin, for example, ask how many were taken. One? Six? Twenty? Then inquire about the consequences of this attempt. For example, was there medical intervention?

4. Ask the student why. Why had he/she previously attempted suicide? Why the suicidal thoughts now?

5. Does the student have a plan? Ask about the details of the plan. The more detailed the thought process, the more lethal. Does the student know when and how the attempt will be made? Assess the lethality of the method. This assessment is critical. Does he/she have a weapon? Using a gun or hanging oneself leaves little time for medical help as compared to taking aspirin.

6. What is the student's preoccupation about an attempt? Does he/she only think about it while at home, or during a particular incident, or does it go beyond all other activities?

7. Ask about drug use. Drug use complicates the seriousness of the situation because the student will tend to be less inhibited while under the influence of drugs. Although the student may deny it, try to get as much information as possible.

8. Observe nonverbal actions. Is the student agitated, tense, sad? Is he/she inebriated? Also keep in mind that caution should be taken if the student seems to be at peace. This may be due to the plans being organized with completion being the next step.

9. Try to gauge the level of depression. Once again, a student may not be depressed because he/she is anxious about completing the plan.

Intervention with the Middle/Secondary School Student

The above process will allow the counselor to determine the level of risk for the student. A low-risk student may have thought about suicide but has never attempted suicide in the past, does not have a plan, is not taking drugs, and is not preoccupied with the ideation. The suicide contract may be sufficient in these cases. Most students at low risk will agree to the counselor's contacting the parents, which should be done. The statements must be monitored closely, as a low-risk student may quickly become a high-risk student.

A typical high-risk student usually has a plan but may or may not have attempted suicide in the past. Of course, a previous attempt is an important factor in assessing lethality, especially if it was recent. But counselors need to keep in mind that many first-time attempts are successful. The current situation must never be minimized. The plan of a high-risk student usually is detailed, and the ideation is of frequent thought preoccupation. At this point, other people need to become involved, including the counselor's supervisor, principal, and school nurse. Ideally, the school will have some type of intervention policy where this issue can be addressed. The goal in a high-risk situation is to have the student undergo a psychiatric evaluation as soon as possible, whether by voluntary or involuntary commitment. The parents will need to be notified, and confidentiality will not be an issue if the limits of confidentiality were explained previously via informed consent. Although confidentiality laws vary from state to state, a counselor usually is not bound by confidentiality if the client intends to harm himself or someone else (Kane & Keeton, 1985). It is absolutely imperative, however, that the practicum/intern student discuss confidentiality limits at the beginning of every client intake session.

A practicum/intern student may encounter a crisis situation in three different ways, and each situation requires some specific guidelines. First, the student may attempt suicide on school premises. As earlier mentioned, the practicum/intern student should refer to the school's policy in regard to this intervention. However, it must be noted that many schools do not have a formal policy outlined. In a recent study by Malley, Kush, & Bogo (1994), 46% of schools surveyed did not have a written formal suicide policy statement. Second, the student may disclose suicidal ideation directly to the practicum/intern student. In this case, the practicum/intern student should assess lethality as in the process outlined above.

Lastly, peers may inform the practicum/intern student of a suicidal student. Seven out of ten students tell a peer about suicide ideation before telling anyone else. It is especially important to take this information seriously. The previously mentioned decision by the Maryland Court of Appeals was in fact in regards to a peer's informing a counselor of another student's intention to kill herself. The counselor confronted the teen, but she denied any problems; so the counselor did not notify the parents. The negligence was considered a failure to inform a parent concerning a potential suicide of a minor

child (Pate, 1992). The following are guidelines to follow for each situation:

If It Occurs on the Premises. Involve appropriate school personnel as previously mentioned; then notify police and/or ambulance service. Also notify parent(s) or guardian. Let them know where their son/daughter is being taken. If the parent(s) or guardian is not available, notify the next closest relative.

See to it that the student receives proper medical and psychiatric care. Very often, the hospital will send the student back to the school after the crisis without a psychiatric evaluation. Practicum/intern students should guard against this phenomenon.

If the Student Discloses to the Practicum/ Intern Student. First, consult the supervisor. Go over the assessment of lethality in the presence of the student. This also will establish the standard of care on behalf of the practicum/intern student.

Call the parent(s) or guardian and tell them that they will be met at the appropriate psychiatric facility with the student and the practicum/intern student. It also would be best if the practicum/intern student's supervisor goes as well.

Explain to the parent(s)/guardian and the student that an evaluation or diagnosis does not necessarily mean commitment. If the parent(s)/guardian resist this process, it is best to contact Children and Youth Services for assistance.

Be sure to contact the parent(s)/guardian in the presence of the child to eliminate the "he/she said" phenomenon. For example, the practicum/intern student could say "I'm sitting in my office with your son. . . ."

Also require a psychologist to determine when it is appropriate for the student to return to school.

If the Peer Tells the Practicum/Intern Student. In this situation, the practicum/intern student should confront the student. If the student admits the suicidal ideation, the same procedure as above may be outlined. If the student denies the ideation, the practicum/intern student should notify the student's parent(s)/guardian. Of course, the student must be informed about this disclosure.

Factors Influencing College/University Student Suicide

Obtaining accurate data on the suicide rates of college student is often very difficult. There are often ineffective record-keeping systems on the part of colleges and universities, and those data that do exist tend to be inconsistent. Because of concern about negative publicity, colleges may be under-reporting or mislabeling suicides (Westefeld, Whitchard, & Range, 1990).

College students carry with them certain issues that seem to be particularly relevant to this setting. Striving for academic success, having unclear vocational goals, and being away from home may cause students to become depressed (Mathiasen, 1988). Also, research has shown poor problem-solving skills under high life stressors to be influential with suicidal college students (Fremouw, Callahan, & Kashden, 1993).

As middle and secondary schools should take more responsibility to prevent student suicides, colleges and universities also have an obligation to respond to and prevent the increase of this epidemic. Campus seminars on suicide prevention and various programming efforts are often beneficial. Offering workshops in dealing with stress, academic concerns, career planning, and problem-solving may be proactive in dealing with the major life stressors of a college student. Educating faculty, staff, students, and administrators about the signs of depression and suicide should be a component in the prevention program that should be outlined in a written formal policy.

It also must be kept in mind that the residence hall staff must be educated in this area, as their exposure to the student body is often extensive (Phillips, 1983).

Intervention with the College/ University Student

When dealing with the college population, there are some special considerations for the practicum/intern student to be aware of. In terms of assessment of lethality and the ways that the practicum/intern student may become aware of a potentially suicidal student, the information outlined above remains the same. However, the main difference with the college student is in terms of parental notification. Some college students may be minors, but the majority are over 18 years old, allowing for a twist in the legal paradigm. Legally, a practicum/intern student is not obligated to contact the parents of a potentially suicidal client if the student is not a minor. However, a psychiatric facility will contact the parents, if for no other reason but insurance purposes. Some universities are referring students to psychiatric institutions earlier in the counseling process for this reason. This area is definitely a gray one. In 1992, Gallagher's National Survey of Counseling Center Directors revealed that 63.8% of the centers notified a third party in regards to a potentially suicidal student. This statistic increased 5% since 1991.

Another complication in this matter is in regard to residence. Out-of-state students and international students sometimes are turned away from psychiatric hospitals because of out-of-state insurance policies. This situation tends to put the responsibility back on the university. In these circumstances, the counseling center needs to take a more active role in helping the student receive the proper psychiatric attention. Contacting the parent(s)/guardian in this situation is a necessity.

Conclusion

With the counseling role comes the responsibility to assess the need for immediacy in a variety of situations. In regard to a potentially suicidal student, this assessment is crucial for appropriate intervention. Fortunately, the practicum and internship experience is fostered by close supervision, in which these essential skills may be learned and monitored.

References

American Counseling Association. (1988). *Ethical standards.* Alexandria, VA: Author.

Barrett, T. (1985). Does suicide prevention in the schools have to be such a "terrifying" concept? *Newslink, 11*(1), 3.

Capuzzi, D., & Golden, L. (1988). *Preventing adolescent suicide.* Muncie, IN: Accelerated Development.

Celotta, B., Golden, J., Keys, S.S., & Cannon, G. (1988). A model prevention program. In D. Capuzzi, & L. Golden, *Preventing adolescent suicide* (pp. 269–296). Muncie, IN: Accelerated Development.

Davis, J.M. (1985). Suicidal crisis in schools. *School Psychology Review, 14*(3).

Eisenberg, L. (1984). The epidemiology of suicide in adolescents. *Pediatric Annals, 13*(1), 47–53.

Fremouw, W., Callahan, T., & Kashden, J. (1993). Adolescent suicidal risk: Psychological, problem solving, and environmental factors. *Suicide and Life-Threatening Behavior, 23*(1).

Gallagher, R.P. (1992). *National survey of counseling center directors.* Alexandria, VA: International Association of Counseling Services, Inc.

Grob, M.C., Klein, A.A., & Eisen, S.V. (1982). The role of the high school professional in identifying and managing adolescent suicide behavior. *Journal of Youth Suicide, 12,* 163–173.

Kane, S., & Keeton, R. (1985). Informed consent. *Campus Voice,* 52–54.

Kush, F.R. (1990). *A descriptive study of school-based adolescent suicide prevention/intervention programs: Program components and the role of the school counselor.* Unpublished doctoral dissertation, University of Pittsburgh.

Malley, P.B., Kush, F., & Bogo, R.J. (1994, November). School-based adolescent suicide prevention/intervention programs: A survey. *The School Counselor, 42,* 130–136.

Mathiasen, R. (1988). Evaluating suicidal risk in the college student. *NASPA Journal, 25,* 257–261.

Pate, R.H. (1992, Summer). Are you liable? *American Counselor.*

Peach, L., & Reddick, T.L. (1991). Counselors can make a difference in preventing adolescent suicide. *The School Counselor, 39.*

Phillips, W. (1983). Suicide education for residence staff: Identification, intervention, and referral. *Journal of College Student Personnel, 24,* 376–378.

Poland, S. (1989). *Suicide intervention in the schools.* New York: The Guilford Press.

Rosenberg, M.L., Smith, J.C., Davidson, L.E., & Conn, J.M. (1987). The emergence of youth suicide: An epidemiological analysis and public health perspective. *Annual Review of Public Health, 8,* 417–440.

Sandoval, J., (1985). Crisis counseling: Conceptualizations and general principles. *School Psychology Review, 14,* 257–265.

Sheeley, V.L., & Herlihy, B. (1989). Counseling suicidal teens: A duty to warn and protect. *The School Counselor, 37.*

Strother, D.B. (1986). Suicide among the very young. *Phi Delta Kappan, 67,* 756–759.

Westefeld, J.S., Whitchard, K.A., & Range, L.M. (1990). College and university student suicide: Trends and implications. *The Counseling Psychologist, 18*(3), 464–476.

Wise, P.S., Smead, V.S., & Huebner, E.S. (1987). Crisis intervention: Involvement and training needs of school psychology personnel. *Journal of School Psychology, 25,* 185–187.

■ ■ ■

HARM TO OTHERS: A GUIDE FOR PRACTICUM STUDENTS AND INTERNS

Patrick B. Malley
Nancy T. Malley

Practicum students and interns should be aware that during the course of their training they may encounter clients who present a serious threat to other people. This counseling situation has ethical and legal implications for students as well as experienced counselors. Purposes of this section are to address these concerns and to offer guidelines to students should this problem occur while they are in training.

The Tarasoff Case

Prosenjit Poddar was an outpatient at the University of California's Cowell Memorial Hospital. He informed his psychotherapist, Dr. Moore, that he planned to kill an unnamed girl, readily identifiable as Tatiana Tarasoff. Ms. Tarasoff was spending the summer in South America. In addition to this revelation, the patient told Dr. Moore he was going to buy a gun. Dr. Moore consulted the psychiatric staff and determined that Poddar should be admitted to a mental institution for observation. The campus police, who took Poddar into custody, were called. After some period of detainment, the campus police judged Poddar as rational and released him. At no point, did Dr. Moore, the police, or any other staff member of the clinic warn Tatiana or her parents about Poddar's expressed intentions of harmful behavior. On October 27, 1969, shortly after her return from Brazil, Tatiana Tarasoff was killed by Poddar in her place of residence (Crocker, 1985).

The Tarasoff parents attempted to sue the Regents of the University of California, the therapist involved, and the police. The case initially was dismissed by the trial court and the court of appeal. Tatiana's parents persisted. They appealed to the Supreme Court of California, arguing that the defendants had a duty to confine Poddar under the provisions of California's Lanterman-Petris-Short civil commitment statute (Stone, 1976). This statute states

> When any person, as a result of mental disorder, is a danger to others . . . a peace officer, member of the attending staff, as defined by regulation, of an evaluation facility designated

by the county, or other professional person designated by the county may, upon probable cause, take, or cause to be taken, the person into custody and place him in a facility . . . for 72-hour treatment and evaluation. (p. 360)

In late 1974, the California Supreme Court decided that a cause for action for negligence did exist against both the therapist and the police for the "Failure to Warn" (Tarasoff, I).

The court, apparently under pressure from various professional groups, agreed to a rehearing. The court's final decision given on July 1, 1976, exempted the police from potential liability but held the plaintiff's suit could be amended to include the therapist alone. The plaintiff ultimately settled out of court. Consequently, the court never found anybody libel. The court did set a standard for therapists, however (Southard & Gross, 1982). The standard is as follows:

> When a therapist determines, or pursuant to the standards of his profession should determine, that his patient presents a serious danger of violence to another, he incurs a serious obligation to use reasonable care to protect the intended victim from such danger. (Tarasoff II, p. 43)

Initially, these two court cases caused a great deal of confusion in the counseling profession. For example, Gehring (1982) stated

> A counselor who is informed by a client that he intends to harm another could easily be held to a standard of knowing that the individual is a real threat to the well-being of another. Once such a disclosure is made and the counselor knows, or by the standards of his profession should know, that the client is serious, then the duty to warn could be applied assuming there is an identifiable victim. . . . (p. 209)

> If the special relationship exists and there is a reasonable knowledge that a client's conduct may be harmful to another, then there is a legal duty to warn the intended victim where that victim is foreseeable. The concept of a duty to warn was initially applied in California but has since been adopted in several other jurisdictions. Failure to fulfill one's duty could result in liability for negligence. (p. 210)

Southard and Gross (1982) reported that the therapist does not have a "Duty to Warn" a potential victim.

> The language in Tarasoff II follows the typical pattern of tort law and relies on a flexible "duty of care," not on a rigid "duty to warn." As already noted, Sadoff (1979, p. 3) writes that Tarasoff established a "legal obligation to protect and warn third parties." This is dangerous because it increases the possibility that clinicians will seek to comply with Tarasoff by rigidly warning, not by seeking other ways of protecting the potential victim. (p. 95)

In summary, the California Supreme Court set a standard for therapists who have a client who expresses a "serious and imminent danger of violence" to others; however, because two interventions were made by the court, one in 1974 and one in 1976, confusion was created in mental health professions. Today, although the confusion still exists, it is accepted widely that mental health professionals do have a duty to protect third parties from the potential violence of their clients (Appelbaum & Rosenbaum, 1989).

Post Tarasoff

Subsequent to the *Tarasoff* case, certain conditions were presented and deemed necessary for the potential imposition of liability on therapists whose clients executed violent and dangerous behavior toward others. They were as follows: (1) the client must make a clear threat, (2) the danger must be serious, (3) the victim must be identifiable, and (4) the danger must be imminent (Gross & Weinberger, 1982). However, subsequent to these initial observations, liability has been imposed on therapists when one or more of the above conditions were not met. In fact, some courts have expanded the original version of the standard, and some have rejected it.

Expansion of the Duty

Some courts have held that the victim did not have to be identifiable, but merely, merely one who was specifically foreseeable. For example, the court ruled in *Jablonski v. United States* (1983) that had the therapist obtained the previous medical records of the client, he would have been able to predict that the client, with his history of violence toward women, would have assaulted the women with whom he lived. Note that in this case, threats were never made against any specific individual. In the same year, the court also allowed liability to be imposed by the son of a woman who suffered emotional trauma when he witnessed the murder of his mother (Hedlund v. Superior Court of Orange County, 1983).

Other courts have ruled in favor of liability when a potential danger was realized to the general public rather than to a specific foreseeable individual or individuals. In *Lipari v. Sears, Roebuck & Co.* (1980), a patient (a former psychiatric patient) terminated therapy and subsequently fired a shotgun into a crowded nightclub, killing Dennis Lipari and severely injuring his wife. Note that there was no clear danger to any particular individual in this case. *Peterson v. the State* (1983) offers a particularly disturbing problem for the profession. In this case, the therapist had released a client who had a drug-related mental problem. The client, under the influence of drugs, ultimately collided with a woman's car and injured her. The court ruled that the therapist should have been able to predict possible harm to the foreseeable public from the patient's dangerous behavior, which was correlated to his drug usage. Because the therapist knew of the patient's tendencies toward drug abuse, yet released him, the therapist was liable for not protecting foreseeable third parties from such.

Another unique twist on the initial *Tarasoff* case was that of John Peck. This client was seeing a therapist who had his master's degree in educational counseling. The client acted out his threatened behavior and burned down the family barn. The barn was 130 feet from the family home where his parents were residing. Liability was imposed on the counselor (Stone, 1986).

Still others have theorized that the willingness of the courts to find therapists liable for harm caused by their patients to third parties puts the therapist treating compulsive sex offenders at risk for tort liability. For instance, by definition, a compulsive and deviant sexual behavior pattern involves coerced or violent sex with a child. Thus, the danger is inherent in the disorder once the diagnosis is made (Melella, Sheldon, & Cullen, 1987). More recently it also has been hypothesized that, the closer the resemblance between researchers and clinicians, the more likely it is that researchers may be held liable for transgressions of deviant and violent behavior on the part of participants in their research (Appelbaum & Rosenbaum, 1989).

Rejection of Tarasoff

A Florida appellate court has held that a psychotherapist whose patient threatened to harm an identifiable third party had no duty to warn the intended victim. The plaintiffs brought an action against a psychiatrist, alleging that their son was murdered by the psychiatrist's patient after the patient threatened to commit that specific crime during a therapy session. The patient was seeing the psychiatrist on a voluntary, outpatient basis. The appellate court affirmed the decision, refusing to recognize a cause of action against a psychotherapist for failure to warn a third party of a patient's threats of violence. The court concluded that it would be fundamentally unfair to impose a duty to warn upon psychotherapists because psychiatry is an inexact science and a patient's dangerousness cannot be predicted with any degree of accuracy. The court added that the relationship of trust and confidence that is necessary for the therapeutic process would be undermined if a psychotherapist were required to warn potential victims whenever a patient expressed hostile feelings toward a third party (*Boynton v. Burglass,* 1991).

It is obvious that confusion still exists regarding clinician liability; however, practicum/intern students, it is advised, should labor (especially in jurisdictions where the Appellate Court has not ruled) under the assumption that some version of *Tarasoff* liability will be imposed (Monahan, 1993).

Assessment of Danger

"Professionals," by definition, possess "specialized knowledge" not available to the general public. This includes knowledge of risk assessment (of potentially violent behavior toward third parties) and knowledge of the laws of the professional's jurisdiction. A resource is available to acquaint the reader with risk assessment (see Appelbaum & Gutheil, 1991).

Practicum/intern students can utilize the following guidelines to assess the potential dangerousness of their clients:

1. Is there a history of violence conducted on the part of the client?

2. Is there a history of violent conduct on the part of the client associated with a previous assessment or diagnosis of mental illness on the part of the client?

3. Does the client have a history of arrest or arrests for violent conduct?

4. Does the client have a history of threats associated with violent conflict?

5. Has the client ever been diagnosed with a mental disorder for which violence is a common symptom?

6. Does the client have any history of at least one inpatient hospitalization associated with dangerous conduct, whether the hospitalization was voluntary or involuntary?

7. Has the client had any history of dangerous conduct, apparently unprovoked, and not stress related?

8. If the client has had a history of dangerous conduct, ask how long ago the incident was. The more recent the dangerous behavior, the more likely the behavior may be repeated.

9. If one considers the client dangerous to the degree of intent or intensity of repeated threats, attempts, or actual harm to others, then these should be noted and the person who may be harmed needs to be notified. Those acts that have a high degree of intent or intensity and/or seriousness are most likely to recur.

10. Determine if the serious threats, attempts, or harm to others have been related to drug and/or alcohol intoxication.

11. Ask the client direct and focussed questions, such as: "What is the most violent thing you have ever done?" or "How close have you ever come to becoming violent?"

12. Check the current records of the client. Make sure to check the nursing notes written on the chart when you were not present.

13. Check the past records of the client if they are reasonably available.

14. Utilize the reports of significant others. A family member is often able to provide valuable information regarding the client's potential for violence. Again, ask direct questions, such as "Are you worried that your loved one is going to hurt someone?"

Taking Action

Students in training should know that when a client is determined to pose a dangerous and imminent threat to another's well-being, serious legal and ethical questions are at issue. The practicum student or intern should pay close attention to the material presented in this section and *immediately* consult the site supervisor regarding a violent client. To defer the supervision until a regularly scheduled conference is due would not be advisable. The institutionalized supervisory conference could be seen as scheduled out of convenience rather than scheduled to meet the client's special needs.

The supervisor is seen in the eyes of the law as acting under the auspices of *respondent superior* (literally, "let the master answer"). This is a form of vicarious liability in which an employer or supervisor is held liable for the wrongful acts of an employee or supervisee. The assumption is that the master or site supervisor is responsible for those negligent acts of his/her agent that take place during the agent's employment or training.

To expedite the supervisory process, a form entitled *Harm to Others* (Form 8.2) has been developed. It can be found at the end of this section. Utilizing this form, the practicum student or intern can list systematically the reasons why he/she believes the client to be potentially dangerous. The practicum student or intern should fill out most of the form before the supervisory session. The supervisor's advice or reactions should be recorded at the conclusion of the conference. At that time, the supervisor should sign the form. The practicum student or intern should keep a copy of the completed form in his/her confidential records. This form serves as documentation that appropriate ethical/legal standards have been followed.

Appelbaum (1985) presented a model for fulfilling the *Tarasoff* obligation. He reported that decisions that have relied on it as a precedent appear to require that clinician's treating potentially dangerous patients undertake a three-stage process of assessment, selection of a course of action, and implementation. The *first stage, assessment,* has two components: (1) therapists must gather those data relevant to an evaluation of dangerousness, and (2) a determination of dangerousness must be made on the basis of those data. The *second stage* of the process asks that the clinician who has determined that a patient is likely to be dangerous *select a course of action to protect potential victims.* The *third stage* of the model requires therapists to *implement* their decisions appropriately. This requirement has two components: (1) the means chosen to protect victims must be carried out effectively and (2) the situation must be monitored on a continuing basis to access the success or failure of the initial response, to access the likelihood that the patient will be violent, and to access the need for further measures to decrease the risk presented by the patient.

When the practicum or internship student and supervisor meet, the following guidelines should be considered:

1. If the danger is not considered imminent, the client may be kept in more intensified therapy. Deal with the aggression as part of the treatment. However, if the client does not adhere to this plan, that is, if they discontinue therapy, the danger should be considered as possibly more imminent.

2. Invite the client to participate in the decision of disclosure. This process very often will make the client feel more in control. It would be prudent also to contact the third party in the presence of the client. This technique may vitiate problems of paranoia after what has been communicated.

3. Attempt environmental manipulations. Medication may be initiated, changed, or increased. Have the client get rid of any lethal weapons.

4. Keep careful records. When recording information relevant to risk, one should note the following: the source of the information (e.g., the name of the spouse), the content of the information (e.g., the character of the threat and the nature and the circumstances under which it was disclosed), and the date on which the information was disclosed. Finally, a rationale for any decision made should be included in the records.

5. If warning a third party is unavoidable, disclose only the minimum amount necessary to protect the victim or the public, stating the specific threat but reserving any opinion or prediction.

6. Consult with your supervisor. Your agency or school should base a contingency plan for such problems that is derived in consultation with an informed attorney, an area psychiatric facility, and local police. Do not practice as a practicum/internship student without liability insurance.

References

Appelbaum, P.S. (1985, April). Tarasoff and the clinician: Problems in fulfilling the duty to protect. *American Journal of Psychiatry, 142*(4), 425–429.

Appelbaum, P., & Rosenbaum, A. (1989). Tarasoff and the researcher: Does the duty to protect apply in the research setting? *American Psychology, 44,* 885–894.

Appelbaum, P., & Gutheil, T. (1991). *Clinical handbook of psychiatry and the law* (2nd ed.). Baltimore: Williams & Wikins.

Boynton v. Burglass. (1991, September 24). Fla. Ct. App., 3d Dist., No. 89-1409.

Crocker, E.M. (1985, Summer). Judicial expansion of the Tarasoff doctrine: Doctor's dilemma. *The Journal of Psychiatry and Law,* 83–99.

Gehring, D.D. (1982, December). The counselor's "duty to warn." *Personnel and Guidance Journal.*

Gross, B.H., & Weinberger, L. (Eds.). (1982). *The mental health professional and the legal system.* San Francisco: Jossey-Bass.

Hedlund v. Superior Court of Orange County. (1983). 34 Cal., 3d. 695, P. 2d. 41, 194 Cal. Rptr. 805.

Jablonski v. United States. (1983). 712 F. 2d. 391 (9th Cir.).

Lanterman-Petris-Short Act. CAL. WELF. and Int. Code 5000–5404:1.

Lipari v. Sears, Roebuck & Co. (1980). 497 F. Supp. 195d. Nebraska.

Melella, F.T., Sheldon, T., & Cullen, K. (1987, Spring). The psychotherapist's third-party liability for sexual assaults committed by his patient. *The Journal of Psychiatry,* 103–104.

Monahan, J. (1993). Limiting therapist exposure to Tarasoff liability: Guidelines for risk containment. *American Psychologist, 48,* 242–243.

Peterson v. the State. (1983). 671, P. 2d., 230. Washington.

Southard, M.J., & Gross, B.H. (1982). In B.H. Gross and L.E. Weinberger (Eds.), *The mental health professional and the legal system.* San Francisco: Jossey-Bass.

Stone, A.A. (1976). The Tarasoff decisions: Suing psychotherapists to safeguard society. *Harvard Law Review, 90,* 358–378.

Stone, A.A. (1986, March). Vermont adapts Tarasoff: A real barnburner. *American Journal of Psychology, 143*(3), 353–354.

Tarasoff v. Regents of the University of California. (1976). 17 Cal. 3rd, 425, 551 P. 2d. 334, 131 Cal. Rptr. 14.

Tarasoff II, vacating 13 Cal. 3rd, 117, 529 P. 2d. 553, 131 Cal. Rptr. 14.

■ ■ ■

HARM TO OTHERS

DIRECTIONS: Student completes the form prior to supervisory sessions, records supervisor's comments and reactions, and student and supervisor sign the completed form. The student should keep the form in his/her confidential records.

1. Student's Name: _____
    Client's Name: _____

2. Number of times the client has been seen: _____

3. Dates client has been seen: _____
    _____
    _____
    _____

4. Client's presenting problem: _____
    _____
    _____
    _____
    _____
    _____
    _____

5. Type of therapy given: _____
    _____
    _____
    _____
    _____
    _____
    _____

6. What did the client do or say to make the counselor concerned that he/she could represent "harm to others"? _____
    _____
    _____
    _____
    _____
    _____
    _____

7. Was a specific victim(s) named? _____
    _____

8. If the victim was not named, what was the relationship of the client to the victim? _____

9. If the victim was not named, did the counselor suspect who the person was? _____
    _____

10. Was a clear threat made? _____

11. Is serious danger present? _____

_____

_____

_____

12. Is the danger believed to be imminent? _____

    If so, why? _____

_____

_____

_____

_____

_____

_____

    If no, why? _____

_____

_____

_____

_____

_____

_____

13. Supervisor's reaction/advice? _____

_____

_____

_____

_____

14. What plan of action is to be taken? _____

_____

_____

_____

_____

_____

_____
Student's Signature

_____
Supervisor's Signature

_____
Date of Conference

Form 8.2, p. 2 of 2, Copy 1

———————— ★ ★ ★ ————————

PSYCHOACTIVE SUBSTANCE USE DISORDERS—DIAGNOSIS, TREATMENT, AND RELAPSE PREVENTION: A GUIDE FOR PRACTICUM STUDENTS AND INTERNS

Francis R. Kush

Clients with psychoactive substance use disorders are among the most complex and difficult to treat. Addictive disorders constitute a serious national health threat with the lifetime incidence of psychoactive substance abuse approaching 20% of the population. Fewer than 10% of individuals with addictive disorders receive professional treatment or belong to self-help groups (Frances & Miller, 1991).

Considerable controversy exists regarding the etiology of psychoactive substance use disorders. Biologically based models emphasize genetic predisposition (Goodwin & Warnock, 1991); psychoanalytic and psychodynamic perspectives suggest that chemical dependency is symptomatic of underlying psychopathology and/or personality dysfunction (Cox, 1987; Forrest, 1985). Leigh (1985) suggested that substance abuse/dependence is the product of a combination of variables that include personality traits, environmental factors, and the immediate self-reinforcing properties of the desired substance. Marlatt (1985) suggested that substance abuse may be an impulse/behavioral (acquired habit pattern) disorder that results in disease states, e.g. cirrhosis. Beck and Emery (1977) and Ellis, McInerney, DiGiuseppe, and Yeager (1988) identified substance-dependent cognitions (belief systems and thinking styles) as critical factors that precipitate substance dependence. Wallace (1991) described the biopsychosocial model, in discussing crack cocaine dependence, which considers genetic predisposition and the pharmacological reinforcing properties of substances, psychological/personality factors, and the social/environmental (learning and reinforcement) component.

Psychoactive substance disordered individuals are a very heterogeneous and complex population. Because of the high frequency of coexisting additional forms of psychopathology, including significant characterologic features, addictive disordered populations are extremely challenging to work with; and success rates with particular clinical subtypes may be modest.

Trends and approaches in the treatment of psychoactive substance disorders are changing, partly out of necessity because of shifting reimbursement patterns of third-party providers and also because of continuing advances in biological, psychological, and psychiatric research. In addition, as there is a growing prominence to view psychoactive substance use disorders as biopsychosocial in nature, greater emphasis is being placed on combining multiple interventions that include the following: detoxification, intense individual and group psychotherapy, social skills training and psychoeducation, psychopharmacological trials, and community-based self-help networks.

This chapter will provide the practicum and internship student who works with addictive disordered populations an overview of the following: an identification of assessment instruments; counseling recommendations; and highlights regarding relapse prevention.

Assessment Instruments

Practicum/internship students who are involved in the counseling of clients for possible psychoactive substance pathology may find it useful to acquaint themselves with standardized assessment instruments as an adjunct to clinical interviews and observation. Two instruments that appear to have good reliability and validity and that can be scored and interpreted in short periods of time are the Drug Abuse Screening Test-20 (DAST-20) (Skinner, 1982) and the Addiction Severity Index (ASI) (McClellan, Luborsky, & Cacciola, 1985; Orvaschel, 1993). The DAST is a 20-item self-report inventory that provides a quantitative index of the degree of consequences and severity of drug abuse. The DAST-20 yields a total cumulative score with severity intervals (i.e., None, Low, Moderate, Substantial, and Severe). The ASI is a structured interview instrument that provides a multidimensional assessment of degree of impairment due to substance use in various areas (medical, employment, severity of chemical use, family/social relationships, legal and psychiatric status). The ASI requires both administration and interviewer severity rating skills; therefore, counselors must have adequate training and orientation to the instrument. The DAST requires only a tabulation of item scores, and the interpretation is objective. Both instruments, although not independently adequate to provide a diagnosis, may be valuable tools for additional information as well as identifying specific areas for treatment focus.

A sample *Substance Abuse Assessment Form* is available in Form 8.3.

Counseling Recommendations

It is important for therapists who work with substance abusing/dependent clients to adopt an objective and factual approach to assessment interviews. As many clients who enter treatment/counseling for substance related problems do so as a result of external pressures (family, employers, legal system), it is important that the counselor convey an impression that he/she is an ally to the client in addressing his/her problems. In asking assessment questions, the therapist should use the objective criteria as a guideline and proceed in a nonjudgmental and matter-of-fact manner and avoid asking leading questions such as: "You don't abuse drugs or alcohol, do you?" (Bukstein, 1990). Initial interviewing goals include establishing a flow of information and disclosure, estimating the client's level of motivation for treatment, and obtaining the necessary information to formulate an objective impression.

The therapist needs to realize that the substance-abusing client frequently enters treatment with a strong sense of ambivalence (anxiety to avoid psychosocial consequences and the drive to continue experiencing the expected desired effects of substance use), which effects treatment motivation. The key to work through ambivalence is to attempt as early as possible to foster *engagement and trust,* which can be done by discussing treatment ambivalence if it is observed and emphasizing the client's presenting negative consequences from his/her history of substance use.

The therapist should relay the results of the assessment interview to the client in the same objective fashion and emphasize that assessment is based on the information that the client provided and also data from assessment instruments. This process may assist the client in working through treatment resistance as well as reinforce the therapeutic alliance.

1. Understand the emotional role that the substance(s) of choice plays for the client. A central challenge for the therapist is to identify the client's rationale for mood-altering substance use. Almost invariably that rationale has an affective base (substance use to avoid or escape negative affect and or tension or to acquire a desired affective state. Once the affective motivation is established, treatment to develop adaptive coping responses can be undertaken. As depth-psychology oriented treatment may be very difficult with substance dependent clients regarding relapse risk, therapists should be cautious in immediately addressing traumatic issues if the client has only a brief period of abstinence or if affect tolerance/modulation appears tenuous.

2. Identify the internal and external triggering events for substance cravings and impulses. Substance-using impulses frequently are precipitated by events that may or may not be evident to the client. The counselor needs to detect the internal (i.e., thoughts, feelings, memories, attitudes) and external (i.e., interpersonal conflicts, social isolation, interpersonal/existential losses) antecedents for the client's substance use impulses and cravings. Helping the client identify his/her triggers when they occur can be used as a signal for the client to implement substance-avoidance behaviors. Once substance triggers are identified, specific operationalized behavior plans for coping with them while abstaining can be constructed and carried, if necessary, by the client for immediate reference and guidance.

3. Confront internal versus external locus of control regarding substance-using behaviors. Many substance-abusing or dependent clients rationalize their substance using behavior by either relinquishing responsibility for control ("I can't help it") or externalizing controls over their behavior ("My boss makes me use—he's so demanding"). The counselor must confront the client by reflecting that the client ultimately chooses to use a substance regardless of the circumstances. Once clients accept this reality, then controlling the impulses to use becomes a treatment focus.

4. Challenge substance-dependence reinforcing cognitions (beliefs and thinking styles). Many substance-abusing/dependent clients will present belief systems that reinforce chemical dependency ("Without my crack, I can't deal with

(Continued on p. 309.)

SUBSTANCE ABUSE ASSESSMENT FORM

Directions: Student asks the client the specific questions addressed on the form. Student, client, and supervisor should sign the form. The completed form is kept in the student's confidential file.

1. What do you or have you used? _____

_____

2. How long have you used (beginning with experimentation)? _____

_____

3. How often are you high in a week? _____

_____

4. How many of your friends use? _____

_____

5. Are you on medication? _____

6. Do you own money for chemicals? How much? _____

7. How much do you spend for chemicals in a month (if you were to pay for all the chemicals)?

_____

8. Who provides if you are broke? _____

_____

9. Have you ever been busted (police, school, home, DWIs)? _____

10. Have you lost a job because of your use? _____

_____

Form 8.3, p. 1 of 4, Copy 1

11. What time of day do you use? _____
_____
_____
_____

12. Do you use on the job or in school? _____
_____
_____
_____

13. Does it take more, less, about the same amount to get you high? _____
_____
_____
_____

14. Have you ever shot up? What? Where on your body? _____
_____
_____

15. Do you sneak using? How do you do it? _____
_____
_____
_____

16. Do you hide stuff? _____
_____

17. Do you have rules for using? What are they? How did they come about? _____
_____
_____
_____
_____
_____
_____

18. Do you use alone? _____
_____
_____
_____

19. Have you ever tried to quit? _____
_____
_____
_____

20. Have you had any withdrawal symptoms? _____
_____
_____
_____

21. Have you lost your "good time highs"? _____

_____

_____

_____

22. Have you ever thought about suicide? _____

_____

_____

_____

23. Do you mix your chemicals when using? _____

_____

_____

_____

24. Do you ever shift from one chemical to another?   Yes _____ No _____

What happened that made you decide to shift? _____

_____

_____

_____

25. Do you avoid people who don't use? _____

_____

_____

_____

26. Do you avoid talking about chemical dependency? _____

_____

_____

_____

27. Have you done things when using that you are ashamed of?   Yes _____ No _____

What happened? _____

_____

_____

_____

28. Who is the most important person in you life, including yourself? _____

_____

29. How are you taking care of him/her? _____

_____

_____

30. On a scale of 1 (low) to 10 (can't use 5), how is your life going? _____

Explain _____

_____

31. Are there any harmful consequences you are aware of in your chemical use other than those touched upon? _____

_____

_____

_____

_____

32. Do you think your chemical is harmful to you?   Yes _____   No _____

     Do you think you have a chemical problem?   Yes _____   No _____

     Explain _____

_____

_____

_____

_____

_____

Student's Signature

_____

Client's Signature

_____

Supervisor's Signature

_____

Date

CONSENT FOR THE RELEASE OF CONFIDENTIAL INFORMATION

    I _____ , authorize _____ (Name or general designation of program making disclosure) to disclose to _____ (Name of person or organization to which disclosure is to be made) the following information: _____ _____ (Nature of the information, as limited as possible).

    The purpose of the disclosure authorized herein is to _____ (Purpose of disclosure, as specific as possible).

    I understand that my records are protected under the Federal regulations governing Confidentiality of Alcohol and Drug Abuse Patient Records, 42 CFR Part 2, and cannot be disclosed without my written consent unless otherwise provided for in the regulations. I also understand that I may revoke this consent at any time except to the extent that action has been taken in reliance on it, and that in any event, this consent expires automatically as follows: _____ (Specification of the date, event, or condition upon which this consent expires).

Dated: _____Signature of participant _____

_____

Signature of parent, guardian, or authorized representative when required

Form 8.3, p. 4 of 4, Copy 1

SUBSTANCE ABUSE ASSESSMENT FORM

Directions: Student asks the client the specific questions addressed on the form. Student, client, and supervisor should sign the form. The completed form is kept in the student's confidential file.

1. What do you or have you used? _____
    _____
    _____
    _____
    _____

2. How long have you used (beginning with experimentation)? _____
    _____
    _____
    _____
    _____

3. How often are you high in a week? _____
    _____
    _____
    _____

4. How many of your friends use? _____
    _____
    _____
    _____
    _____

5. Are you on medication? _____
    _____

6. Do you own money for chemicals? How much? _____
    _____

7. How much do you spend for chemicals in a month (if you were to pay for all the chemicals)?
    _____
    _____

8. Who provides if you are broke? _____
    _____
    _____

9. Have you ever been busted (police, school, home, DWIs)? _____
    _____

10. Have you lost a job because of your use? _____
    _____
    _____

11. What time of day do you use? _____
_____
_____
_____

12. Do you use on the job or in school? _____
_____
_____
_____

13. Does it take more, less, about the same amount to get you high? ____
_____
_____
_____

14. Have you ever shot up? What? Where on your body? _____
_____
_____

15. Do you sneak using? How do you do it? _____
_____
_____
_____

16. Do you hide stuff? _____
_____

17. Do you have rules for using? What are they? How did they come about? ____
_____
_____
_____
_____
_____
_____

18. Do you use alone? _____
_____
_____
_____

19. Have you ever tried to quit? _____
_____
_____
_____

20. Have you had any withdrawal symptoms? _____
_____
_____
_____

21. Have you lost your "good time highs"? _____
_____
_____
_____

22. Have you ever thought about suicide? _____
_____
_____
_____

23. Do you mix your chemicals when using? _____
_____
_____
_____

24. Do you ever shift from one chemical to another?   Yes _____ No _____

   What happened that made you decide to shift? _____
_____
_____
_____

25. Do you avoid people who don't use? _____
_____
_____
_____

26. Do you avoid talking about chemical dependency? _____
_____
_____
_____

27. Have you done things when using that you are ashamed of?   Yes _____ No _____

   What happened? _____
_____
_____
_____

28. Who is the most important person in you life, including yourself? _____
_____

29. How are you taking care of him/her? _____
_____
_____

30. On a scale of 1 (low) to 10 (can't use 5), how is your life going? _____

   Explain _____
_____

31. Are there any harmful consequences you are aware of in your chemical use other than those touched upon? _____

_____

_____

_____

_____

32. Do you think your chemical is harmful to you?   Yes _____   No _____

Do you think you have a chemical problem?   Yes _____   No _____

Explain _____

_____

_____

_____

_____

_____

Student's Signature

_____

Client's Signature

_____

Supervisor's Signature

_____

Date

CONSENT FOR THE RELEASE OF CONFIDENTIAL INFORMATION

I _____ , authorize _____ (Name or general designation of program making disclosure) to disclose to _____ (Name of person or organization to which disclosure is to be made) the following information: _____ _____ (Nature of the information, as limited as possible).

The purpose of the disclosure authorized herein is to _____ (Purpose of disclosure, as specific as possible).

I understand that my records are protected under the Federal regulations governing Confidentiality of Alcohol and Drug Abuse Patient Records, 42 CFR Part 2, and cannot be disclosed without my written consent unless otherwise provided for in the regulations. I also understand that I may revoke this consent at any time except to the extent that action has been taken in reliance on it, and that in any event, this consent expires automatically as follows: _____ (Specification of the date, event, or condition upon which this consent expires).

Dated: _____Signature of participant _____

_____

Signature of parent, guardian, or authorized representative when required

Form 8.3, p. 4 of 4, Copy 2

life."; "I need a drink to control myself."). The counselor should challenge maladaptive cognitions.

5. Help the client to learn and apply abstaining behaviors (thinking through cravings and impulses). Coping with cravings and impulses is a vital therapeutic goal. A useful resistance skill is for the client to focus on previous negative consequences of substance use when the client experiences substance cravings or impulses. This technique shifts psychological focus from the desired and expected immediate mood altering effect of the substance to associating the substance with an emotionally negative event(s). This technique of "thinking the craving through" can divert clients from impulsiveness and make them aware of adaptive options. It is important for counselors to review with clients the distinctions between thinking, feeling, and physical action (doing). Clients need to realize that they can have substance-oriented cravings and impulses (feelings) and not carry them out.

6. Practice therapeutic rather than antagonistic confrontation. As treatment engagement on the part of the client is critical, the counselor must be careful not to confuse confrontation with intolerance. Therapeutic confrontation occurs when the counselor presents the client with concrete examples of clinical material that is representative of the disorder. Therapeutic confrontation is based upon the objective data or behavior that the client presents and not upon a conflict of personal values. Attempts to impose guilt or shame upon the client may increase the potential for treatment dropout. Reflecting clinical observations back to the client in a nonthreatening and constructive fashion may increase the probability that the client will accept and work with the intervention.

7. Establish healthy developmental goals. An important part of counseling substance-abusing clients is addressing the frequent developmental disturbances that accompany maladaptive patterns of substance use (dropping out of school, termination from employment, family disruption, etc.). Part of the treatment plan should include a return (perhaps gradually) to normal and productive functioning. Frustration and anxiety tolerance may be a central focus depending on the severity and duration of psychosocial disturbances.

Relapse Prevention

Relapse prevention is defined as "a self-management program designed to enhance the maintenance stage of the habit-change process" (Marlatt, 1985a, 1985b). Behaviorally, relapse prevention can be seen as one set of operationalized target behaviors implemented and practiced consistently over time that results in another set of targeted undesired behaviors being discontinued. Below are general framework suggestions for an operationalized psychoactive substance relapse prevention program. Therapists should help the clients

1. Identify high-risk situations. This suggestion helps the client realize what environmental stimuli have served as external triggers for substance cravings, impulses, and use. High-risk situations may be attending particular social events where substance use is prominent or spending time at places where substances are readily available. The awareness of high-risk situations alerts the client to consider avoidance or to apply specific behavior plans for increasing controls to maintain abstinence.

2. Make necessary lifestyle changes and relationship modifications. Gaining awareness of specific lifestyle behaviors (theft, prostitution, drug sales, etc.) that are specifically related to the substance-using pattern is important, as those behavior patterns may need to change also in order to maximize the prognosis for abstinence. Likewise, specific relationships that reinforce substance use must also be confronted, modified, or even discontinued until the client has gained sufficient behavioral and impulse controls to withstand the influence of others who advocate substance use.

3. Reduce access to psychoactive substances. A strategic component of relapse prevention is reducing access to psychoactive substances. This may occur by removing psychoactive substances from the client's residence, eliminating routine purchasing of substances (alcohol) or identifying specific places (high-risk situations) where substances are readily available and/or promoted.

4. Address any underlying psychopathology. Untreated psychiatric disorders, or psychopathology, is one of the most common reasons for

psychoactive substance relapse (McClellan, 1986). Mood, anxiety, or personality disorders, or other forms of psychopathology that persist into the abstinence period, should be formally evaluated and treated. The use of simultaneous combination treatments (psychotherapy, pharmacotherapy, family therapy, and self-help groups) may be most advantageous.

5. Rebound from a relapse. In the treatment of substance-abusing/dependent clients, relapses occur; and in specific patient subtypes, they may be common (i.e., severe personality disorders, untreated mood or anxiety disorders). It is important for the counselor to be clinically prepared for relapse and to promote to the client that a relapse should not be viewed fatalistically but rather simply as a mistake with the current treatment focus. The client should be encouraged to resume abstinence and to gain an understanding of the dynamics of the relapse. Relapses can be utilized as a restarting point in treatment if therapeutic engagement is maintained.

References

American Psychiatric Association. (1987). *Diagnostic and statistical manual of mental disorders* (3rd ed., revised). Washington, DC: Author.

Beck, A., & Emery, G.D. (1977). *Cognitive therapy of substance abuse.* Philadelphia, PA: Center for Cognitive Therapy.

Bukstein, O.G. (1990). A primer on psychoactive substance use disorders in DSM-III-R. Unpublished paper, Western Psychiatric Institute and Clinic.

Cox, M. (1987). Personality theory and research. In H.T. Blane & K.E. Leonard (Eds.), *Psychological theories of drinking and alcoholism* (pp. 55–84). New York: Guilford Press.

Ellis, A., McInerney, J., DiGiuseppe, R., Yeager, R. (1988). *Rational-emotive therapy with alcoholics and substance abusers.* Elmsford, NY: Pergamon Press.

Frances, R.J., & Miller, S.I. (Eds.). (1991). Clinical textbook of addictive disorders. New York: Guilford Press.

Forrest, G.G. (1985). Psychodynamically oriented treatment of alcoholism and substance abuse. In T.E. Bratter & G.G. Forrest (Eds.), *Alcoholism and substance abuse* (pp. 307–336). New York: Free Press.

Goodwin, D.W., & Warnock, J.K. (1991). Alcoholism: A family disease. In R.J. Frances & S.I. Miller (Eds.), *Clinical textbook of addictive disorders* (pp. 485–500). New York: Guilford Press.

Leigh, G. (1985). Psychosocial factors in the etiology of substance abuse. In T.E. Bratter & G.G. Forrest (Eds.), *Alcoholism and substance abuse* (pp. 3–48). New York: Free Press.

Marlatt, A. (1985a). Cognitive factors in the relapse process. In G.A. Marlatt & J.R. Gordon (Eds.), *Relapse prevention* (pp. 128–193). New York: Guilford Press.

Marlatt, A. (1985b). Relapse prevention, theoretical rationale, and overview of the model. In G.A. Marlatt & J.R. Gordon (Eds.), *Relapse prevention* (pp. 3–67). New York: Guilford Press.

McClellan, A.T. (1986). "Psychiatric severity" as a predictor of outcome from substance abuse treatments. In R.E. Meyer (Ed.), *Psychopathology and addictive disorders* (pp. 97–135). New York: Guilford Press.

McClellan, A.T., Luborsky, L., & Cacciola, M.A. (1985). New data from the Addiction Severity Index, reliability and validity in three centers. *The Journal of Nervous and Mental Disease, 173*(7).

Orvaschel, H. (1993). *Social functioning and social supports: A review of measures suitable for use with substance abusers.* Diagnostic source book on drug abuse research and treatment. National Institute on Drug Abuse, U.S. Department of Health and Human Services.

Ray, O., & Ksir, C. (1990). *Drugs, society and human behavior.* Newport Beach, CA: Times Mirror/Mosby.

Skinner, H.A. (1982). *The drug abuse screening test-20 (DAST-20): Guidelines for administering and scoring.* Toronto, Ontario: Addiction Research Foundation.

Wallace, B. (1991). *Crack cocaine.* New York: Brunner-Mazel.

CHILD ABUSE AND NEGLECT: A GUIDE FOR PRACTICUM STUDENTS AND INTERNS

Lou Ann Schrock-Brutz
Patrick B. Malley

In dealing with the issue of child abuse and/or neglect in clinical settings, student counselors must bear in mind the unique relationship they have with their field supervisors, the responsibility they have to the institution at which they are working, and clients they serve. A close working relationship with the field site supervisor is imperative to the learning process to ensure that proper and quality care is afforded to clients.

In all instances regarding child abuse, an immediate report should be made to the field site supervisor, and a review of the institution's policy should be completed. The following guide is just that, and should only be utilized in conjunction with the institution's policy and at the discretion of the field supervisor.

Definition

Child abuse legislation first appeared around the turn of the century in New York State. Compared to present day statutes it was quite vague and weak (Guyer, 1982). Currently all 50 states have enacted child abuse laws requiring mandatory reporting. The laws in some states remain vague and allow for a degree of variation in judicial and regulatory responses. This is also true of the confidentiality issues involved in mandatory reporting (Erickson, McEvoy, & Colucci, 1984). Therefore, the student counselor will need to be familiar with the particular legislation in the state where he/she is completing the field study.

For purposes of this article, the Pennsylvania "Child Protective Services Law" Act of 1975, P.L. 438, No. 124 was utilized in conjunction with Act 136 of 1982 and Act 42 of 1983. This Act defines child abuse and neglect in Section 3 as follows:

> As used in this act: "Child abuse" means serious physical or mental injury which is not explained by the available medical history as being accidental, or sexual abuse or sexual exploitation, or serious physical neglect, of a child under 18 years of age, of the injury, abuse or neglect has been caused by the acts or omissions of the child's parents or by a person responsible for the child's welfare, or any individual residing in the same home as the child, or a paramour of a child's parent provided, however, no child shall be deemed to be physically or mentally abused for the sole reason he is in good faith being furnished treatment by spiritual means through prayer alone in accordance with the tenets and practices of a recognized church or religious denomination by a duly accredited practitioner thereof or is not provided specified medical treatment in the practice of religious beliefs, or solely on the grounds of environmental factors which are beyond the control of the person responsible for the child's welfare such as inadequate housing, furnishing, income, clothing, and medical care. (p. 1)

Recognition

Child abuse and/or neglect becomes apparent to the counselor in one of two ways: either by direct verbal report or by being uncovered indirectly via the counseling process. When uncovered directly via report either the victim, perpetrator, or some other party involved with the victim or perpetrator reports such. This is the most direct method, and the position of the counselor is not to evaluate the authenticity of the report, at least not at this phase. This is the job of the children and youth authorities.

What about when the counselor is not told directly but suspects abuse and/or neglect may be occurring? Erickson et al. (1984) referred to some general "characteristics" of child abuse applicable to the victim and perpetrator. Of these, the most

widely accepted for the abusive and/or neglectful parent are as follows:

1. abused as children themselves,

2. socially and emotionally immature,

3. low self-esteem,

4. expect children to act as adults,

5. cannot express frustration or anger via acceptable behaviors,

6. expectations of their children are not realistic given their ages,

7. violent marital discord,

8. abuse of drugs and/or alcohol,

9. inability to tolerate stress,

10. lack adequate parenting skills,

11. ignore child's needs,

12. are guarded in discussing family relationships, and

13. lack an appropriate role model.

The most widely accepted general characteristics of the abused and/or neglected child are as follows:

1. inappropriate hostility directed toward authority figures;

2. disruptive and destructive;

3. passive and withdrawn, crying easily;

4. fearful at times, not wanting to go home (or to the place where abuse occurs);

5. habitual absence or tardiness from school;

6. inappropriately dressed for the weather;

7. failure to thrive symptoms;

8. bruises, burns, or other unexplainable marks;

9. chronically untreated medical needs;

10. constant hunger;

11. sexually oriented remarks;

12. sexually suggestive behavior; and

13. discomfort of genital areas.

One must exercise caution in evaluating these "general characteristics." The counselor needs to be concerned when several of the characteristics of the abusive parent and abused child are present. The presence of only a few characteristics may only be indicative of a dysfunctional family. In observing these characteristics, keep documented records for specifically addressing these issues for future reference.

Reporting

The "Child Protective Services Law," Section 4(a-d), deals with mandatory reporting of suspected child abuse. The one in Pennsylvania is representative of those in other states. This section specifies that any person who, in the course of their professional occupation, has reason to believe that child coming before them is a victim of suspected child abuse must report this to the appropriate children and youth agency. The local county office numbers can be obtained by contacting the hotline office. Other national sources of information can be found at the end of this section.

A report of child abuse is to be made to the state hotline number immediately upon discovery. They in turn will notify the appropriate county agency who will be in touch with you in the future. This is done via a verbal report and followed up on within 48 hours by the submission of a suspected Child Abuse Form. In Pennsylvania, the form number is CY 47, which should be available at the facility at which the student is working or can be obtained from a children and youth agency. In some cases, more than one county office will work in conjunction with another during an investigation.

Privileged communication is referred to in the "Child Protective Services Law," Section 4(c). This section stipulates that confidentiality does not apply to situations involving child abuse, and this cannot be used as an excuse for failure to report. Issues regarding confidentiality should be dealt with during the first counseling session. During this phase of the counseling relationship, the client(s) become(s) aware of the counselor's

ethical and legal obligations regarding the reporting of suspected child abuse. Thus, if such a report becomes necessary, the client(s) already has been "forewarned." In such instances, the belief is that the damage to the therapeutic relationship can be kept at a minimum. this is further facilitated by encouraging the suspected perpetrators, if they are involved in counseling sessions with you, to call children and youth authorities themselves to report the incident. this is only possible when they have admitted to such.

If the client does not feel comfortable placing the call to the appropriate agency, the counselor can arrange for an immediate appointment with children and youth authorities and offer to attend the session with the client. Cooperation from the alleged perpetrator is ideal and facilitated behavioral change; however, if the client refuses to voluntarily participate in reporting, the student counselor has the responsibility to do so. This is also true when the perpetrator is not in counseling and the victim is. In some instances, the counselor may choose to involve the perpetrator at the time of the report; however, this becomes an individual issue that is best discussed with the field supervisor.

Regardless of the manner in which the reporting is done, time is of the essence. Abuse and/or neglect must be reported immediately to ensure the safety of the alleged victim. Children and youth authorities will require some basic information during the initial oral report. Sample 8 shows the required information a student should have prior to calling the authorities. According to Schroeder (1979), two cases occurred in the state of California where a professional, a physician, was held liable in a civil suit for allowing children to return to their parents' care without reporting suspected child abuse. This occurred when the children were subsequently injured by the parents. Both cases serve as precedents for liability in not reporting suspected child abuse.

Counseling Relationship

Dealing with child abuse is not easy for the counselor. Muehlemann and Kimmons (1981) addressed the difficulties psychologists have in making decisions regarding child abuse reporting. Oftentimes, this is due to the impact reporting will have on the counseling relationship.

A SAMPLE FOR CHILD ABUSE REPORTING

Practicum Counselor and Position _____

Date and Time _____

Alleged Perpetrator _____ d.o.b. _____

    Address _____ S.S.# _____

Alleged Victim _____ d.o.b. _____

    Address _____ S.S.# _____

Information obtained from _____ d.o.b. _____

    Address _____

    Relationship to alleged perpetrator _____

    Relationship to alleged victim _____

Brief description of incident or concern _____

_____

_____

_____

Incident(s) ongoing _____ or specific date _____

Reported to immediate supervisor on _____

    Supervisor's name and position _____

Reported to children and youth services on _____ time _____

    Children and youth worker name _____

Alleged perpetrator aware of report?   Yes _____ No _____

Alleged victim aware of report?   Yes _____ No _____

Alleged perpetrator in counseling?   Yes _____ No _____

    Where _____

Alleged victim in counseling?   Yes _____ No _____

    Where _____

Results _____

_____

_____

Student Counselor Signature _____

Field Supervisor Signature _____

    cc: client's file
        agency file

Sample 8. A sample for child abuse reporting.

CHILD ABUSE AND NEGLECT SOCIAL SERVICE AGENCIES

Resources

National Committee for the Prevention of
  Child Abuse
  332 S. Michigan, Suite 1600
  Chicago, IL 60604   312-663-3520

Child Welfare League of America
  440 1st Street, N.W., Suite 310
  Washington, DC 20001-2085   202-638-3952

TMG Childhelp U.S.A.
  P. O. Box 2816
  Van Nuys, CA 91401   1-800-422-4453

International Society for the Prevention of
  Child Abuse and Neglect
  1205 Oneida Street
  Denver, CO 80220   303-321-3963

What happens to the counseling relationship after a report of suspected child abuse is made too the authorities is dependent upon what happened during the counseling prior to the report. If mandatory reporting as it relates to the breach of confidentiality was discussed with clients when counseling was initiated, the likelihood of the continuance of a trusting relationship is enhanced. The same is also true when the counselor is supportive to client(s) during the process.

The degree of support afforded the client, whether perpetrator and/or victim, is very crucial in child abuse cases. More often than not, the degree of empathy a counselor has in this situation is a culmination of education, experience, and the counselor's personal values. Although a counselor's personal values are not to enter actively into the counseling relationship, in many ways they do indirectly. During the learning process, the student counselor needs to become aware of his/her own value system and evaluate, with the cooperation of the field instructor, how it impacts the counseling relationship. As Lippitt (1985) pointed out, counselors cannot function value free. The secret lies in not imposing one's values on others. If you do not feel comfortable dealing with these issues, which at times become quite emotional, be honest with yourself and your field supervisor. Enlist his/her assistance in learning how to participate in this type of counseling. The victim and/or the perpetrator are your clients. You have ethical and legal responsibilities to them.

References

Child Protective Services Law Act of 1975, P.L. 438, No. 124, Act of 1982, No. 136, Act of 1983, No. 42.

Erickson, E.L., McEvoy, A., & Colucci, N.D. (1984). *Child abuse and neglect: A guidebook for educators and community leaders* (2nd ed.). Holmes Beach, FL: Learning Publications.

Guyer, M.J. (1982). Child abuse and neglect statutes: Legal and clinical implications. *American Journal of Orthopsychiatry, 52*(1), 73–81.

Lippitt, D.N. (1985). The ethical task in family therapy. *Family Therapy, XII*(3), 297–301.

Muehlemann, T., & Kimmons, C. (1981). Psychologists' views on child abuse reporting, confidentiality, life, and the law: An exploratory study. *Professional Psychology, 12*(5), 631–638.

Schroeder, L.O. (1979). Legal liability: A professional concern. *Clinical Social Work Journal, 7*(3), 194–199.

SOCIAL PHOBIA: A GUIDE FOR PRACTICUM STUDENTS AND INTERNS
David E. Botwin, Ph.D.

Social phobia has been, until quite recently, the overlooked anxiety disorder. In large part, it infrequently was diagnosed because clinicians did not look for it and their clients or patients did not describe themselves in terms that would suggest this disorder. Also, as noted by Uhde, Tancer, Black, and Brown (1991),

> Because almost everyone has experienced social anxiety or discomfort, it is easy for the lay public and clinicians alike to overlook the potential anguish and incapacitating nature of this disorder. Patients with social phobia often feel ashamed, frustrated, demoralized, and overwhelmed by their symptomatology. (p. 31)

A 1985 review article (Liebowitz, Gorman, Fyer, & Klein) observed that

> While social phobia has received some attention from British investigators, it has been dramatically neglected in the

US mental health literature, except by behavior therapists. Interest in social phobia among American clinicians and researchers can be expected to grow, however, as the specialized anxiety clinics now being established continue to proliferate. (p. 735)

The recent proliferation of studies on social phobia in the clinical research literature confirms the accuracy of this predication.

This parallels with the transformation in professional and public awareness about panic disorder and agoraphobia that occurred in the 1980s. As the media publicized these conditions, people who suffered from panic disorder and agoraphobia learned that there was available treatment for their condition and that it was a recognized disorder with a name. The latter is especially important, for there is nothing as isolating or frightening as living with distressing and incapacitating symptoms that are unrecognized and invalidated by those from whom help has been sought. When "experts," whether in clinical consultation or in the media, supply a name for what you suffer from, it suggests that you are not alone, and even more important, that there are people who understand what you are experiencing and suffering and can help you. In short, such naming is hope eliciting. When panic disorder, or agoraphobia, started receiving general media attention, concerned family members and friends began to recognize that this was what persons they lived with or knew suffered from and then to encourage, or even initiate, their seeking professional treatment.

Typically, individuals with social phobia have tended to think that this was just the way they were, that they were simply painfully shy, or especially sensitive—that they were people for whom certain kinds of interpersonal situations were especially stressful and difficult. A fairly recent national newspaper article publicized the prevalence of phobic disorders, and the Phobia Society of America (now the Anxiety Disorders Association of America) did not mention social phobia, although it gave a long list of specific simple phobias, many of them relatively rare and, unlike social phobia, imposing considerably less restriction or disability.

Social phobia should be of special interest and concern to practicum and internship students in counseling and psychotherapy for the following reasons:

1. Early age of reported onset.

2. Impact on students and their school attendance, performance, and behavior.

3. Disabling vocational and social consequences.

4. High comorbidity with other anxiety disorders, depression, alcohol, and other substance abuse.

5. Social phobia may predispose individuals to major depression.

6. Since effective treatments for social phobia are available, early diagnosis, treatment, or referral is important and can have powerful preventive as well as ameliorative impact on individuals' lives.

Age at Onset

DSM-III-R (APA, 1987) reported age at onset of social phobia as late childhood or early adolescence. A more recent epidemiologic community based study of over 13,000 adults reported mean age at onset of the subsample of 106 subjects with social phobia who did not have comorbid agoraphobia or simple phobia as 15.5 years, with peaks at the interval of 0 to 5 years and at age 13 (Schneier, Johnson, Hornig, Liebowitz, & Weissman, 1992). Onset prior to age 25 was reported for 90% of these subjects, prior to age 15 for 62%, and prior to age 5 for 21%. Inclusion of subjects with comorbid agoraphobia or simple phobia did not alter these findings significantly. Scholing and Emmelkamp (1990), in considering patient samples, concluded

> most patients first noticed their problems between 10 and 14 years, followed by the group where onset was between 15 and 19 years. Taken together, about 70% of the patients reported that their social phobia started between 10 and 19 years. (p. 279)

It therefore behooves counselors to consider developmental events that occur in this period of vulnerability for social phobia.

As children confront the developmental tasks of adolescence, they also are making school transitions that are challenging and, for some, threatening. In moving to middle or junior high school, they leave the relatively more structured, or protective, elementary school environment for one where they have contact with more teachers, new teachers, and with new, unfamiliar classmates. Gym, group showers, lavatories, and the locker room often are mentioned as threats to children who are embarrassed or concerned about their physical appearance and development. For appearance-sensitive others, the classroom, halls, and schoolyard do almost as well.

This is a period when same sex and opposite sex friendships different from those of childhood are formed, when the presence or absence of conversational skills facilitates or impedes this formation of friendships and when there are more opportunities to join and participate in extracurricular activities and sports than before. Dating and sexual exploration occurs during this interval. Becoming part of a peer group is an important task for adolescents. The experience gained here, and some of the relationships formed, may become both model and substance of later social support networks.

For the insecure, for those lacking self-confidence and self-esteem, for those oversensitive to perceived or actual critical regard of others, for those fearful of any scrutiny by others, or for the painfully self-conscious, this can be a very stressful and difficult period characterized by social withdrawal and lack of engagement in those peer group interactions and activities that develop a sense of personal and social competence and worth. The outcome can be adult social anxiety, isolation, loneliness and depression.

In addition to awareness of early onset, counselors need to know that in adolescents, especially males, social phobia is believed to be a significant, and generally unrecognized, cause of school refusal. A clinical anxiety disorder coupled with persistent school refusal, especially in older adolescents, has been cited as having serious prognosis for future problems of adjustment. Social phobia is hardly confined to grades 1–12, however. One survey estimated that approximately 3% to 10% of students at a British college manifested typical social phobic symptoms (Bryant & Trower, 1974).

Socially phobic students find class recitation very anxiety provoking. Courses where students are required to deliver oral reports are especially threatening. They may avoid taking such classes when they have an option, absent themselves when they expect to be called upon, and experience great emotional distress, as well as disturbing physiological symptoms, on anticipation of class performance as well as during it. Practicum and internship students

in counseling and psychotherapy may conclude, on interviewing such students, that their problem is simply one of performance anxiety or stage fright and may not actively interview for social phobia— that is, for a more pervasive pattern of anxiety eliciting situations and avoidance. The anguish and extent of disability experienced by some students is described poignantly in the following adult retrospective account:

> I've suffered from severe anxiety since as far back as I can remember. Grammar school and high school were absolute torture for me. Even though I did my homework, studied, and knew the answers most of the time, I spent the whole day, every single day for 12 long years, living in mortal fear and dread of being called on and singled out by the teacher. If I was called on, I froze with panic and anxiety to the extent my mind literally went blank. I couldn't think or give an answer even if a gun had been pointed at my head. (Uhde et al., 1991, p. 31)

Social phobia has also been cited as a factor in failure to achieve occupational status for which individuals are otherwise qualified. Greater individual visibility and increased performance expectations tend to accompany promotion and the assumption of more responsible work roles. One might then be expected to speak up at planning sessions, or give reports or presentations in other group settings. Being asked to take the minutes at a conference or meeting is a contingency to be greatly avoided by those fearful of writing in the scrutiny or presence of others. For socially phobic persons, such occasions are fraught with dread and the source of awful anticipatory as well as actual performance anxiety. Increased status in the workplace or at school often involves more, or closer, interaction with superiors and thus becomes something to be avoided by the anxious social phobic. Some socially phobic individuals may avoid attaining a level of performance that might make them recipients of unwanted focus and attention.

Patients seeking treatment have described the trauma of being selected for public recognition of their outstanding work performance and even leaving good jobs to avoid impending recognition. Highly competent professionals have described how their achievement of status led to situations that terrified them, namely invitations to speak to their peers. Mahoney (1991, pp. 351–353) gave a poignant account of a world famous psychologist and distinguished scholar who shared with Mahoney his well kept secret, an excruciating public-speaking anxiety. For years he had avoided lecture invitations and proposed banquets and award ceremonies in his honor. Doing so was cause of considerable personal anguish for him. What should be understood from these examples is that individuals such as these do not just have a situational performance problem. They suffer in anticipation, from the threat of recognition, from the stress of inventing excuses that will not expose their real reasons, and finally, from feeling bad about turning down or deceiving others whom they recognize meant well by them. The last part (feeling bad) certainly does not bolster their self-esteem.

Although a slightly higher prevalence of social phobia in females in the general population has been reported (Barlow, 1988), among clinical populations gender distribution has been reported as equal, or having a 60/40 male to female ratio (Amies, Gelder, & Shaw, 1983). The proportion of males seeking treatment, strikingly higher than with other anxiety disorders, has been speculated to be a function of the impact of social phobia on traditional male role expectations and performance, ranging from leadership functions and other assertive or publicly visible work roles to initiating of social interaction with women, such as asking for dates. Most dating or heterosexual anxiety does not meet current DSM-III-R or DSM-IV criteria for social phobia; however, dating commonly is reported by social phobics as a feared situation. Because dating anxiety frequently occurs in high school and college students, is very distressing to them, and may have impairing effects on their future as well as current lives, it is suggested that practicum or internship counselors read Hope and Heimberg (1990). This is an excellent, comprehensive guide to the treatment of dating anxiety.

One of the distinctions drawn between social phobia and avoidant personality disorder by current clinical researchers is in regard to desire to engage in social relationships. Whereas avoidant personalities are seen as coming to terms with their lifestyle, or as lacking desire for interaction, social phobics are seen as yearning for contact or relationships, and as often continuing to make painful and unsuccessful attempts. Some social phobics, male and female, report remaining in unsatisfying relationships because establishing them was such a difficult process and they both dreaded the ordeal of attempts with new persons and doubted their ability to find another partner. Others express loneliness, yearning, desire for marriage, and

dread of being approached for a date or approaching others. Some report only being able to approach or respond to others, or allow approach, after use of enough alcohol to alleviate their anxiety.

No wonder alcohol frequently has been called the social lubricant. Because of alcohol's effect in reducing social discomfort, abuse as well as use has significant incidence. High rates of social phobia (21%-39%) have been reported in both abstinent and hospitalized alcoholics (Smail, Stockwell, Canter, & Hodgson, 1984; Chambliss, Cherney, Caputo, & Rheinstein, 1987). Because of the tendency to focus on the most visible or prominent disorder, especially one that has attained a higher level of popular and professional awareness, the severe anxiety that preceded alcohol abuse may be overlooked, not diagnosed, and not included in a treatment plan. This is a recipe for relapse.

Striking comorbidity findings are an especially important reason why practicum and internship students in counseling and psychotherapy should be able to assess for social phobia. One important community-based study concluded that "only 31% of subjects with social phobia had no other lifetime disorder (Schneier et al., 1992). A recent study of a clinical population concluded that

> A large majority (70.2%) suffered from, at least, one other anxiety disorder in their lifetime and in particular, panic disorder with or without agoraphobia (49.1%). Alcohol (28.1%) and substance (15.8%) abuse or dependence were also common lifetime diagnoses. Social phobia usually predated any episode of mood disorder (81.7%) or any other anxiety disorder (62.7%). Social phobia may predispose individuals to other psychiatric illnesses, in particular major depression. (Van Ameringen, Mancini, Styan, & Donison, 1991, p. 93)

Fear of scrutiny by others has been described as the distinguishing characteristic of social phobics. Clinical descriptions of these patients mention their exaggerated fear of "looking foolish," embarrassment, humiliation, or any negative evaluation by others, and their "exquisite sensitivity" to these issues. These individuals are thus typically avoidant of any situations where their anxiety may become manifest to others through blushing, trembling, shaking, or voice tremors. Speaking, eating in public, drinking (the cup or glass may shake or spill), writing one's name in the presence of others such as at banks, and the use of public lavatories all may be sources of great personal threat to be avoided.

Clinical authorities have previously distinguished between individuals who experience more discrete or circumscribed performance anxiety, where the activities that are avoided can be performed readily in private away from the scrutiny of others, and those who experience more pervasive social anxiety and tend to avoid social interaction. Lives of loneliness and relative isolation are not uncommon consequences of this form of social phobia. Some individuals may form one primary relationship, including marriage, but they may never develop other relationships. Those who do marry frequently may not mingle with relatives, attend family functions and gatherings, or have any other friends. (See Liebowitz, Schneier, Hollander, Welkowitz, Saoud, Feerick, Campeas, Fallon, Street, & Gitow, 1991.)

The expanded conceptualization of social phobia can be seen in a comparison of diagnostic criteria in DSM-III (APA, 1980), DSM-III-R (APA, 1987), and DSM-IV (APA, 1994). Prior to DSM-III (1980), social phobia was viewed as a type of simple phobia, now called specific phobia. The DSM-III-R definition emphasized fear and avoidance of situations involving possible scrutiny by others as the essential feature of social phobia. DSM-IV, however, gives equal emphasis to "social or performance situations in which the person is exposed to unfamiliar people or to possible scrutiny by others" (p. 416). It explicitly mentions, for the first time, significant interference "with the person's normal routine, occupational (academic) functioning, or social activities or relationships) (p. 417).

For younger individuals, "unfamiliar people" may well translate to social phobia being manifested in inhibition about dating and the development of peer friendships. Their social phobia may be expressed in avoidance of, or difficulty in, interacting with authority figures or superiors in school or work settings. The negative implications of such anxiety, inhibition, or avoidance for personal fulfillment, success, and happiness are obvious.

Diagnosis and Assessment

Whereas social anxiety is a more generic descriptor of a range of arousal and response patterns, of fears relating to exposure to and evaluation by others, and schema regarding embarrassment and humiliation, social phobia is the severe and symptomatically specific end of the gamut. DSM-IV, in fact, gives the subtitle "Social Anxiety Disorder" under Social Phobia (p. 411).

The diagnostic difficulties most frequently cited in the literature relate to discriminating social phobia from panic disorder, and social phobia from avoidant personality disorder (Barlow, 1988; Herbert, Hope, & Bellack, 1992; Liebowitz et al., 1985; Scholing & Emmelkamp, 1990; Taylor & Arnow, 1988; Widiger, 1992). While both social phobics and panic disorder patients do panic, the latter have panic attacks in many nonsocial situations. Panic disorder patients usually are comforted by the presence of familiar others, while social phobics often prefer to be alone. Travelling alone is feared by panic disorder patients, whereas some social phobics may feel comfortable using public transportation only during off hours when they are relatively alone. Barlow (1988) stated

> Social phobics had little difficulty being alone, crossing streets, riding public transport, or the like, but consistently rated situations such as being introduced, using the telephone, and being teased as more 'phobic' than did patients with panic disorder with agoraphobia. (p. 544)

Patients who have panic disorder with agoraphobia not uncommonly have social phobic fears and display avoidance of social functions and performance situations. However, this is related to the fear of having a panic attack in a situation where escape is not readily available and where they may suffer public humiliation by panicking in the presence of others. Loss of control is a primary issue for panic disorder with agoraphobia patients, and embarrassment is viewed as one of the dreaded consequences. Social phobics are more likely to be concerned with displaying signs of anxiety that are visible to others, such as blushing or trembling, or performing inadequately, and thus suffering embarrassment. Having spontaneous panic attacks, or panic attacks in uncued situations that do not involve social evaluation, has been cited as discriminating of panic disorder.

Panic disorder patients express fear of the panic attack itself, suffering loss of control, "going crazy," or having a heart attack. Social phobics, on the other hand, express fear of negative evaluation by others, of failure when exposed to scrutiny, and consequent shame and embarrassment. Panic disorder patients are specific about where they fear (i.e., crowds; driving or travelling alone; restaurants; places where they may be "trapped" or unable to make a quick or unobtrusive exit, such as movies, church, or the beauty parlor; and elevators). They commonly fear and avoid department stores, malls, supermarkets and banks. Places with checkout or teller lines are perceived as restraints to quick exit and escape.

In contrast, listed below are situations most commonly feared by social phobics. Social phobics are usually even more explicit and specific about what they fear.

> Talking or performing in front of others;
>
> Being the center of attention (e.g., at a birthday party);
>
> Meetings (attending and/or speaking);
>
> Eating/writing/drinking/working while being observed;
>
> Using public urinals;
>
> Conversations (initiating and/or being on a date);
>
> Attending a party;
>
> Using the telephone (answering and/or making calls);
>
> Talking to authority figures;
>
> Entering a situation where others are seated (e.g., entering a room, an airplane, or a crowded bus);
>
> Being assertive (e.g., expressing disagreement or making a request);
>
> Compliments (receiving and/or giving); and
>
> Shaking hands. (Hope, 1993, p. 8)

When a client or student has mentioned inhibition, discomfort, or difficulty in one or more of these situations, the counselor should inquire about other situations that may be problematic. The counselor next could consider use of one of the existing scales that measure social phobia.

The widely used *Fear Questionnaire* (FQ), developed by Marks and Mathews (1979), is most suitable for brief screening. This short standardized instrument has a 5-item social phobia subscale consisting of items 3, 7, 9, 11 and 14. All are rated on a 0 to 8 point scale, the higher number reflecting greatest severity. The other 5-item subscales are agoraphobia and blood and injury phobia. There are also 5 items that measure anxiety and depression symptoms or reactions associated with a phobic reaction (See Form 8.4).

The *Brief Social Phobia Scale* (BSPS) (Davidson, Potts, Richichi, Ford, Krishman, Smith, & Wilson, 1991) measures fear and avoidance in seven situations common to social phobia and also measures the severity of four physiologic symptoms that commonly are experienced. It thus has two dimensions: "symptoms of fear/avoidance behavior, and physiologic reactions" (p.48). (See Form 8.5.) The authors recommended

> that the scale be used after a clinical or semi-structured interview through which the interviewer may become familiar with the patient's primary symptoms. After the initial interview, the interviewer administers the scale in checklist fashion to the patient, who looks at a copy of the scale during the interview. Each item is addressed in sequence, and any ambiguities or inconsistencies are brought to the patient's notice and addressed appropriately. (p. 49)

Liebowitz has developed a 24-item social phobia scale that has separate subscales for performance and social anxiety, with separate ratings for fear and avoidance (Papp, Gorman, & Liebowitz, 1988). The range of situations covered is quite comprehensive.

The ADIS-R (Anxiety Disorders Interview Schedule-Revised) provides an especially thorough set of clinical assessment questions for social phobia. A special strength and unique feature is the section dealing with origins of the phobia. This information could be important to treatment. It can be found in Barlow (1988, pp. 545–546).

Before administering these, it would be well to give the client a rationale for doing so, something like: "We want to select the best method of treatment to help you with this problem. This questionnaire (inventory) can help us." Telling a client what you are doing, and why, is both threat reducing and alliance building. Practicum and internship students might well consult Cormier and Cormier (1991, pp. 144–215) for a thorough discussion of these issues and processes.

Treatment

Both psychopharmacologic and psychosocial treatments for social phobia are available. Only a psychiatrist who specializes in the treatment of anxiety disorders, or an anxiety disorders clinic, can properly prescribe and monitor psychopharmacologic treatments. While support for their efficacy is still equivocal, very recent studies have yielded promising outcome results.

Scholing and Emmelkamp (1990) concluded that "there is little evidence yet that psychopharmacological drugs are effective in the treatment of social phobia" (p. 300).

(Continued on p. 322.)

FEAR QUESTIONNAIRE (FQ)

Choose a number from the scale below to show how much you would avoid each of the situations listed below because of fear or other unpleasant feelings. Then write the number you chose in the blank opposite each situation.

0	1	2	3	4	5	6	7	8

Would not avoid it		Slightly avoid it		Definitely avoid it		Markedly avoid it		Always avoid it

_____	1. Main phobia you want treated (describe in your own words)
_____	2. Injections or minor surgery
_____	3. Eating or drinking with other people
_____	4. Hospitals
_____	5. Traveling alone by bus or coach
_____	6. Walking alone in busy streets
_____	7. Being watched or stared at
_____	8. Going into crowded shops
_____	9. Talking to people in authority
_____	10. Sight of blood
_____	11. Being criticized
_____	12. Going alone far from home
_____	13. Thought of injury or illness
_____	14. Speaking or acting to an audience
_____	15. Large open spaces
_____	16. Going to the dentist
_____	17. Other situations (describe)

Now choose a number from the scale below to show how much you are troubled by each problem listed, and write the number in the blank.

0	1	2	3	4	5	6	7	8

Hardly at all		Slightly troublesome		Definitely troublesome		Markedly troublesome		Very severely troublesome

_____	18. Feeling miserable or depressed
_____	19. Feeling irritable or angry
_____	20. Feeling tense or panicky
_____	21. Upsetting thoughts coming into your mind
_____	22. Feeling you or your surroundings are strange or unreal
_____	23. Other feelings (describe)

How would you rate the present state of your phobic symptoms on the scale below? Please circle one number between 0 and 8.

0	1	2	3	4	5	6	7	8

Reprinted from *Behaviour Research and Therapy,* Vol. 17, I.M. Marks and A.M. Mathews, "Brief Standard Self-rating Scale for Phobic Patients, pp. 263–267. Copyright 1979, with kind permission from Elsevier Science Ltd, The Boulevard, Langford Lane, Kidlington 0X5 1GB, UK.

Form 8.4., p. 1 of 1, Copy 1.

THE BRIEF SOCIAL PHOBIA SCALE

Instructions: It is recommended that the interviewer give a copy of this scale to the client for the interview. The time period will cover the previous week, unless otherwise specified (e.g., at the initial evaluation interview, when it could be the previous month).

Part I: Fear/Avoidance (F/A)

How much do you fear and avoid the following situations? Please give separate ratings for fear and avoidance.

	Fear rating	Avoidance rating
	0 = None	0 = None
	1 = Mild	1 = Rare
	2 = Moderate	2 = Sometimes
	3 = Severe	3 = Frequent
	4 = Extreme	4 = Always
	Fear (F)	Avoidance (A)
1. Speaking in public or in front of others	_____	_____
2. Talking to people in authority	_____	_____
3. Talking to strangers	_____	_____
4. Being embarrassed or humiliated	_____	_____
5. Being criticized	_____	_____
6. Social gatherings	_____	_____
7. Doing something while being watched (this does not include speaking)	_____	_____

Part II: Physiologic (P)

When you are in a situation that involves contact with other people, or when you are thinking about such a situation, do you experience the following symptoms?

	0 = None
	1 = Mild
	2 = Moderate
	3 = Severe
	4 = Extreme
8. Blushing	_____
9. Palpitations	_____
10. Trembling	_____
11. Sweating	_____

Total scores: F =   A =   P =   Total =

This form was developed by J.R.T. Davidson et al. (Copyright 1991) and appeared in *The Journal of Clinical Psychiatry,* Vol. 52, Number 11 (supplement), pp. 48–51. Reprinted with permission.

Form 8.5., p. 1 of 1, Copy 1.

On the other hand, Uhde et al. (1991), in endorsing the use of the MAO inhibitor phenelzine, reported that it is particularly effective with the general type of social phobia. Liebowitz, Schneier, Hollander et al. (1991) reported significant gains in their patients on phenelzine, and also in clinical trials conducted by others. One case described by them may be of special interest to counselors.

After placement on phenelzine, a severely anxious 19-year-old male who had dropped out of school because of extreme discomfort with teachers and classmates was able to complete high school and go on to college. These authors "now consider phenelzine an established form of therapy for social phobia" (p. 12). They also cited successful outcomes for the experimental reversible MAO inhibitor moclobemide, a drug with less severe side effects.

The successful use of Beta-adrenergic blockers for discrete or circumscribed performance anxiety situations also has been reported (Liebowitz, Schneier, Hollander et al., 1991). These situations include tasks that involve fine motor coordination like the playing of a stringed instrument, archery, and pistol shooting, as well as public speaking. The main benefit of the medication is autonomic arousal reduction, in particular, tremor. The reduction in heart rate and perspiration effect is especially comforting to speakers who are distracted by these symptoms and also concerned that others may notice.

The spiraling cycle of anxiety leading to symptoms leading to symptom induced distraction leading to symptom increase, etc., is thus curtailed by the medication effects.

Persons with these discrete performance problems only take propanolol (Inderal, Inderide) an hour or so before performance rather than on a continued maintenance basis. Many of them are individuals who function at a high level in other circumstances.

Drug and psychosocial treatments are certainly not mutually exclusive, and combinations of drug therapy are used and are currently being evaluated in clinical trials.

Psychosocial Treatment

A number of behavioral and cognitive strategies, alone and in combination, have effectively been used for treatment of social phobia. These include exposure treatment, social skills training, applied relaxation training, cognitive restructuring, self-instructional training, systematic rational restructuring, rational-emotive therapy, and anxiety management training (a combination of relaxation training, distraction training, and rational self-talk).

Hope (1993) described some of the advantages that groups treatment offers over individual therapy for social phobia. Among these are that the group sessions themselves provide an in vivo experience of interaction with others, and that extended role-play becomes possible, providing opportunities for simulated exposure and habituation. (Habituation is the process opposite to sensitization. It refers to the lessening, or decline, in responses to a stimulus situation, especially physiological reactions.)

Group treatment can facilitate cognitive changes since people usually can see cognitive distortions, such as exaggerated negative self-appraisals of performance, in others more readily than they can in themselves. In plain terms, people, especially clients, tend to be much tougher on themselves than they are on others because of distortions in self-perception and use of elastic standards for performance.

Butler (1989, pp. 94–96) has emphasized the importance of preparing the client for treatment. A common mistake of beginning counselors and therapists is to engage in treatment procedures without thorough exploration of the client expectations and goals for treatment and without providing a thorough rationale for proposed strategies and procedures. (See Cormier & Cormier, 1991, pp. 297–298, 301–303, for excellent discussion and illustration of these points).

Clients who have suffered distress and constraints in their lives for a long time may have the unrealistic goal of becoming highly competent performers who rarely, if ever, experience anxiety, in a fairly short time, with minimal discomfort in the transition process. The before and after commercial diet program ads do not suggest intermediate stages of body change, nor do they suggest the stress, discomfort, and discipline involved in significant lifestyle alteration. The scripts that clients have for themselves are personal and often contain unrealistic elements, and their elicitation requires patient, probing inquiry on the part of the counselor or therapist.

Counselors and therapists need to explain thoroughly the rationale for treatment subgoals and their sequence, while listening for and addressing unvoiced as well as expressed doubts, fears, and reservations of the client. Failure to do so contributes to preventable lack of client commitment, or follow-through on an action level, to a treatment plan that is conceptually sound. Frequently the counselor or therapist then describes the treatment failure to the supervisor as an instance of "lack of motivation" on the client's part. Sometimes such treatment failures are attributed unwarrantedly to a personality disorder in the client.

Exposure to feared situations has been a cornerstone of behavioral treatment for a long time. The treatment of social phobia presents special problems and challenges, however, because of the central role of cognitive distortion in social phobics self-appraisal and in their attributions to the reactions, real or imagined, of others (Butler, 1989; Scholing and Emmelkamp, 1990). For these reasons, combinations of therapist guided exposure with cognitive restructuring have yielded significantly better results than single treatment protocols.

The application of exposure procedures to social phobia poses more difficulties and challenges for the therapist than their application in the treatment of agoraphobic avoidance. Butler (1989), in particular, has described these in detail. Before practicum or internship students undertake the use of these procedures, they should be familiar with her clinical recommendations and should have read Hope's excellent article on the employment of exposure treatment (1993). A fine current reference source for counselors wishing to learn how to treat social phobia with cognitive-behavioral group therapy (CBGT) is Hope and Heimberg (1993).

An intervention that practicum and internship students might be better prepared to undertake is social skills training. This is not to imply that all persons with generalized social phobia do have significant skill deficits. Understandably, as a consequence of inadequate social interaction experience, many of them do. On the other hand, some social phobics have adequate, or even good, social skills. Their problems stem more from cognitive

distortions such as perfectionistic and unrealistic self-standards, polarized thinking, mental filtering, and emotional reasoning from appraisal rather than performance factors. Practicum and internship students could work with such clients to change their maladaptive and self-defeating cognitive patterns.

For those clients who do have social skill deficits, modeling approaches, with the counselor or in group settings, combined with in-session practice and graduated homework assignments, can be most helpful in building competency based confidence.

Practicum and internship students in counseling might well bear in mind that in addition to the distress caused by a problem and its direct ramifications, people frequently suffer from damaged self-esteem or lessened feelings of personal worth because they have the problem. Therefore, by explaining to socially phobic clients that they do have a recognized disorder that many very distinguished and prominent persons, past and present, have also struggled with, that they are neither mentally ill nor doomed to lifelong distress, and that there is available treatment, counselors can make a positive contribution to the welfare of clients and students. Information and support can be quite reassuring.

Counseling practicum and internship students also can facilitate socially phobic clients' or students' connecting with clinicians or clinics who can offer current, state of the art treatment. Under proper supervision, students could help clients with public speaking anxiety, and use other institutional and community resources to this end. Under supervision, students could engage in social skill development and cognitive restructuring activities on both an individual and group basis. After all, assertion training is a social and interactional activity that involves changes in cognitive schema about oneself and others.

References

American Psychological Association. (1980). *Diagnostic and statistical manual of mental disorders* (3rd ed.). Washington, DC: Author.

American Psychological Association. (1987). *Diagnostic and statistical manual of mental disorders* (3rd ed., revised). Washington, DC: Author.

American Psychological Association. (1994). *Diagnostic and statistical manual of mental disorders* (4th ed.). Washington, DC: Author.

Amies, P.L., Gelder, M.G., & Shaw, P.M. (1983). *British Journal of Psychiatry, 142,* 174–179.

Barlow, D.H. (1988). *Anxiety and its disorders.* New York: Guilford Press.

Bryant, B., & Trower, P.E. (1974). Social difficulty in a student sample. *British Journal of Educational Psychology, 44,* 13–21.

Butler, G. (1989). Issues in the application of cognitive and behavioral strategies to the treatment of social phobia. *Clinical Psychology Review 9,* 91–106.

Chambliss, D.L., Cherney, J., Caputo, G.C., & Rheinstein, B.J.C. (1987). Anxiety disorders and alcoholism: A study with in-patient alcoholics. *Journal of Anxiety Disorders, 1,* 29–40.

Cormier, W.H., & Cormier, L.S. (1991). *Interviewing strategies for helpers* (3rd ed.). Pacific Grove, CA: Brooks/Cole.

Davidson, J.R.T., Potts, N.L.S., Richichi, E.A., Ford, S.M., Krishman, K.R.R., Smith, R.D., & Wilson, W. (1991). The brief social phobia scale. *Journal of Clinical Psychiatry, 52*(11)(supplement), 48–51.

Herbert, J.D., Hope, D.A., & Bellack, A.S. (1992). Validity of the distinction between generalized social phobia and avoidant personality disorder. *Journal of Abnormal Psychology, 101*(2), 332–339.

Hope, D.A. (1993). Exposure and social phobia: Assessment and treatment considerations. *The Behavior Therapist, 16,* 7–12.

Hope, D.A., & Heimberg, R.G. (1990). Dating anxiety. In H. Leitenberg (Ed.), *Handbook of social and evaluative anxiety* (pp. 217–246). New York: Plenum.

Hope, D.A., & Heimberg, R.G. (1993). Social phobia and social anxiety. In D.H. Barlow (Ed.), *Clinical handbook of psychological disorders.* New York: Guilford Press.

Liebowitz, M.R., Gorman, J.M., Fyer, A.J., & Klein, D.F. (1985). Social phobia: Review of a neglected anxiety disorder. *Archives of General Psychiatry, 42,* 729–736.

Liebowitz, M.R., Schneier, F.R., Hollander, E., Welkowitz, L.A., Saoud, J.B., Feerick, J., Campeas, R., Fallon, B.A., Street, L., & Gitow, A. (1991). Treatment of social phobia with drugs other than benzodiazepines. *Journal of Clinical Psychiatry, 52*(11)(supplement), 10–15.

Mahoney, M.J. (1991). *Human change processes.* New York: Basic Books.

Marks, I.M., & Mathews, A.M. (1979). Brief standard self-rating scale for phobic patients. *Behaviour Research and Therapy, 17,* 263–267.

Papp, L.A., Gorman, J.M., & Liebowitz, M.R. (1988). Social phobia. In R. Noyes, Jr., M. Roth, & G.D. Burrows (Eds.), *Handbook of anxiety, Vol. 2: Classification, etiological factors and associated disturbances.* Amsterdam: Elsevier.

Schneier, F.R., Johnson, J., Hornig, C.D., Liebowitz, M.R., & Weissman, M.M. (1992). Social phobia. *Archives of General Psychiatry, 49,* 282–288.

Scholing, A., & Emmelkamp, P.M.G. (1990). Social phobia: Nature and treatment. In H. Leitenberg (Ed.), *Handbook of social and evaluation anxiety* (pp. 269–324). New York: Plenum Press.

Smail, P., Stockwell, T., Canter, S., & Hodgson, R. (1984). Alcohol dependence and phobic anxiety states: I. A. prevalence study. *British Journal of Psychiatry, 144,* 53–77.

Taylor, C.B., & Arnow, B. (1988). *The nature and treatment of anxiety disorders.* New York: The Free Press.

Uhde, T.W., Tancer, M.E., Black, B., & Brown, T.M. (1991). Phenomenology and neurobiology of social phobia: Comparison with panic disorder. *Journal of Clinical Psychiatry, 52*(11)(supplement), 31–40.

Van Ameringen, M., Mancini, C., Styan, G., & Donison, D. (1991). Relationship of social phobia with other psychiatric illness. *Journal of Affective Disorders, 23,* 93–99.

Widiger, T.A. (1992). Generalized social phobia versus avoidant personality disorder: A commentary on three studies. *Journal of Abnormal Psychology, 101*(2), 340–343.

■ ◣ ■

Chapter 9

FINAL EVALUATION

The preceding chapters in this text primarily addressed facilitating a student's process through the practicum/internship experience. Theoretical aspects integral to the counselor's training were integrated with various forms and sample formats in order to maximize the learning process for practicum students and interns.

This chapter is organized to help those involved in the practicum/internship to formally evaluate it. This process will help practicum students and interns determine their strengths and weaknesses. It also serves as a vehicle to help site personnel formally evaluate their training structures.

The *Monthly Practicum Log* (Chapter 2, Form 2.6) permits the student to quantify the number of hours spent in particular counseling areas while in the practicum. The practicum student should detail the time spent in the various training activities. The student should have his/her supervisor sign the practicum log monthly in recognition of these activities.

The function of the remaining evaluation forms (Forms 9.1 through 9.5) is explained in the information that follows.

The *Internship Log* (Form 9.1) parallels the function of the practicum log and is used by interns.

The *Student Evaluation* (Form 9.2) complements the practicum and internship logs. The supervisor utilizes this form to evaluate the student's work in each relevant and appropriate category.

The *Client's Personal/Social Satisfaction with Counseling* (Form 9.3) allows the practicum student's or intern's clients to address the degree of satisfaction experienced during the counseling process. The student should have his/her client sign and fill out the form when counseling has been terminated.

The *Student Counselor Evaluation of Supervisor* (Form 9.4) is filled out by the practicum student or intern at the midpoint and conclusion of their supervisory contract. Both the student and his/her supervisor should sign the form.

A *Site Evaluation* (Form 9.5) is to be used so that site personnel and university program faculty can assess the quality of their training sites.

INTERNSHIP LOG

DIRECTIONS:

1. Record the dates of each week at the site where indicated.
2. Record the total number of hours per week activity under the appropriate column.
3. Total the number of hours for the week and indicate at the bottom of the week column.
4. At the end of the month, total the hours spent in each activity by adding the hours across each activity and indicate the total in the monthly totals column.
5. Get the supervisor's signature. Keep this in your file to be submitted to the university internship coordinator at the completion of the internship.

ACTIVITIES	Week 1 from: to:	Week 2 from: to:	Week 3 from: to:	Week 4 from: to:	Monthly Totals
Intake Interview					
Individual Counseling					
Group Counseling					
Family Counseling					
Consulting/ Intervention					
Psychoeducation					
Community Work					
Career Counseling					
Report Writing					
Case Conference					
Supervision peer individual group					
Other					
Weekly Totals					

Intern's Name _____ Date _____

Supervisor's Signature _____ Date _____

Form 9.1, p. 1 of 1, Copy 1

INTERNSHIP LOG

DIRECTIONS:

1. Record the dates of each week at the site where indicated.
2. Record the total number of hours per week activity under the appropriate column.
3. Total the number of hours for the week and indicate at the bottom of the week column.
4. At the end of the month, total the hours spent in each activity by adding the hours across each activity and indicate the total in the monthly totals column.
5. Get the supervisor's signature. Keep this in your file to be submitted to the university internship coordinator at the completion of the internship.

ACTIVITIES	Week 1 from: to:	Week 2 from: to:	Week 3 from: to:	Week 4 from: to:	Monthly Totals
Intake Interview					
Individual Counseling					
Group Counseling					
Family Counseling					
Consulting/ Intervention					
Psychoeducation					
Community Work					
Career Counseling					
Report Writing					
Case Conference					

Supervision
  peer
  individual
  group					

Other					
Weekly Totals					

Intern's Name _____ Date _____

Supervisor's Signature _____ Date _____

Form 9.1, p. 1 of 1, Copy 2

INTERNSHIP LOG

DIRECTIONS:

1. Record the dates of each week at the site where indicated.
2. Record the total number of hours per week activity under the appropriate column.
3. Total the number of hours for the week and indicate at the bottom of the week column.
4. At the end of the month, total the hours spent in each activity by adding the hours across each activity and indicate the total in the monthly totals column.
5. Get the supervisor's signature. Keep this in your file to be submitted to the university internship coordinator at the completion of the internship.

ACTIVITIES	Week 1 from: to:	Week 2 from: to:	Week 3 from: to:	Week 4 from: to:	Monthly Totals
Intake Interview					
Individual Counseling					
Group Counseling					
Family Counseling					
Consulting/ Intervention					
Psychoeducation					
Community Work					
Career Counseling					
Report Writing					
Case Conference					
Supervision peer individual group					
Other					
Weekly Totals					

Intern's Name _____   Date _____

Supervisor's Signature _____   Date _____

Form 9.1, p. 1 of 1, Copy 3

INTERNSHIP LOG

DIRECTIONS:

1. Record the dates of each week at the site where indicated.
2. Record the total number of hours per week activity under the appropriate column.
3. Total the number of hours for the week and indicate at the bottom of the week column.
4. At the end of the month, total the hours spent in each activity by adding the hours across each activity and indicate the total in the monthly totals column.
5. Get the supervisor's signature. Keep this in your file to be submitted to the university internship coordinator at the completion of the internship.

ACTIVITIES	Week 1 from: to:	Week 2 from: to:	Week 3 from: to:	Week 4 from: to:	Monthly Totals
Intake Interview					
Individual Counseling					
Group Counseling					
Family Counseling					
Consulting/ Intervention					
Psychoeducation					
Community Work					
Career Counseling					
Report Writing					
Case Conference					
Supervision peer individual group					
Other					
Weekly Totals					

Intern's Name _____   Date _____

Supervisor's Signature _____   Date _____

Form 9.1, p. 1 of 1, Copy 4

INTERNSHIP LOG

DIRECTIONS:

1. Record the dates of each week at the site where indicated.
2. Record the total number of hours per week activity under the appropriate column.
3. Total the number of hours for the week and indicate at the bottom of the week column.
4. At the end of the month, total the hours spent in each activity by adding the hours across each activity and indicate the total in the monthly totals column.
5. Get the supervisor's signature. Keep this in your file to be submitted to the university internship coordinator at the completion of the internship.

ACTIVITIES	Week 1 from: to:	Week 2 from: to:	Week 3 from: to:	Week 4 from: to:	Monthly Totals
Intake Interview					
Individual Counseling					
Group Counseling					
Family Counseling					
Consulting/ Intervention					
Psychoeducation					
Community Work					
Career Counseling					
Report Writing					
Case Conference					
Supervision peer individual group					
Other					
Weekly Totals					

Intern's Name _____ Date _____

Supervisor's Signature _____ Date _____

INTERNSHIP LOG

DIRECTIONS:

1. Record the dates of each week at the site where indicated.
2. Record the total number of hours per week activity under the appropriate column.
3. Total the number of hours for the week and indicate at the bottom of the week column.
4. At the end of the month, total the hours spent in each activity by adding the hours across each activity and indicate the total in the monthly totals column.
5. Get the supervisor's signature. Keep this in your file to be submitted to the university internship coordinator at the completion of the internship.

ACTIVITIES	Week 1 from: to:	Week 2 from: to:	Week 3 from: to:	Week 4 from: to:	Monthly Totals
Intake Interview					
Individual Counseling					
Group Counseling					
Family Counseling					
Consulting/ Intervention					
Psychoeducation					
Community Work					
Career Counseling					
Report Writing					
Case Conference					
Supervision peer individual group					
Other					
Weekly Totals					

Intern's Name _____ Date _____

Supervisor's Signature _____ Date _____

Form 9.1, p. 1 of 1, Copy 6

INTERNSHIP LOG

DIRECTIONS:

1. Record the dates of each week at the site where indicated.
2. Record the total number of hours per week activity under the appropriate column.
3. Total the number of hours for the week and indicate at the bottom of the week column.
4. At the end of the month, total the hours spent in each activity by adding the hours across each activity and indicate the total in the monthly totals column.
5. Get the supervisor's signature. Keep this in your file to be submitted to the university internship coordinator at the completion of the internship.

ACTIVITIES	Week 1 from: to:	Week 2 from: to:	Week 3 from: to:	Week 4 from: to:	Monthly Totals
Intake Interview					
Individual Counseling					
Group Counseling					
Family Counseling					
Consulting/ Intervention					
Psychoeducation					
Community Work					
Career Counseling					
Report Writing					
Case Conference					
Supervision peer individual group					
Other					
Weekly Totals					

Intern's Name _____ Date _____

Supervisor's Signature _____ Date _____

Form 9.1, p. 1 of 1, Copy 7

INTERNSHIP LOG

DIRECTIONS:

1. Record the dates of each week at the site where indicated.
2. Record the total number of hours per week activity under the appropriate column.
3. Total the number of hours for the week and indicate at the bottom of the week column.
4. At the end of the month, total the hours spent in each activity by adding the hours across each activity and indicate the total in the monthly totals column.
5. Get the supervisor's signature. Keep this in your file to be submitted to the university internship coordinator at the completion of the internship.

ACTIVITIES	Week 1 from: to:	Week 2 from: to:	Week 3 from: to:	Week 4 from: to:	Monthly Totals
Intake Interview					
Individual Counseling					
Group Counseling					
Family Counseling					
Consulting/ Intervention					
Psychoeducation					
Community Work					
Career Counseling					
Report Writing					
Case Conference					
Supervision peer individual group					
Other					
Weekly Totals					

Intern's Name _____ Date _____

Supervisor's Signature _____ Date _____

Form 9.1, p. 1 of 1, Copy 8

STUDENT EVALUATION

DIRECTIONS: Site supervisor is to complete this form in duplicate. One copy is to go to the student; the other copy is sent to the faculty liaison.

The areas listed below serve as a general guide for the activities typically engaged in during counselor/psychologist training. Please rate the student on the activities in which he/she has engaged using the following scale.

A—Functions extremely well and/or independently.

B—Functions adequately and/or requires occasional supervision.

C—Requires close supervision in this area.

NA—Not applicable to this training experience.

_____	_____
Student Name	Supervisor Signature
_____	_____
Site	Date

TRAINING ACTIVITIES

_____   1. Intake Interviewing

_____   2. Individual Counseling/Psychotherapy

_____   3. Group Counseling/Psychotherapy

_____   4. Testing: Administration and Interpretation

_____   5. Report Writing

_____   6. Consultation

_____   7. Psychoeducational Activities

_____   8. Career Counseling

_____   9. Family/Couple Counseling

_____   10. Case Conference/Staff Presentation

            11. Other (please list) _____

                _____

                _____

                _____

Compared with other graduate students in counseling at this level of training and experience, this student performs overall at the following level (check) one:

☐	☐	☐	☐	☐
99th %ile	80th %ile	60th %ile	40th %ile	20th %ile

Additional Comments:

Please use the additional space for any comments that would help us evaluate this student's progress. Student may comment upon exceptions to ratings, if any.

STUDENT EVALUATION

DIRECTIONS: Site supervisor is to complete this form in duplicate. One copy is to go to the student; the other copy is sent to the faculty liaison.

The areas listed below serve as a general guide for the activities typically engaged in during counselor/psychologist training. Please rate the student on the activities in which he/she has engaged using the following scale.

A—Functions extremely well and/or independently.

B—Functions adequately and/or requires occasional supervision.

C—Requires close supervision in this area.

NA—Not applicable to this training experience.

_____   _____
Student Name   Supervisor Signature

_____   _____
Site   Date

TRAINING ACTIVITIES

_____   1. Intake Interviewing

_____   2. Individual Counseling/Psychotherapy

_____   3. Group Counseling/Psychotherapy

_____   4. Testing: Administration and Interpretation

_____   5. Report Writing

_____   6. Consultation

_____   7. Psychoeducational Activities

_____   8. Career Counseling

_____   9. Family/Couple Counseling

_____   10. Case Conference/Staff Presentation

              11. Other (please list) _____

              _____

              _____

              _____

Compared with other graduate students in counseling at this level of training and experience, this student performs overall at the following level (check) one:

☐	☐	☐	☐	☐
99th %ile	80th %ile	60th %ile	40th %ile	20th %ile

Additional Comments:

Please use the additional space for any comments that would help us evaluate this student's progress. Student may comment upon exceptions to ratings, if any.

STUDENT EVALUATION

DIRECTIONS: Site supervisor is to complete this form in duplicate. One copy is to go to the student; the other copy is sent to the faculty liaison.

The areas listed below serve as a general guide for the activities typically engaged in during counselor/psychologist training. Please rate the student on the activities in which he/she has engaged using the following scale.

A—Functions extremely well and/or independently.

B—Functions adequately and/or requires occasional supervision.

C—Requires close supervision in this area.

NA—Not applicable to this training experience.

_____   _____
           Student Name   Supervisor Signature

_____   _____
                Site   Date

TRAINING ACTIVITIES

_____   1. Intake Interviewing

_____   2. Individual Counseling/Psychotherapy

_____   3. Group Counseling/Psychotherapy

_____   4. Testing: Administration and Interpretation

_____   5. Report Writing

_____   6. Consultation

_____   7. Psychoeducational Activities

_____   8. Career Counseling

_____   9. Family/Couple Counseling

_____   10. Case Conference/Staff Presentation

            11. Other (please list) _____

                _____

                _____

                _____

Compared with other graduate students in counseling at this level of training and experience, this student performs overall at the following level (check) one:

☐	☐	☐	☐	☐
99th %ile	80th %ile	60th %ile	40th %ile	20th %ile

Additional Comments:

Please use the additional space for any comments that would help us evaluate this student's progress. Student may comment upon exceptions to ratings, if any.

STUDENT EVALUATION

DIRECTIONS: Site supervisor is to complete this form in duplicate. One copy is to go to the student; the other copy is sent to the faculty liaison.

The areas listed below serve as a general guide for the activities typically engaged in during counselor/psychologist training. Please rate the student on the activities in which he/she has engaged using the following scale.

A—Functions extremely well and/or independently.

B—Functions adequately and/or requires occasional supervision.

C—Requires close supervision in this area.

NA—Not applicable to this training experience.

_____   _____
         Student Name   Supervisor Signature

_____   _____
             Site   Date

TRAINING ACTIVITIES

_____   1. Intake Interviewing

_____   2. Individual Counseling/Psychotherapy

_____   3. Group Counseling/Psychotherapy

_____   4. Testing: Administration and Interpretation

_____   5. Report Writing

_____   6. Consultation

_____   7. Psychoeducational Activities

_____   8. Career Counseling

_____   9. Family/Couple Counseling

_____   10. Case Conference/Staff Presentation

             11. Other (please list) _____

                 _____

                 _____

Compared with other graduate students in counseling at this level of training and experience, this student performs overall at the following level (check) one:

☐	☐	☐	☐	☐
99th %ile	80th %ile	60th %ile	40th %ile	20th %ile

Additional Comments:

Please use the additional space for any comments that would help us evaluate this student's progress. Student may comment upon exceptions to ratings, if any.

CLIENT'S PERSONAL/SOCIAL SATISFACTION WITH COUNSELING

Client Name _____   Counselor Name _____

Client ID Number _____   Counselor ID Number _____

Date _____

Please read each of the following questions carefully and **circle** the response for each one that most nearly reflects your honest opinion.

1. How much help did you get with your concern?

   1   None
   2   A little
   3   Some
   4   Much
   5   All I needed

2. How satisfied are you with the relationship with your counselor?

   1   Not at all
   2   Slightly
   3   Some
   4   Pretty well
   5   Completely

3. How much help have you received with concerns other than your original reasons for entering counseling?

   1   None
   2   A little worse
   3   Some
   4   Much
   5   All I needed

4. How do you feel now compared to when you first came to counseling?

   1   Much worse
   2   A little worse
   3   The same
   4   Quite a bit better
   5   Greatly improved

5. How much has counseling helped you in understanding yourself?

   1   None
   2   A little
   3   Moderately
   4   Quite a bit
   5   Greatly

6. How willing would you be to return to your counselor if you wanted help with another concern?

   1   Unwilling
   2   Reluctant
   3   Slightly inclined
   4   Moderately willing
   5   Very willing

7. How willing would you be to recommend your counselor to one of your friends?

   1   Unwilling
   2   Reluctant
   3   Slightly inclined
   4   Moderately willing
   5   Very willing

Used by permission from Dr. Roger Hutchinson, Professor of Psychology-Counseling and Director, Counseling Practicum Clinic, Department of Counseling Psychology and Guidance Services, Ball State University. This form originally was printed in Chapter 10 in the *Practicum Manual for Counseling and Psychotherapy* by K. Dimick and F. Krause, Accelerated Development, 1980.

Form 9.3, p. 1 of 2, Copy 1

8. How much did your counselor differ from what you might consider to be an ideal counselor?

1 Greatly
2 In many ways
3 Somewhat
4 A little
5 Not at all

9. Based on your experiences at this clinic, how did you judge the counselors to be?

1 Incompetent
2 Little competence
3 Moderately competent
4 Competent
5 Highly competent

10. To what extent could the relationship you had with your counselor have been improved?

1 Greatly
2 Quite a bit
3 Moderately
4 Slightly
5 Not at all

11. How sensitive was your counselor to the way you felt?

1 Insensitive
2 Slightly insensitive
3 Sometimes sensitive
4 Usually sensitive
5 Very sensitive

12. To what extent do you still lack self-understanding about the things that trouble you?

1 Great
2 Quite a bit
3 Moderate
4 Slight
5 Not at all

13. If counseling were available only on a fee-paying basis, how likely would you be to return if you had other concerns?

1 I would not return
2 It would be unlikely for me to return
3 I might return
4 I probably would return
5 I would return

14. In general , how satisfied are you with your counseling experience?

1 Not satisfied
2 Moderately dissatisfied
3 Slightly satisfied
4 Moderately satisfied
5 Completely satisfied

15. The technique most used by your counselor was?

1 Left it to me
2 Interested listener
3 Gave opinions and suggestions
4 Gave interpretations
5 Counselor was vague and unclear

16. Your reactions while being counseled.

1 Found it unpleasant and upsetting at times
2 Found it very interesting, enjoyed it
3 Got angry often at my counselor
4 Often felt discouraged at lack of progress
5 Felt relaxed and looked forward to sessions
6 Felt that I could not get my story across, that I couldn't get counselor to understand me

Form 9.3, p. 2 of 2, Copy 1

CLIENT'S PERSONAL/SOCIAL SATISFACTION WITH COUNSELING

Client Name _____   Counselor Name _____

Client ID Number _____   Counselor ID Number _____

Date _____

Please read each of the following questions carefully and **circle** the response for each one that most nearly reflects your honest opinion.

1. How much help did you get with your concern?

    1 None
    2 A little
    3 Some
    4 Much
    5 All I needed

2. How satisfied are you with the relationship with your counselor?

    1 Not at all
    2 Slightly
    3 Some
    4 Pretty well
    5 Completely

3. How much help have you received with concerns other than your original reasons for entering counseling?

    1 None
    2 A little worse
    3 Some
    4 Much
    5 All I needed

4. How do you feel now compared to when you first came to counseling?

    1 Much worse
    2 A little worse
    3 The same
    4 Quite a bit better
    5 Greatly improved

5. How much has counseling helped you in understanding yourself?

    1 None
    2 A little
    3 Moderately
    4 Quite a bit
    5 Greatly

6. How willing would you be to return to your counselor if you wanted help with another concern?

    1 Unwilling
    2 Reluctant
    3 Slightly inclined
    4 Moderately willing
    5 Very willing

7. How willing would you be to recommend your counselor to one of your friends?

    1 Unwilling
    2 Reluctant
    3 Slightly inclined
    4 Moderately willing
    5 Very willing

Used by permission from Dr. Roger Hutchinson, Professor of Psychology-Counseling and Director, Counseling Practicum Clinic, Department of Counseling Psychology and Guidance Services, Ball State University. This form originally was printed in Chapter 10 in the *Practicum Manual for Counseling and Psychotherapy* by K. Dimick and F. Krause, Accelerated Development, 1980.

Form 9.3, p. 1 of 2, Copy 2

8. How much did your counselor differ from what you might consider to be an ideal counselor?

1 Greatly
2 In many ways
3 Somewhat
4 A little
5 Not at all

9. Based on your experiences at this clinic, how did you judge the counselors to be?

1 Incompetent
2 Little competence
3 Moderately competent
4 Competent
5 Highly competent

10. To what extent could the relationship you had with your counselor have been improved?

1 Greatly
2 Quite a bit
3 Moderately
4 Slightly
5 Not at all

11. How sensitive was your counselor to the way you felt?

1 Insensitive
2 Slightly insensitive
3 Sometimes sensitive
4 Usually sensitive
5 Very sensitive

12. To what extent do you still lack self-understanding about the things that trouble you?

1 Great
2 Quite a bit
3 Moderate
4 Slight
5 Not at all

13. If counseling were available only on a fee-paying basis, how likely would you be to return if you had other concerns?

1 I would not return
2 It would be unlikely for me to return
3 I might return
4 I probably would return
5 I would return

14. In general , how satisfied are you with your counseling experience?

1 Not satisfied
2 Moderately dissatisfied
3 Slightly satisfied
4 Moderately satisfied
5 Completely satisfied

15. The technique most used by your counselor was?

1 Left it to me
2 Interested listener
3 Gave opinions and suggestions
4 Gave interpretations
5 Counselor was vague and unclear

16. Your reactions while being counseled.

1 Found it unpleasant and upsetting at times
2 Found it very interesting, enjoyed it
3 Got angry often at my counselor
4 Often felt discouraged at lack of progress
5 Felt relaxed and looked forward to sessions
6 Felt that I could not get my story across, that I couldn't get counselor to understand me

CLIENT'S PERSONAL/SOCIAL SATISFACTION WITH COUNSELING

Client Name _____   Counselor Name _____

Client ID Number _____   Counselor ID Number _____

Date _____

Please read each of the following questions carefully and **circle** the response for each one that most nearly reflects your honest opinion.

1. How much help did you get with your concern?

   1 None
   2 A little
   3 Some
   4 Much
   5 All I needed

2. How satisfied are you with the relationship with your counselor?

   1 Not at all
   2 Slightly
   3 Some
   4 Pretty well
   5 Completely

3. How much help have you received with concerns other than your original reasons for entering counseling?

   1 None
   2 A little worse
   3 Some
   4 Much
   5 All I needed

4. How do you feel now compared to when you first came to counseling?

   1 Much worse
   2 A little worse
   3 The same
   4 Quite a bit better
   5 Greatly improved

5. How much has counseling helped you in understanding yourself?

   1 None
   2 A little
   3 Moderately
   4 Quite a bit
   5 Greatly

6. How willing would you be to return to your counselor if you wanted help with another concern?

   1 Unwilling
   2 Reluctant
   3 Slightly inclined
   4 Moderately willing
   5 Very willing

7. How willing would you be to recommend your counselor to one of your friends?

   1 Unwilling
   2 Reluctant
   3 Slightly inclined
   4 Moderately willing
   5 Very willing

Used by permission from Dr. Roger Hutchinson, Professor of Psychology-Counseling and Director, Counseling Practicum Clinic, Department of Counseling Psychology and Guidance Services, Ball State University. This form originally was printed in Chapter 10 in the *Practicum Manual for Counseling and Psychotherapy* by K. Dimick and F. Krause, Accelerated Development, 1980.

Form 9.3, p. 1 of 2, Copy 3

8. How much did your counselor differ from what you might consider to be an ideal counselor?

1 Greatly
2 In many ways
3 Somewhat
4 A little
5 Not at all

9. Based on your experiences at this clinic, how did you judge the counselors to be?

1 Incompetent
2 Little competence
3 Moderately competent
4 Competent
5 Highly competent

10. To what extent could the relationship you had with your counselor have been improved?

1 Greatly
2 Quite a bit
3 Moderately
4 Slightly
5 Not at all

11. How sensitive was your counselor to the way you felt?

1 Insensitive
2 Slightly insensitive
3 Sometimes sensitive
4 Usually sensitive
5 Very sensitive

12. To what extent do you still lack self-understanding about the things that trouble you?

1 Great
2 Quite a bit
3 Moderate
4 Slight
5 Not at all

13. If counseling were available only on a fee-paying basis, how likely would you be to return if you had other concerns?

1 I would not return
2 It would be unlikely for me to return
3 I might return
4 I probably would return
5 I would return

14. In general , how satisfied are you with your counseling experience?

1 Not satisfied
2 Moderately dissatisfied
3 Slightly satisfied
4 Moderately satisfied
5 Completely satisfied

15. The technique most used by your counselor was?

1 Left it to me
2 Interested listener
3 Gave opinions and suggestions
4 Gave interpretations
5 Counselor was vague and unclear

16. Your reactions while being counseled.

1 Found it unpleasant and upsetting at times
2 Found it very interesting, enjoyed it
3 Got angry often at my counselor
4 Often felt discouraged at lack of progress
5 Felt relaxed and looked forward to sessions
6 Felt that I could not get my story across, that I couldn't get counselor to understand me

Form 9.3, p. 2 of 2, Copy 3

CLIENT'S PERSONAL/SOCIAL SATISFACTION WITH COUNSELING

Client Name _____   Counselor Name _____

Client ID Number _____   Counselor ID Number _____

Date _____

Please read each of the following questions carefully and **circle** the response for each one that most nearly reflects your honest opinion.

1. How much help did you get with your concern?

   1 None
   2 A little
   3 Some
   4 Much
   5 All I needed

2. How satisfied are you with the relationship with your counselor?

   1 Not at all
   2 Slightly
   3 Some
   4 Pretty well
   5 Completely

3. How much help have you received with concerns other than your original reasons for entering counseling?

   1 None
   2 A little worse
   3 Some
   4 Much
   5 All I needed

4. How do you feel now compared to when you first came to counseling?

   1 Much worse
   2 A little worse
   3 The same
   4 Quite a bit better
   5 Greatly improved

5. How much has counseling helped you in understanding yourself?

   1 None
   2 A little
   3 Moderately
   4 Quite a bit
   5 Greatly

6. How willing would you be to return to your counselor if you wanted help with another concern?

   1 Unwilling
   2 Reluctant
   3 Slightly inclined
   4 Moderately willing
   5 Very willing

7. How willing would you be to recommend your counselor to one of your friends?

   1 Unwilling
   2 Reluctant
   3 Slightly inclined
   4 Moderately willing
   5 Very willing

Used by permission from Dr. Roger Hutchinson, Professor of Psychology-Counseling and Director, Counseling Practicum Clinic, Department of Counseling Psychology and Guidance Services, Ball State University. This form originally was printed in Chapter 10 in the *Practicum Manual for Counseling and Psychotherapy* by K. Dimick and F. Krause, Accelerated Development, 1980.

Form 9.3, p. 1 of 2, Copy 4

8. How much did your counselor differ from what you might consider to be an ideal counselor?

1 Greatly
2 In many ways
3 Somewhat
4 A little
5 Not at all

9. Based on your experiences at this clinic, how did you judge the counselors to be?

1 Incompetent
2 Little competence
3 Moderately competent
4 Competent
5 Highly competent

10. To what extent could the relationship you had with your counselor have been improved?

1 Greatly
2 Quite a bit
3 Moderately
4 Slightly
5 Not at all

11. How sensitive was your counselor to the way you felt?

1 Insensitive
2 Slightly insensitive
3 Sometimes sensitive
4 Usually sensitive
5 Very sensitive

12. To what extent do you still lack self-understanding about the things that trouble you?

1 Great
2 Quite a bit
3 Moderate
4 Slight
5 Not at all

13. If counseling were available only on a fee-paying basis, how likely would you be to return if you had other concerns?

1 I would not return
2 It would be unlikely for me to return
3 I might return
4 I probably would return
5 I would return

14. In general , how satisfied are you with your counseling experience?

1 Not satisfied
2 Moderately dissatisfied
3 Slightly satisfied
4 Moderately satisfied
5 Completely satisfied

15. The technique most used by your counselor was?

1 Left it to me
2 Interested listener
3 Gave opinions and suggestions
4 Gave interpretations
5 Counselor was vague and unclear

16. Your reactions while being counseled.

1 Found it unpleasant and upsetting at times
2 Found it very interesting, enjoyed it
3 Got angry often at my counselor
4 Often felt discouraged at lack of progress
5 Felt relaxed and looked forward to sessions
6 Felt that I could not get my story across, that I couldn't get counselor to understand me

Form 9.3, p. 2 of 2, Copy 4

CLIENT'S PERSONAL/SOCIAL SATISFACTION WITH COUNSELING

Client Name _____   Counselor Name _____

Client ID Number _____   Counselor ID Number _____

Date _____

Please read each of the following questions carefully and **circle** the response for each one that most nearly reflects your honest opinion.

1. How much help did you get with your concern?

   1 None
   2 A little
   3 Some
   4 Much
   5 All I needed

2. How satisfied are you with the relationship with your counselor?

   1 Not at all
   2 Slightly
   3 Some
   4 Pretty well
   5 Completely

3. How much help have you received with concerns other than your original reasons for entering counseling?

   1 None
   2 A little worse
   3 Some
   4 Much
   5 All I needed

4. How do you feel now compared to when you first came to counseling?

   1 Much worse
   2 A little worse
   3 The same
   4 Quite a bit better
   5 Greatly improved

5. How much has counseling helped you in understanding yourself?

   1 None
   2 A little
   3 Moderately
   4 Quite a bit
   5 Greatly

6. How willing would you be to return to your counselor if you wanted help with another concern?

   1 Unwilling
   2 Reluctant
   3 Slightly inclined
   4 Moderately willing
   5 Very willing

7. How willing would you be to recommend your counselor to one of your friends?

   1 Unwilling
   2 Reluctant
   3 Slightly inclined
   4 Moderately willing
   5 Very willing

Used by permission from Dr. Roger Hutchinson, Professor of Psychology-Counseling and Director, Counseling Practicum Clinic, Department of Counseling Psychology and Guidance Services, Ball State University. This form originally was printed in Chapter 10 in the *Practicum Manual for Counseling and Psychotherapy* by K. Dimick and F. Krause, Accelerated Development, 1980.

Form 9.3, p. 1 of 2, Copy 5

8. How much did your counselor differ from what you might consider to be an ideal counselor?

    1 Greatly
    2 In many ways
    3 Somewhat
    4 A little
    5 Not at all

9. Based on your experiences at this clinic, how did you judge the counselors to be?

    1 Incompetent
    2 Little competence
    3 Moderately competent
    4 Competent
    5 Highly competent

10. To what extent could the relationship you had with your counselor have been improved?

    1 Greatly
    2 Quite a bit
    3 Moderately
    4 Slightly
    5 Not at all

11. How sensitive was your counselor to the way you felt?

    1 Insensitive
    2 Slightly insensitive
    3 Sometimes sensitive
    4 Usually sensitive
    5 Very sensitive

12. To what extent do you still lack self-understanding about the things that trouble you?

    1 Great
    2 Quite a bit
    3 Moderate
    4 Slight
    5 Not at all

13. If counseling were available only on a fee-paying basis, how likely would you be to return if you had other concerns?

    1 I would not return
    2 It would be unlikely for me to return
    3 I might return
    4 I probably would return
    5 I would return

14. In general , how satisfied are you with your counseling experience?

    1 Not satisfied
    2 Moderately dissatisfied
    3 Slightly satisfied
    4 Moderately satisfied
    5 Completely satisfied

15. The technique most used by your counselor was?

    1 Left it to me
    2 Interested listener
    3 Gave opinions and suggestions
    4 Gave interpretations
    5 Counselor was vague and unclear

16. Your reactions while being counseled.

    1 Found it unpleasant and upsetting at times
    2 Found it very interesting, enjoyed it
    3 Got angry often at my counselor
    4 Often felt discouraged at lack of progress
    5 Felt relaxed and looked forward to sessions
    6 Felt that I could not get my story across, that I couldn't get counselor to understand me

STUDENT COUNSELOR EVALUATION OF SUPERVISOR*

SUGGESTED USE: The practicum or internship supervisor could obtain feedback on the supervision by asking student counselors to complete this form. The evaluation could be done at midterm and/or final. The purposes are twofold: (1) to provide feedback for improving supervision and (2) to encourage communication between the supervisor and the student counselor.

Name of Practicum or Internship Supervisor: _____

Period covered _____ to _____

DIRECTIONS: The student counselor when asked to do so is to make an evaluation of the supervision received. Circle the number that best represents how you, the student counselor, feel about the supervision received. After the form is completed, the supervisor may suggest a meeting to discuss the supervision received. After the form is completed, the supervisor may suggest a meeting to discuss the supervision desired.

		Poor	Adequate	Good
1.	Gives time and energy in observing, tape processing and case conferences	1 2	3 4	5 6
2.	Accepts and respects me as a person.	1 2	3 4	5 6
3.	Recognizes and encourages further development of my strengths and capabilities.	1 2	3 4	5 6
4.	Gives me useful feedback when I do something well.	1 2	3 4	5 6
5.	Provides me the freedom to develop flexible and effective counseling styles.	1 2	3 4	5 6
6.	Encourages and listens to my ideas and suggestions for developing my counseling skills.	1 2	3 4	5 6
7.	Provides suggestions for developing my counseling skills.	1 2	3 4	5 6
8.	Helps me understand the implications and dynamics of the counseling approaches I use.	1 2	3 4	5 6
9.	Encourages me to use new and different techniques when appropriate	1 2	3 4	5 6
10.	Is spontaneous and flexible in the supervisory sessions.	1 2	3 4	5 6
11.	Helps me define and achieve specific concrete goals for myself during the practicum experience.	1 2	3 4	5 6
12.	Gives me useful feedback when I do something wrong.	1 2	3 4	5 6
13.	Allows me to discuss problems I encounter in my practicum setting.	1 2	3 4	5 6

*Printed by permission from Dr. Harold Hackney, Assistant Professor, Purdue University. This form was designed by two graduate students based upon material drawn from Counseling Strategies and Objectives by H. Hackney and S. Nye, Prentice-Hall, 1973. This form originally was printed in Chapter 10 in the *Practicum Manual for Counseling and Psychotherapy,* by K. Dimick and F. Krause, Muncie, IN: Accelerated Development, 1980.

		Poor	Adequate	Good
14.	Pays amount of attention to both me and my clients.	1 2	3 4	5 6
15.	Focuses on both verbal and nonverbal behavior in me and in my clients.	1 2	3 4	5 6
16.	Helps me define and maintain ethical behavior in counseling and case management.	1 2	3 4	5 6
17.	Encourages me to engage in professional behavior.	1 2	3 4	5 6
18.	Maintains confidentiality in material discussed in supervisory sessions.	1 2	3 4	5 6
19.	Deals with both content and effect when supervising.	1 2	3 4	5 6
20.	Focuses on the implications, consequences, and contingencies of specific behaviors in counseling and supervision.	1 2	3 4	5 6
21.	Helps me organize relevant case data in planning goals and strategies with my client.	1 2	3 4	5 6
22.	Helps me formulate a theoretically sound rationale of human behavior.	1 2	3 4	5 6
23.	Offers resource information when I request or need it.	1 2	3 4	5 6
24.	Helps me develop increased skill in critiquing and gaining insight from my counseling tapes.	1 2	3 4	5 6
25.	Allows and encourages me to evaluate myself.	1 2	3 4	5 6
26.	Explains his/her criteria for evaluation clearly and in behavioral terms.	1 2	3 4	5 6
27.	Applies his/her criteria fairly in evaluating my counseling performance.	1 2	3 4	5 6

ADDITIONAL COMMENTS AND/OR SUGGESTIONS

_____

_____

_____   _____
        Date   Practicum Student/Intern

My signature indicates that I have read the above report and have discussed the content with my supervisee. It does not necessarily indicate that I agree with the report in part or in whole.

_____   _____
        Date   Signature of Supervisor

Form 9.4, p. 2 of 2, Copy 1

STUDENT COUNSELOR EVALUATION OF SUPERVISOR*

SUGGESTED USE: The practicum or internship supervisor could obtain feedback on the supervision by asking student counselors to complete this form. The evaluation could be done at midterm and/or final. The purposes are twofold: (1) to provide feedback for improving supervision and (2) to encourage communication between the supervisor and the student counselor.

Name of Practicum or Internship Supervisor: _____

Period covered _____ to _____

DIRECTIONS: The student counselor when asked to do so is to make an evaluation of the supervision received. Circle the number that best represents how you, the student counselor, feel about the supervision received. After the form is completed, the supervisor may suggest a meeting to discuss the supervision received. After the form is completed, the supervisor may suggest a meeting to discuss the supervision desired.

		Poor	Adequate	Good
1.	Gives time and energy in observing, tape processing and case conferences	1 2	3 4	5 6
2.	Accepts and respects me as a person.	1 2	3 4	5 6
3.	Recognizes and encourages further development of my strengths and capabilities.	1 2	3 4	5 6
4.	Gives me useful feedback when I do something well.	1 2	3 4	5 6
5.	Provides me the freedom to develop flexible and effective counseling styles.	1 2	3 4	5 6
6.	Encourages and listens to my ideas and suggestions for developing my counseling skills.	1 2	3 4	5 6
7.	Provides suggestions for developing my counseling skills.	1 2	3 4	5 6
8.	Helps me understand the implications and dynamics of the counseling approaches I use.	1 2	3 4	5 6
9.	Encourages me to use new and different techniques when appropriate	1 2	3 4	5 6
10.	Is spontaneous and flexible in the supervisory sessions.	1 2	3 4	5 6
11.	Helps me define and achieve specific concrete goals for myself during the practicum experience.	1 2	3 4	5 6
12.	Gives me useful feedback when I do something wrong.	1 2	3 4	5 6
13.	Allows me to discuss problems I encounter in my practicum setting.	1 2	3 4	5 6

---

*Printed by permission from Dr. Harold Hackney, Assistant Professor, Purdue University. This form was designed by two graduate students based upon material drawn from Counseling Strategies and Objectives by H. Hackney and S. Nye, Prentice-Hall, 1973. This form originally was printed in Chapter 10 in the *Practicum Manual for Counseling and Psychotherapy,* by K. Dimick and F. Krause, Muncie, IN: Accelerated Development, 1980.

		Poor		Adequate		Good	
14.	Pays amount of attention to both me and my clients.	1	2	3	4	5	6
15.	Focuses on both verbal and nonverbal behavior in me and in my clients.	1	2	3	4	5	6
16.	Helps me define and maintain ethical behavior in counseling and case management.	1	2	3	4	5	6
17.	Encourages me to engage in professional behavior.	1	2	3	4	5	6
18.	Maintains confidentiality in material discussed in supervisory sessions.	1	2	3	4	5	6
19.	Deals with both content and effect when supervising.	1	2	3	4	5	6
20.	Focuses on the implications, consequences, and contingencies of specific behaviors in counseling and supervision.	1	2	3	4	5	6
21.	Helps me organize relevant case data in planning goals and strategies with my client.	1	2	3	4	5	6
22.	Helps me formulate a theoretically sound rationale of human behavior.	1	2	3	4	5	6
23.	Offers resource information when I request or need it.	1	2	3	4	5	6
24.	Helps me develop increased skill in critiquing and gaining insight from my counseling tapes.	1	2	3	4	5	6
25.	Allows and encourages me to evaluate myself.	1	2	3	4	5	6
26.	Explains his/her criteria for evaluation clearly and in behavioral terms.	1	2	3	4	5	6
27.	Applies his/her criteria fairly in evaluating my counseling performance.	1	2	3	4	5	6

ADDITIONAL COMMENTS AND/OR SUGGESTIONS

_____

_____

_____   _____
Date   Practicum Student/Intern

My signature indicates that I have read the above report and have discussed the content with my supervisee. It does not necessarily indicate that I agree with the report in part or in whole.

_____   _____
Date   Signature of Supervisor

Form 9.4, p. 2 of 2, Copy 2

SITE EVALUATION

DIRECTIONS: Student completes this form at the end of the practicum and/or internship. This should be turned in to the university supervisor or internship coordinator as indicated by the university program.

_____

Name: _____   Site: _____

Dates of Placement: _____   Site Supervisor: _____

Faculty Liaison: _____

Rate the following questions about your site and experiences by the following:

1) _____	Amount of on-site supervision.
2) _____	Quality and usefulness of on-site supervision.
3) _____	Usefulness and helpfulness of faculty liaison.
4) _____	Relevance of experience to career goals.

A. Very satisfactory   5) _____   Exposure to and communication of school/agency goals.

B. Moderately satisfactory 6) _____   Exposure to and communication of school/agency procedures.

C. Moderately unsatisfactory 7) _____   Exposure to professional roles and functions within the school/agency.

D. Very unsatisfactory   8) _____   Exposure to information about community resources.

9) _____   Rate all applicable experiences that you had at your site:

_____   Report writing

_____   Intake interviewing

_____   Administration and interpretation of tests

_____   Staff presentations/case conferences

_____   Individual counseling

_____   Group counseling

_____   Family/couple counseling

_____   Psychoeducational activities

_____   Consultation

_____   Career counseling

_____   Other _____

10) _____   Overall evaluation of the site.

COMMENTS: Include any suggestions for improvements in the experiences you have rated moderately (C) or very unsatisfactory (D).

Form 9.5, p. 1 of 1, Copy 1

SITE EVALUATION

DIRECTIONS: Student completes this form at the end of the practicum and/or internship. This should be turned in to the university supervisor or internship coordinator as indicated by the university program.

Name: _____ Site: _____

Dates of Placement: _____ Site Supervisor: _____

Faculty Liaison: _____

Rate the following questions about your site and experiences by the following:

	1) _____	Amount of on-site supervision.
	2) _____	Quality and usefulness of on-site supervision.
	3) _____	Usefulness and helpfulness of faculty liaison.
	4) _____	Relevance of experience to career goals.
A. Very satisfactory	5) _____	Exposure to and communication of school/agency goals.
B. Moderately satisfactory	6) _____	Exposure to and communication of school/agency procedures.
C. Moderately unsatisfactory	7) _____	Exposure to professional roles and functions within the school/agency.
D. Very unsatisfactory	8) _____	Exposure to information about community resources.
	9) _____	Rate all applicable experiences that you had at your site:

       _____ Report writing

       _____ Intake interviewing

       _____ Administration and interpretation of tests

       _____ Staff presentations/case conferences

       _____ Individual counseling

       _____ Group counseling

       _____ Family/couple counseling

       _____ Psychoeducational activities

       _____ Consultation

       _____ Career counseling

       _____ Other _____

    10) _____ Overall evaluation of the site.

COMMENTS: Include any suggestions for improvements in the experiences you have rated moderately (C) or very unsatisfactory (D).

INDEX

ABOUT THE AUTHORS

John Charles Boylan

John Charles Boylan is a professor of counseling and psychology at Marywood College, Scranton, Pennsylvania. He was granted his bachelor's degree from the University of Scranton and his M.Ed. and Ph.D. from the University of Pittsburgh. He completed a post-doctoral residency in Sex Therapy at Mount Sinai Medical School, New York City.

Dr. Boylan is a Licensed Psychologist, Certified Sex Therapist, Diplomat of the American Board of Sexology, and Certified School Counselor. Dr. Boylan has served as secondary school counselor and Director of Pupil Personnel Services at Delaware Valley School District, Milford, Pennsylvania. Dr. Boylan has been with Marywood College for the last 23 years. During that time, he has served as Director of Career Planning and Placement, chairperson of the Department of Counseling and Psychology, and of the Graduate School.

Dr. Boylan has served as a consultant to the Pennsylvania Department of Education—Adult Education Section and has been the author and program director of several major grants in adult education. He has written several resource guides in adult education: Boylan, J.C., Golden, J., & Curran, B., *Career Resource Guide for Emotionally Impaired, Physically Handicapped and Mentally Retarded Adults,* Pennsylvania Department of education; and Boylan, J.C., & Mrykalo, F., *Resource Guide for Adult Education Counselors.*

Currently, Dr. Boylan has a part-time private practice in Scranton and Clarks Summit, Pennsylvania, specializing in marital and sex therapy.

Patrick Brendan Malley

Patrick Brendan Malley is an associate professor in the Department of Psychology in Education at the University of Pittsburgh. He was granted his B.A. degree from Saint Francis College in Loretta, Pennsylvania, his M.Ed. degree from Duquesne University, and his Ph.D. from the University of Pittsburgh. Dr. Malley is a Licensed Psychologist and a Certified School Counselor. He has been with the University of Pittsburgh for the last 20 years. During this period of time, Dr. Malley has served as chairman of the master's, internship, and doctoral programs in the School Counseling Program, in the Department of Psychology in Education. He also is recognized widely as a specialist in ethical issues as they relate to counseling theory and practice.

Dr. Malley has acted as a consultant to the United States Office of Education, and has served as the project director of several dissemination projects funded by the United States Office of Education and granted to the University of Pittsburgh. He also has served as coordinator for the United States Office of Education and Cleveland State University, Boston University, and State University of New York at Brockport.

As a result of his interest in professional/ethical issues in counseling theory and practice, Dr. Malley has produced a number of videotapes: *When a Colleague Practices Unethically; Counseling the Client Who Is Potentially Harmful to Others;* and *Counseling and Child Abuse.*

Judith Scott

Judith Scott is an associate professor in the Department of Psychology in Education at the University of Pittsburgh, Pittsburgh, Pennsylvania. She was granted her B.B.A. from the University of Pittsburgh and completed her M.Ed. and Ph.D. at the University of Pittsburgh.

Dr. Scott is a Licensed Psychologist, Certified School Counselor, Certified School Psychologist, and National Certified Counselor. She has served as school counselor at Keystone Oaks School District and Penn Hills School District in Pittsburgh. Dr. Scott has been with the Counselor Education Program at the University of Pittsburgh since 1968. During that time she served as coordinator of the full- and part-time master's degree programs in counseling, as coordinator of the part-time doctoral program, and as field site coordinator.

Dr. Scott has served as a consultant to several school districts and also has been a consultant on several major grants funded by the United States Office of Education. She has been a presenter at numerous state, regional, and national conferences of ACA and APA and served as Pennsylvania State Coordinator of Sex Equality in Guidance Opportunities Project. She has published articles on counseling supervision, women's adult development, and career development. Dr. Scott has held various offices at the state and regional levels in ACA and is past-president of Pennsylvania Association of Counselor Education and Supervision.

Currently, Dr. Scott has a part-time private practice in Pittsburgh specializing in development counseling with adults.